Something Chocolate This Way Comes

Other *Baby Blues®* Books from Andrews McMeel Publishing

Guess Who Didn't Take a Nap?
I Thought Labor Ended When the Baby Was Born
We Are Experiencing Parental Difficulties . . . Please Stand By
Night of the Living Dad
I Saw Elvis in My Ultrasound
One More and We're Outnumbered!
Check, Please . . .
threats, bribes & videotape
If I'm a Stay-at-Home Mom, Why Am I Always in the Car?
Lift and Separate
I Shouldn't Have to Scream More Than Once!
Motherhood Is Not for Wimps
Baby Blues®: Unplugged
Dad to the Bone
Never a Dry Moment
Two Plus One Is Enough
Playdate: Category 5
Our Server Is Down

Treasuries

The Super-Absorbent Biodegradable Family-Size Baby Blues®
Baby Blues®: Ten Years and Still in Diapers
Butt-Naked Baby Blues®
Wall-to-Wall Baby Blues®
Driving Under the Influence of Children

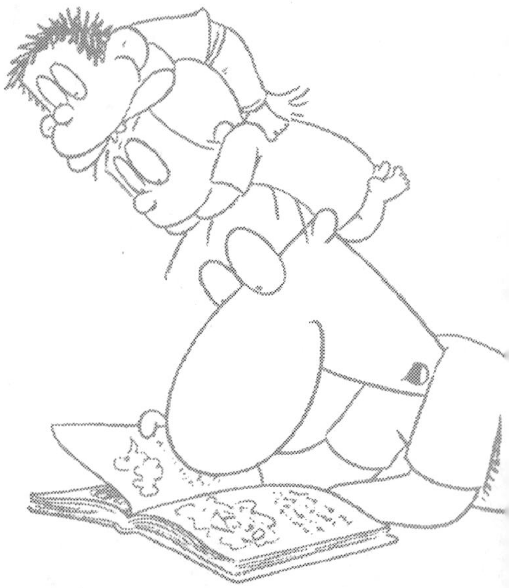

Baby Blues 21 Scrapbook

Something Chocolate This Way Comes

By Rick Kirkman & Jerry Scott

Andrews McMeel
Publishing, LLC
Kansas City

Baby Blues® is syndicated internationally by King Features Syndicate, Inc. For information, write King Features Syndicate, Inc., 888 Seventh Avenue, New York, New York 10019.

06 07 08 09 10 BBG 10 9 8 7 6 5 4 3 2 1

ISBN-13: 978-0-7407-5686-3
ISBN-10: 0-7407-5686-9

Library of Congress Catalog Card Number: 2005936083

www.andrewsmcmeel.com

Find *Baby Blues*® on the Web at
www.babyblues.com.

ATTENTION: SCHOOLS AND BUSINESSES

Andrews McMeel books are available at quantity discounts with bulk purchase for educational, business, or sales promotional use. For information, please write to: Special Sales Department, Andrews McMeel Publishing, LLC, 4520 Main Street, Kansas City, Missouri 64111.

To Sukey: Nest builder to empty nester, a mother extraordinaire.
—R.K.

To Cady Lane, our confectionery specialist.
—J.S.

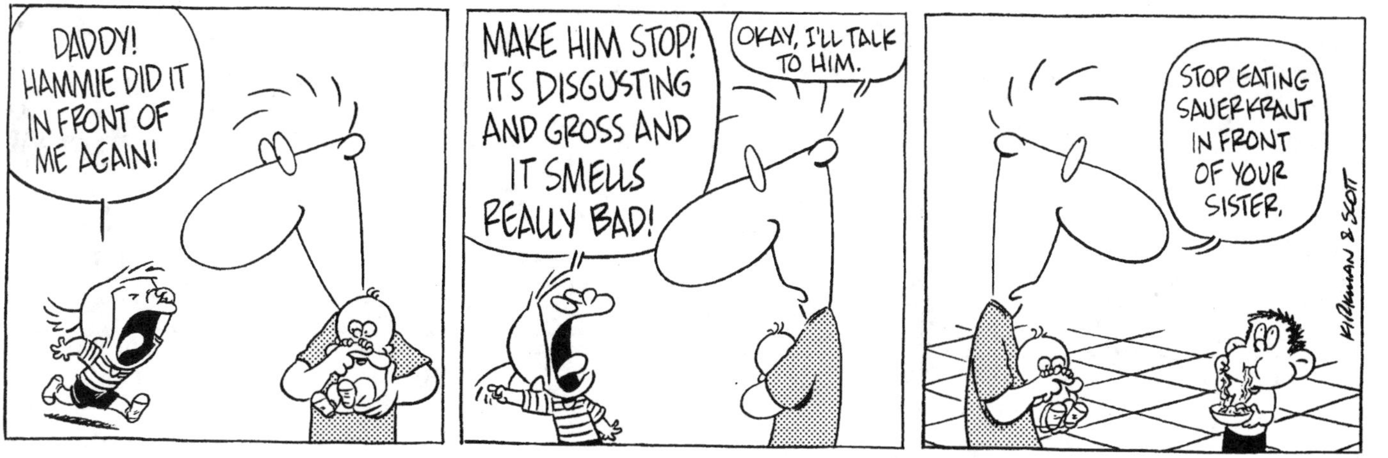
DADDY! HAMMIE DID IT IN FRONT OF ME AGAIN!
MAKE HIM STOP! IT'S DISGUSTING AND GROSS AND IT SMELLS REALLY BAD!
OKAY, I'LL TALK TO HIM.
STOP EATING SAUERKRAUT IN FRONT OF YOUR SISTER.
KIRKMAN & SCOTT

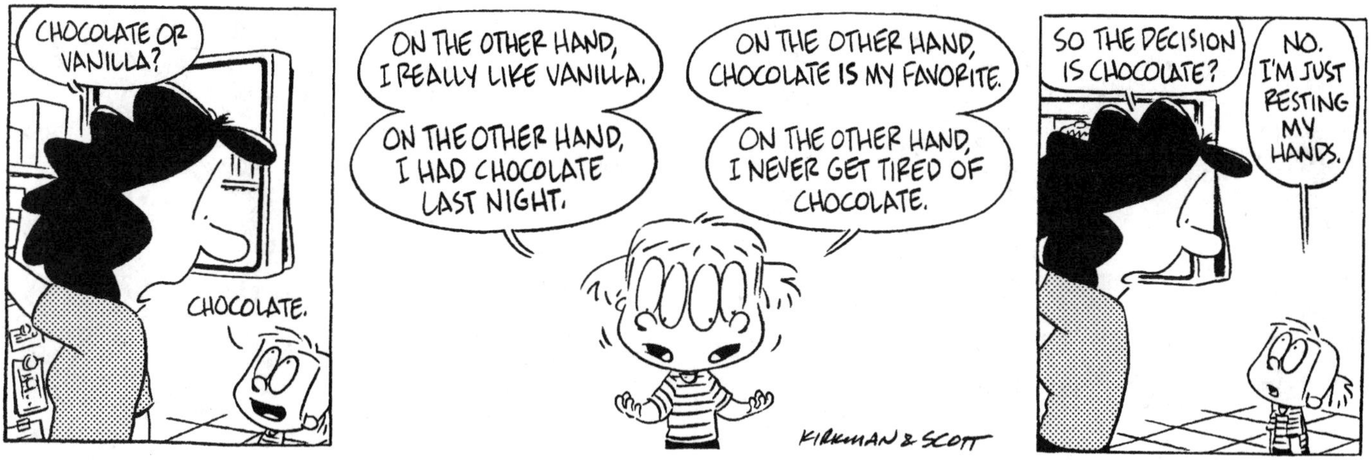
CHOCOLATE OR VANILLA?
CHOCOLATE.
ON THE OTHER HAND, I REALLY LIKE VANILLA.
ON THE OTHER HAND, I HAD CHOCOLATE LAST NIGHT.
ON THE OTHER HAND, CHOCOLATE IS MY FAVORITE.
ON THE OTHER HAND, I NEVER GET TIRED OF CHOCOLATE.
KIRKMAN & SCOTT
SO THE DECISION IS CHOCOLATE?
NO. I'M JUST RESTING MY HANDS.

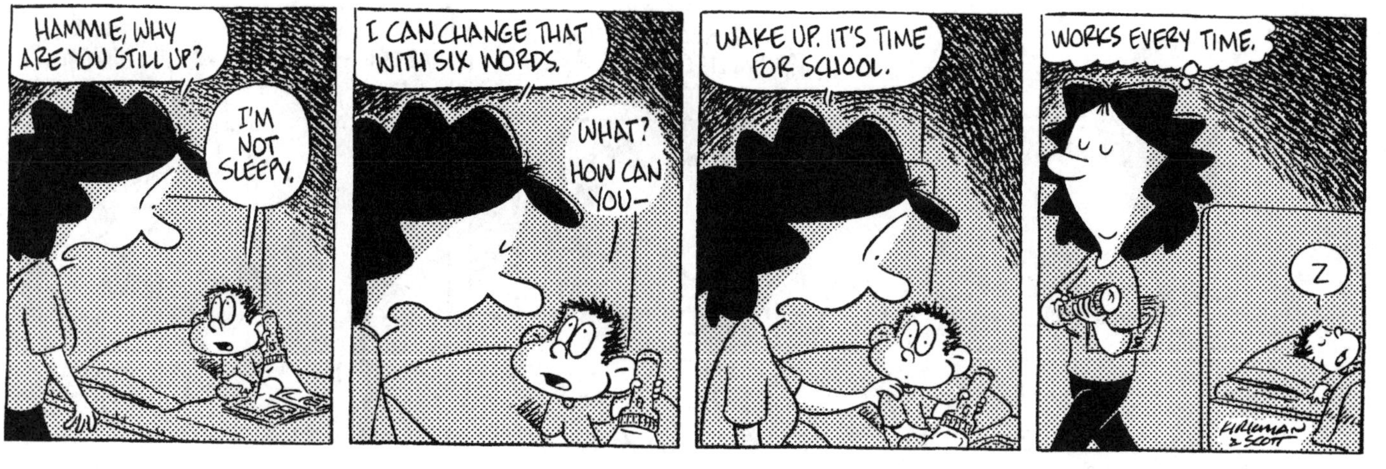
HAMMIE, WHY ARE YOU STILL UP?
I'M NOT SLEEPY.
I CAN CHANGE THAT WITH SIX WORDS.
WHAT? HOW CAN YOU–
WAKE UP. IT'S TIME FOR SCHOOL.
WORKS EVERY TIME.
Z
KIRKMAN & SCOTT

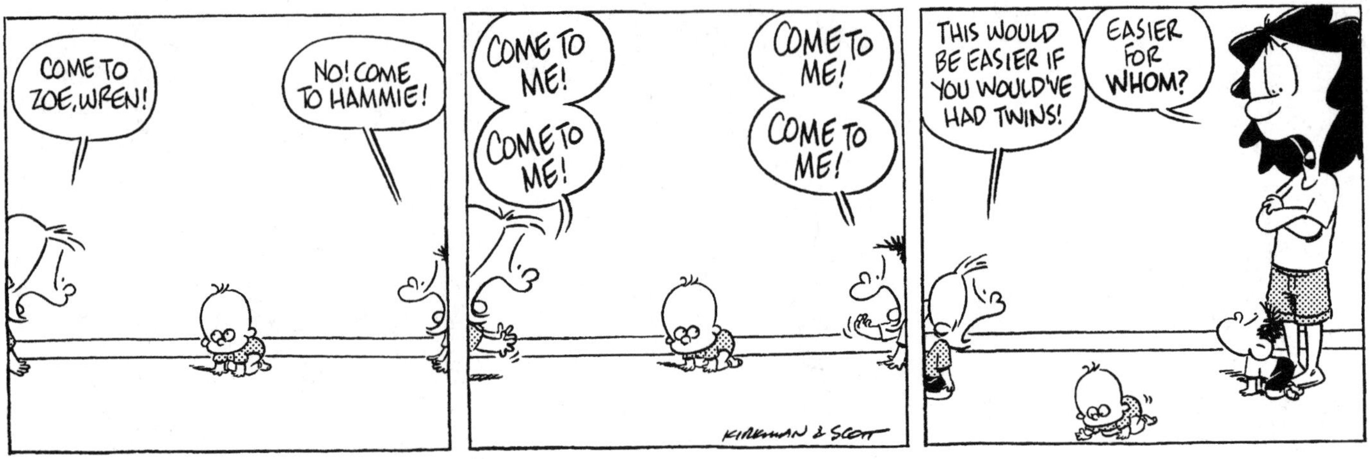
COME TO ZOE, WREN!
NO! COME TO HAMMIE!
COME TO ME!
COME TO ME!
COME TO ME!
COME TO ME!
KIRKMAN & SCOTT
THIS WOULD BE EASIER IF YOU WOULD'VE HAD TWINS!
EASIER FOR WHOM?

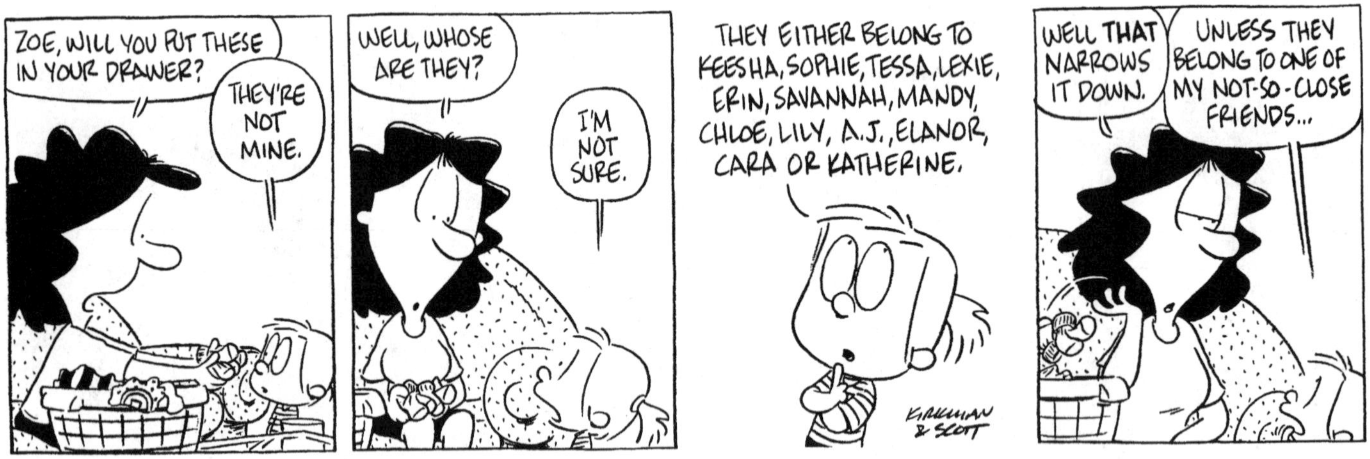
ZOE, WILL YOU PUT THESE IN YOUR DRAWER?
THEY'RE NOT MINE.
WELL, WHOSE ARE THEY?
I'M NOT SURE.
THEY EITHER BELONG TO KEESHA, SOPHIE, TESSA, LEXIE, ERIN, SAVANNAH, MANDY, CHLOE, LILY, A.J., ELANOR, CARA OR KATHERINE.
KIRKMAN & SCOTT
WELL THAT NARROWS IT DOWN.
UNLESS THEY BELONG TO ONE OF MY NOT-SO-CLOSE FRIENDS...

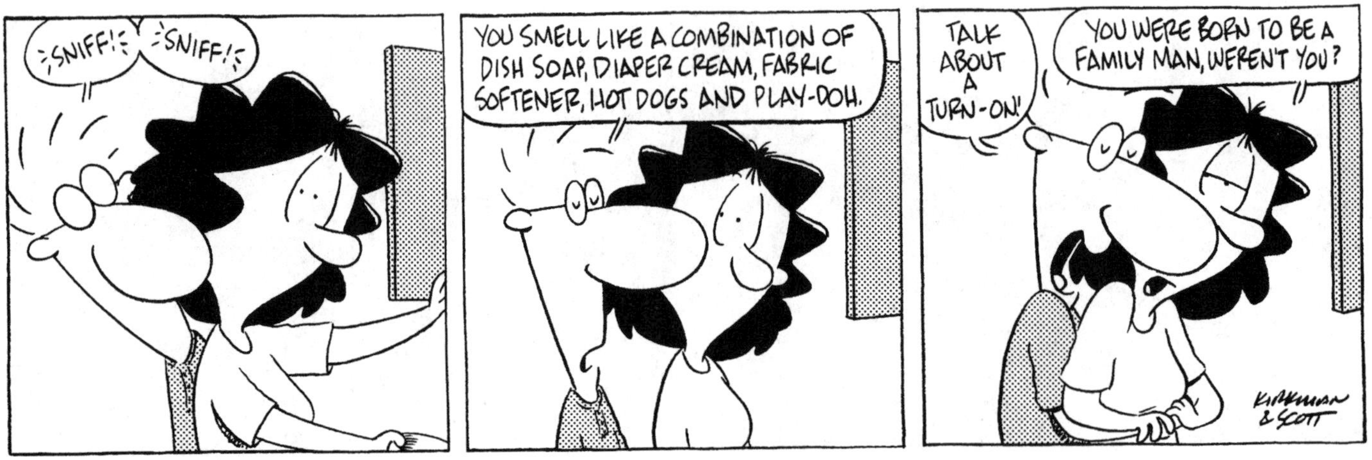
SNIFF!
SNIFF!
YOU SMELL LIKE A COMBINATION OF DISH SOAP, DIAPER CREAM, FABRIC SOFTENER, HOT DOGS AND PLAY-DOH.
TALK ABOUT A TURN-ON!
YOU WERE BORN TO BE A FAMILY MAN, WEREN'T YOU?
KIRKMAN & SCOTT

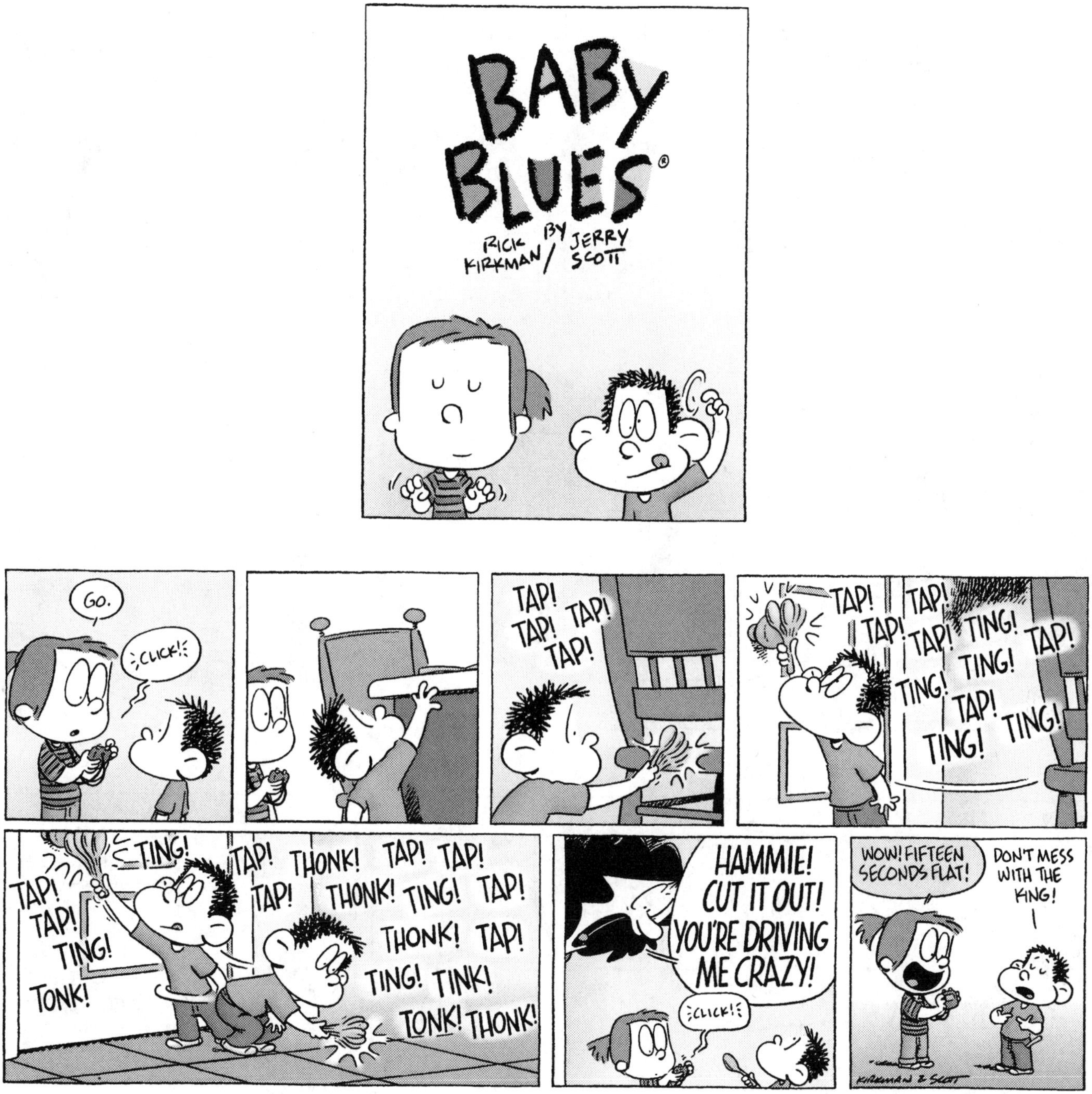
BABY BLUES®
BY RICK KIRKMAN / JERRY SCOTT
GO.
CLICK!
TAP! TAP! TAP! TAP!
TAP! TAP! TAP! TAP! TING! TAP! TING! TING! TAP! TING! TING!
TING! TAP! TAP! TING! TONK! TAP! THONK! TAP! TAP! TAP! THONK! TING! TAP! THONK! TAP! TING! TINK! TONK! THONK!
HAMMIE! CUT IT OUT! YOU'RE DRIVING ME CRAZY!
CLICK!
WOW! FIFTEEN SECONDS FLAT!
DON'T MESS WITH THE KING!
KIRKMAN & SCOTT

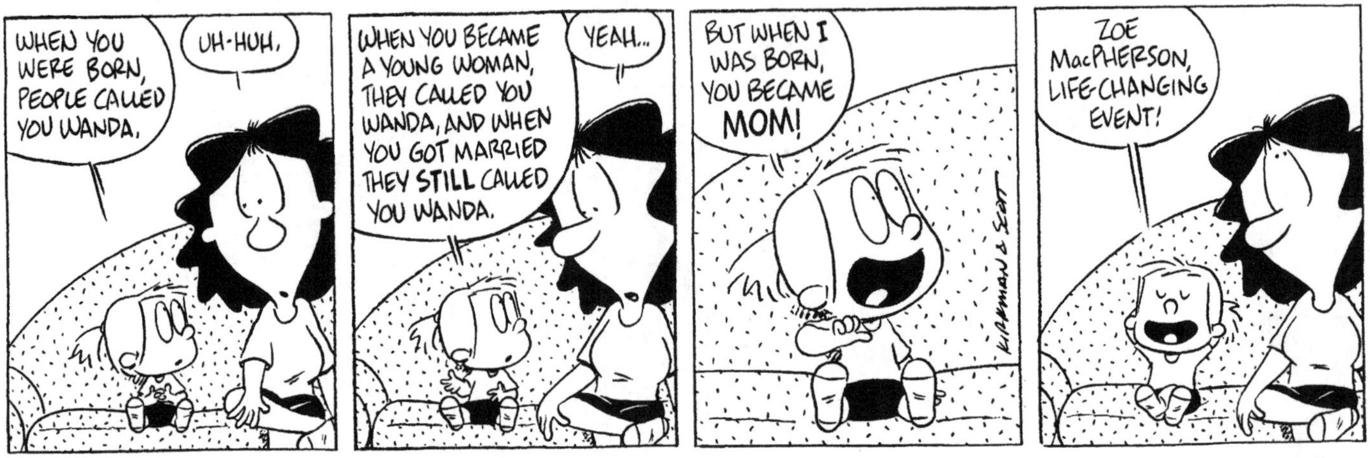
WHEN YOU WERE BORN, PEOPLE CALLED YOU WANDA.
UH-HUH.
WHEN YOU BECAME A YOUNG WOMAN, THEY CALLED YOU WANDA, AND WHEN YOU GOT MARRIED THEY STILL CALLED YOU WANDA.
YEAH...
BUT WHEN I WAS BORN, YOU BECAME MOM!
KIRKMAN & SCOTT
ZOE MacPHERSON, LIFE-CHANGING EVENT!

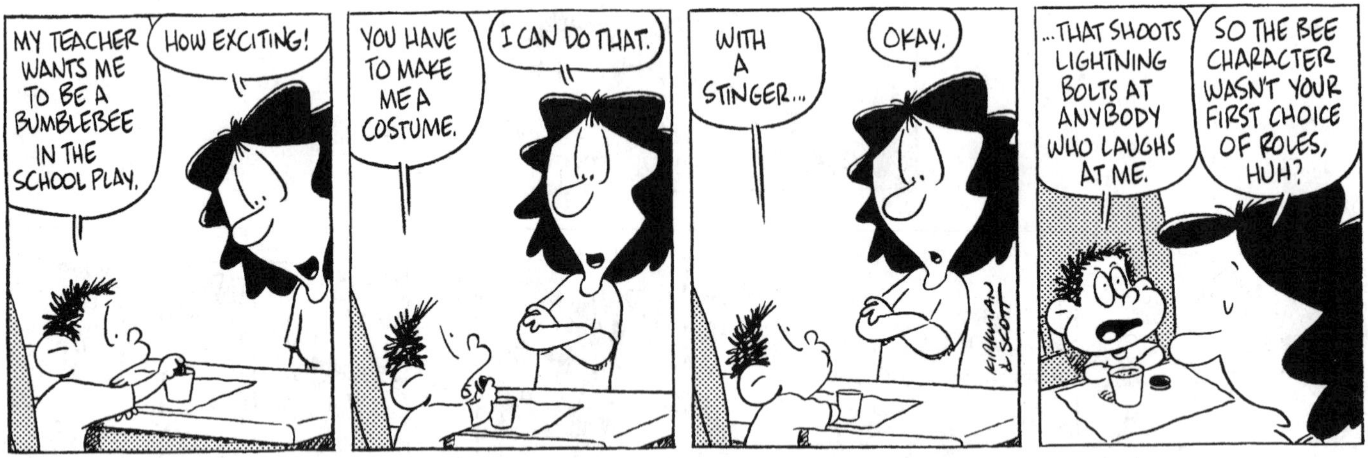
MY TEACHER WANTS ME TO BE A BUMBLEBEE IN THE SCHOOL PLAY.
HOW EXCITING!
YOU HAVE TO MAKE ME A COSTUME.
I CAN DO THAT.
WITH A STINGER...
OKAY.
KIRKMAN & SCOTT
...THAT SHOOTS LIGHTNING BOLTS AT ANYBODY WHO LAUGHS AT ME.
SO THE BEE CHARACTER WASN'T YOUR FIRST CHOICE OF ROLES, HUH?

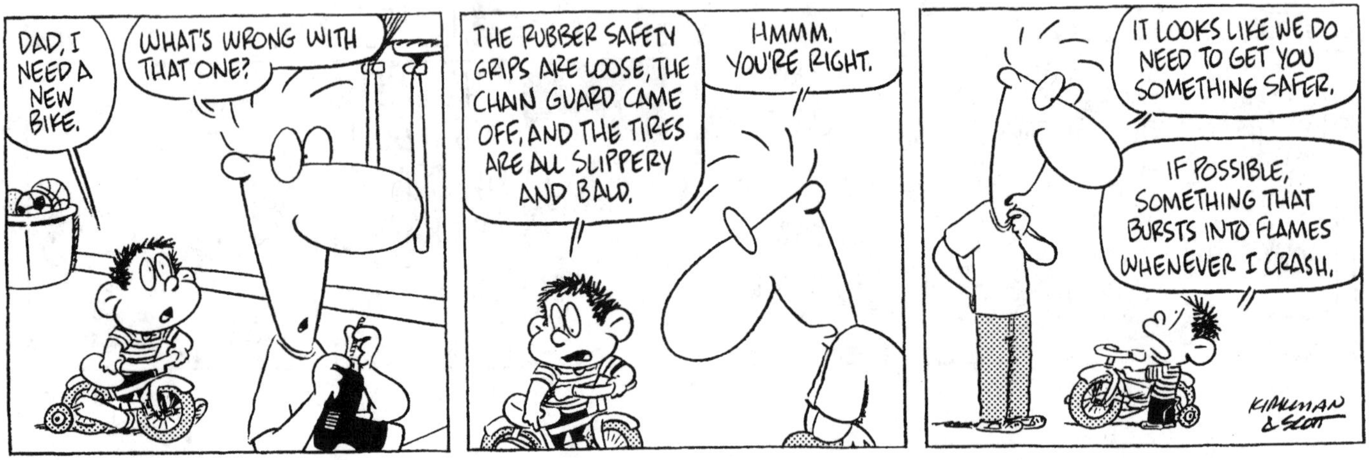
DAD, I NEED A NEW BIKE.
WHAT'S WRONG WITH THAT ONE?
THE RUBBER SAFETY GRIPS ARE LOOSE, THE CHAIN GUARD CAME OFF, AND THE TIRES ARE ALL SLIPPERY AND BALD.
HMMM. YOU'RE RIGHT.
IT LOOKS LIKE WE DO NEED TO GET YOU SOMETHING SAFER.
IF POSSIBLE, SOMETHING THAT BURSTS INTO FLAMES WHENEVER I CRASH.
KIRKMAN & SCOTT

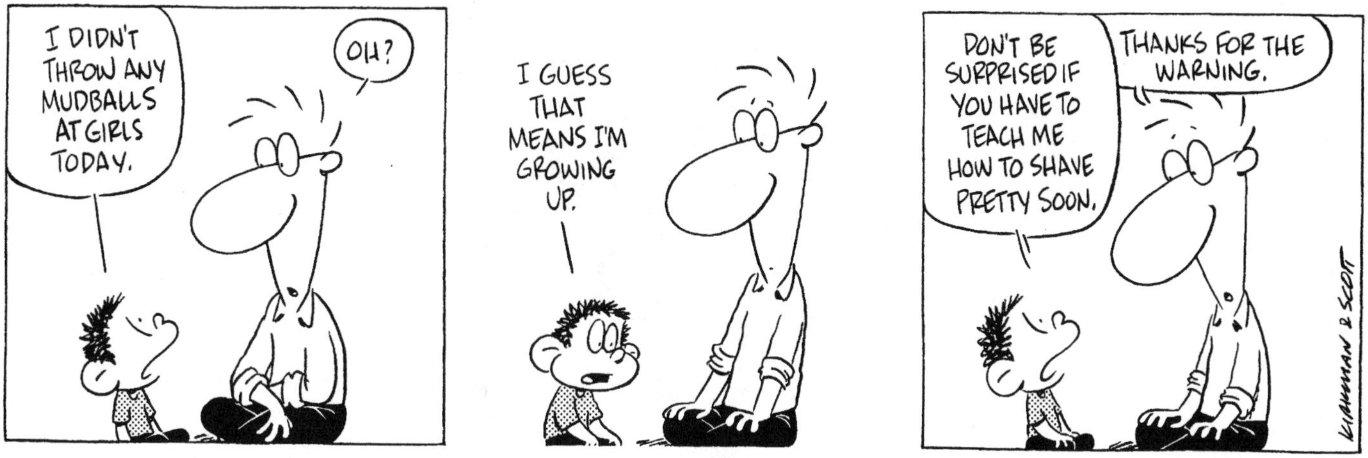
I DIDN'T THROW ANY MUDBALLS AT GIRLS TODAY.
OH?
I GUESS THAT MEANS I'M GROWING UP.
DON'T BE SURPRISED IF YOU HAVE TO TEACH ME HOW TO SHAVE PRETTY SOON.
THANKS FOR THE WARNING.
KIRKMAN & SCOTT

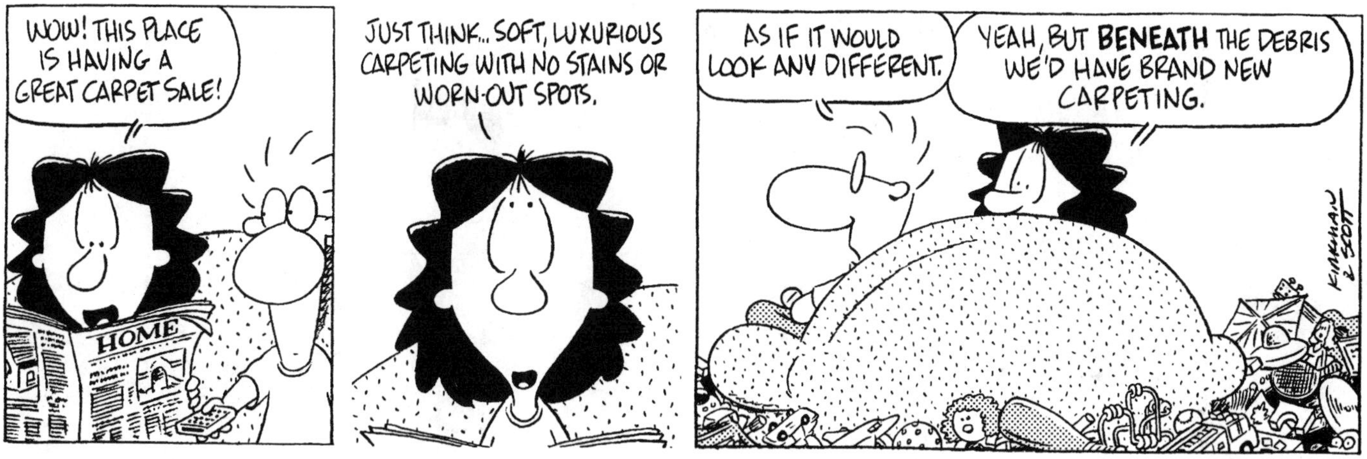
WOW! THIS PLACE IS HAVING A GREAT CARPET SALE!
HOME
JUST THINK... SOFT, LUXURIOUS CARPETING WITH NO STAINS OR WORN-OUT SPOTS.
AS IF IT WOULD LOOK ANY DIFFERENT.
YEAH, BUT **BENEATH** THE DEBRIS WE'D HAVE BRAND NEW CARPETING.
KIRKMAN & SCOTT

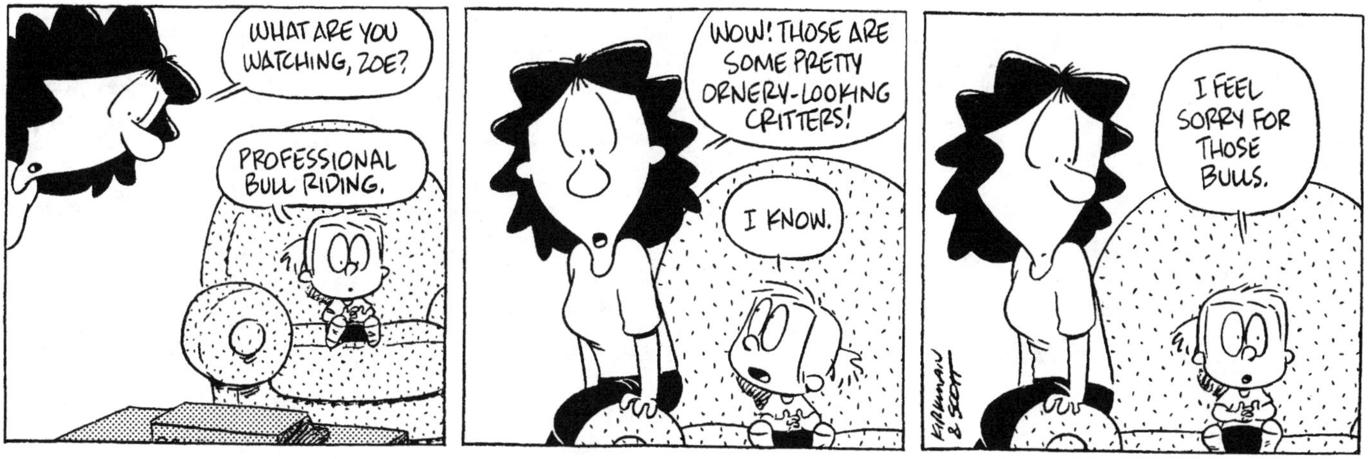
WHAT ARE YOU WATCHING, ZOE?
PROFESSIONAL BULL RIDING.
WOW! THOSE ARE SOME PRETTY ORNERY-LOOKING CRITTERS!
I KNOW.
KIRKMAN & SCOTT
I FEEL SORRY FOR THOSE BULLS.

BABY BLUES®
BY RICK KIRKMAN / JERRY SCOTT

I WISH I HAD CURLY HAIR LIKE WREN'S.
BUT NOT AS CURLY. MORE STRAIGHTISH-LY CURLY.
AND LONGER.
AND THICKER.
AND NOT AS BLOND.
SO BASICALLY, YOU WISH THAT YOU HAD THE HAIR YOU ALREADY HAVE.
YEAH... EXACTLY!
THANKS, DADDY! YOU'RE SUCH A GOOD LISTENER!
WELL, LISTENING IS MY SPECIALTY.
IT'S THE UNDERSTANDING PART THAT NEEDS WORK.

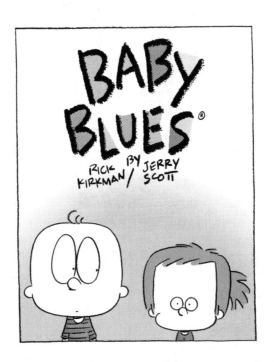

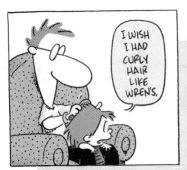

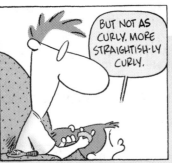

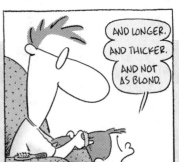

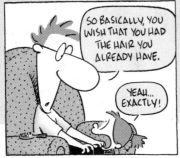

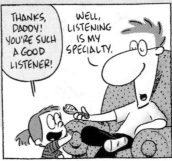

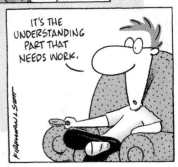

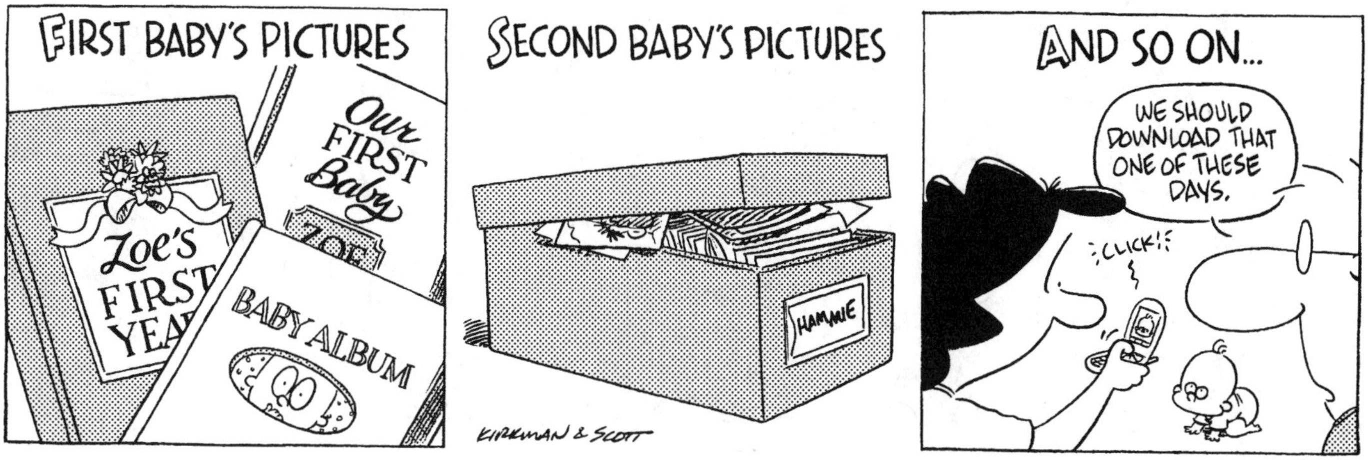
FIRST BABY'S PICTURES
Our FIRST Baby
ZOE
Zoe's FIRST YEAR
BABY ALBUM
SECOND BABY'S PICTURES
HAMMIE
KIRKMAN & SCOTT
AND SO ON...
WE SHOULD DOWNLOAD THAT ONE OF THESE DAYS.
CLICK!

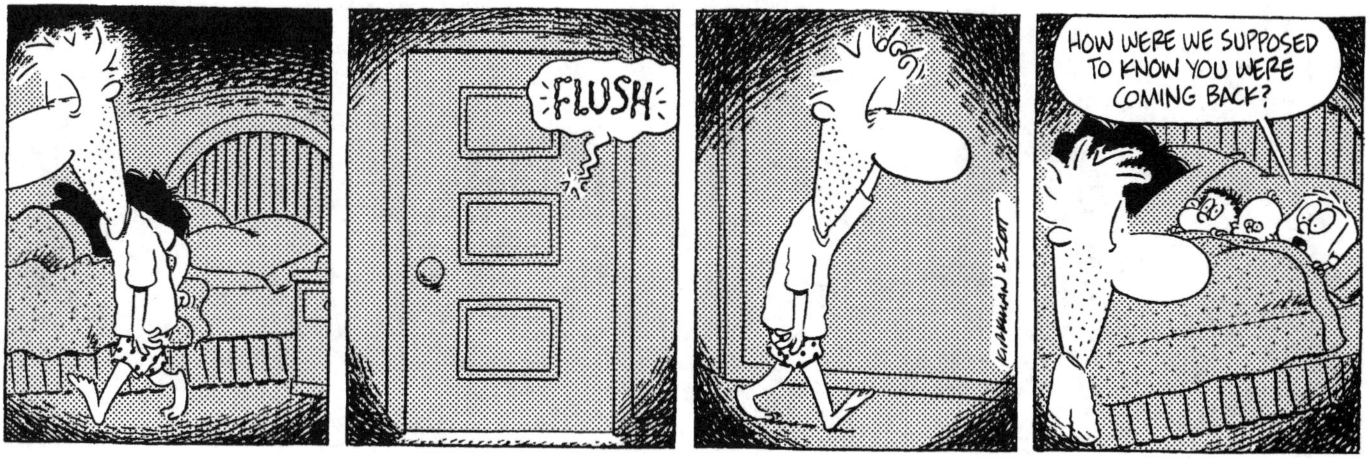
FLUSH
KIRKMAN & SCOTT
HOW WERE WE SUPPOSED TO KNOW YOU WERE COMING BACK?

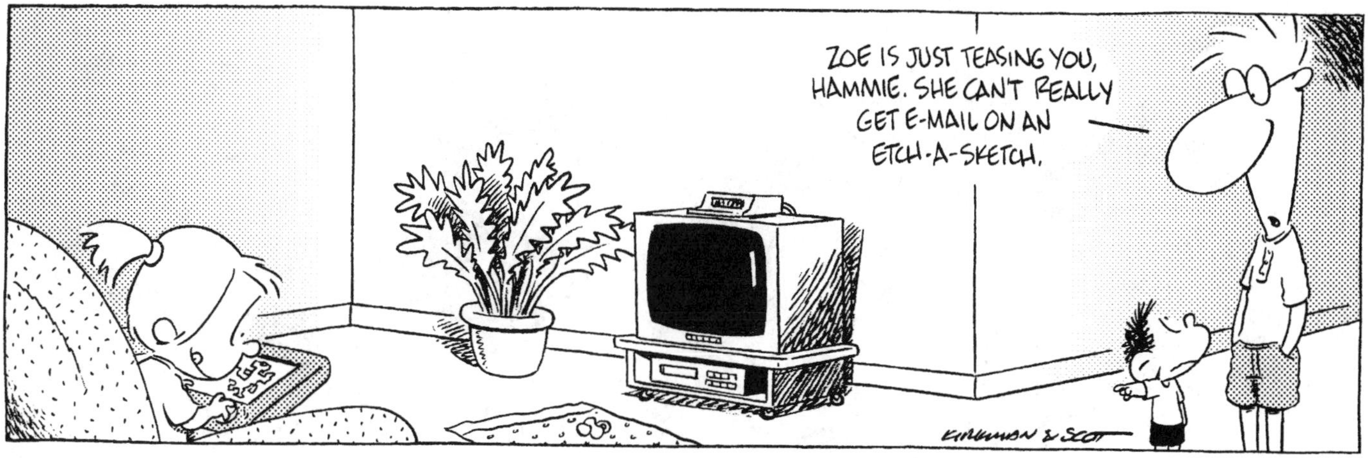
ZOE IS JUST TEASING YOU, HAMMIE. SHE CAN'T REALLY GET E-MAIL ON AN ETCH-A-SKETCH.
KIRKMAN & SCOTT

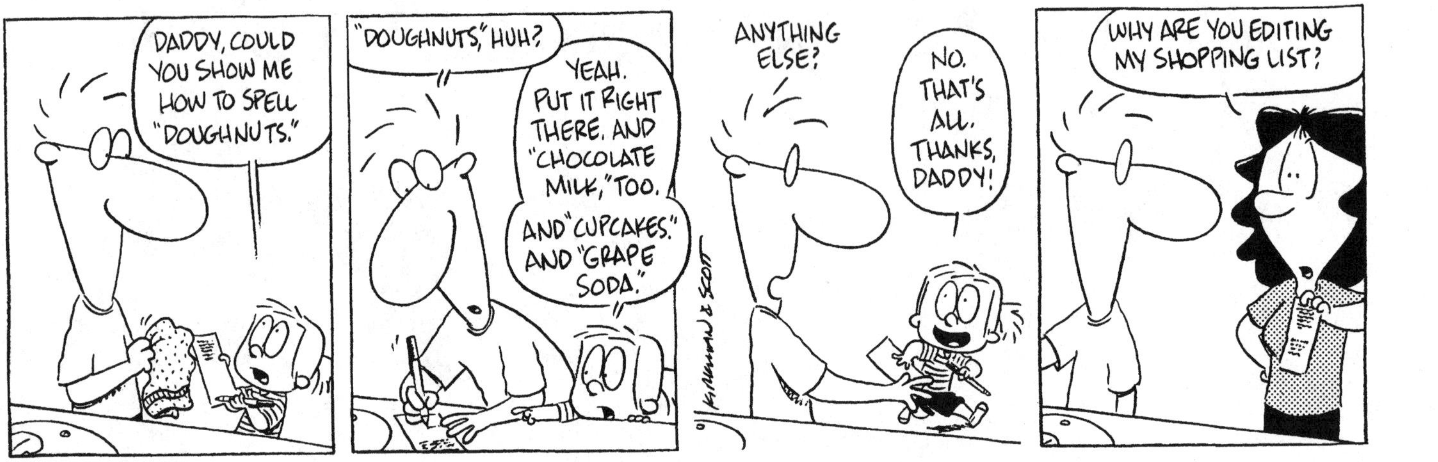
DADDY, COULD YOU SHOW ME HOW TO SPELL "DOUGHNUTS."
"DOUGHNUTS," HUH?
YEAH. PUT IT RIGHT THERE. AND "CHOCOLATE MILK," TOO.
AND "CUPCAKES." AND "GRAPE SODA."
KIRKMAN & SCOTT
ANYTHING ELSE?
NO. THAT'S ALL. THANKS, DADDY!
WHY ARE YOU EDITING MY SHOPPING LIST?

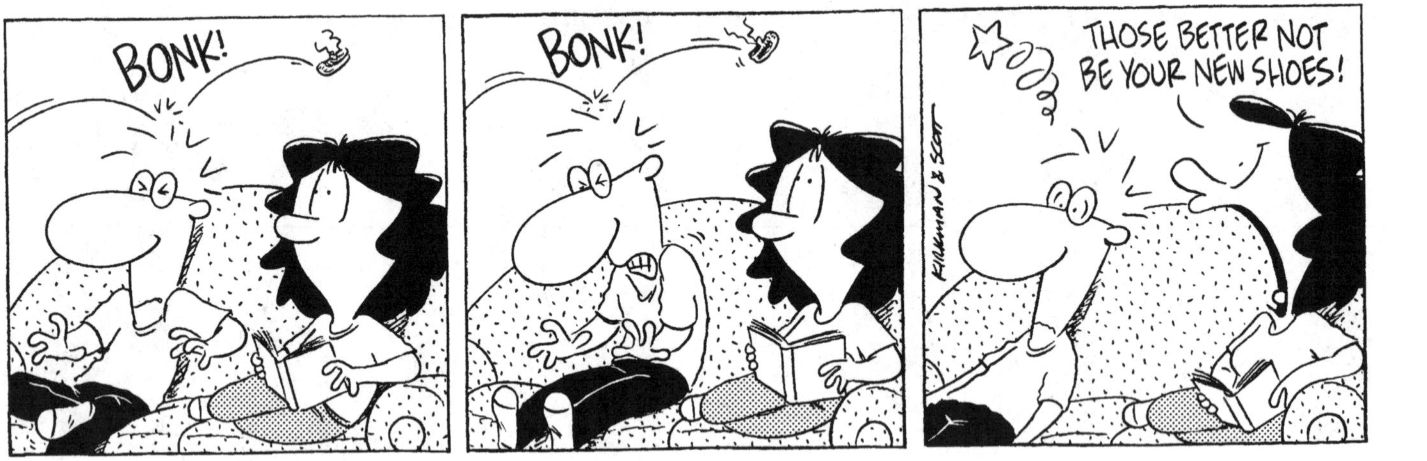
BONK!
BONK!
KIRKMAN & SCOTT
THOSE BETTER NOT BE YOUR NEW SHOES!

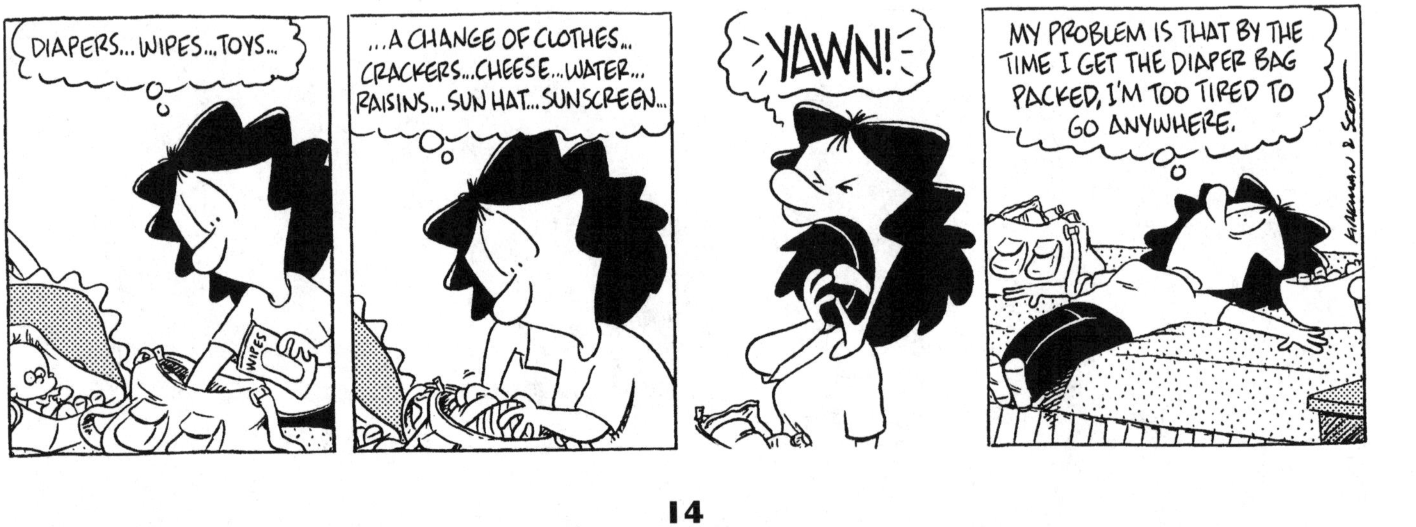
DIAPERS... WIPES... TOYS...
WIPES
...A CHANGE OF CLOTHES... CRACKERS... CHEESE... WATER... RAISINS... SUN HAT... SUNSCREEN...
YAWN!
MY PROBLEM IS THAT BY THE TIME I GET THE DIAPER BAG PACKED, I'M TOO TIRED TO GO ANYWHERE.
KIRKMAN & SCOTT

BABY BLUES®
BY
RICK KIRKMAN / JERRY SCOTT

OH, SURE! PUNISH ME!
WHY NOT? EVERYTHING IS ZOE'S FAULT, RIGHT?
JUST PUT ME IN MY ROOM— PROBLEM SOLVED!
I'LL BET YOU'RE ALL REALLY ENJOYING THIS!
THERE'S A BET SHE'D LOSE.
KIRKMAN & SCOTT

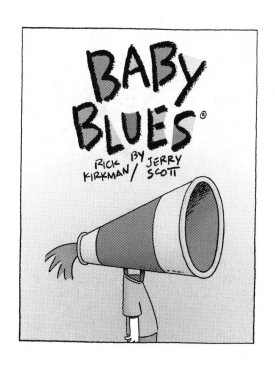

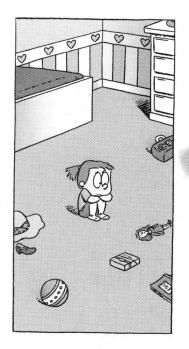

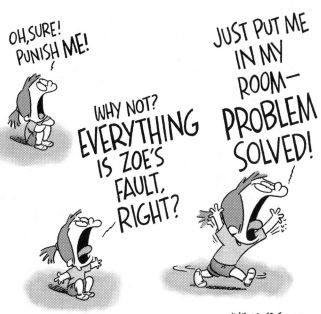

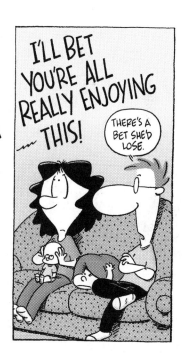

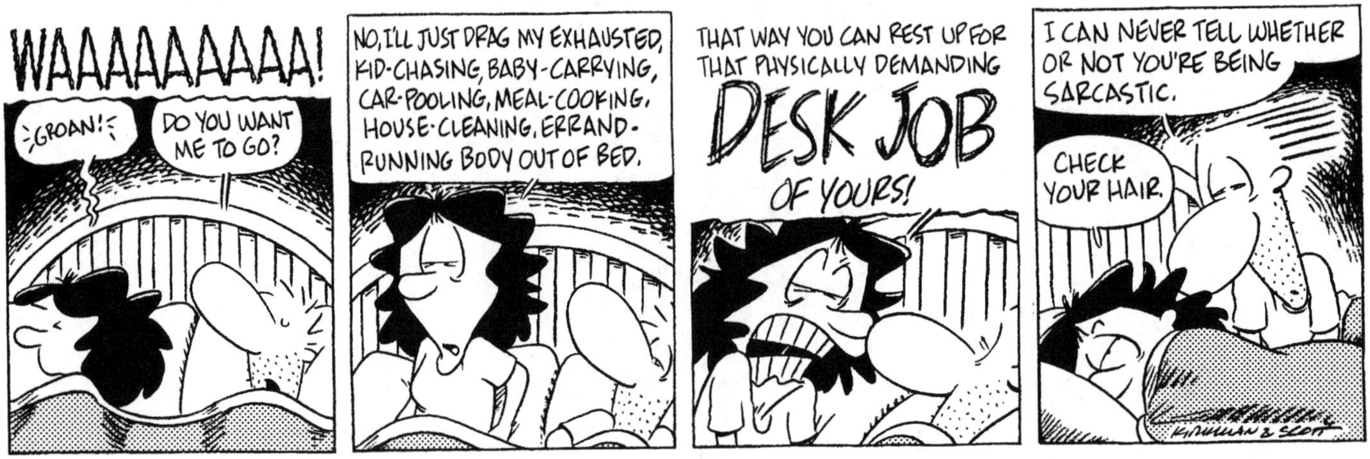
WAAAAAAAAA!
GROAN!
DO YOU WANT ME TO GO?
NO, I'LL JUST DRAG MY EXHAUSTED, KID-CHASING, BABY-CARRYING, CAR-POOLING, MEAL-COOKING, HOUSE-CLEANING, ERRAND-RUNNING BODY OUT OF BED.
THAT WAY YOU CAN REST UP FOR THAT PHYSICALLY DEMANDING DESK JOB OF YOURS!
I CAN NEVER TELL WHETHER OR NOT YOU'RE BEING SARCASTIC.
CHECK YOUR HAIR.
KIRKMAN & SCOTT

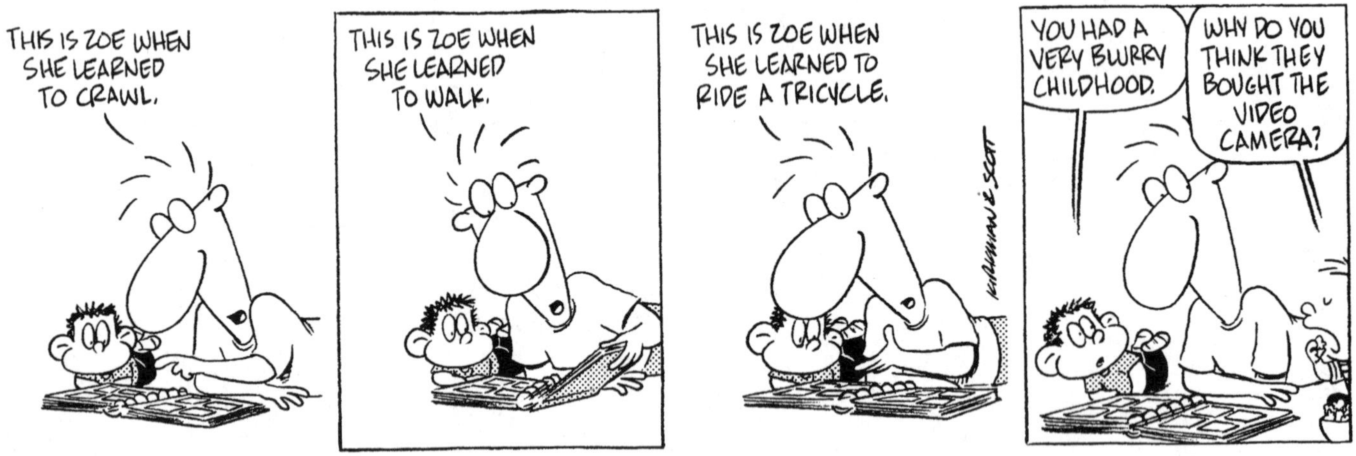
THIS IS ZOE WHEN SHE LEARNED TO CRAWL.
THIS IS ZOE WHEN SHE LEARNED TO WALK.
THIS IS ZOE WHEN SHE LEARNED TO RIDE A TRICYCLE.
KIRKMAN & SCOTT
YOU HAD A VERY BLURRY CHILDHOOD.
WHY DO YOU THINK THEY BOUGHT THE VIDEO CAMERA?

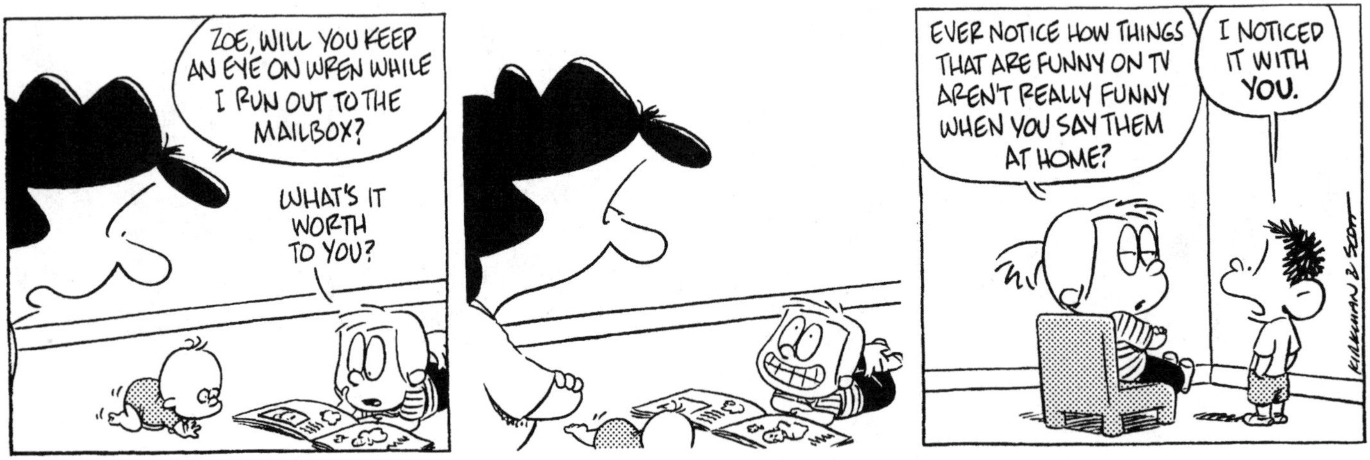
ZOE, WILL YOU KEEP AN EYE ON WREN WHILE I RUN OUT TO THE MAILBOX?
WHAT'S IT WORTH TO YOU?
EVER NOTICE HOW THINGS THAT ARE FUNNY ON TV AREN'T REALLY FUNNY WHEN YOU SAY THEM AT HOME?
I NOTICED IT WITH YOU.
KIRKMAN & SCOTT

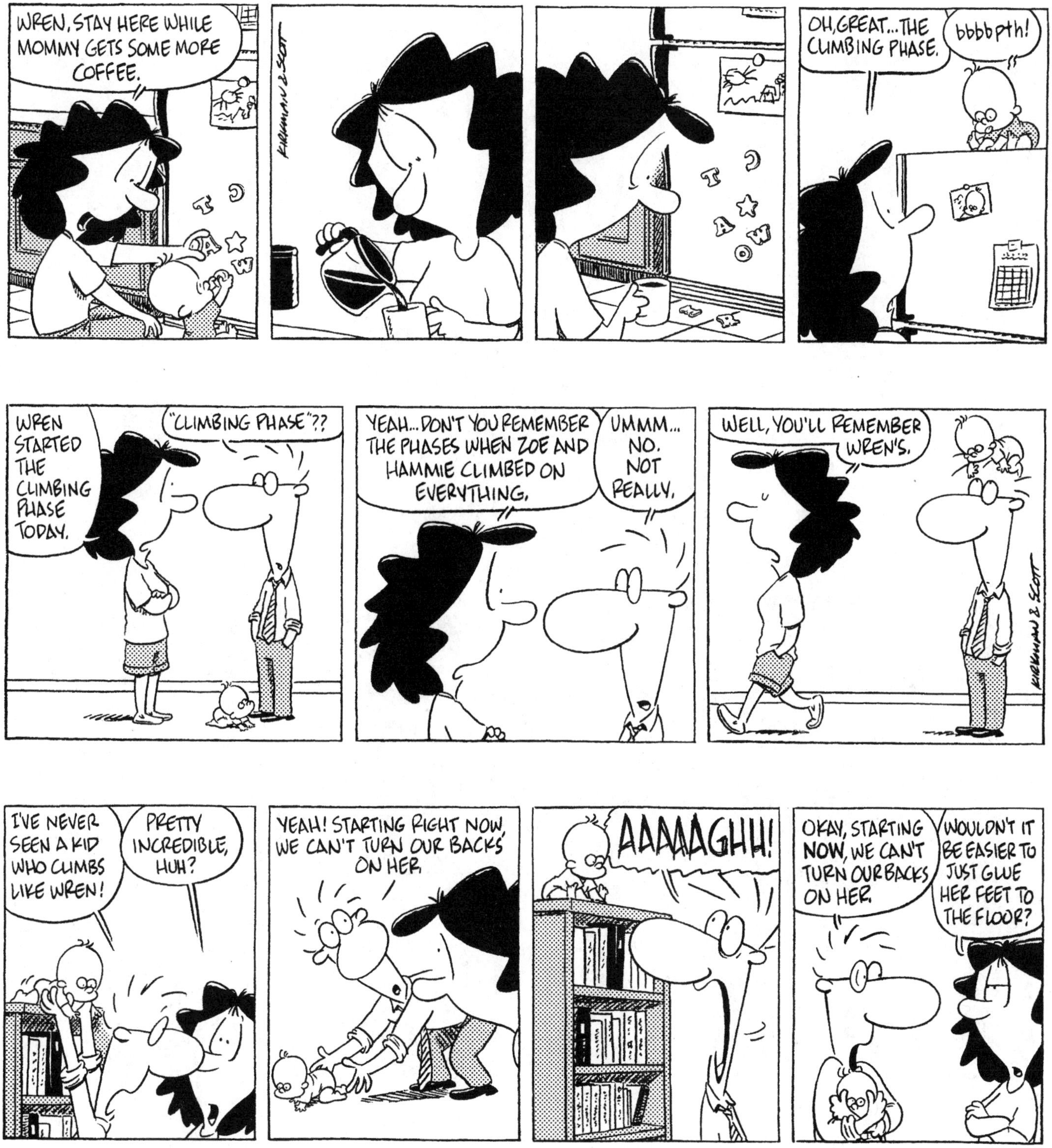
WREN, STAY HERE WHILE MOMMY GETS SOME MORE COFFEE.
KIRKMAN & SCOTT
OH, GREAT... THE CLIMBING PHASE.
bbbbpth!
WREN STARTED THE CLIMBING PHASE TODAY.
"CLIMBING PHASE"??
YEAH... DON'T YOU REMEMBER THE PHASES WHEN ZOE AND HAMMIE CLIMBED ON EVERYTHING.
UMMM... NO. NOT REALLY.
WELL, YOU'LL REMEMBER WREN'S.
KIRKMAN & SCOTT
I'VE NEVER SEEN A KID WHO CLIMBS LIKE WREN!
PRETTY INCREDIBLE, HUH?
YEAH! STARTING RIGHT NOW, WE CAN'T TURN OUR BACKS ON HER.
AAAAAGHH!
OKAY, STARTING NOW, WE CAN'T TURN OUR BACKS ON HER.
WOULDN'T IT BE EASIER TO JUST GLUE HER FEET TO THE FLOOR?

BABY BLUES®
BY RICK KIRKMAN / JERRY SCOTT
WORLD'S GREATEST MOM

MONDAY
Remember Mom This Sunday
Chocolate
TUESDAY
MOTHER DAY HINTS
SPORTS
GIFTS FOR MOM
MOTHER'S DAY SALE!
WEDNESDAY
WORLD'S GREATEST MOM
Mother's Day IS MAY 8th!
Place your orders today
THURSDAY
MOTHERS DAY BRUNCH 11-2 SUNDAY
FRIDAY
Mother's Day
SATURDAY NIGHT
THIS HOLIDAY SURE HAS A WAY OF SNEAKING UP ON YOU.
YEAH. THEY SHOULD ADVERTISE IT OR SOMETHING!

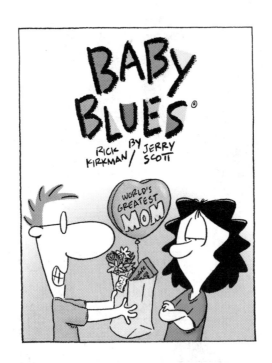

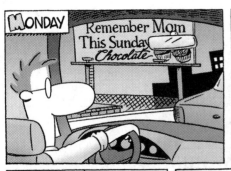

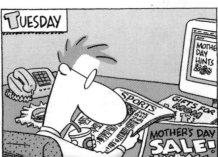

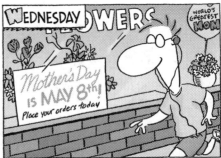

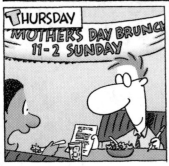

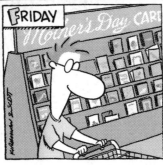

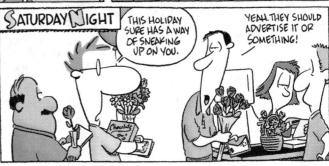

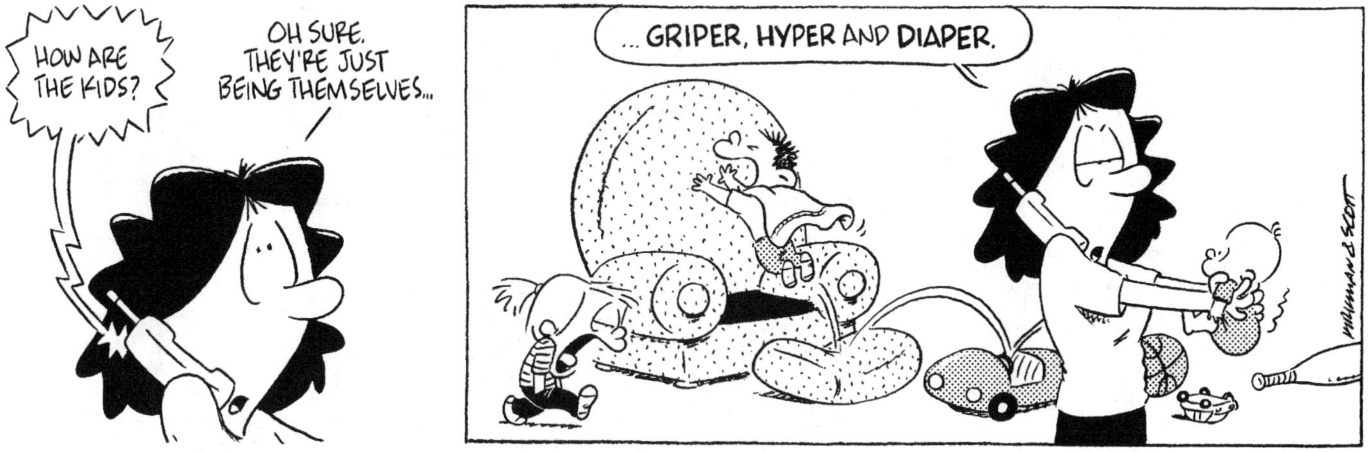
HOW ARE THE KIDS?
OH SURE. THEY'RE JUST BEING THEMSELVES...
...GRIPER, HYPER AND DIAPER.
KIRKMAN & SCOTT

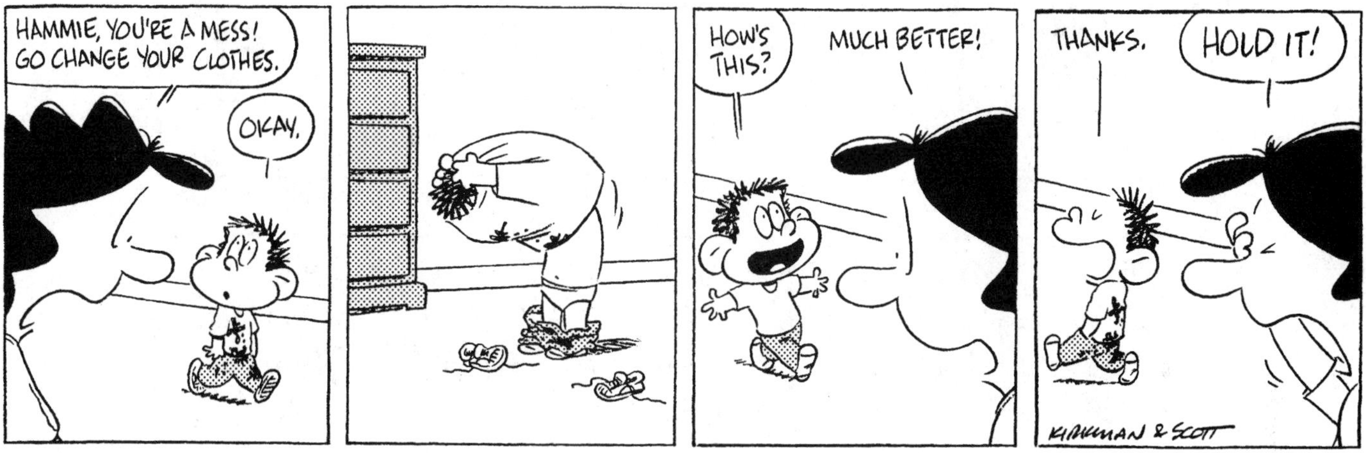
HAMMIE, YOU'RE A MESS! GO CHANGE YOUR CLOTHES.
OKAY.
HOW'S THIS?
MUCH BETTER!
THANKS.
HOLD IT!
KIRKMAN & SCOTT

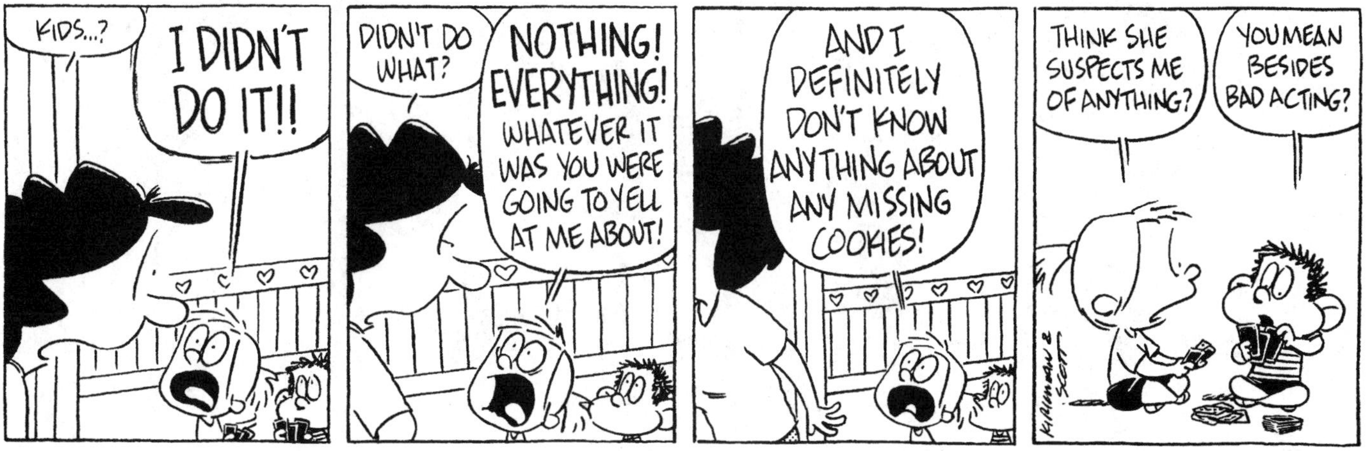
KIDS...?
I DIDN'T DO IT!!
DIDN'T DO WHAT?
NOTHING! EVERYTHING! WHATEVER IT WAS YOU WERE GOING TO YELL AT ME ABOUT!
AND I DEFINITELY DON'T KNOW ANYTHING ABOUT ANY MISSING COOKIES!
THINK SHE SUSPECTS ME OF ANYTHING?
YOU MEAN BESIDES BAD ACTING?
KIRKMAN & SCOTT

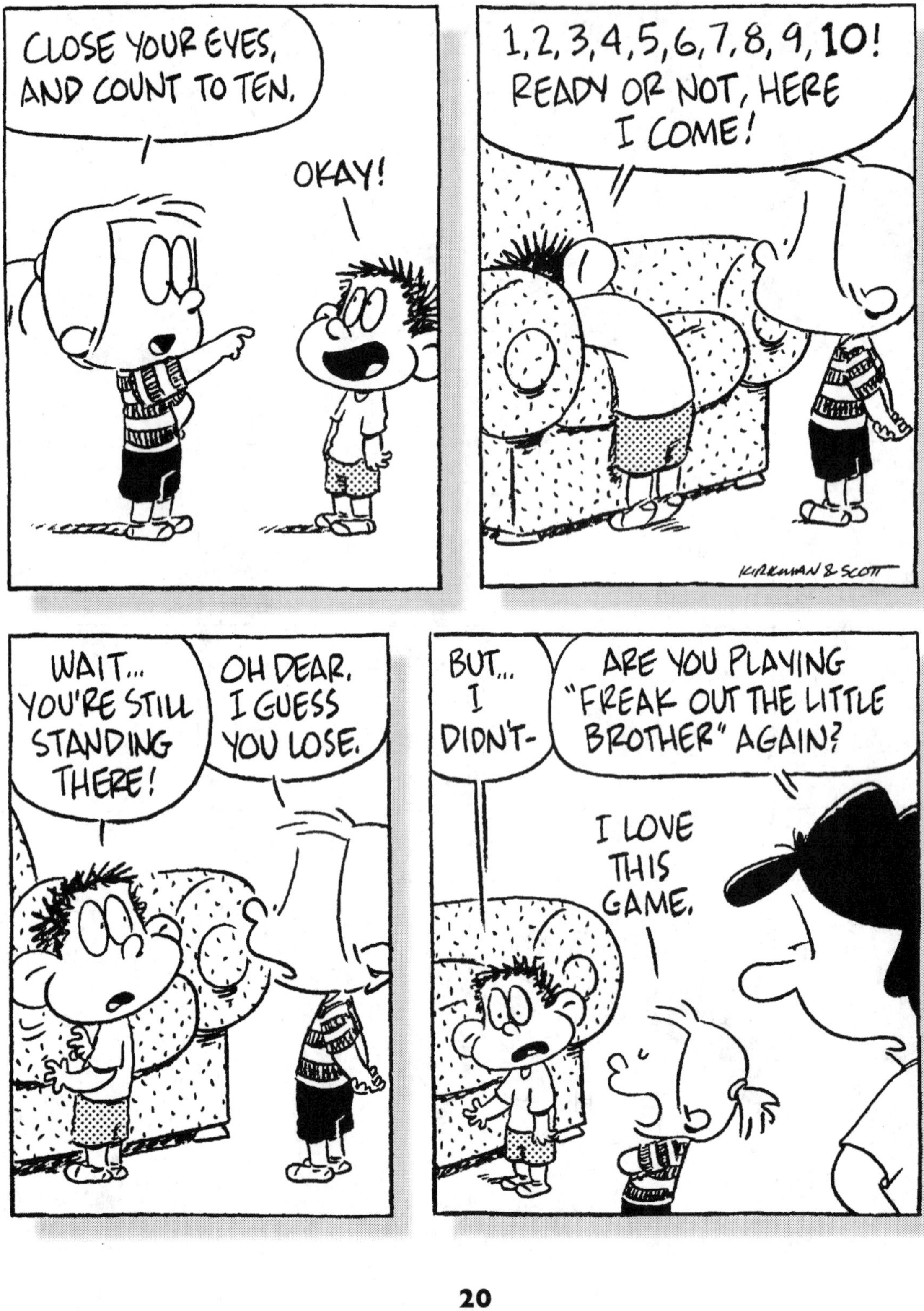
CLOSE YOUR EYES, AND COUNT TO TEN.
OKAY!
1,2,3,4,5,6,7,8,9,10! READY OR NOT, HERE I COME!
KIRKMAN & SCOTT
WAIT... YOU'RE STILL STANDING THERE!
OH DEAR. I GUESS YOU LOSE.
BUT... I DIDN'T-
ARE YOU PLAYING "FREAK OUT THE LITTLE BROTHER" AGAIN?
I LOVE THIS GAME.

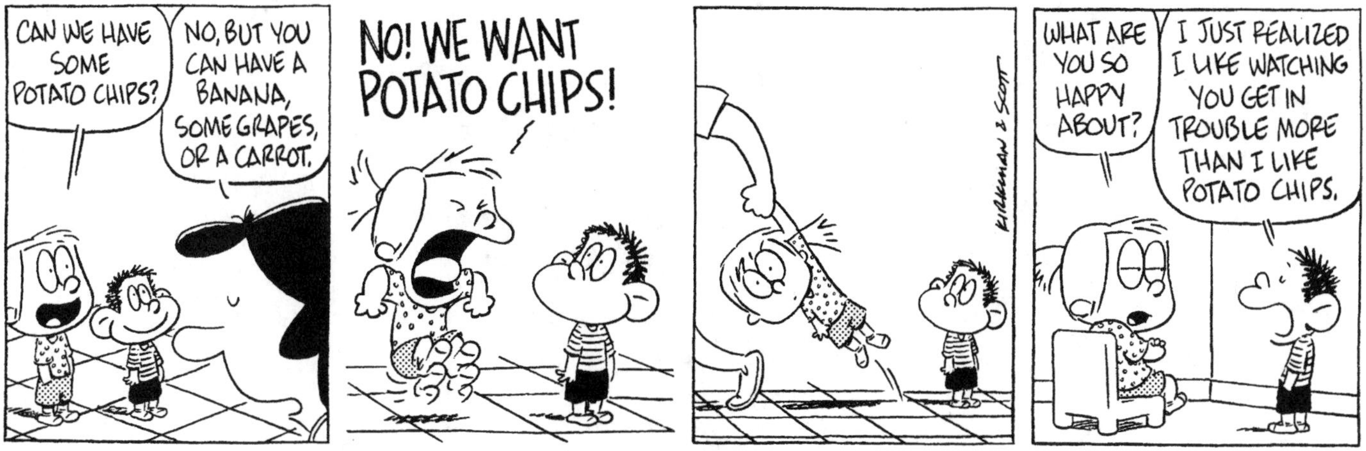
CAN WE HAVE SOME POTATO CHIPS?
NO, BUT YOU CAN HAVE A BANANA, SOME GRAPES, OR A CARROT.
NO! WE WANT POTATO CHIPS!
KIRKMAN & SCOTT
WHAT ARE YOU SO HAPPY ABOUT?
I JUST REALIZED I LIKE WATCHING YOU GET IN TROUBLE MORE THAN I LIKE POTATO CHIPS.

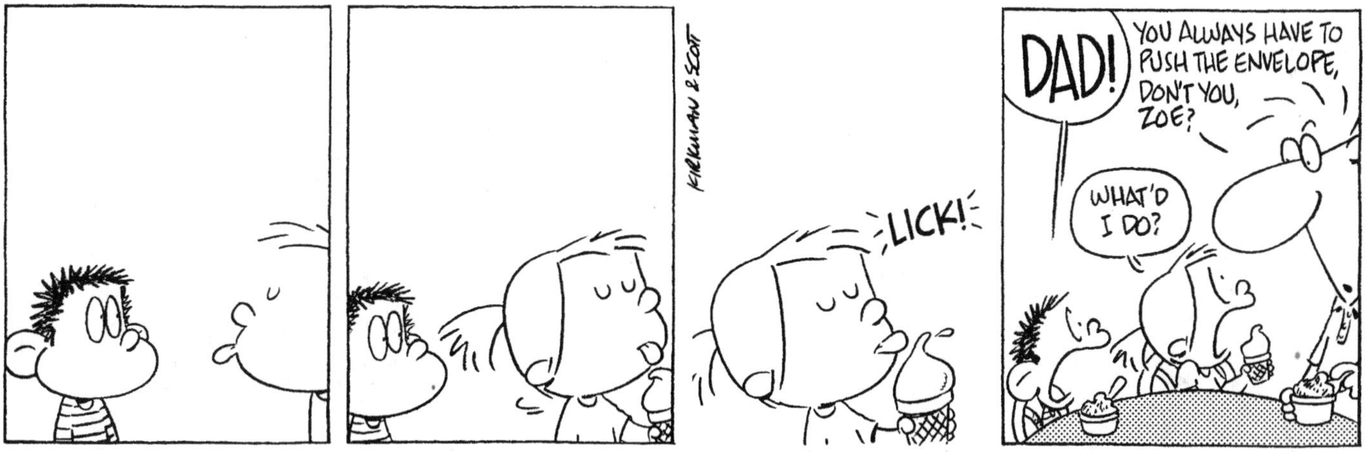
KIRKMAN & SCOTT
LICK!
DAD!
YOU ALWAYS HAVE TO PUSH THE ENVELOPE, DON'T YOU, ZOE?
WHAT'D I DO?

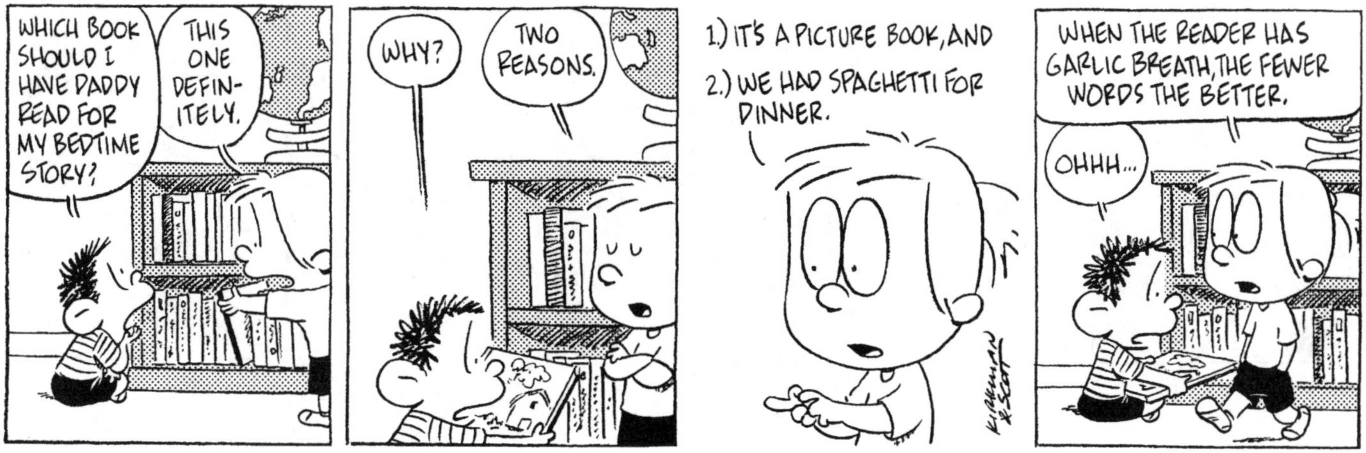
WHICH BOOK SHOULD I HAVE DADDY READ FOR MY BEDTIME STORY?
THIS ONE DEFIN-ITELY.
WHY?
TWO REASONS.
1.) IT'S A PICTURE BOOK, AND
2.) WE HAD SPAGHETTI FOR DINNER.
KIRKMAN & SCOTT
WHEN THE READER HAS GARLIC BREATH, THE FEWER WORDS THE BETTER.
OHHH...

BABY BLUES®
BY RICK KIRKMAN / JERRY SCOTT

LET'S GO GUYS!! STORY TIME!
COMING!
WHAT KIND OF STORY DO YOU WANT ME TO READ TONIGHT, HAMMIE... FICTION OR NON-FICTION?
HUH?
WHAT'S "FICTION"?
IT MEANS MADE UP.
RIGHT. FICTION COMES FROM THE WRITER'S IMAGINATION.
OH.
LIKE MOM'S WEIGHT ON HER DRIVER'S LICENSE.
WELL, TECHNICALLY THAT'S FANTASY...
I CAN HEAR YOU!!
KIRKMAN & SCOTT

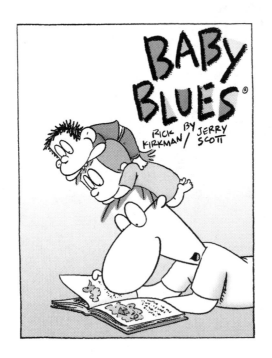

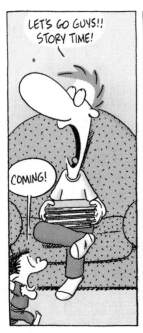

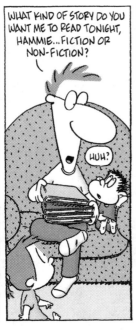

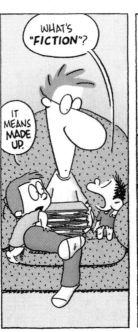

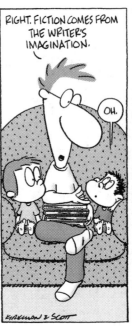

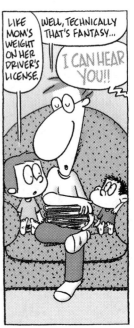

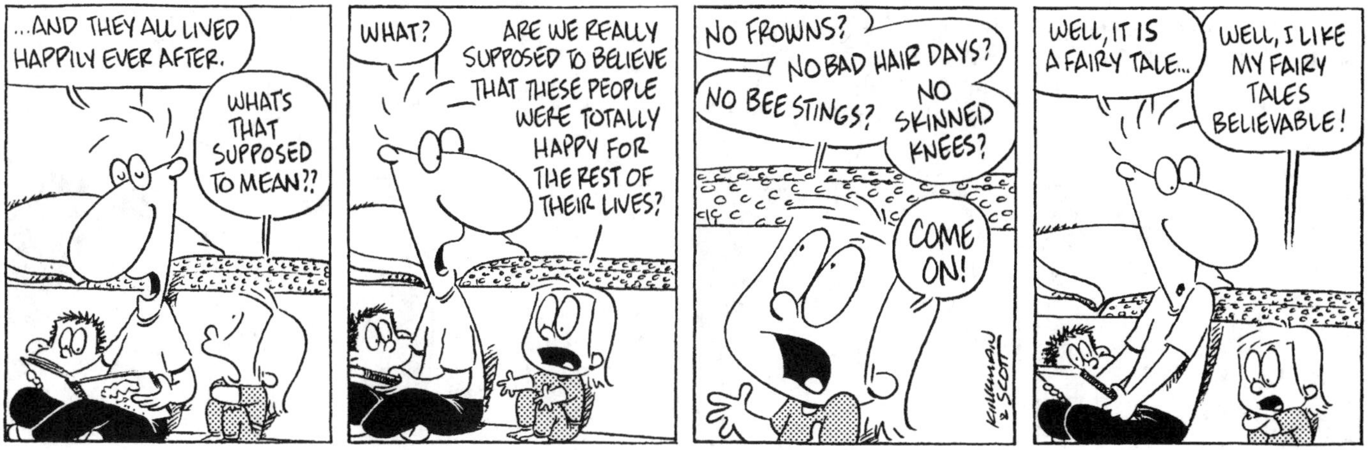
...AND THEY ALL LIVED HAPPILY EVER AFTER.
WHAT'S THAT SUPPOSED TO MEAN??
WHAT?
ARE WE REALLY SUPPOSED TO BELIEVE THAT THESE PEOPLE WERE TOTALLY HAPPY FOR THE REST OF THEIR LIVES?
NO FROWNS?
NO BAD HAIR DAYS?
NO BEE STINGS?
NO SKINNED KNEES?
COME ON!
WELL, IT IS A FAIRY TALE...
WELL, I LIKE MY FAIRY TALES BELIEVABLE!

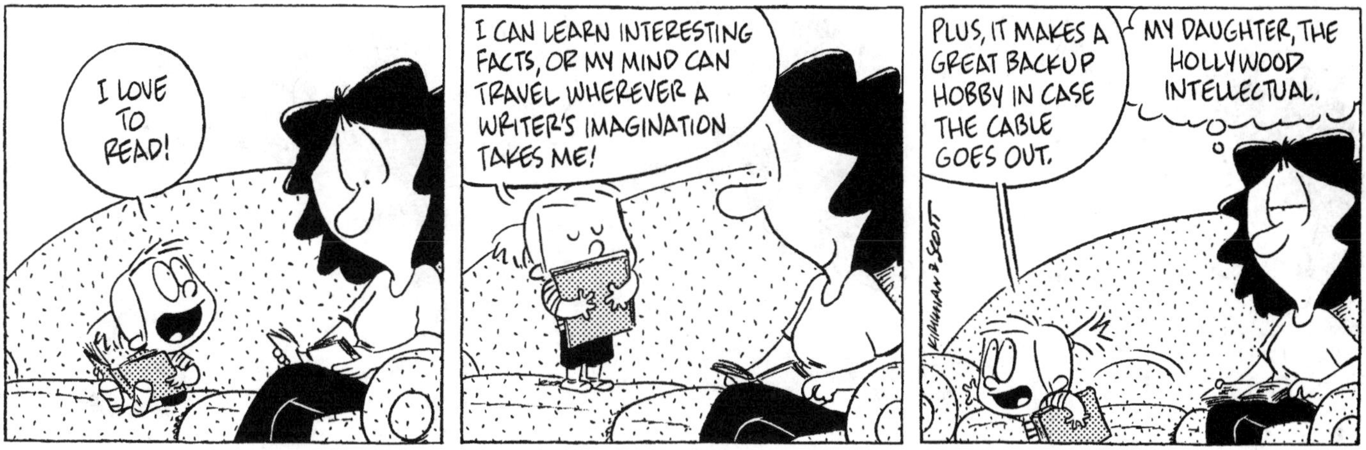
I LOVE TO READ!
I CAN LEARN INTERESTING FACTS, OR MY MIND CAN TRAVEL WHEREVER A WRITER'S IMAGINATION TAKES ME!
PLUS, IT MAKES A GREAT BACKUP HOBBY IN CASE THE CABLE GOES OUT.
MY DAUGHTER, THE HOLLYWOOD INTELLECTUAL.

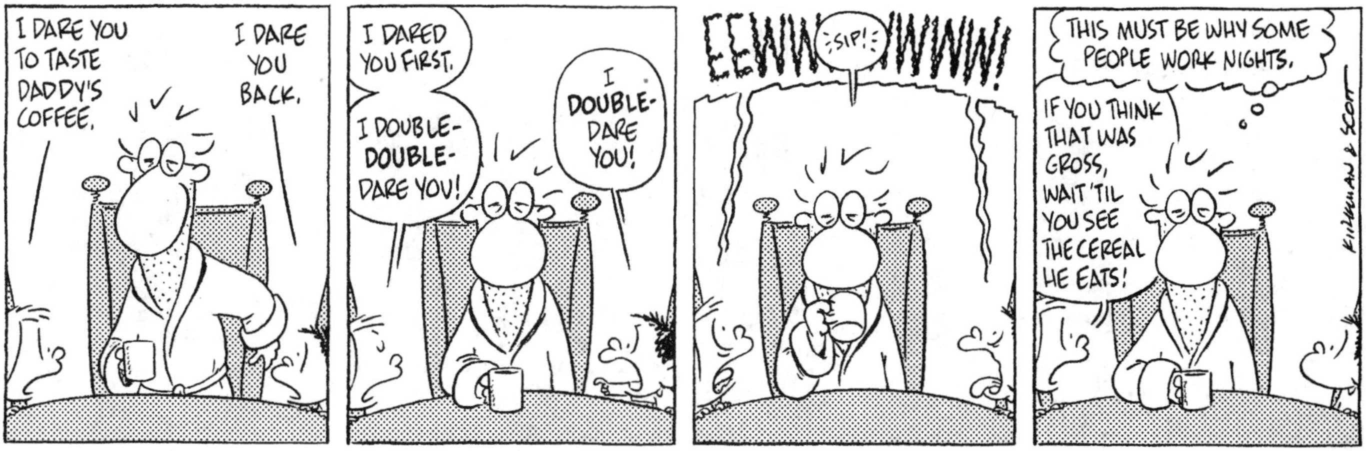
I DARE YOU TO TASTE DADDY'S COFFEE.
I DARE YOU BACK.
I DARED YOU FIRST.
I DOUBLE-DARE YOU!
I DOUBLE-DOUBLE-DARE YOU!
EEWW
SIP!
WWWW!
THIS MUST BE WHY SOME PEOPLE WORK NIGHTS.
IF YOU THINK THAT WAS GROSS, WAIT 'TIL YOU SEE THE CEREAL HE EATS!

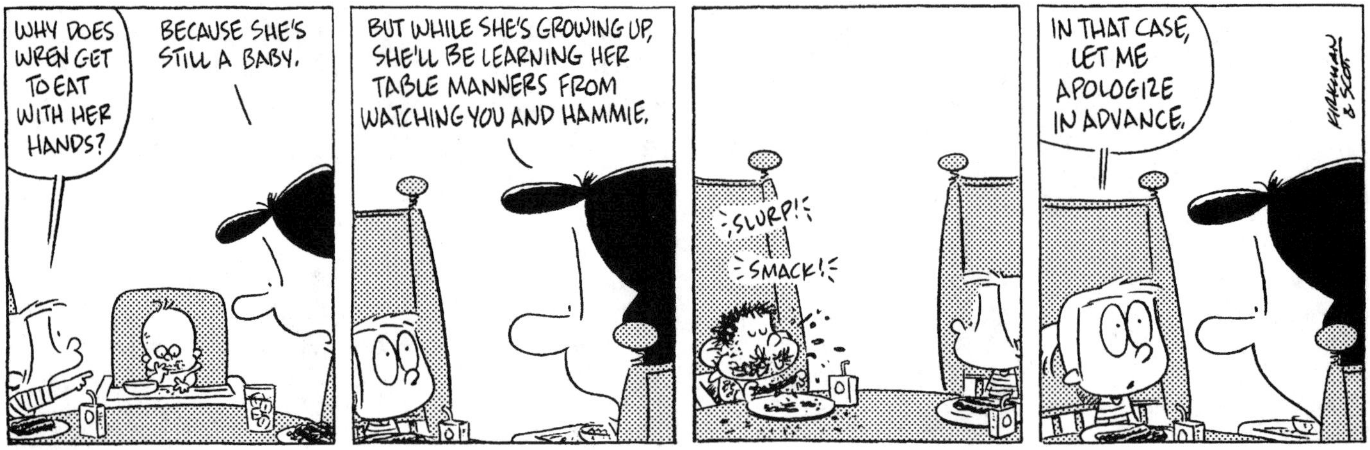
WHY DOES WREN GET TO EAT WITH HER HANDS?
BECAUSE SHE'S STILL A BABY.
BUT WHILE SHE'S GROWING UP, SHE'LL BE LEARNING HER TABLE MANNERS FROM WATCHING YOU AND HAMMIE.
SLURP!
SMACK!
IN THAT CASE, LET ME APOLOGIZE IN ADVANCE.
KIRKMAN & SCOTT

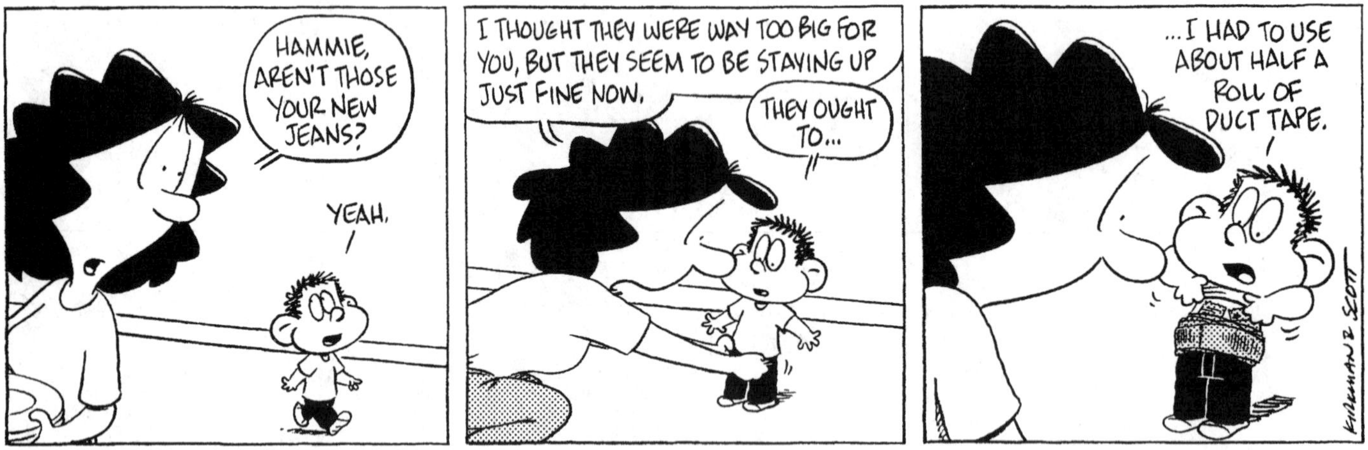
HAMMIE, AREN'T THOSE YOUR NEW JEANS?
YEAH.
I THOUGHT THEY WERE WAY TOO BIG FOR YOU, BUT THEY SEEM TO BE STAYING UP JUST FINE NOW.
THEY OUGHT TO...
...I HAD TO USE ABOUT HALF A ROLL OF DUCT TAPE.
KIRKMAN & SCOTT

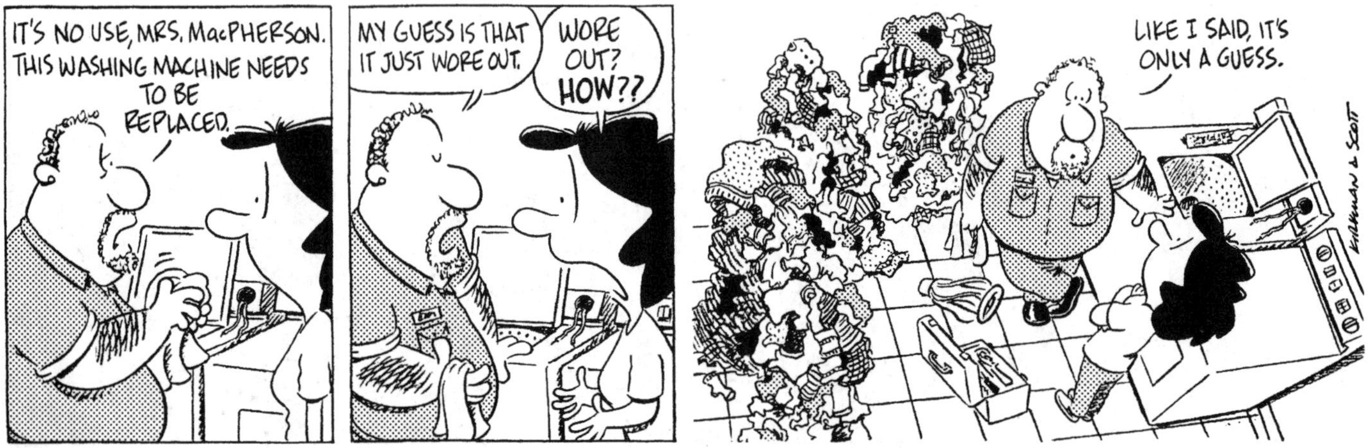
IT'S NO USE, MRS. MacPHERSON. THIS WASHING MACHINE NEEDS TO BE REPLACED.
MY GUESS IS THAT IT JUST WORE OUT.
WORE OUT? HOW??
LIKE I SAID, IT'S ONLY A GUESS.
KIRKMAN & SCOTT

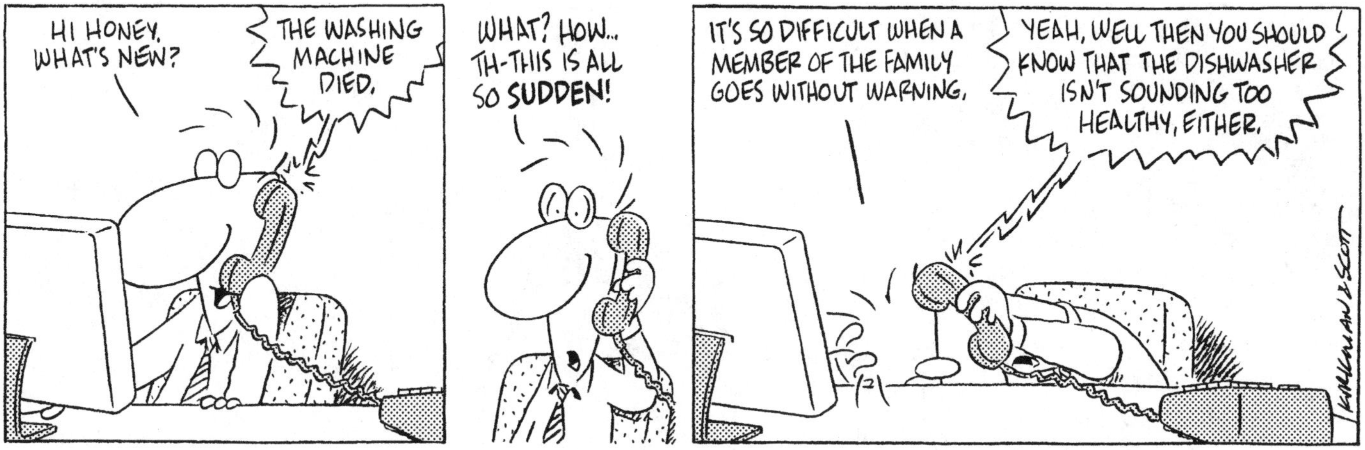
HI HONEY. WHAT'S NEW?
THE WASHING MACHINE DIED.
WHAT? HOW... TH-THIS IS ALL SO **SUDDEN**!
IT'S SO DIFFICULT WHEN A MEMBER OF THE FAMILY GOES WITHOUT WARNING.
YEAH, WELL THEN YOU SHOULD KNOW THAT THE DISHWASHER ISN'T SOUNDING TOO HEALTHY, EITHER.
KIRKMAN & SCOTT

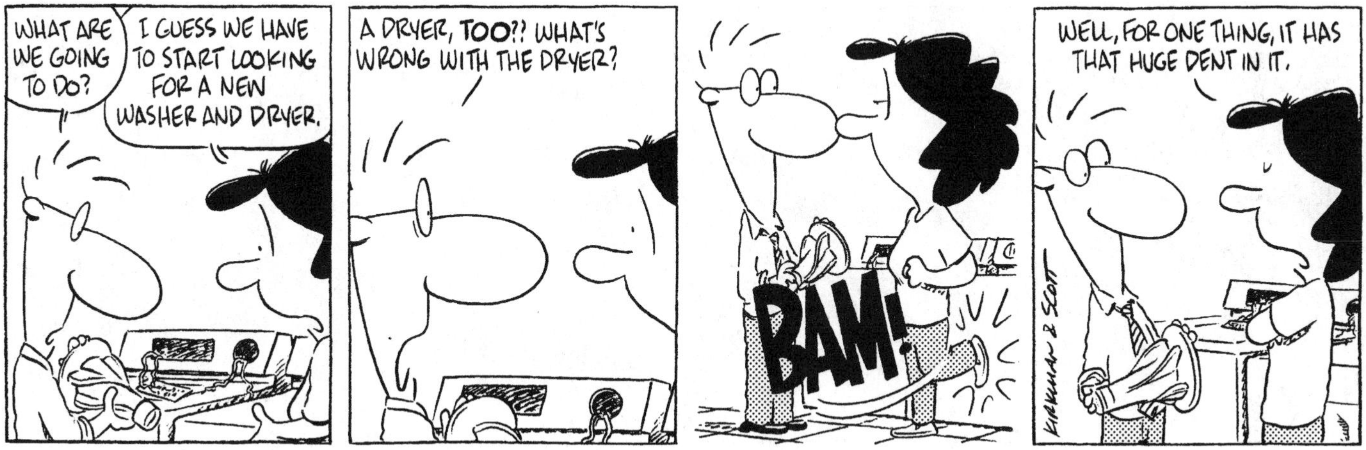
WHAT ARE WE GOING TO DO?
I GUESS WE HAVE TO START LOOKING FOR A NEW WASHER AND DRYER.
A DRYER, **TOO**?? WHAT'S WRONG WITH THE DRYER?
BAM!
KIRKMAN & SCOTT
WELL, FOR ONE THING, IT HAS THAT HUGE DENT IN IT.

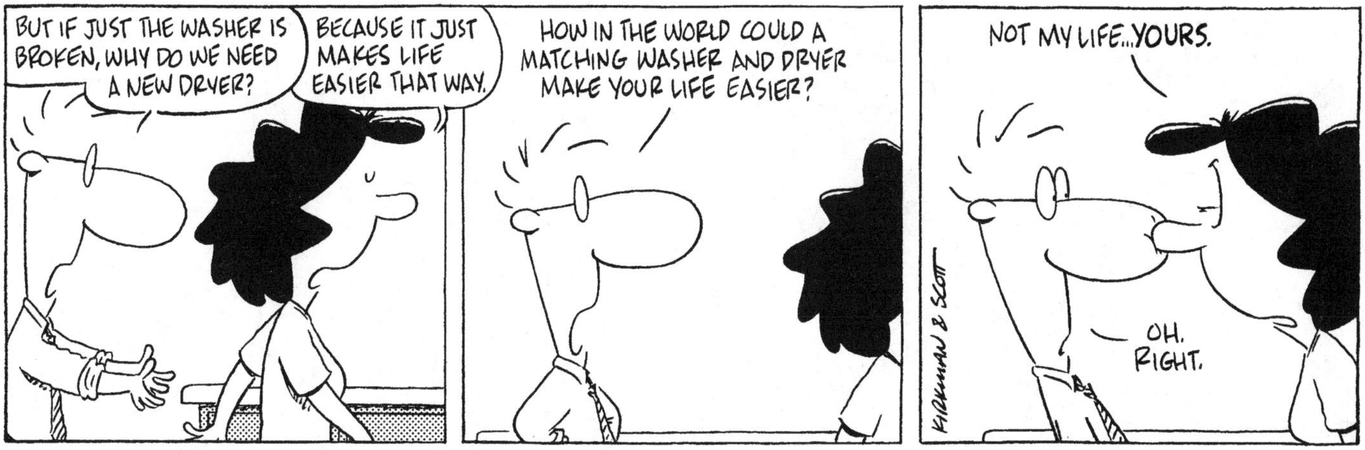
BUT IF JUST THE WASHER IS BROKEN, WHY DO WE NEED A NEW DRYER?
BECAUSE IT JUST MAKES LIFE EASIER THAT WAY.
HOW IN THE WORLD COULD A MATCHING WASHER AND DRYER MAKE YOUR LIFE EASIER?
KIRKMAN & SCOTT
NOT MY LIFE...**YOURS**.
OH. RIGHT.

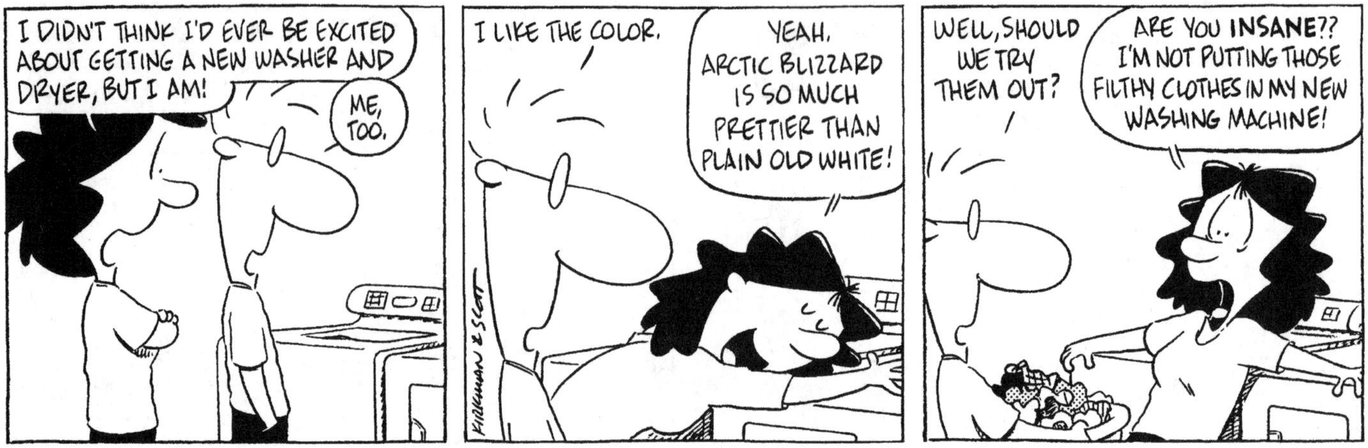
I DIDN'T THINK I'D EVER BE EXCITED ABOUT GETTING A NEW WASHER AND DRYER, BUT I AM!
ME, TOO.
I LIKE THE COLOR.
YEAH. ARCTIC BLIZZARD IS SO MUCH PRETTIER THAN PLAIN OLD WHITE!
KIRKMAN & SCOTT
WELL, SHOULD WE TRY THEM OUT?
ARE YOU **INSANE**?? I'M NOT PUTTING THOSE FILTHY CLOTHES IN MY NEW WASHING MACHINE!

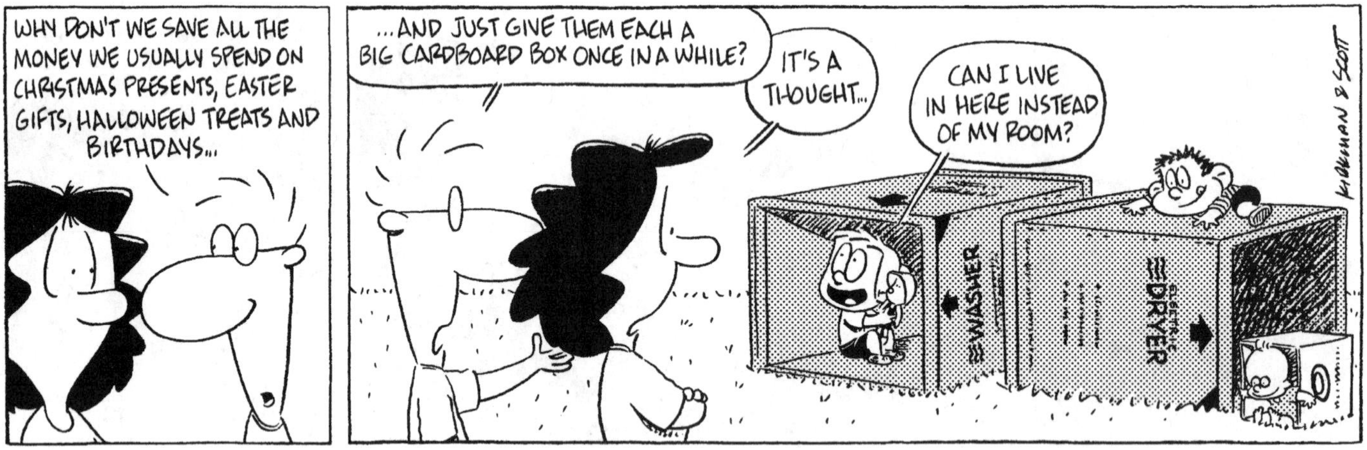
WHY DON'T WE SAVE ALL THE MONEY WE USUALLY SPEND ON CHRISTMAS PRESENTS, EASTER GIFTS, HALLOWEEN TREATS AND BIRTHDAYS...
...AND JUST GIVE THEM EACH A BIG CARDBOARD BOX ONCE IN A WHILE?
IT'S A THOUGHT...
CAN I LIVE IN HERE INSTEAD OF MY ROOM?
WASHER
DRYER
KIRKMAN & SCOTT

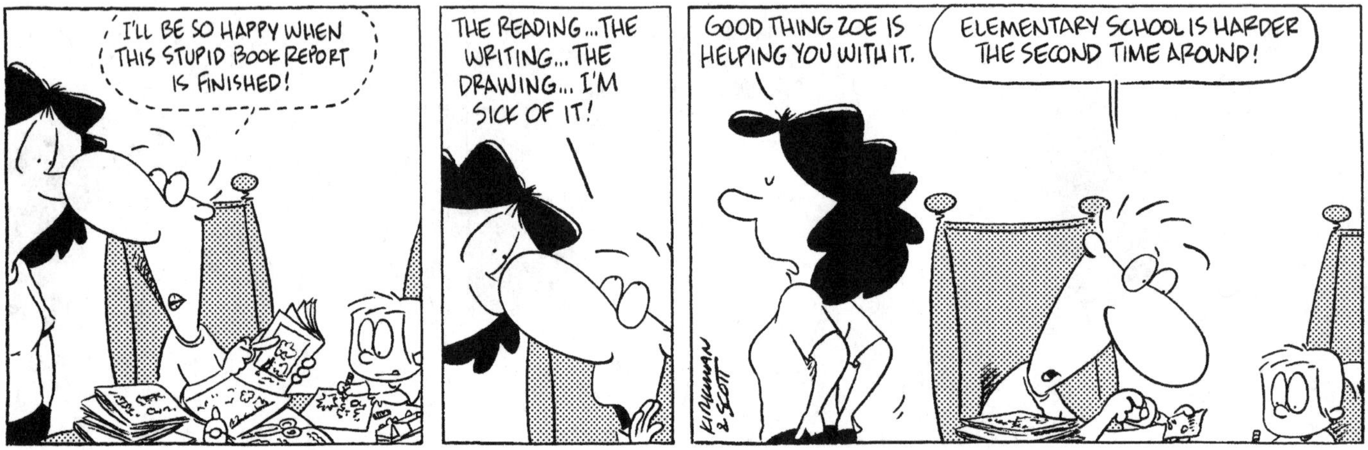
I'LL BE SO HAPPY WHEN THIS STUPID BOOK REPORT IS FINISHED!
THE READING... THE WRITING... THE DRAWING... I'M SICK OF IT!
GOOD THING ZOE IS HELPING YOU WITH IT.
ELEMENTARY SCHOOL IS HARDER THE SECOND TIME AROUND!
KIRKMAN & SCOTT

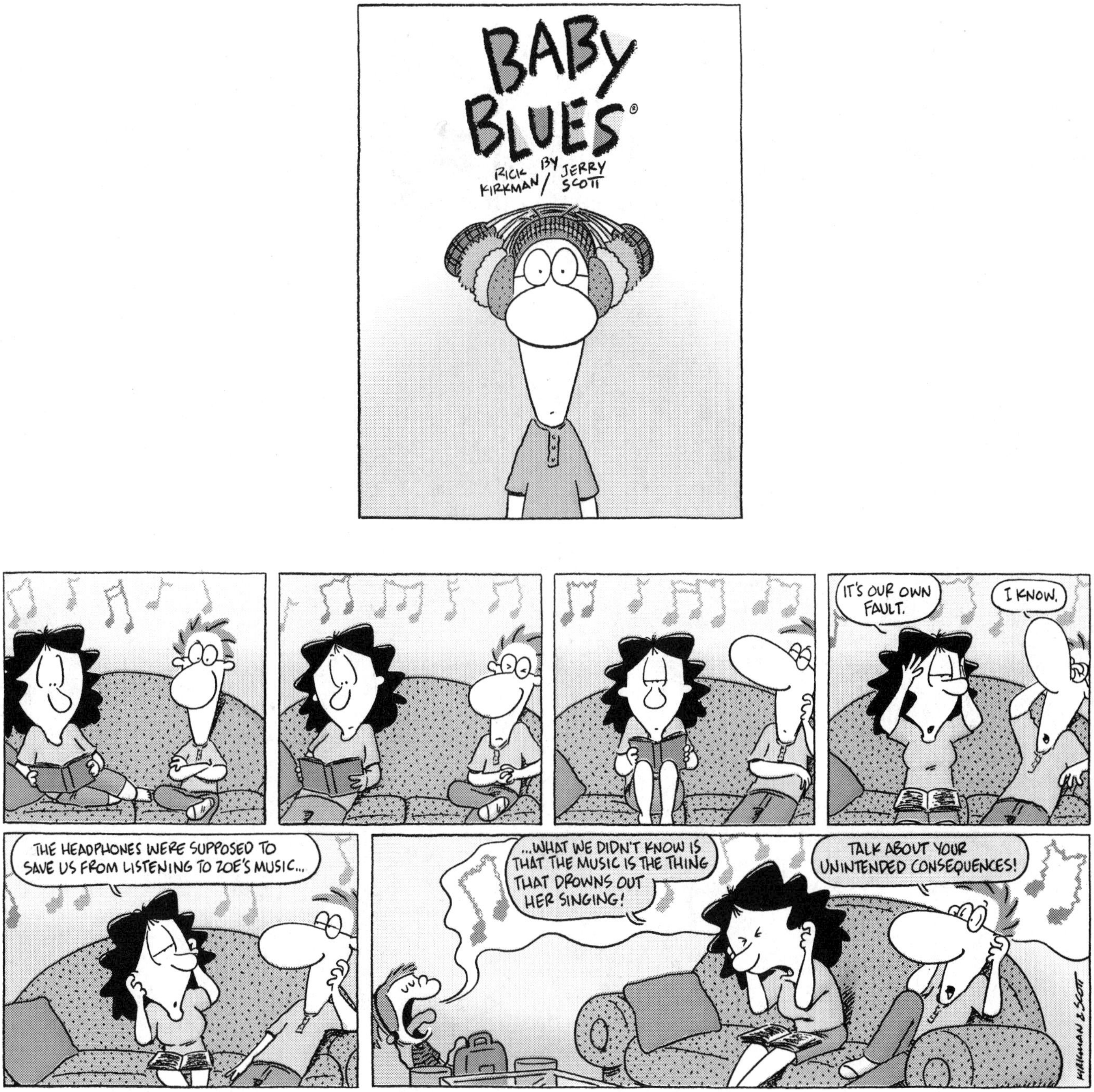
BABY BLUES®
BY RICK KIRKMAN / JERRY SCOTT
IT'S OUR OWN FAULT.
I KNOW.
THE HEADPHONES WERE SUPPOSED TO SAVE US FROM LISTENING TO ZOE'S MUSIC...
...WHAT WE DIDN'T KNOW IS THAT THE MUSIC IS THE THING THAT DROWNS OUT HER SINGING!
TALK ABOUT YOUR UNINTENDED CONSEQUENCES!
KIRKMAN & SCOTT

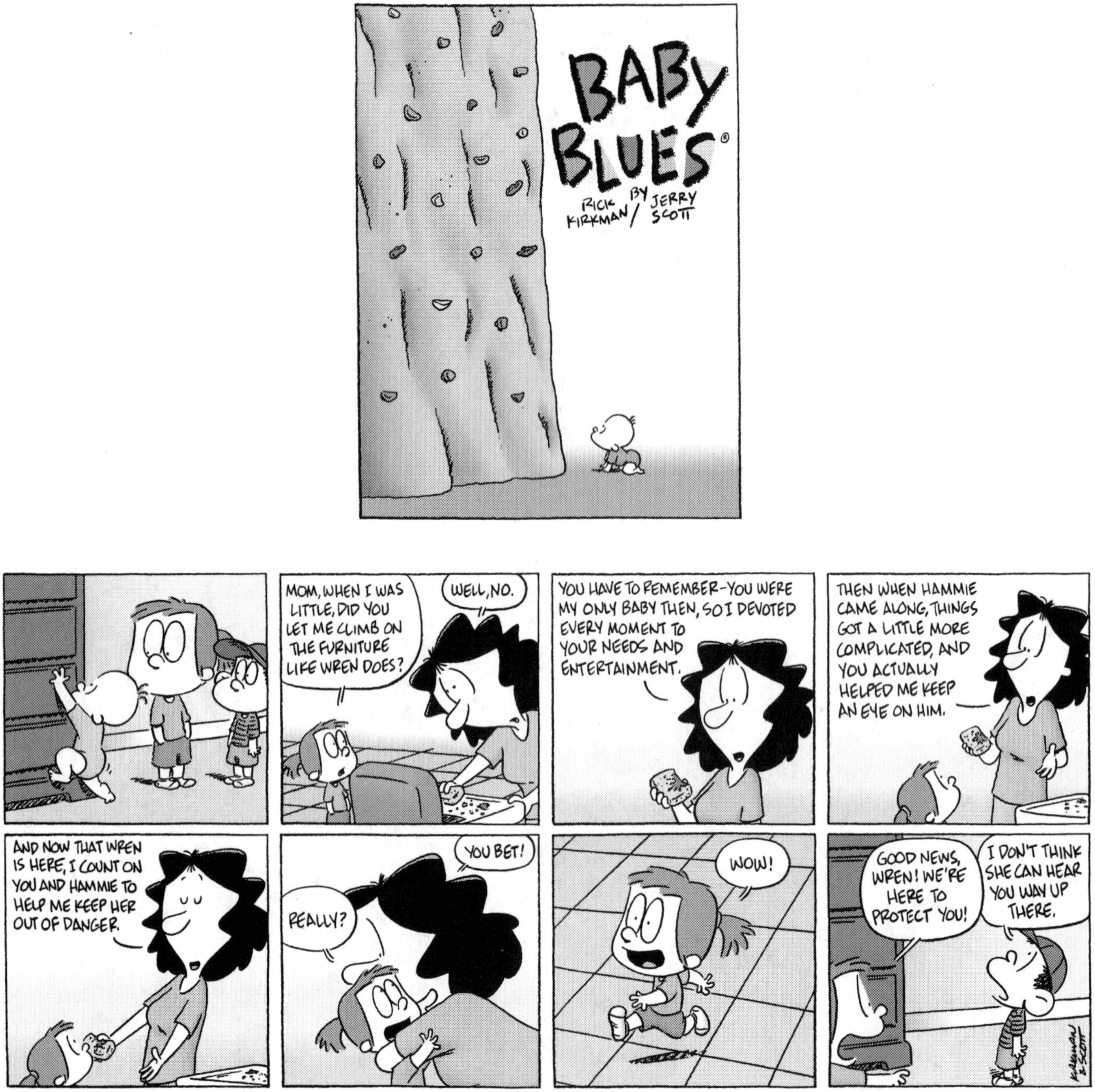
BABY BLUES®
BY RICK KIRKMAN / JERRY SCOTT
MOM, WHEN I WAS LITTLE, DID YOU LET ME CLIMB ON THE FURNITURE LIKE WREN DOES?
WELL, NO.
YOU HAVE TO REMEMBER–YOU WERE MY ONLY BABY THEN, SO I DEVOTED EVERY MOMENT TO YOUR NEEDS AND ENTERTAINMENT.
THEN WHEN HAMMIE CAME ALONG, THINGS GOT A LITTLE MORE COMPLICATED, AND YOU ACTUALLY HELPED ME KEEP AN EYE ON HIM.
AND NOW THAT WREN IS HERE, I COUNT ON YOU AND HAMMIE TO HELP ME KEEP HER OUT OF DANGER.
YOU BET!
REALLY?
WOW!
GOOD NEWS, WREN! WE'RE HERE TO PROTECT YOU!
I DON'T THINK SHE CAN HEAR YOU WAY UP THERE.

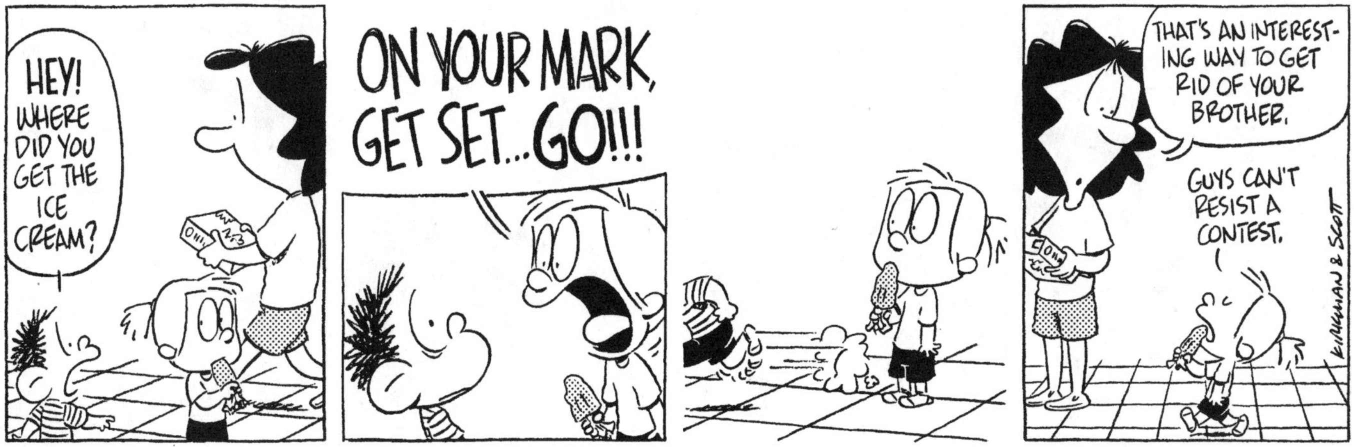
HEY! WHERE DID YOU GET THE ICE CREAM?
ON YOUR MARK, GET SET...GO!!!
THAT'S AN INTEREST-ING WAY TO GET RID OF YOUR BROTHER.
GUYS CAN'T RESIST A CONTEST.
KIRKMAN & SCOTT

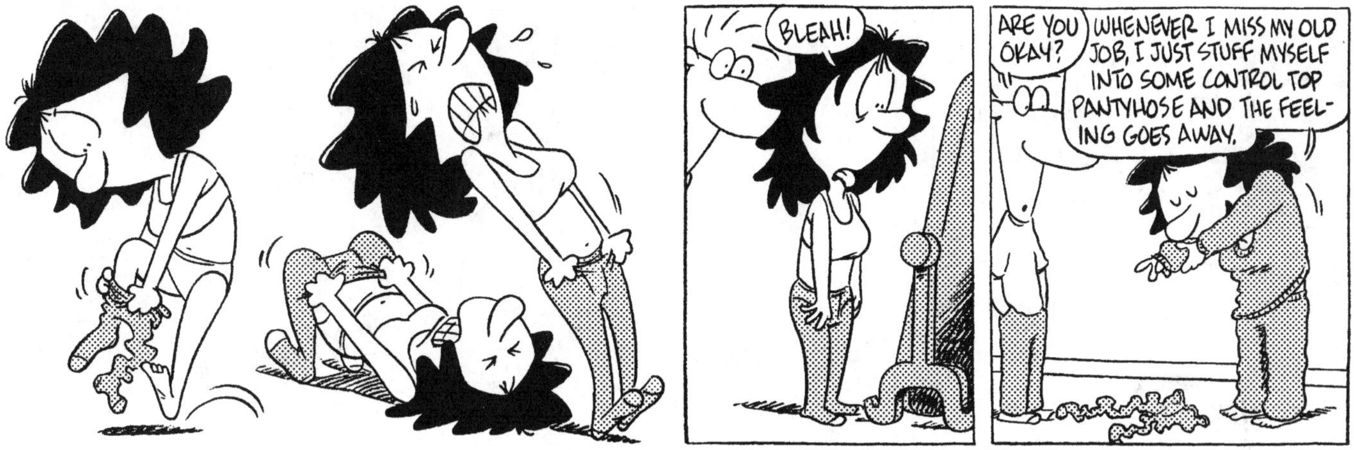
BLEAH!
ARE YOU OKAY?
WHENEVER I MISS MY OLD JOB, I JUST STUFF MYSELF INTO SOME CONTROL TOP PANTYHOSE AND THE FEEL-ING GOES AWAY.

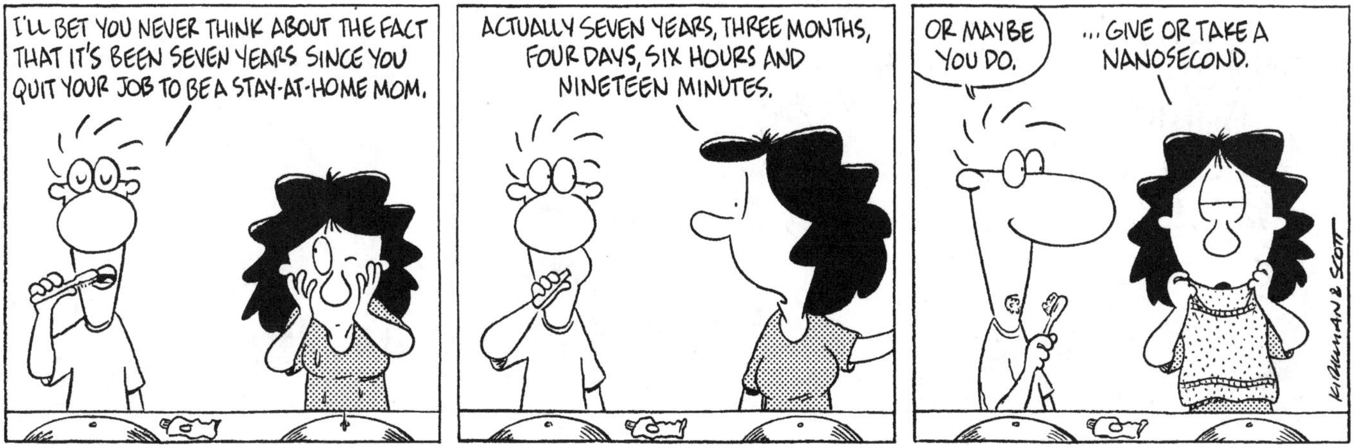
I'LL BET YOU NEVER THINK ABOUT THE FACT THAT IT'S BEEN SEVEN YEARS SINCE YOU QUIT YOUR JOB TO BE A STAY-AT-HOME MOM.
ACTUALLY SEVEN YEARS, THREE MONTHS, FOUR DAYS, SIX HOURS AND NINETEEN MINUTES.
OR MAYBE YOU DO.
...GIVE OR TAKE A NANOSECOND.
KIRKMAN & SCOTT

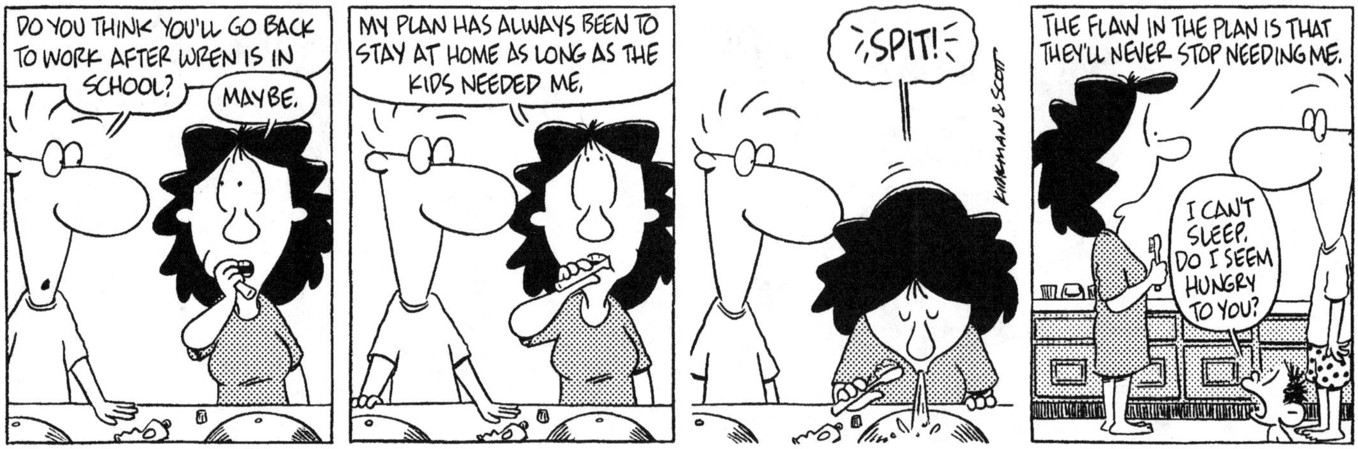
DO YOU THINK YOU'LL GO BACK TO WORK AFTER WREN IS IN SCHOOL?
MAYBE.
MY PLAN HAS ALWAYS BEEN TO STAY AT HOME AS LONG AS THE KIDS NEEDED ME.
SPIT!
KIRKMAN & SCOTT
THE FLAW IN THE PLAN IS THAT THEY'LL NEVER STOP NEEDING ME.
I CAN'T SLEEP. DO I SEEM HUNGRY TO YOU?

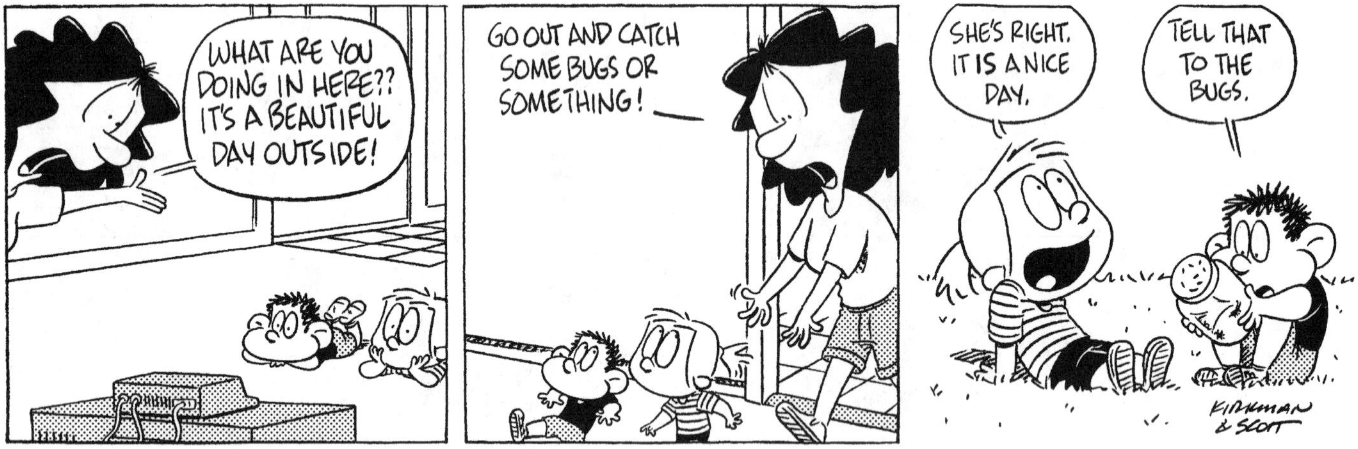
WHAT ARE YOU DOING IN HERE?? IT'S A BEAUTIFUL DAY OUTSIDE!
GO OUT AND CATCH SOME BUGS OR SOMETHING!
SHE'S RIGHT. IT IS A NICE DAY.
TELL THAT TO THE BUGS.
KIRKMAN & SCOTT

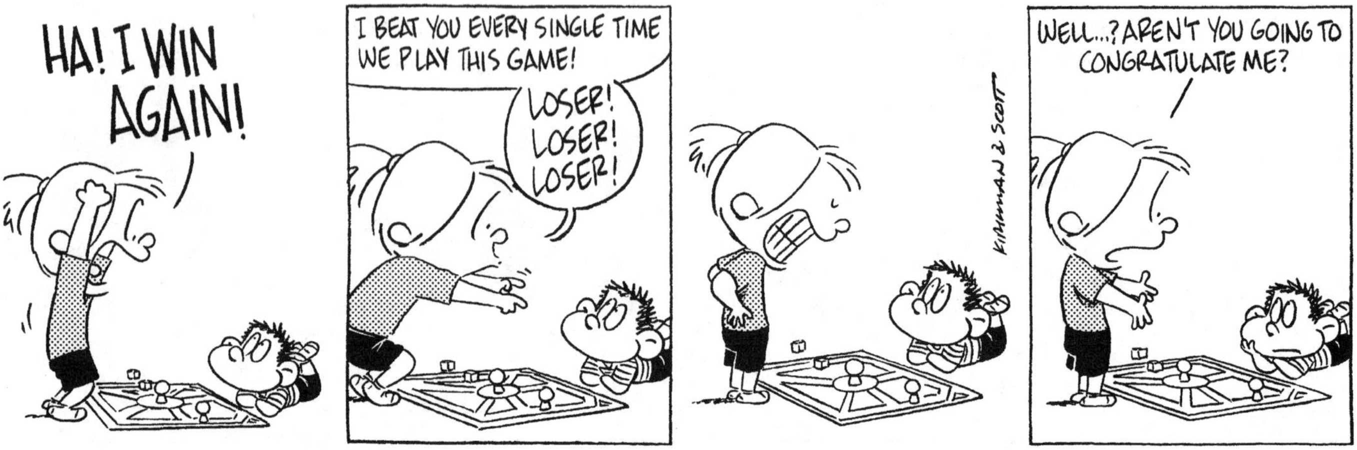
HA! I WIN AGAIN!
I BEAT YOU EVERY SINGLE TIME WE PLAY THIS GAME!
LOSER! LOSER! LOSER!
KIRKMAN & SCOTT
WELL...? AREN'T YOU GOING TO CONGRATULATE ME?

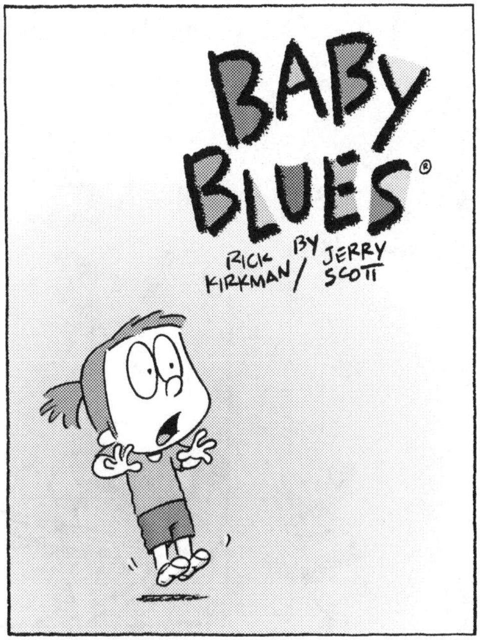
BABY BLUES®
BY
RICK KIRKMAN / JERRY SCOTT

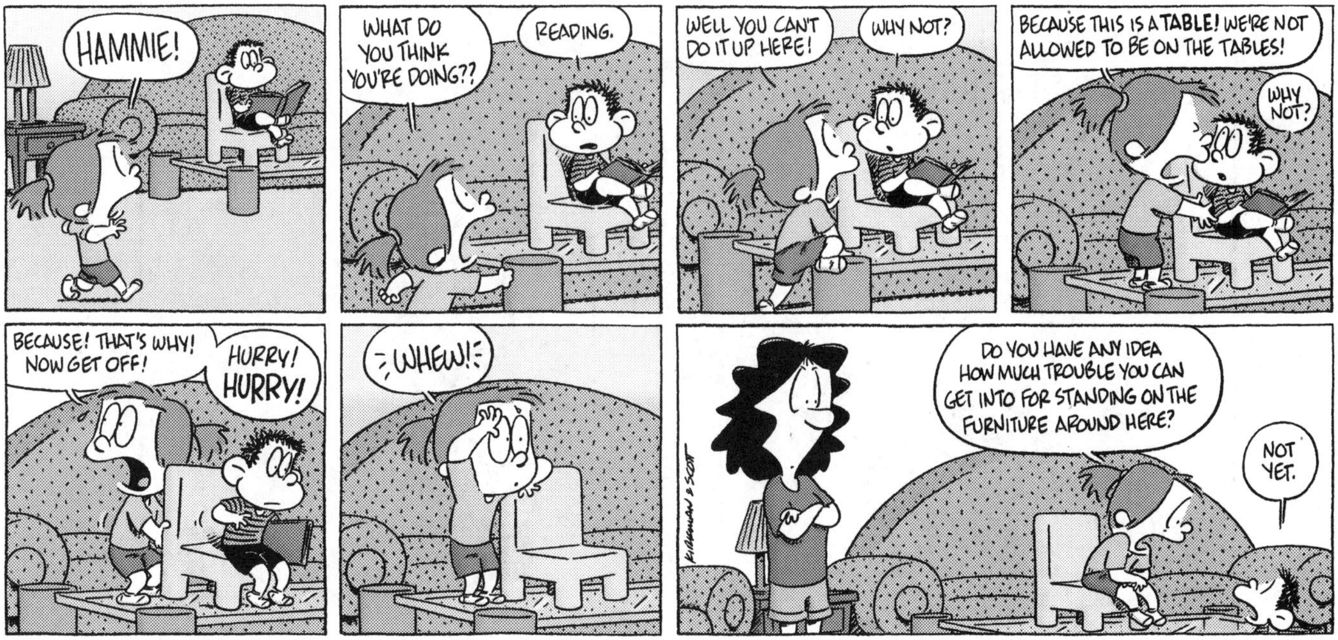
HAMMIE!
WHAT DO YOU THINK YOU'RE DOING??
READING.
WELL YOU CAN'T DO IT UP HERE!
WHY NOT?
BECAUSE THIS IS A TABLE! WE'RE NOT ALLOWED TO BE ON THE TABLES!
WHY NOT?
BECAUSE! THAT'S WHY! NOW GET OFF!
HURRY! HURRY!
WHEW!
KIRKMAN & SCOTT
DO YOU HAVE ANY IDEA HOW MUCH TROUBLE YOU CAN GET INTO FOR STANDING ON THE FURNITURE AROUND HERE?
NOT YET.

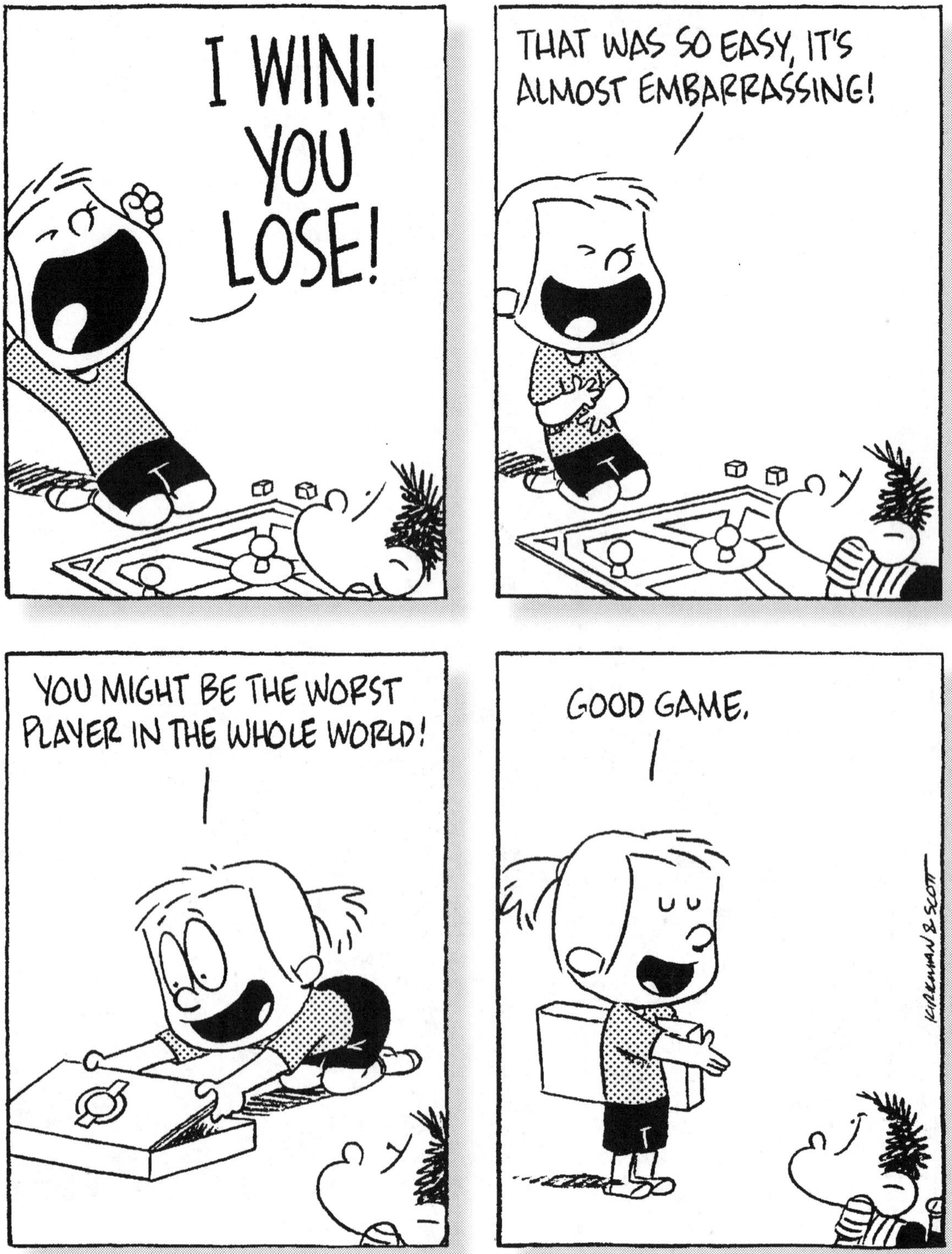
I WIN! YOU LOSE!
THAT WAS SO EASY, IT'S ALMOST EMBARRASSING!
YOU MIGHT BE THE WORST PLAYER IN THE WHOLE WORLD!
GOOD GAME.
KIRKMAN & SCOTT

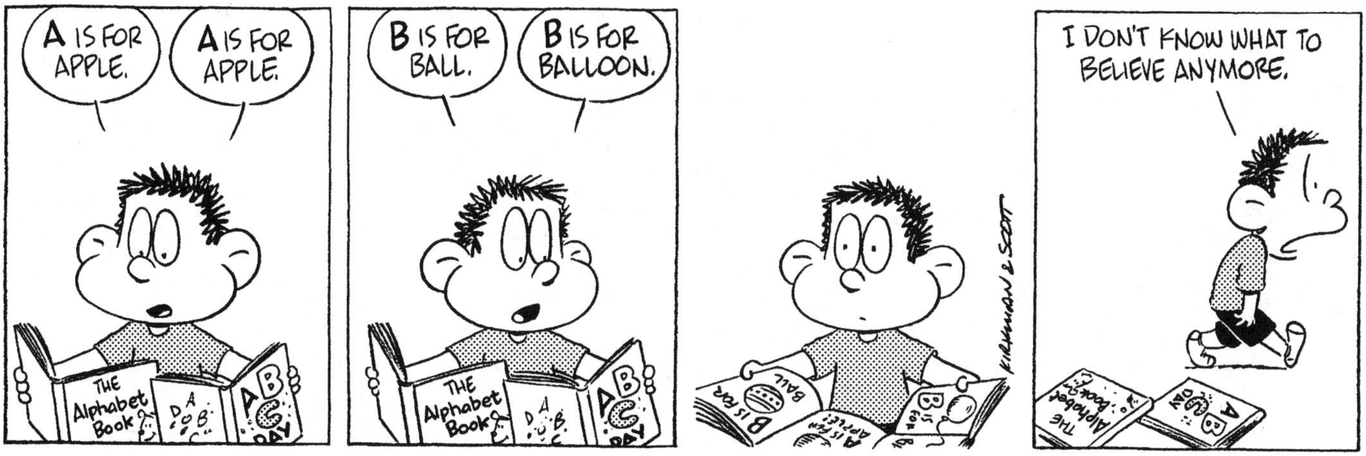
A IS FOR APPLE.
A IS FOR APPLE.
B IS FOR BALL.
B IS FOR BALLOON.
KIRKMAN & SCOTT
I DON'T KNOW WHAT TO BELIEVE ANYMORE.

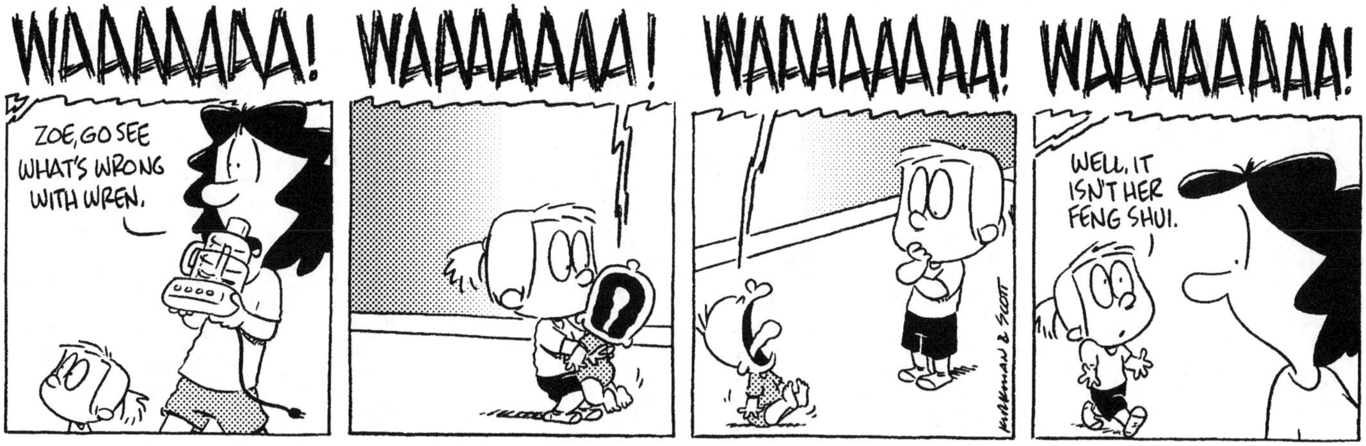
WAAAAAAA!
WAAAAAAAA!
WAAAAAAAAA!
WAAAAAAAAAA!
ZOE, GO SEE WHAT'S WRONG WITH WREN.
KIRKMAN & SCOTT
WELL, IT ISN'T HER FENG SHUI.

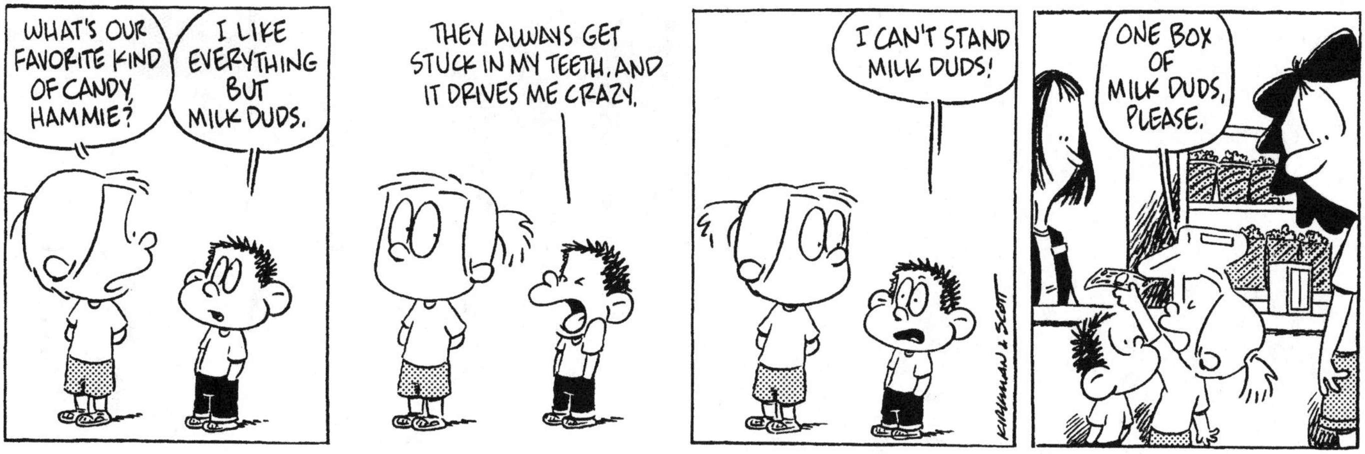
WHAT'S OUR FAVORITE KIND OF CANDY, HAMMIE?
I LIKE EVERYTHING BUT MILK DUDS.
THEY ALWAYS GET STUCK IN MY TEETH, AND IT DRIVES ME CRAZY.
I CAN'T STAND MILK DUDS!
KIRKMAN & SCOTT
ONE BOX OF MILK DUDS, PLEASE.

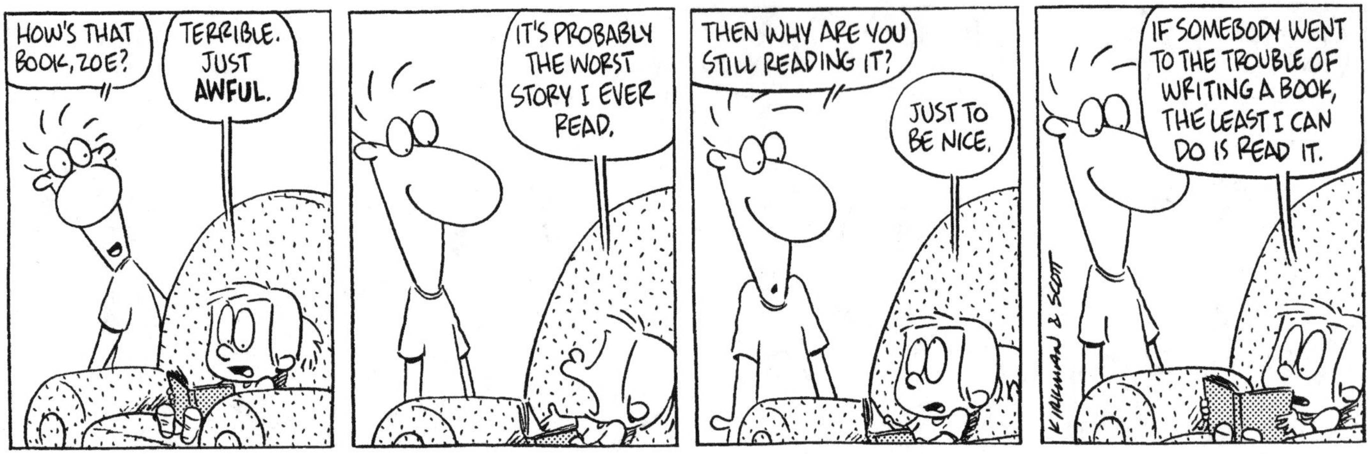
HOW'S THAT BOOK, ZOE?
TERRIBLE. JUST **AWFUL.**
IT'S PROBABLY THE WORST STORY I EVER READ.
THEN WHY ARE YOU STILL READING IT?
JUST TO BE NICE.
KIRKMAN & SCOTT
IF SOMEBODY WENT TO THE TROUBLE OF WRITING A BOOK, THE LEAST I CAN DO IS READ IT.

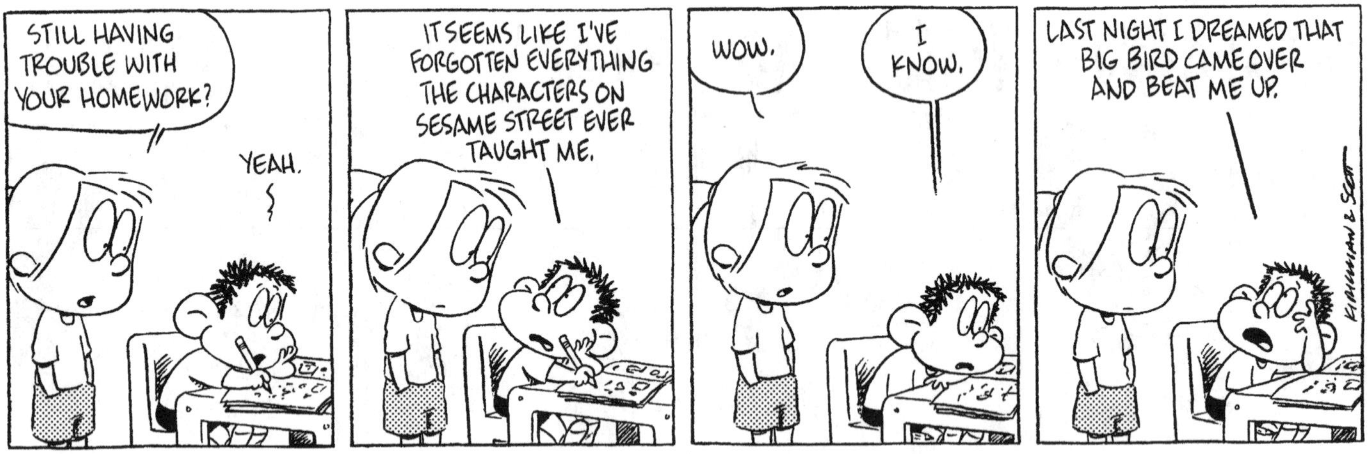
STILL HAVING TROUBLE WITH YOUR HOMEWORK?
YEAH.
IT SEEMS LIKE I'VE FORGOTTEN EVERYTHING THE CHARACTERS ON SESAME STREET EVER TAUGHT ME.
WOW.
I KNOW.
LAST NIGHT I DREAMED THAT BIG BIRD CAME OVER AND BEAT ME UP.
KIRKMAN & SCOTT

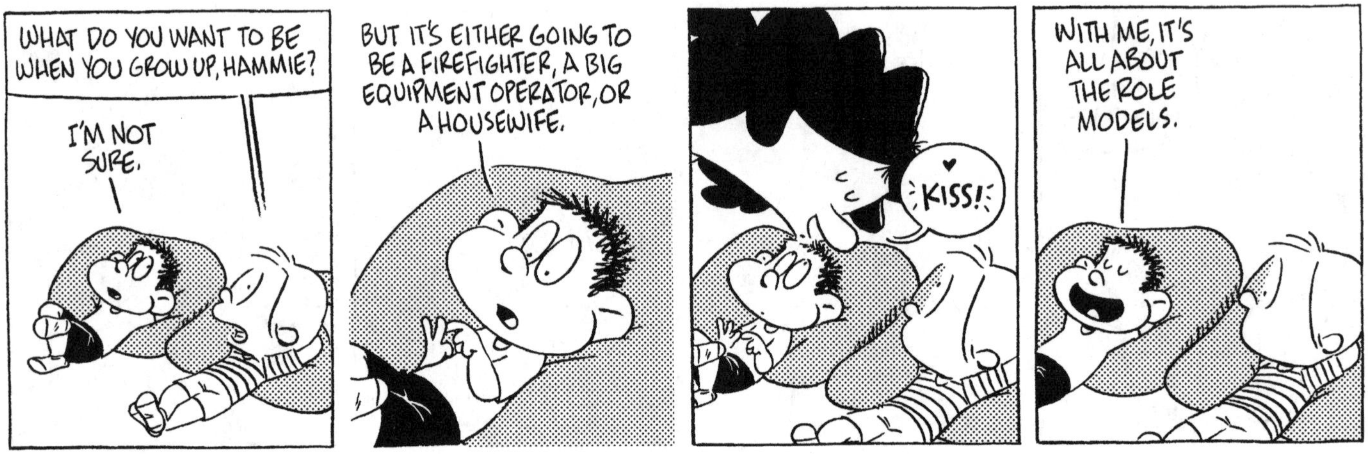
WHAT DO YOU WANT TO BE WHEN YOU GROW UP, HAMMIE?
I'M NOT SURE.
BUT IT'S EITHER GOING TO BE A FIREFIGHTER, A BIG EQUIPMENT OPERATOR, OR A HOUSEWIFE.
KISS!
WITH ME, IT'S ALL ABOUT THE ROLE MODELS.

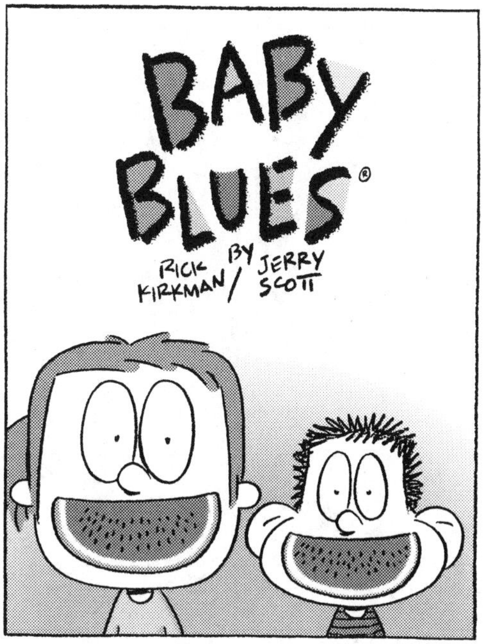
BABY BLUES®
BY
RICK KIRKMAN / JERRY SCOTT

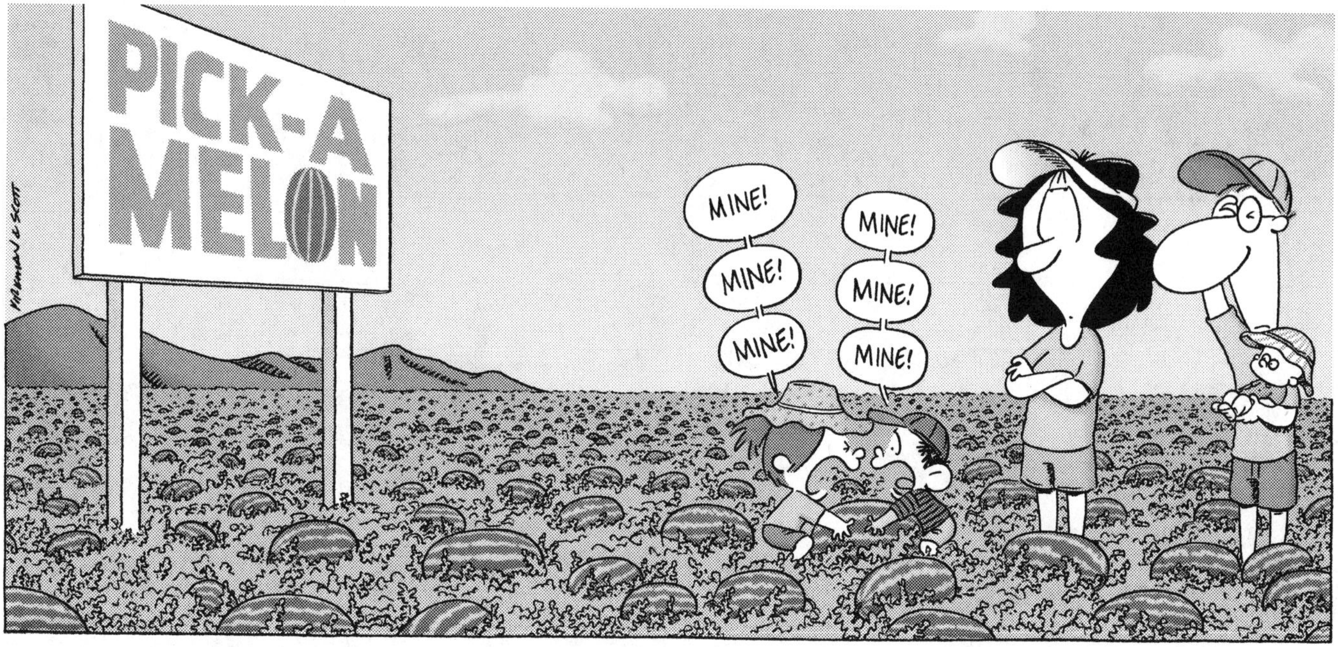
PICK-A MELON
MINE!
MINE!
MINE!
MINE!
MINE!
MINE!

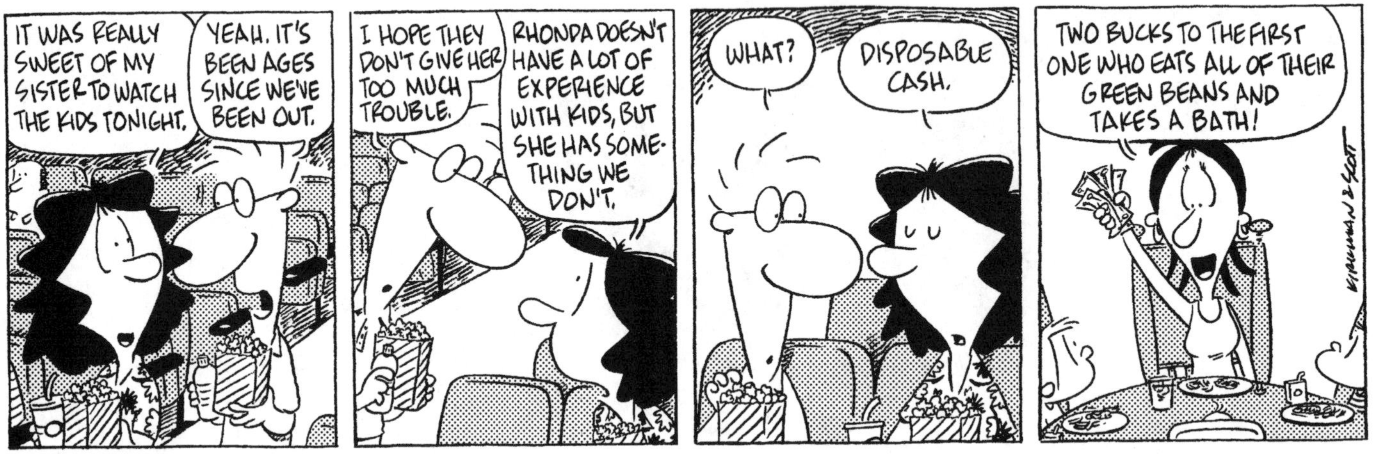
IT WAS REALLY SWEET OF MY SISTER TO WATCH THE KIDS TONIGHT.
YEAH. IT'S BEEN AGES SINCE WE'VE BEEN OUT.
I HOPE THEY DON'T GIVE HER TOO MUCH TROUBLE.
RHONDA DOESN'T HAVE A LOT OF EXPERIENCE WITH KIDS, BUT SHE HAS SOMETHING WE DON'T.
WHAT?
DISPOSABLE CASH.
TWO BUCKS TO THE FIRST ONE WHO EATS ALL OF THEIR GREEN BEANS AND TAKES A BATH!
KIRKMAN & SCOTT

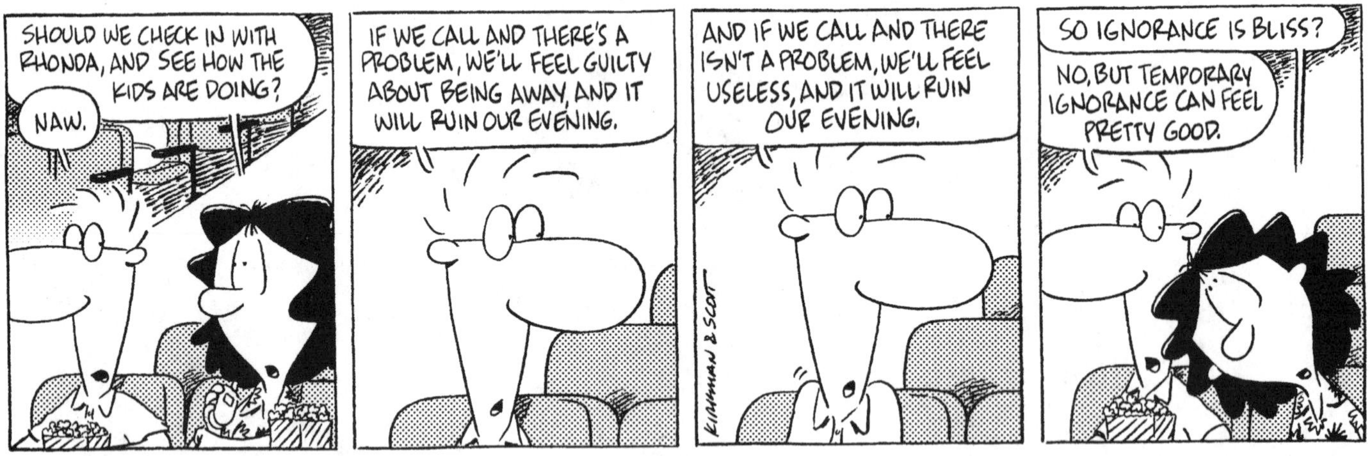
SHOULD WE CHECK IN WITH RHONDA, AND SEE HOW THE KIDS ARE DOING?
NAW.
IF WE CALL AND THERE'S A PROBLEM, WE'LL FEEL GUILTY ABOUT BEING AWAY, AND IT WILL RUIN OUR EVENING.
AND IF WE CALL AND THERE ISN'T A PROBLEM, WE'LL FEEL USELESS, AND IT WILL RUIN OUR EVENING.
SO IGNORANCE IS BLISS?
NO, BUT TEMPORARY IGNORANCE CAN FEEL PRETTY GOOD.
KIRKMAN & SCOTT

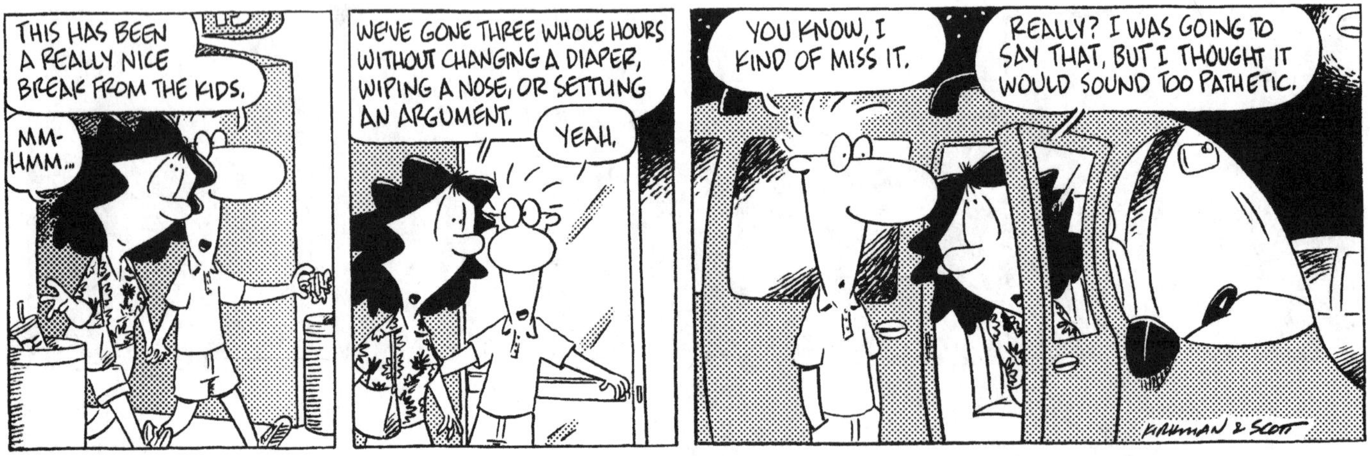
THIS HAS BEEN A REALLY NICE BREAK FROM THE KIDS.
MM-HMM...
WE'VE GONE THREE WHOLE HOURS WITHOUT CHANGING A DIAPER, WIPING A NOSE, OR SETTLING AN ARGUMENT.
YEAH.
YOU KNOW, I KIND OF MISS IT.
REALLY? I WAS GOING TO SAY THAT, BUT I THOUGHT IT WOULD SOUND TOO PATHETIC.
KIRKMAN & SCOTT

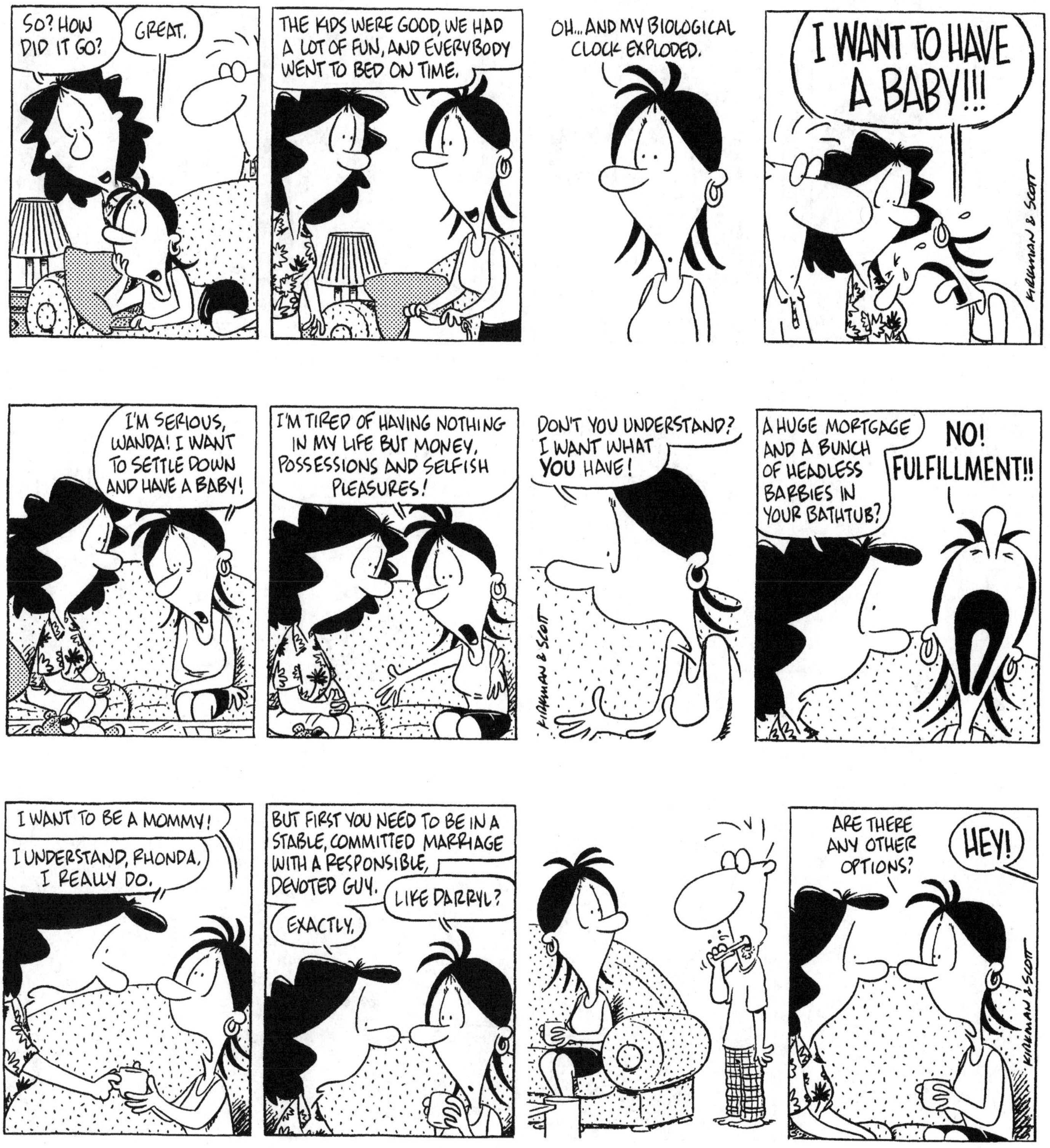
SO? HOW DID IT GO?
GREAT.
THE KIDS WERE GOOD, WE HAD A LOT OF FUN, AND EVERYBODY WENT TO BED ON TIME.
OH... AND MY BIOLOGICAL CLOCK EXPLODED.
I WANT TO HAVE A BABY!!!
KIRKMAN & SCOTT
I'M SERIOUS, WANDA! I WANT TO SETTLE DOWN AND HAVE A BABY!
I'M TIRED OF HAVING NOTHING IN MY LIFE BUT MONEY, POSSESSIONS AND SELFISH PLEASURES!
DON'T YOU UNDERSTAND? I WANT WHAT YOU HAVE!
KIRKMAN & SCOTT
A HUGE MORTGAGE AND A BUNCH OF HEADLESS BARBIES IN YOUR BATHTUB?
NO! FULFILLMENT!!
I WANT TO BE A MOMMY!
I UNDERSTAND, RHONDA, I REALLY DO.
BUT FIRST YOU NEED TO BE IN A STABLE, COMMITTED MARRIAGE WITH A RESPONSIBLE, DEVOTED GUY.
LIKE DARRYL?
EXACTLY.
KIRKMAN & SCOTT
ARE THERE ANY OTHER OPTIONS?
HEY!
KIRKMAN & SCOTT

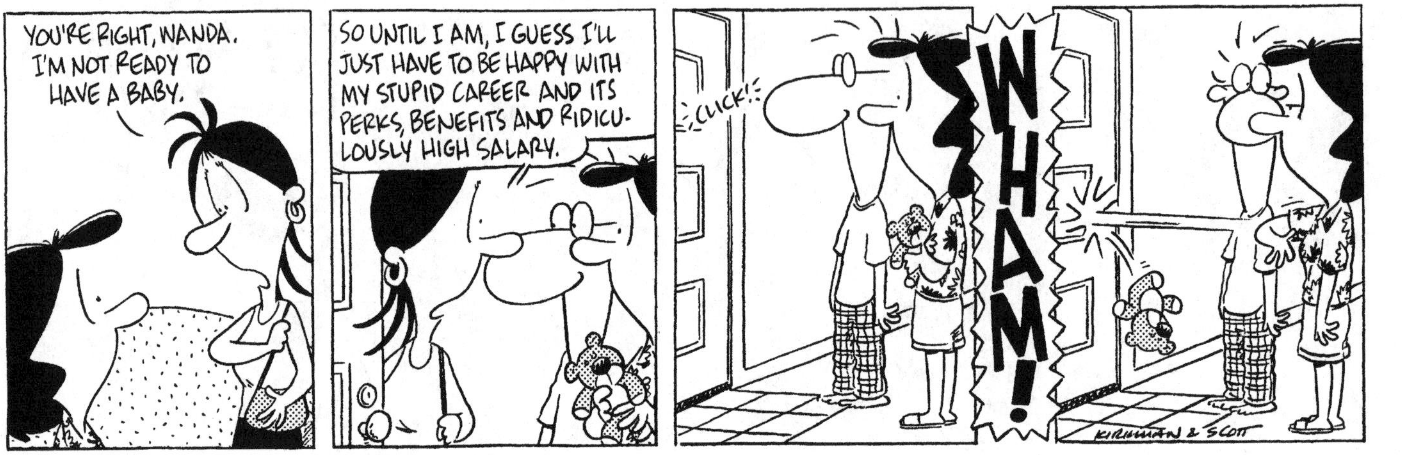
YOU'RE RIGHT, WANDA. I'M NOT READY TO HAVE A BABY.
SO UNTIL I AM, I GUESS I'LL JUST HAVE TO BE HAPPY WITH MY STUPID CAREER AND ITS PERKS, BENEFITS AND RIDICULOUSLY HIGH SALARY.
CLICK!
WHAM!
KIRKMAN & SCOTT

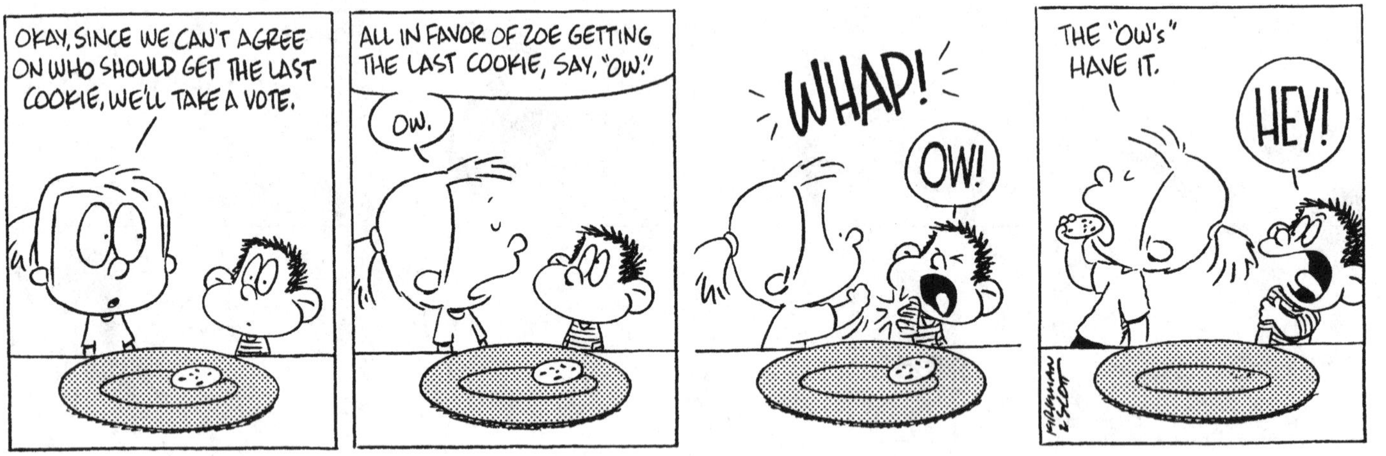
OKAY, SINCE WE CAN'T AGREE ON WHO SHOULD GET THE LAST COOKIE, WE'LL TAKE A VOTE.
ALL IN FAVOR OF ZOE GETTING THE LAST COOKIE, SAY, "OW."
OW.
WHAP!
OW!
THE "OW's" HAVE IT.
HEY!
KIRKMAN & SCOTT

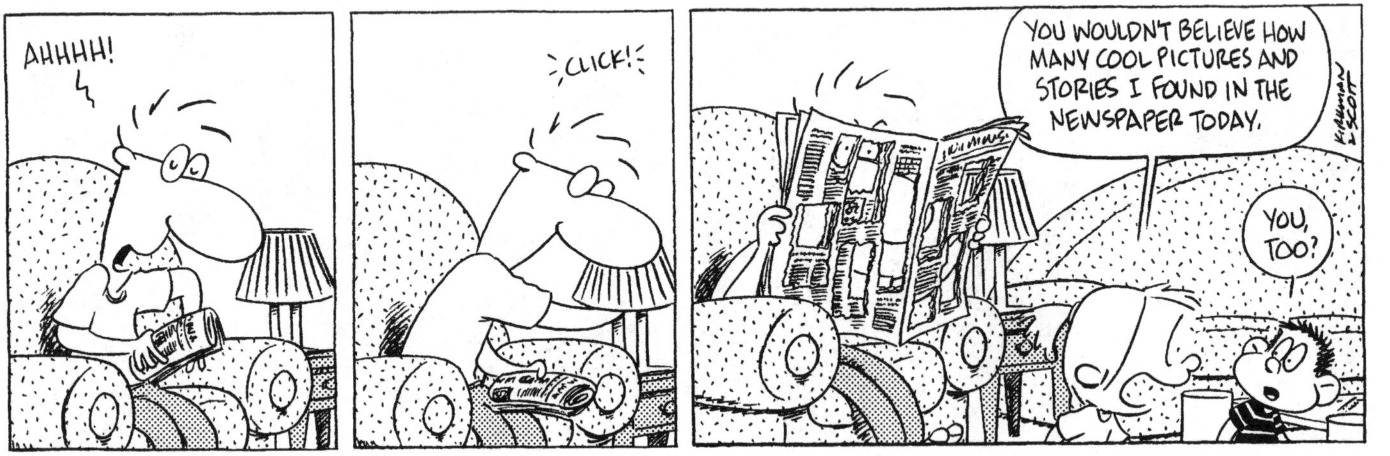
AHHHH!
CLICK!
YOU WOULDN'T BELIEVE HOW MANY COOL PICTURES AND STORIES I FOUND IN THE NEWSPAPER TODAY.
YOU, TOO?
KIRKMAN & SCOTT

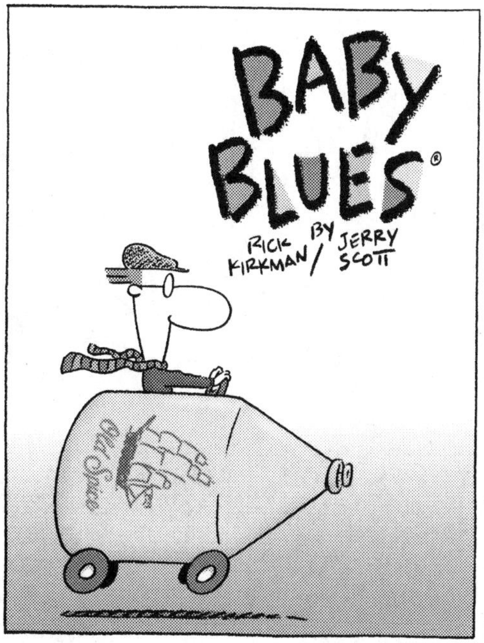
BABY BLUES®
BY RICK KIRKMAN / JERRY SCOTT

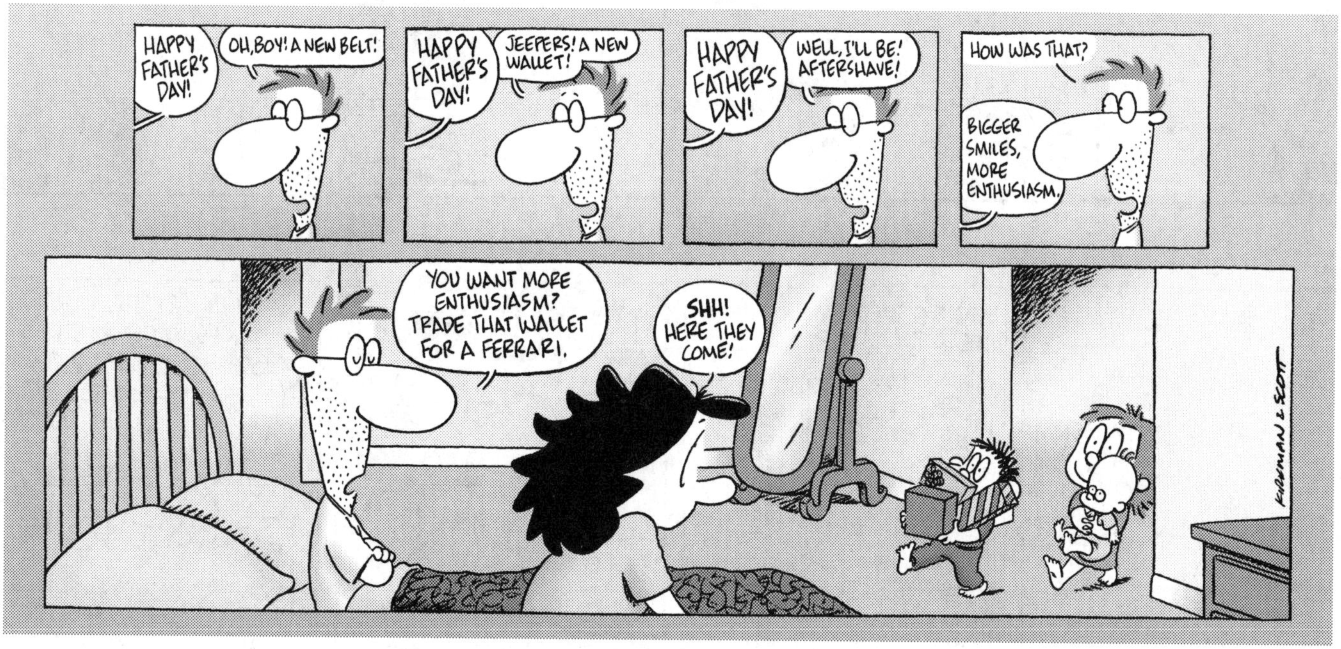
HAPPY FATHER'S DAY!
OH, BOY! A NEW BELT!
HAPPY FATHER'S DAY!
JEEPERS! A NEW WALLET!
HAPPY FATHER'S DAY!
WELL, I'LL BE! AFTERSHAVE!
HOW WAS THAT?
BIGGER SMILES, MORE ENTHUSIASM.
YOU WANT MORE ENTHUSIASM? TRADE THAT WALLET FOR A FERRARI.
SHH! HERE THEY COME!
KIRKMAN & SCOTT

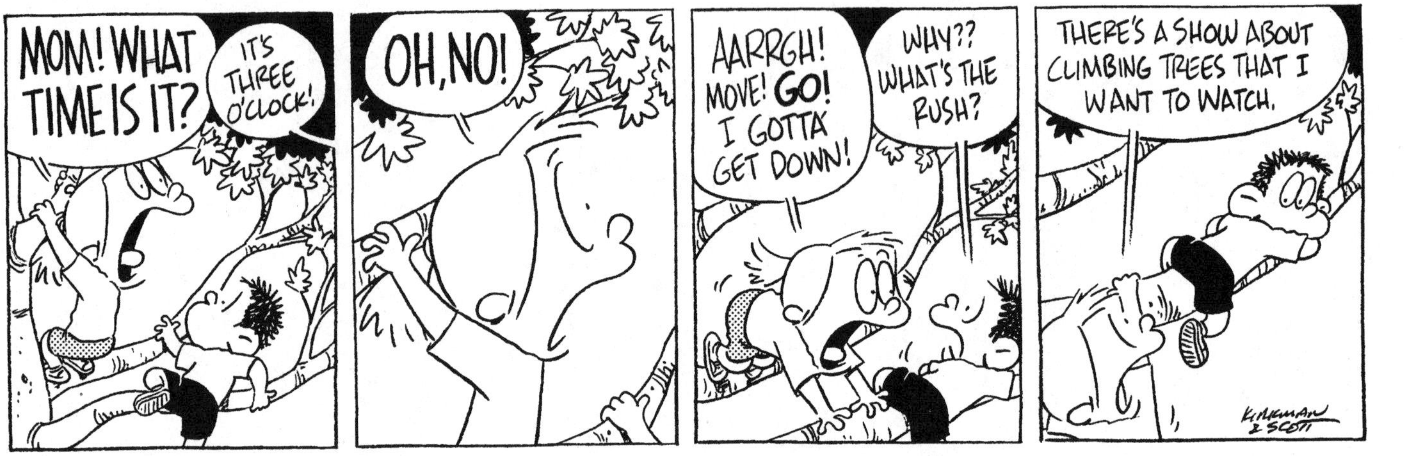
MOM! WHAT TIME IS IT?
IT'S THREE O'CLOCK!
OH, NO!
AARRGH! MOVE! GO! I GOTTA GET DOWN!
WHY?? WHAT'S THE RUSH?
THERE'S A SHOW ABOUT CLIMBING TREES THAT I WANT TO WATCH.
KIRKMAN & SCOTT

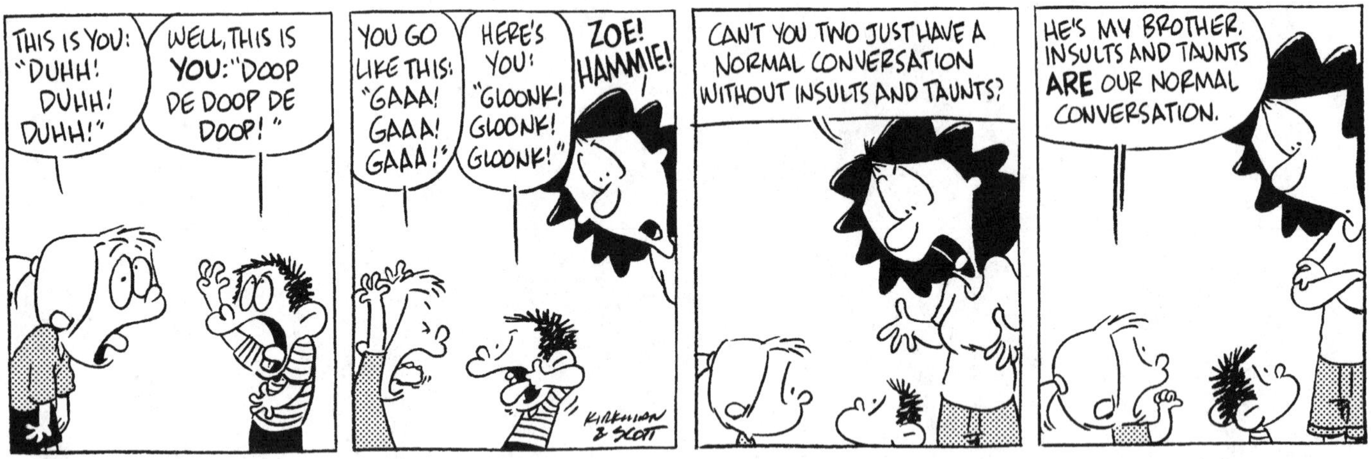
THIS IS YOU: "DUHH! DUHH! DUHH!"
WELL, THIS IS YOU: "DOOP DE DOOP DE DOOP!"
YOU GO LIKE THIS: "GAAA! GAAA! GAAA!"
HERE'S YOU: "GLOONK! GLOONK! GLOONK!"
ZOE! HAMMIE!
KIRKMAN & SCOTT
CAN'T YOU TWO JUST HAVE A NORMAL CONVERSATION WITHOUT INSULTS AND TAUNTS?
HE'S MY BROTHER. INSULTS AND TAUNTS ARE OUR NORMAL CONVERSATION.

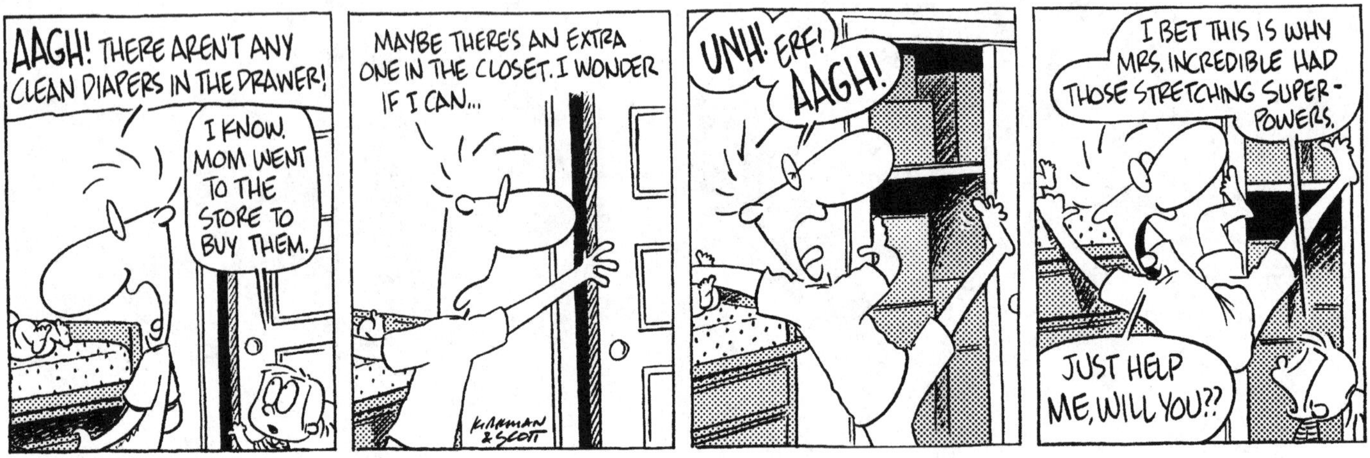
AAGH! THERE AREN'T ANY CLEAN DIAPERS IN THE DRAWER!
I KNOW. MOM WENT TO THE STORE TO BUY THEM.
MAYBE THERE'S AN EXTRA ONE IN THE CLOSET. I WONDER IF I CAN...
KIRKMAN & SCOTT
UNH! ERF! AAGH!
I BET THIS IS WHY MRS. INCREDIBLE HAD THOSE STRETCHING SUPER-POWERS.
JUST HELP ME, WILL YOU??

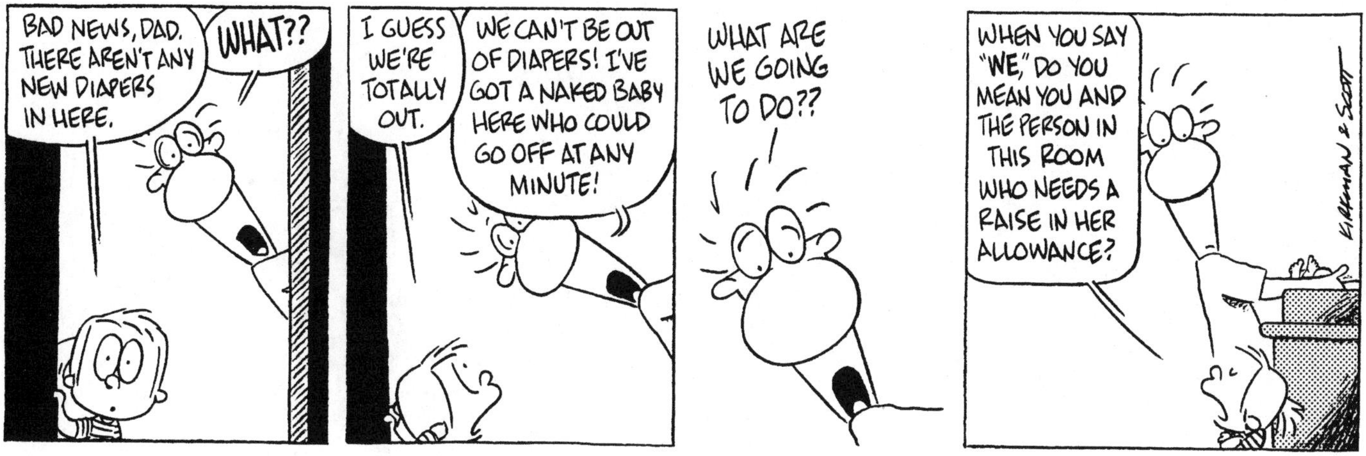
BAD NEWS, DAD. THERE AREN'T ANY NEW DIAPERS IN HERE.
WHAT??
I GUESS WE'RE TOTALLY OUT.
WE CAN'T BE OUT OF DIAPERS! I'VE GOT A NAKED BABY HERE WHO COULD GO OFF AT ANY MINUTE!
WHAT ARE WE GOING TO DO??
WHEN YOU SAY "WE," DO YOU MEAN YOU AND THE PERSON IN THIS ROOM WHO NEEDS A RAISE IN HER ALLOWANCE?
KIRKMAN & SCOTT

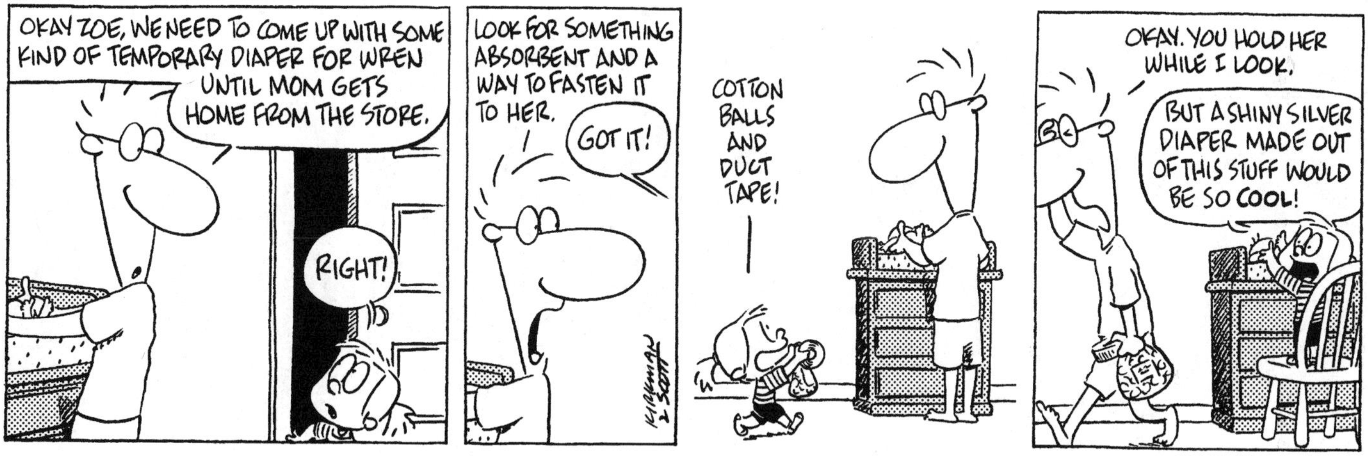
OKAY ZOE, WE NEED TO COME UP WITH SOME KIND OF TEMPORARY DIAPER FOR WREN UNTIL MOM GETS HOME FROM THE STORE.
RIGHT!
LOOK FOR SOMETHING ABSORBENT AND A WAY TO FASTEN IT TO HER.
GOT IT!
KIRKMAN & SCOTT
COTTON BALLS AND DUCT TAPE!
OKAY. YOU HOLD HER WHILE I LOOK.
BUT A SHINY SILVER DIAPER MADE OUT OF THIS STUFF WOULD BE SO COOL!

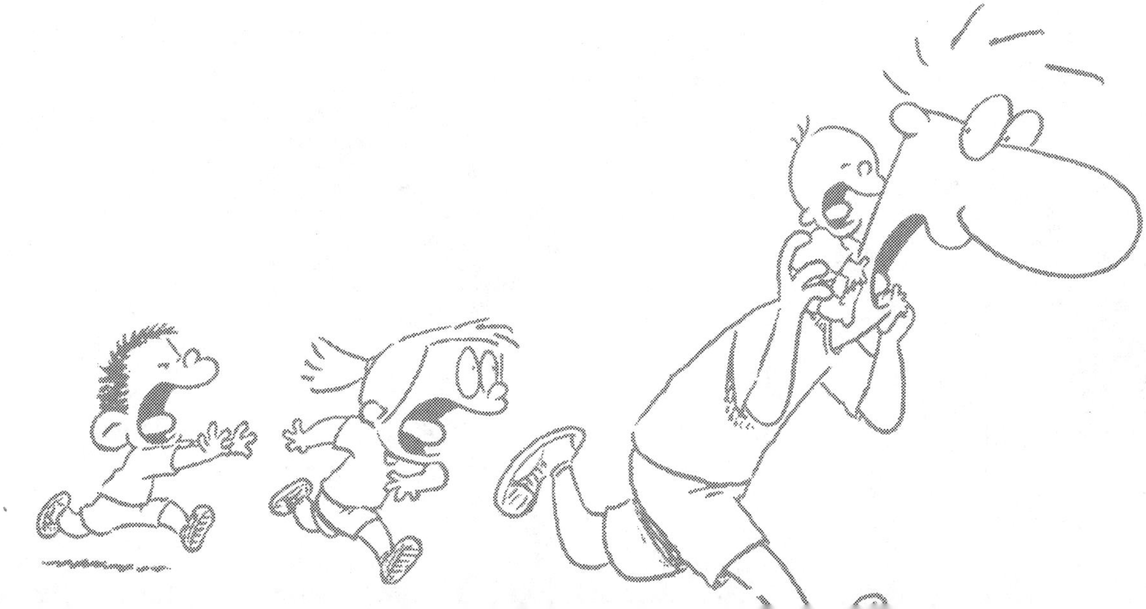

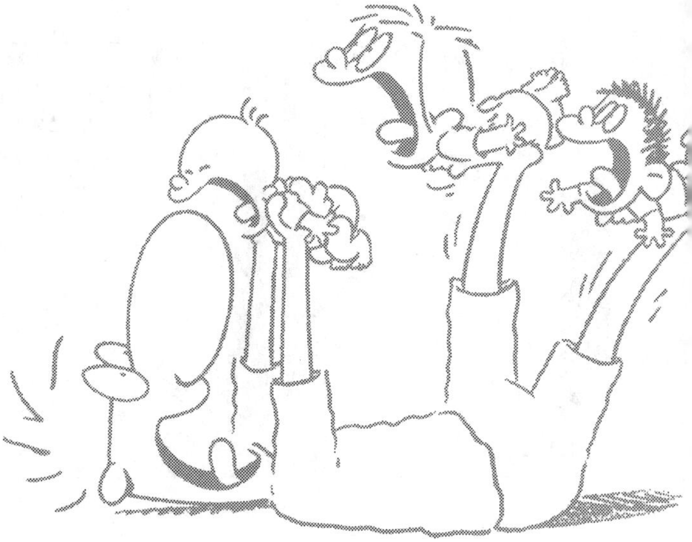

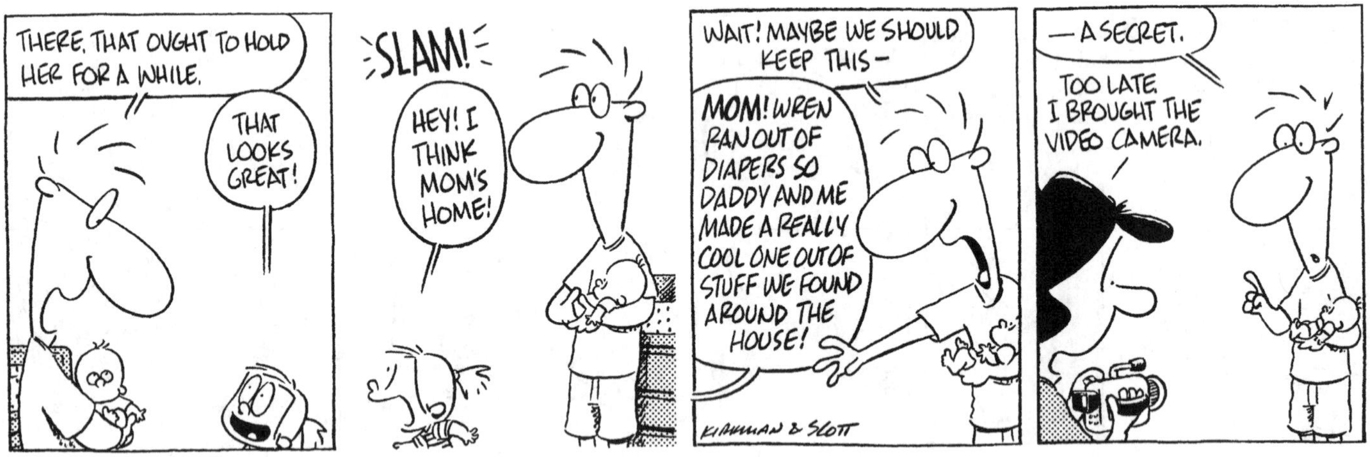
THERE. THAT OUGHT TO HOLD HER FOR A WHILE.
THAT LOOKS GREAT!
SLAM!
HEY! I THINK MOM'S HOME!
WAIT! MAYBE WE SHOULD KEEP THIS—
MOM! WREN RAN OUT OF DIAPERS SO DADDY AND ME MADE A REALLY COOL ONE OUT OF STUFF WE FOUND AROUND THE HOUSE!
KIRKMAN & SCOTT
—A SECRET.
TOO LATE. I BROUGHT THE VIDEO CAMERA.

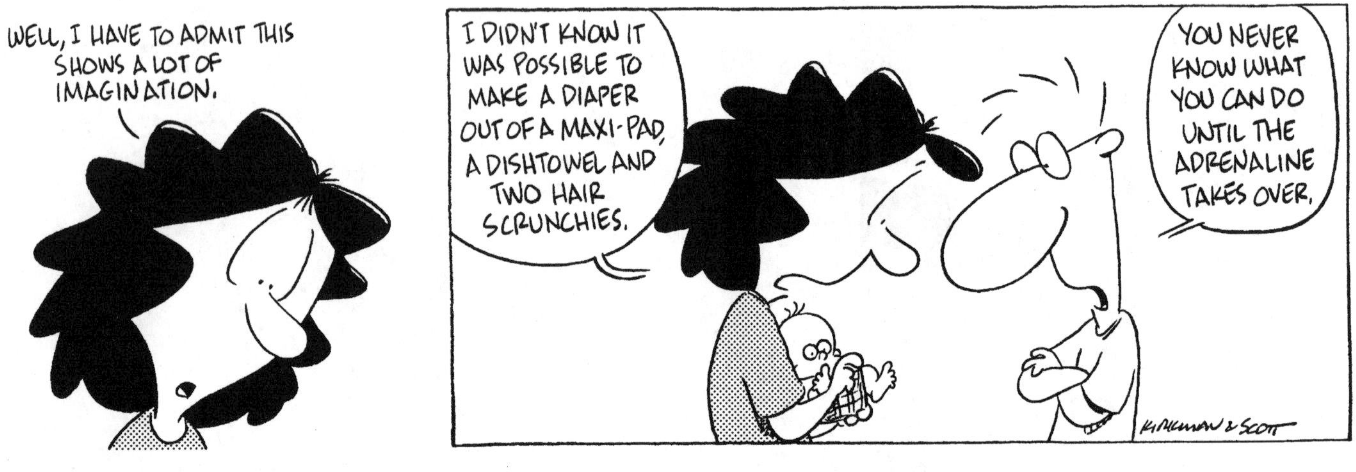
WELL, I HAVE TO ADMIT THIS SHOWS A LOT OF IMAGINATION.
I DIDN'T KNOW IT WAS POSSIBLE TO MAKE A DIAPER OUT OF A MAXI-PAD, A DISHTOWEL AND TWO HAIR SCRUNCHIES.
YOU NEVER KNOW WHAT YOU CAN DO UNTIL THE ADRENALINE TAKES OVER.
KIRKMAN & SCOTT

BABY BLUES®
BY RICK KIRKMAN / JERRY SCOTT

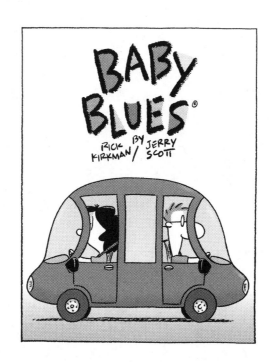

I GOT AN INVITATION TO KEESHA'S BIRTHDAY PARTY!
LET ME SEE!
UH-OH.. KEESHA'S PARTY IS ON THE SAME DAY AS BECCA'S PARTY.
BUT BECCA'S IS IN THE MORNING, AND KEESHA'S IS IN THE AFTERNOON.
OH, RIGHT. I GUESS THAT MEANS YOU AND HAMMIE ARE EACH GOING TO TWO BIRTHDAY PARTIES NEXT SATURDAY.
YAY!
HOW ARE WE GOING TO DO THAT?
WELL, I CAN TAKE ZOE TO BECCA'S PARTY AT 10, AND DROP HAMMIE OFF AT TRENT'S PARTY BY 10:30.
THEN I'LL TAKE WREN TO THE PARK AND GO TO THE GROCERY STORE IF YOU'LL PICK UP HAMMIE, DROP HIM OFF AT LOGAN'S PARTY, THEN PICK UP ZOE AND TAKE HER TO KEESHA'S.
I CAN PICK UP HAMMIE UP ON MY WAY FROM THE STORE, AND YOU CAN WALK OVER TO KEESHA'S TO GET ZOE AFTER WE PUT AWAY THE GROCERIES.
WOW! BUSY WEEKEND.
YEP. T.G.I.O.T.
WHAT?
THANK GOODNESS IT'S ONLY TUESDAY.
KIRKMAN & SCOTT

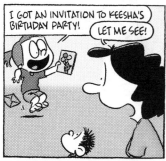

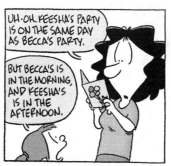

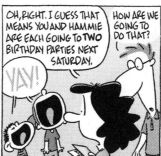

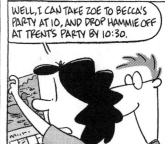

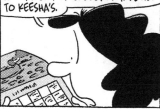

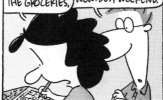

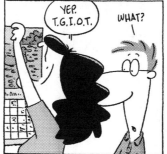

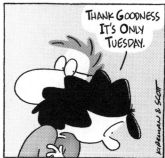

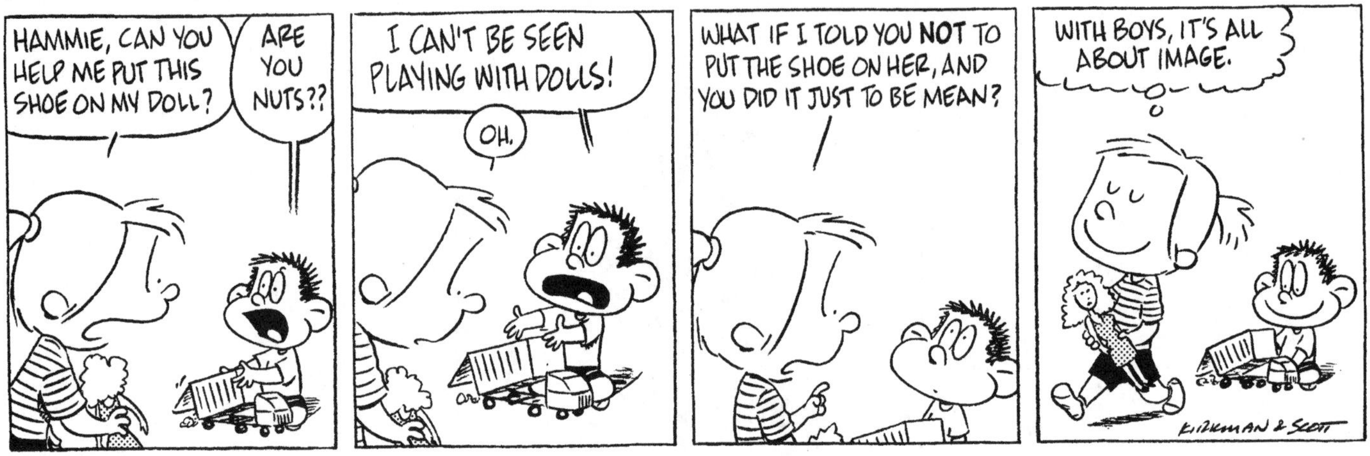
HAMMIE, CAN YOU HELP ME PUT THIS SHOE ON MY DOLL?
ARE YOU NUTS??
I CAN'T BE SEEN PLAYING WITH DOLLS!
OH.
WHAT IF I TOLD YOU **NOT** TO PUT THE SHOE ON HER, AND YOU DID IT JUST TO BE MEAN?
WITH BOYS, IT'S ALL ABOUT IMAGE.
KIRKMAN & SCOTT

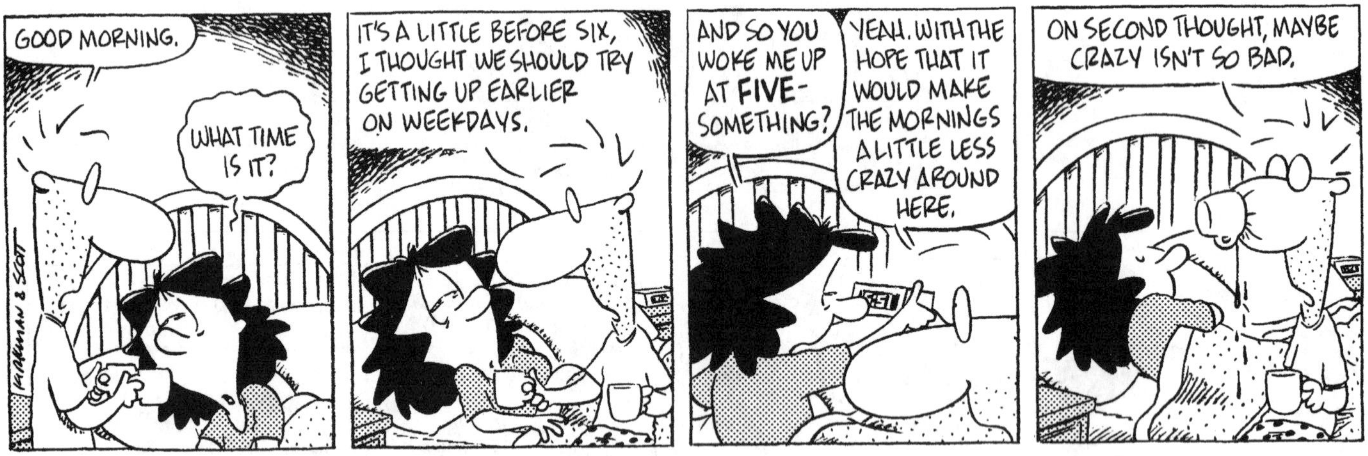
GOOD MORNING.
WHAT TIME IS IT?
KIRKMAN & SCOTT
IT'S A LITTLE BEFORE SIX, I THOUGHT WE SHOULD TRY GETTING UP EARLIER ON WEEKDAYS.
AND SO YOU WOKE ME UP AT **FIVE**-SOMETHING?
YEAH. WITH THE HOPE THAT IT WOULD MAKE THE MORNINGS A LITTLE LESS CRAZY AROUND HERE.
ON SECOND THOUGHT, MAYBE CRAZY ISN'T SO BAD.

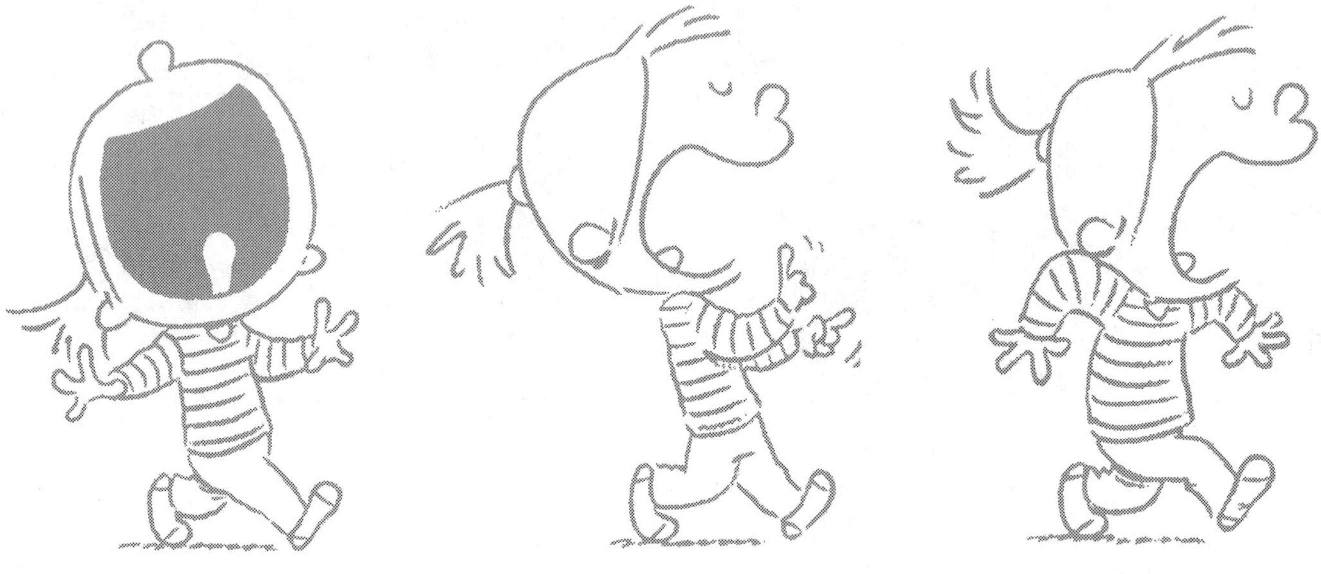

BABY BLUES®
BY RICK KIRKMAN / JERRY SCOTT

YOU KNOW, THAT SONG WAS ORIGINALLY RECORDED BY BOBBY VINTON IN LIKE, 1964.
A LOT OF NEW MUSIC IS SAMPLING OLD CLASSICS.
THAT'S TRUE.
AND IT'S NOT JUST MUSIC. THE SAME GOES FOR MOVIES, BOOKS, AND TELEVISION, TOO.
DON'T FORGET VIDEO GAMES.
A LOT OF THE STUFF THAT WAS AROUND WHEN WE WERE KIDS IS JUST BEING REPACKAGED AND SOLD TO YOU GUYS AS IF IT WERE ALL BRAND NEW.
TSK!
IF YOU IGNORE WHAT THEY'RE SAYING, IT SORTA LOOKS LIKE THEY'RE LIP-SYNCING TO THE MUSIC.
COOL.

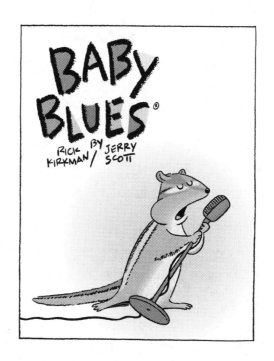

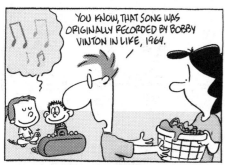

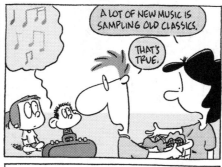

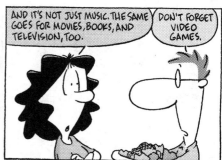

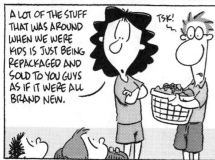

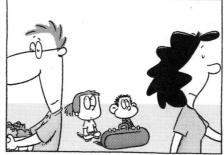

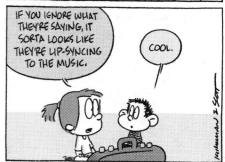

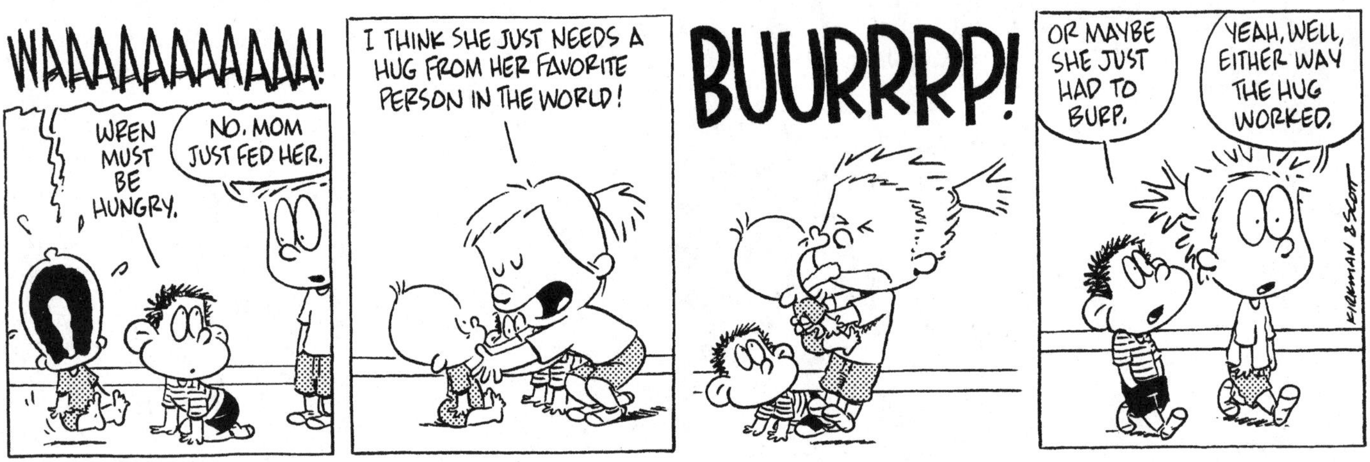
WAAAAAAAAAAA!
WREN MUST BE HUNGRY.
NO. MOM JUST FED HER.
I THINK SHE JUST NEEDS A HUG FROM HER FAVORITE PERSON IN THE WORLD!
BUURRRP!
OR MAYBE SHE JUST HAD TO BURP.
YEAH, WELL, EITHER WAY THE HUG WORKED.
KIRKMAN & SCOTT

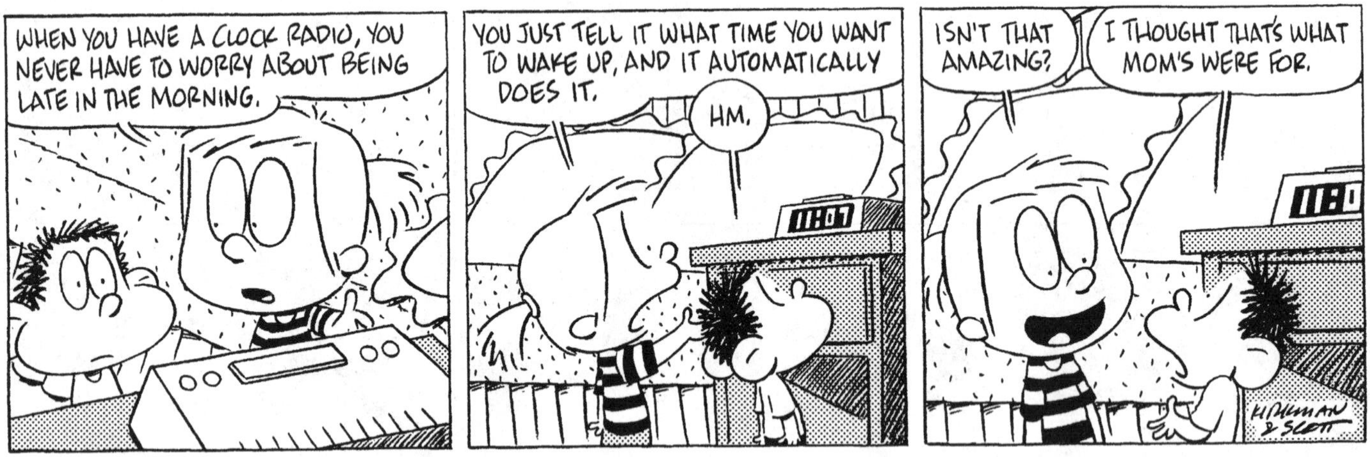
WHEN YOU HAVE A CLOCK RADIO, YOU NEVER HAVE TO WORRY ABOUT BEING LATE IN THE MORNING.
YOU JUST TELL IT WHAT TIME YOU WANT TO WAKE UP, AND IT AUTOMATICALLY DOES IT.
HM.
ISN'T THAT AMAZING?
I THOUGHT THAT'S WHAT MOM'S WERE FOR.
KIRKMAN & SCOTT

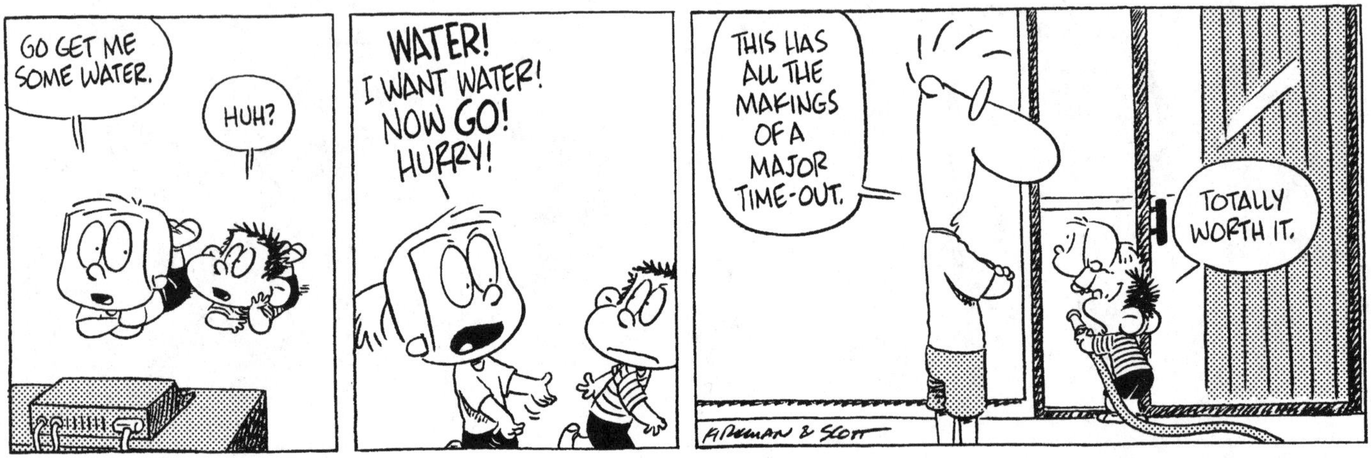
GO GET ME SOME WATER.
HUH?
WATER! I WANT WATER! NOW GO! HURRY!
THIS HAS ALL THE MAKINGS OF A MAJOR TIME-OUT.
TOTALLY WORTH IT.
KIRKMAN & SCOTT

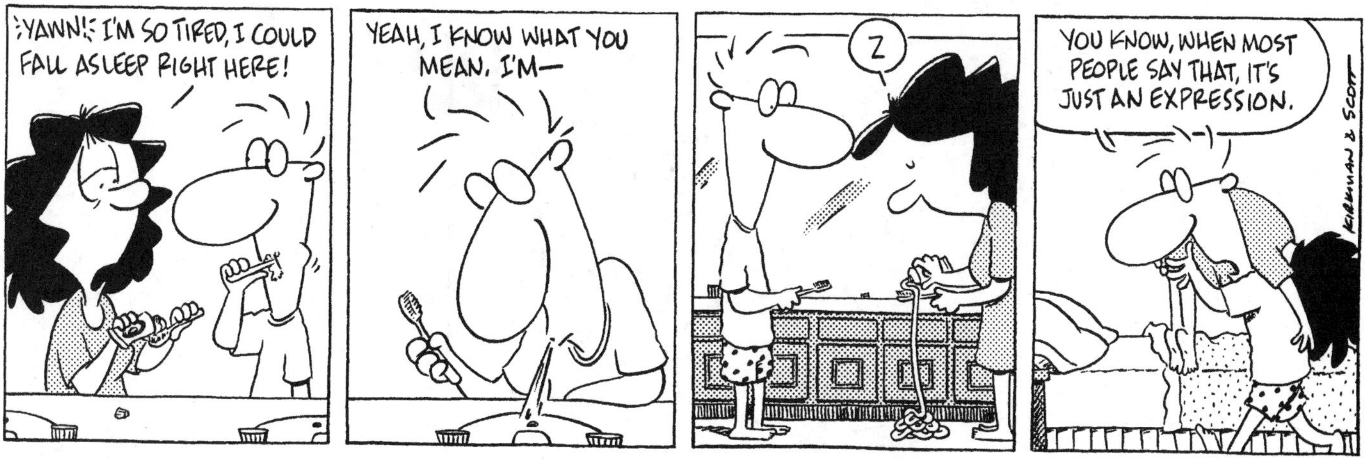
YAWN! I'M SO TIRED, I COULD FALL ASLEEP RIGHT HERE!
YEAH, I KNOW WHAT YOU MEAN. I'M—
Z
YOU KNOW, WHEN MOST PEOPLE SAY THAT, IT'S JUST AN EXPRESSION.
KIRKMAN & SCOTT

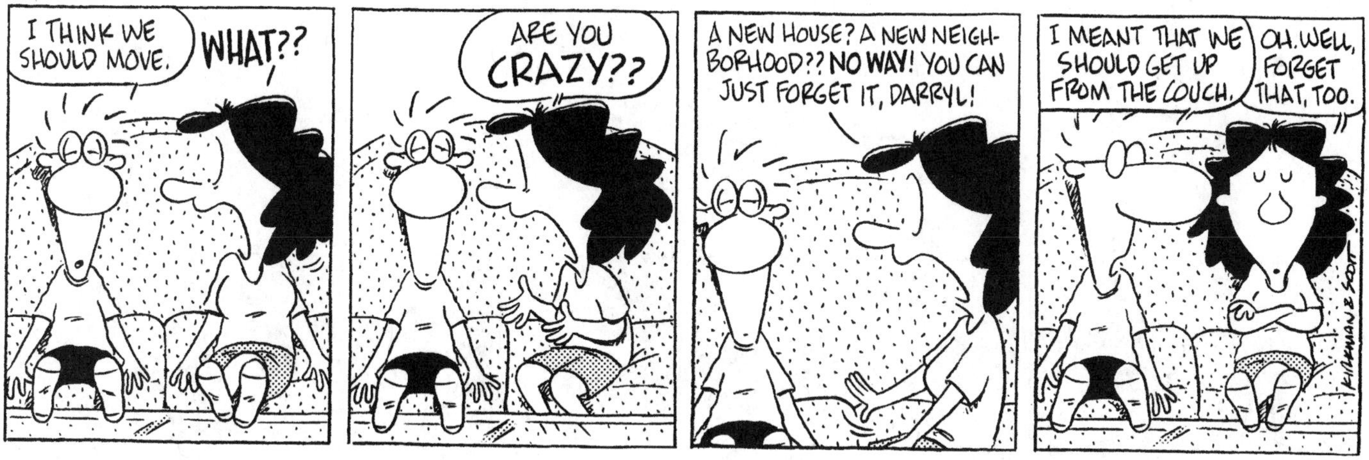
I THINK WE SHOULD MOVE.
WHAT??
ARE YOU CRAZY??
A NEW HOUSE? A NEW NEIGHBORHOOD?? NO WAY! YOU CAN JUST FORGET IT, DARRYL!
I MEANT THAT WE SHOULD GET UP FROM THE COUCH.
OH. WELL, FORGET THAT, TOO.
KIRKMAN & SCOTT

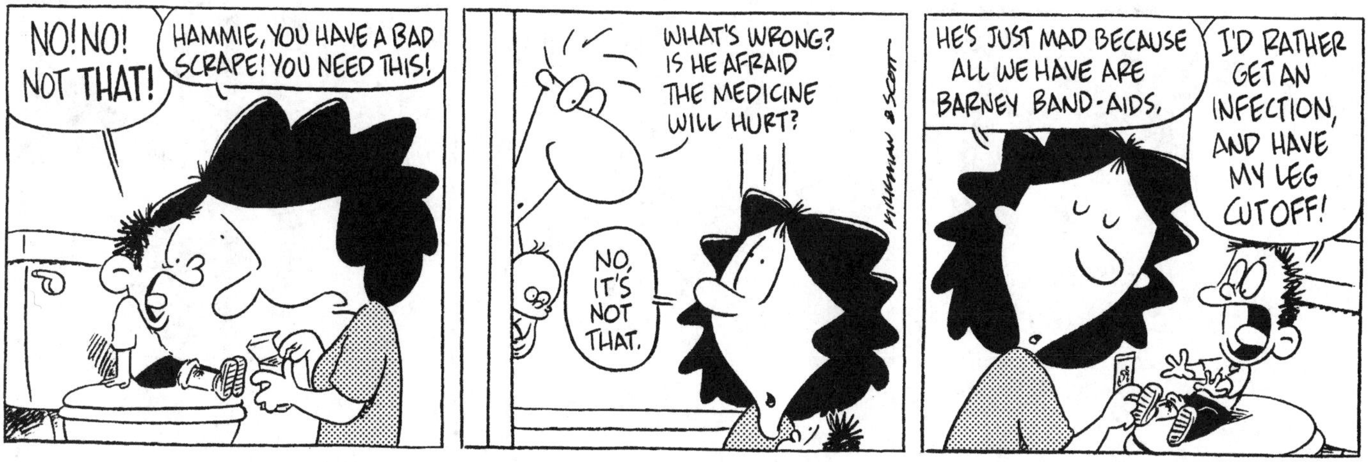
NO! NO! NOT THAT!
HAMMIE, YOU HAVE A BAD SCRAPE! YOU NEED THIS!
WHAT'S WRONG? IS HE AFRAID THE MEDICINE WILL HURT?
NO, IT'S NOT THAT.
KIRKMAN & SCOTT
HE'S JUST MAD BECAUSE ALL WE HAVE ARE BARNEY BAND-AIDS.
I'D RATHER GET AN INFECTION, AND HAVE MY LEG CUT OFF!

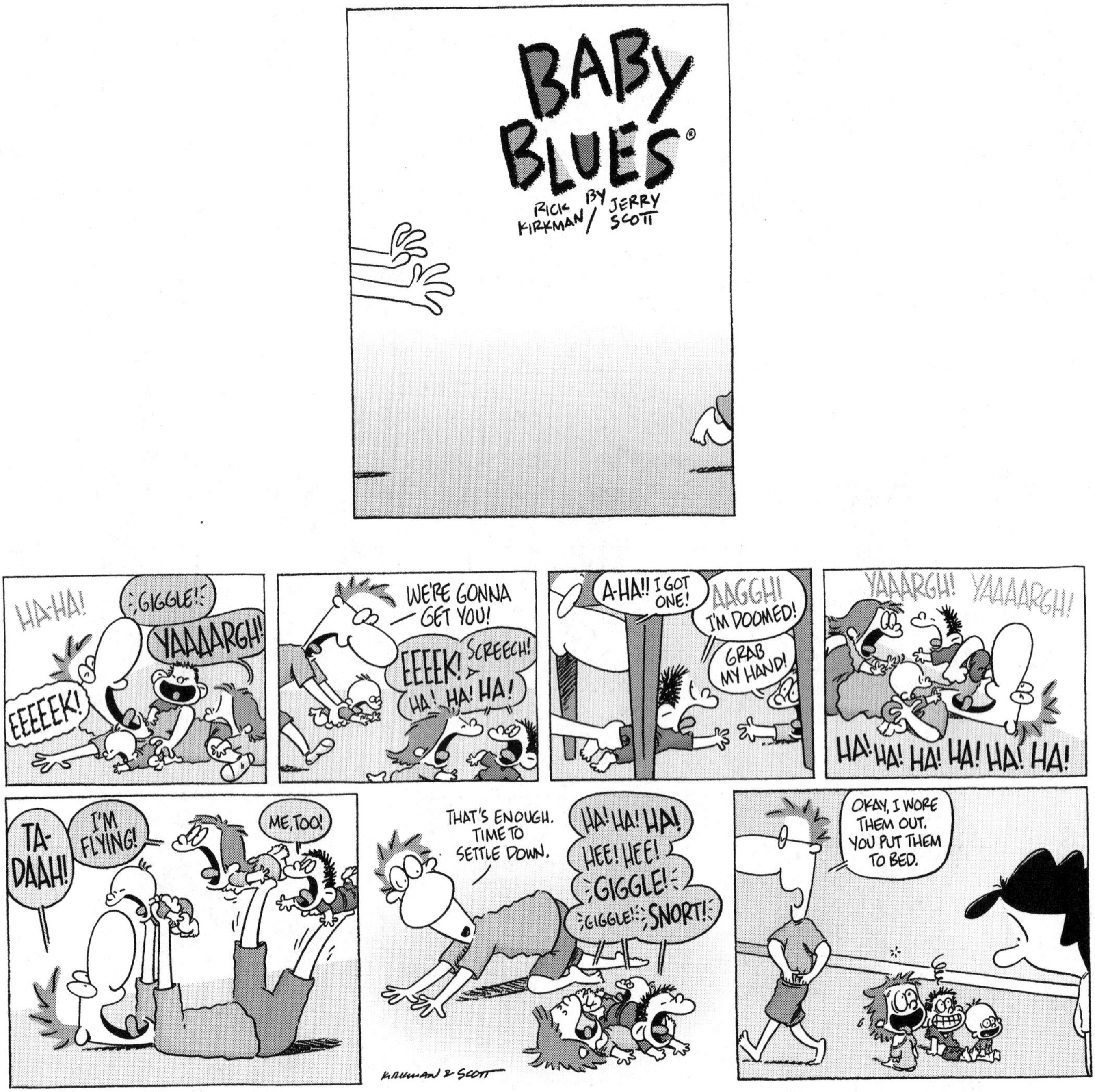

BABY BLUES®
BY RICK KIRKMAN / JERRY SCOTT
HA-HA!
GIGGLE!
YAAAARGH!
EEEEEK!
WE'RE GONNA GET YOU!
EEEEK!
SCREECH!
HA! HA! HA!
A-HA!! I GOT ONE!
AAGGH! I'M DOOMED!
GRAB MY HAND!
YAAARGH!
YAAAARGH!
HA! HA! HA! HA! HA! HA!
TA-DAAH!
I'M FLYING!
ME, TOO!
THAT'S ENOUGH. TIME TO SETTLE DOWN.
HA! HA! HA!
HEE! HEE!
GIGGLE!
GIGGLE!
SNORT!
KIRKMAN & SCOTT
OKAY, I WORE THEM OUT. YOU PUT THEM TO BED.

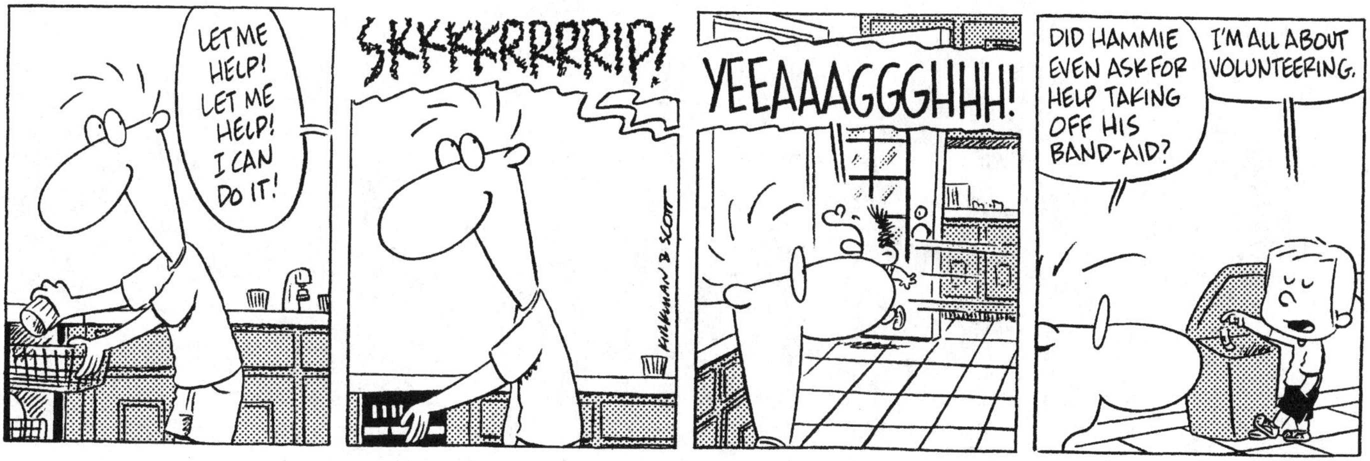
LET ME HELP! LET ME HELP! I CAN DO IT!
SKKKKRRRRIP!
YEEAAAGGGHHH!
DID HAMMIE EVEN ASK FOR HELP TAKING OFF HIS BAND-AID?
I'M ALL ABOUT VOLUNTEERING.

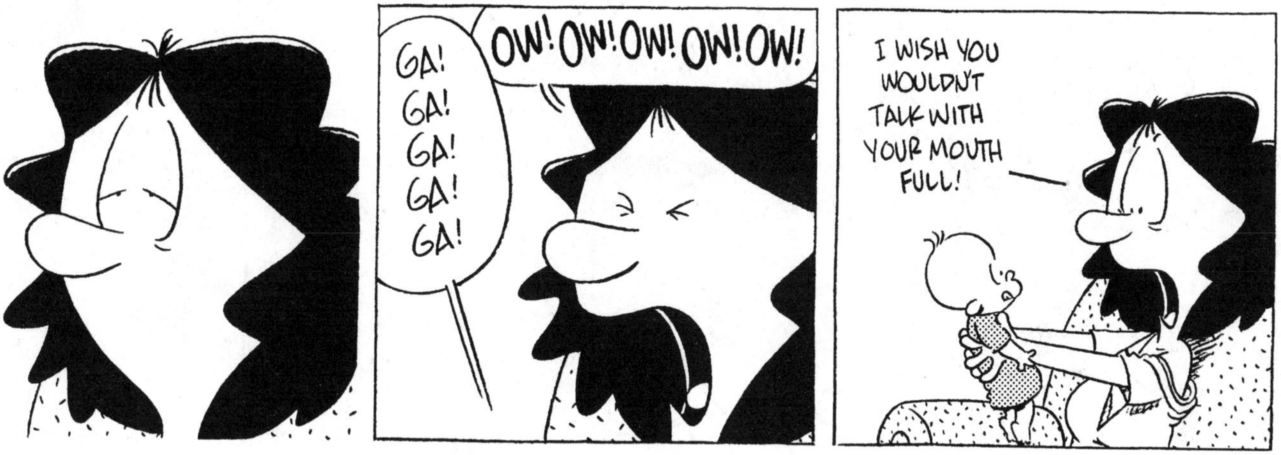
GA! GA! GA! GA! GA!
OW! OW! OW! OW! OW!
I WISH YOU WOULDN'T TALK WITH YOUR MOUTH FULL!

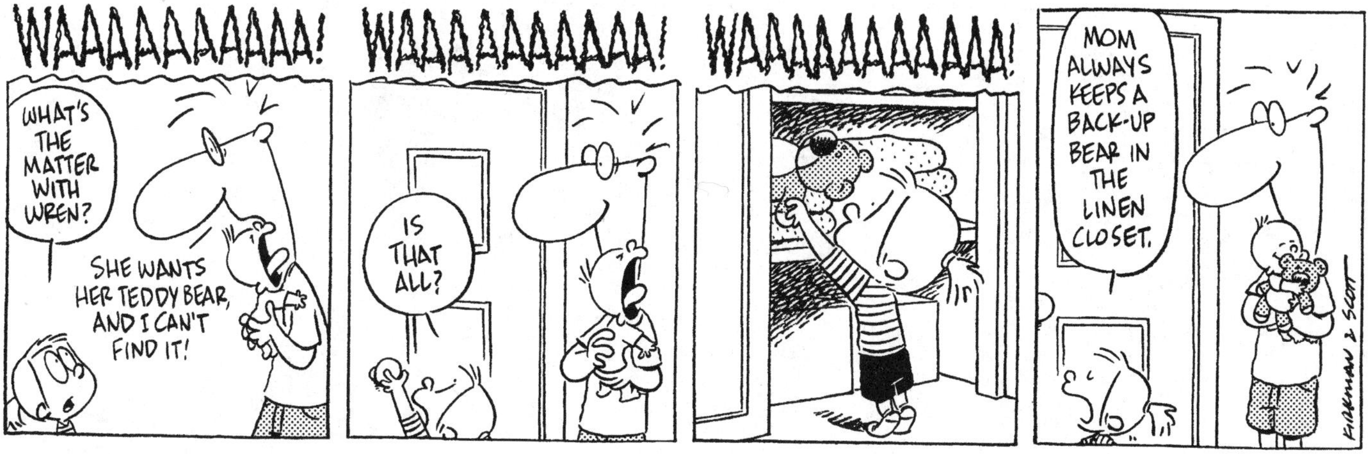
WAAAAAAAAAA!
WHAT'S THE MATTER WITH WREN?
SHE WANTS HER TEDDY BEAR, AND I CAN'T FIND IT!
WAAAAAAAAAA!
IS THAT ALL?
WAAAAAAAAAAA!
MOM ALWAYS KEEPS A BACK-UP BEAR IN THE LINEN CLOSET.

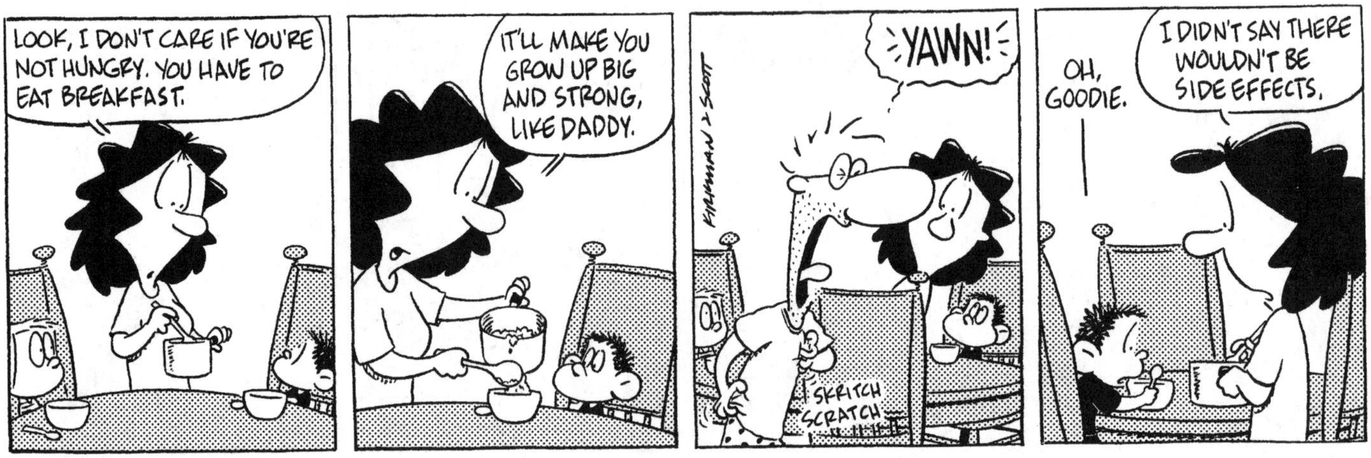
LOOK, I DON'T CARE IF YOU'RE NOT HUNGRY. YOU HAVE TO EAT BREAKFAST.
IT'LL MAKE YOU GROW UP BIG AND STRONG, LIKE DADDY.
YAWN!
SKRITCH SCRATCH
OH, GOODIE.
I DIDN'T SAY THERE WOULDN'T BE SIDE EFFECTS.

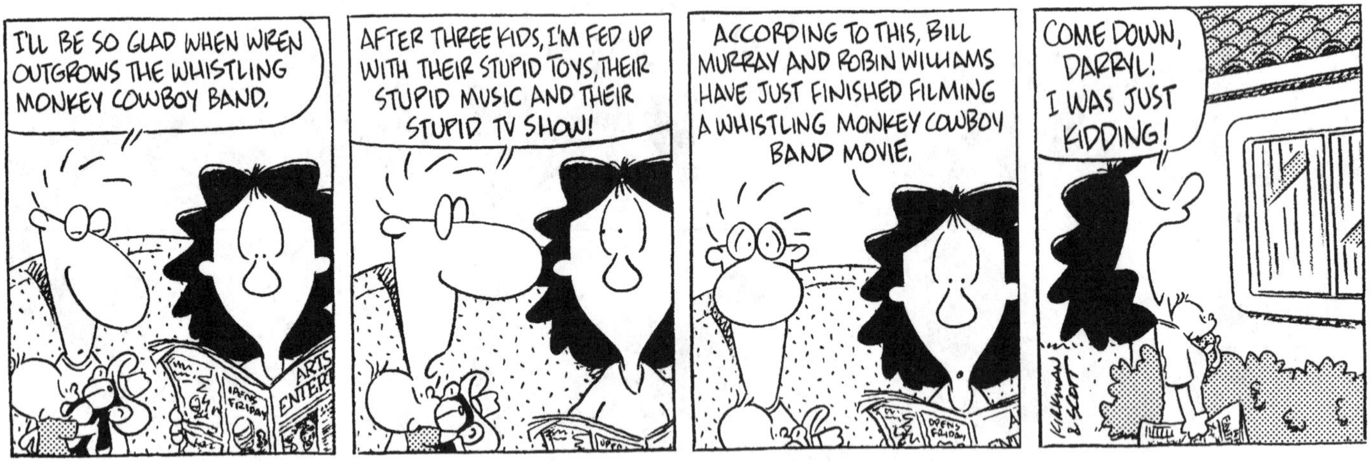
I'LL BE SO GLAD WHEN WREN OUTGROWS THE WHISTLING MONKEY COWBOY BAND.
AFTER THREE KIDS, I'M FED UP WITH THEIR STUPID TOYS, THEIR STUPID MUSIC AND THEIR STUPID TV SHOW!
ACCORDING TO THIS, BILL MURRAY AND ROBIN WILLIAMS HAVE JUST FINISHED FILMING A WHISTLING MONKEY COWBOY BAND MOVIE.
COME DOWN, DARRYL! I WAS JUST KIDDING!

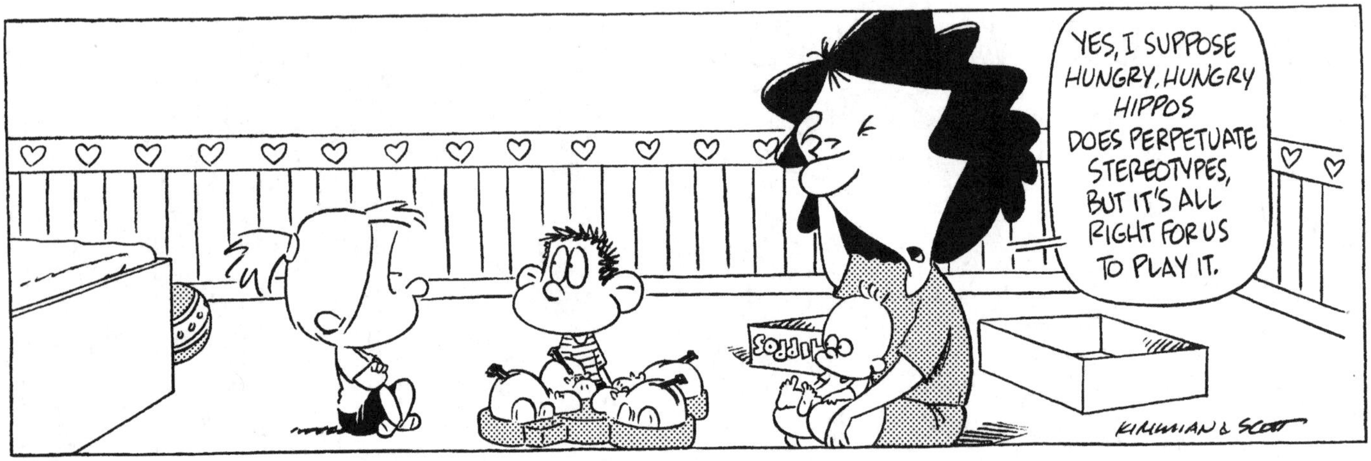
YES, I SUPPOSE HUNGRY, HUNGRY HIPPOS DOES PERPETUATE STEREOTYPES, BUT IT'S ALL RIGHT FOR US TO PLAY IT.
HIPPOS
KIRKMAN & SCOTT

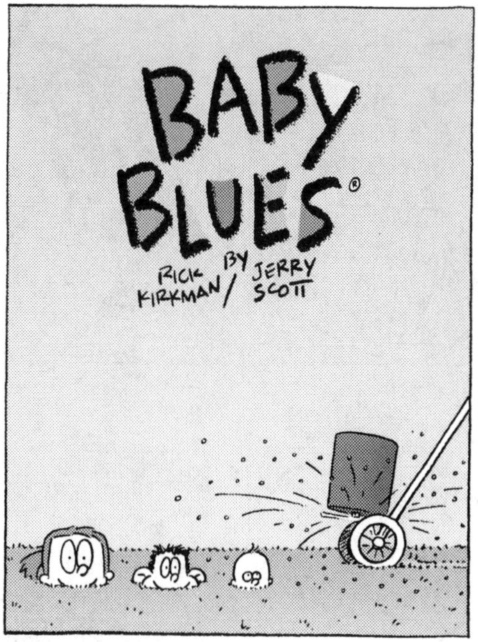
BABY BLUES®
BY RICK KIRKMAN/ JERRY SCOTT

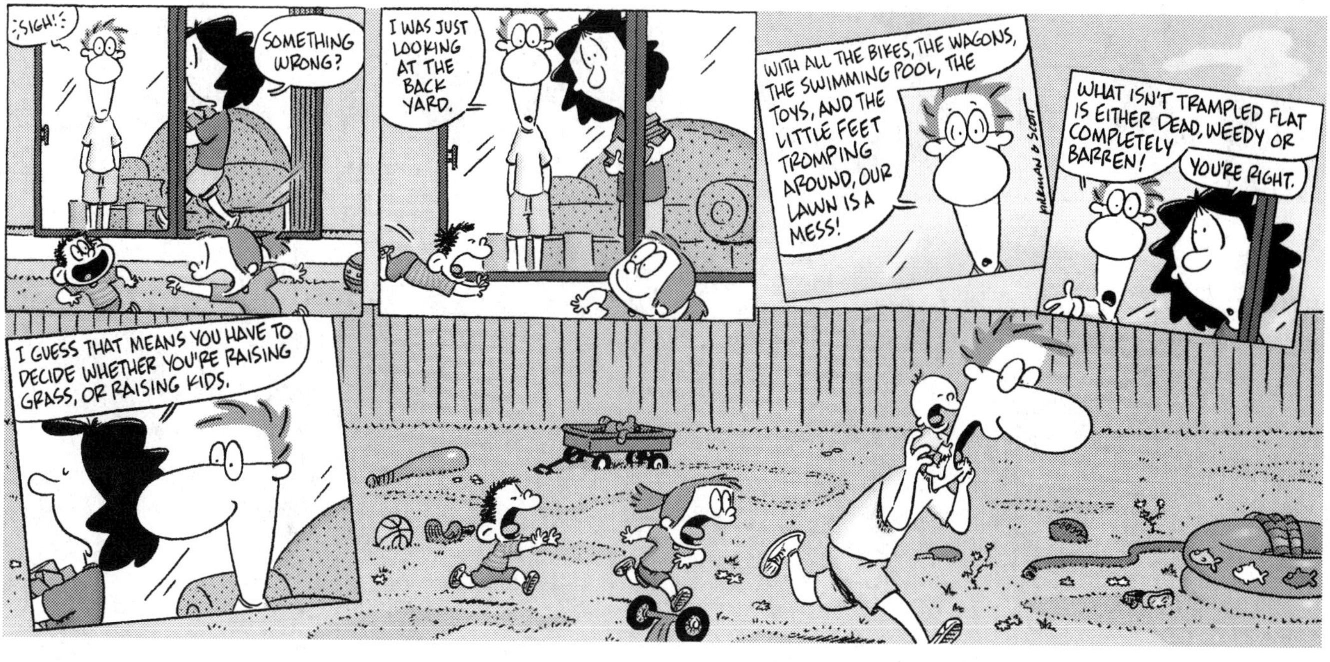
SIGH!
SOMETHING WRONG?
I WAS JUST LOOKING AT THE BACK YARD.
WITH ALL THE BIKES, THE WAGONS, THE SWIMMING POOL, THE TOYS, AND THE LITTLE FEET TROMPING AROUND, OUR LAWN IS A MESS!
WHAT ISN'T TRAMPLED FLAT IS EITHER DEAD, WEEDY OR COMPLETELY BARREN!
YOU'RE RIGHT.
I GUESS THAT MEANS YOU HAVE TO DECIDE WHETHER YOU'RE RAISING GRASS, OR RAISING KIDS.

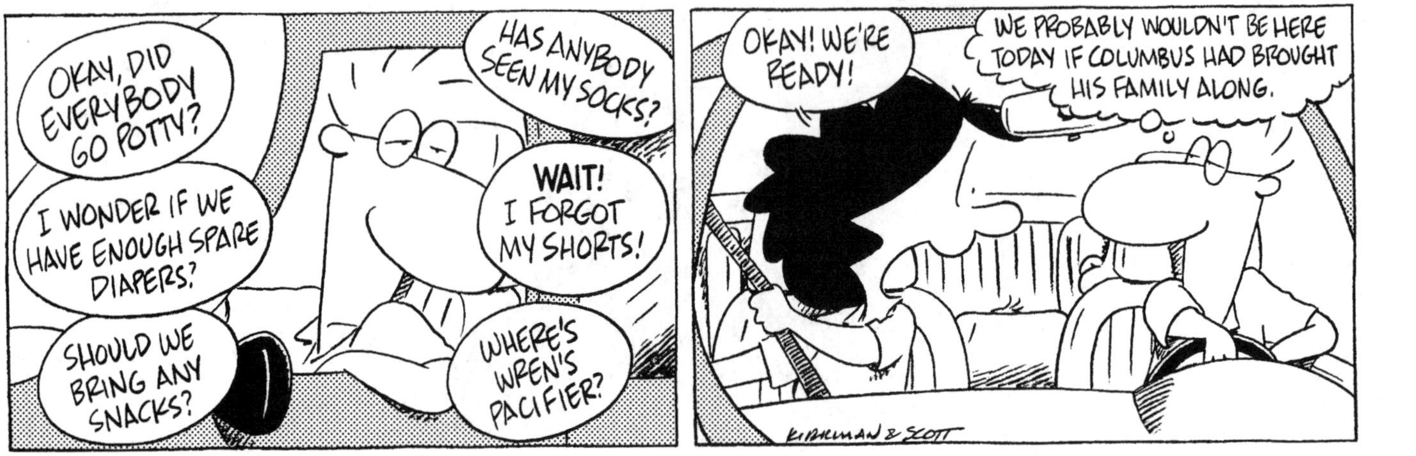
OKAY, DID EVERYBODY GO POTTY?
HAS ANYBODY SEEN MY SOCKS?
I WONDER IF WE HAVE ENOUGH SPARE DIAPERS?
WAIT! I FORGOT MY SHORTS!
SHOULD WE BRING ANY SNACKS?
WHERE'S WREN'S PACIFIER?
OKAY! WE'RE READY!
WE PROBABLY WOULDN'T BE HERE TODAY IF COLUMBUS HAD BROUGHT HIS FAMILY ALONG.
KIRKMAN & SCOTT

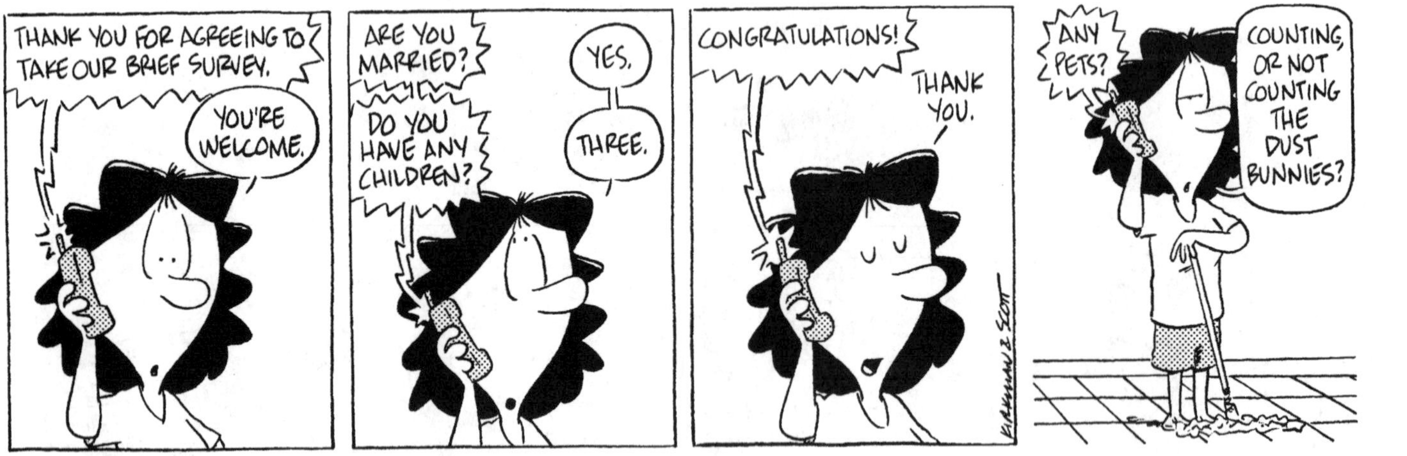
THANK YOU FOR AGREEING TO TAKE OUR BRIEF SURVEY.
YOU'RE WELCOME.
ARE YOU MARRIED?
YES.
DO YOU HAVE ANY CHILDREN?
THREE.
CONGRATULATIONS!
THANK YOU.
KIRKMAN & SCOTT
ANY PETS?
COUNTING, OR NOT COUNTING THE DUST BUNNIES?

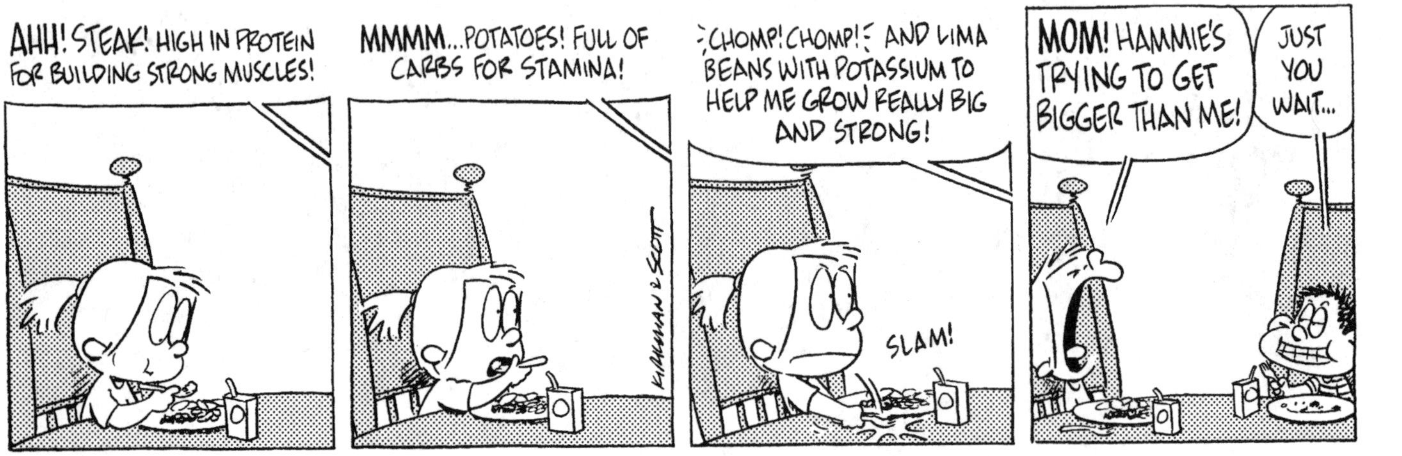
AHH! STEAK! HIGH IN PROTEIN FOR BUILDING STRONG MUSCLES!
MMMM...POTATOES! FULL OF CARBS FOR STAMINA!
KIRKMAN & SCOTT
CHOMP! CHOMP! AND LIMA BEANS WITH POTASSIUM TO HELP ME GROW REALLY BIG AND STRONG!
SLAM!
MOM! HAMMIE'S TRYING TO GET BIGGER THAN ME!
JUST YOU WAIT...

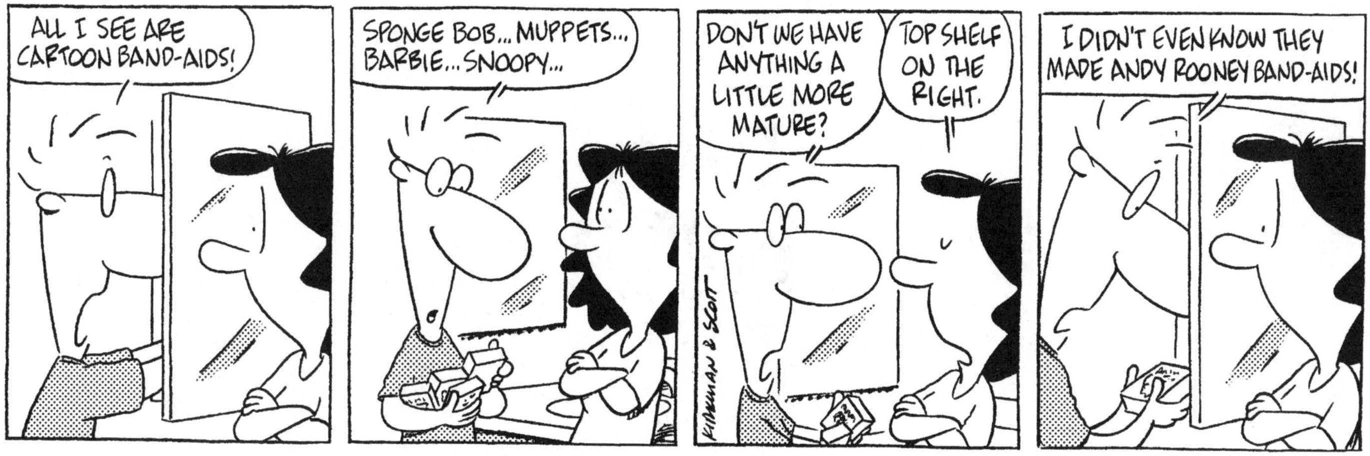
ALL I SEE ARE CARTOON BAND-AIDS!
SPONGE BOB... MUPPETS... BARBIE... SNOOPY...
DON'T WE HAVE ANYTHING A LITTLE MORE MATURE?
TOP SHELF ON THE RIGHT.
KIRKMAN & SCOTT
I DIDN'T EVEN KNOW THEY MADE ANDY ROONEY BAND-AIDS!

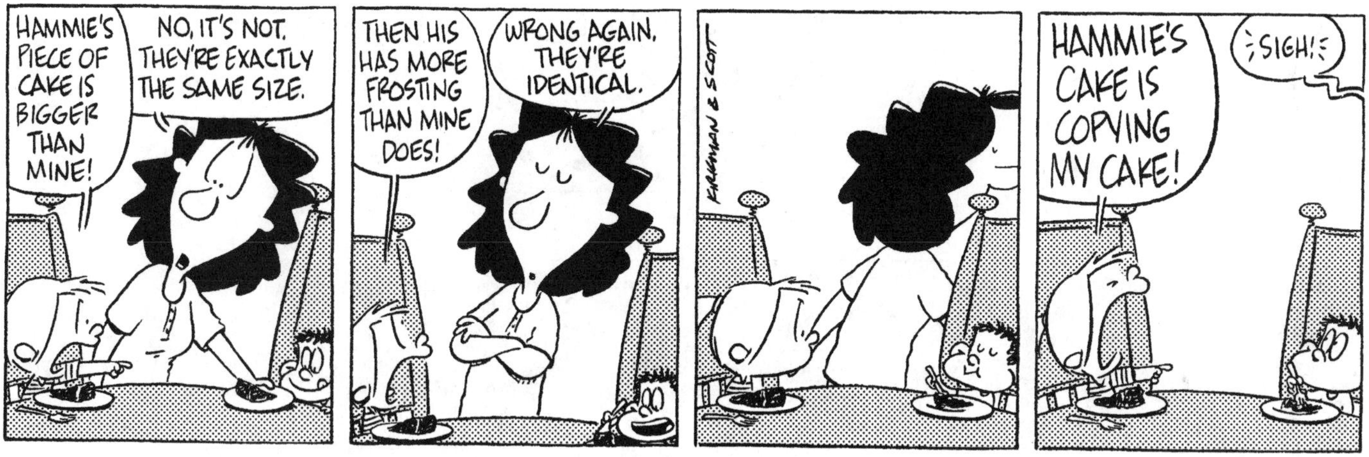
HAMMIE'S PIECE OF CAKE IS BIGGER THAN MINE!
NO, IT'S NOT. THEY'RE EXACTLY THE SAME SIZE.
THEN HIS HAS MORE FROSTING THAN MINE DOES!
WRONG AGAIN. THEY'RE IDENTICAL.
KIRKMAN & SCOTT
HAMMIE'S CAKE IS COPYING MY CAKE!
SIGH!

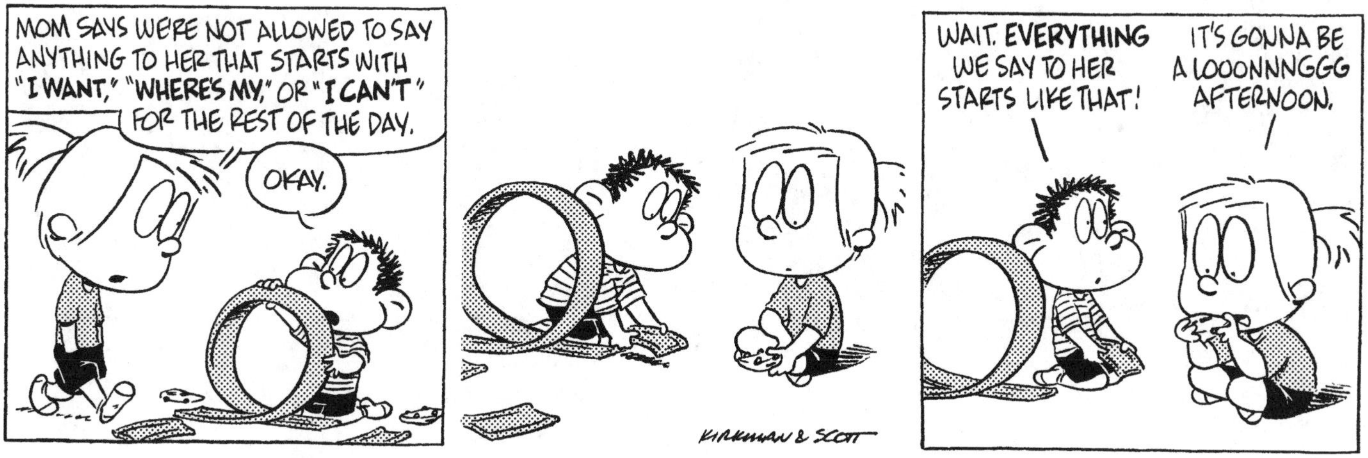
MOM SAYS WE'RE NOT ALLOWED TO SAY ANYTHING TO HER THAT STARTS WITH "I WANT," "WHERE'S MY," OR "I CAN'T" FOR THE REST OF THE DAY.
OKAY.
KIRKMAN & SCOTT
WAIT. EVERYTHING WE SAY TO HER STARTS LIKE THAT!
IT'S GONNA BE A LOOONNNGGG AFTERNOON.

BABY BLUES®
BY RICK KIRKMAN / JERRY SCOTT

WWAAAAAAAA AAAAAAAAAA AAAAAAAAA!
KIRKMAN & SCOTT

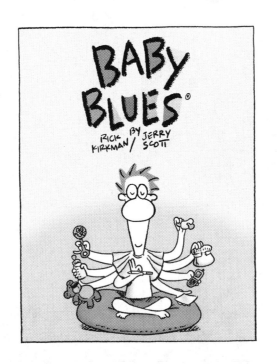

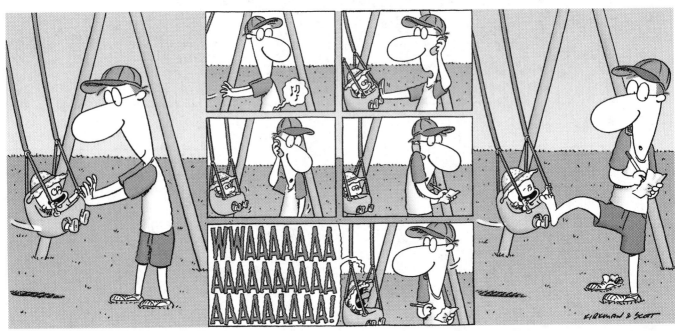

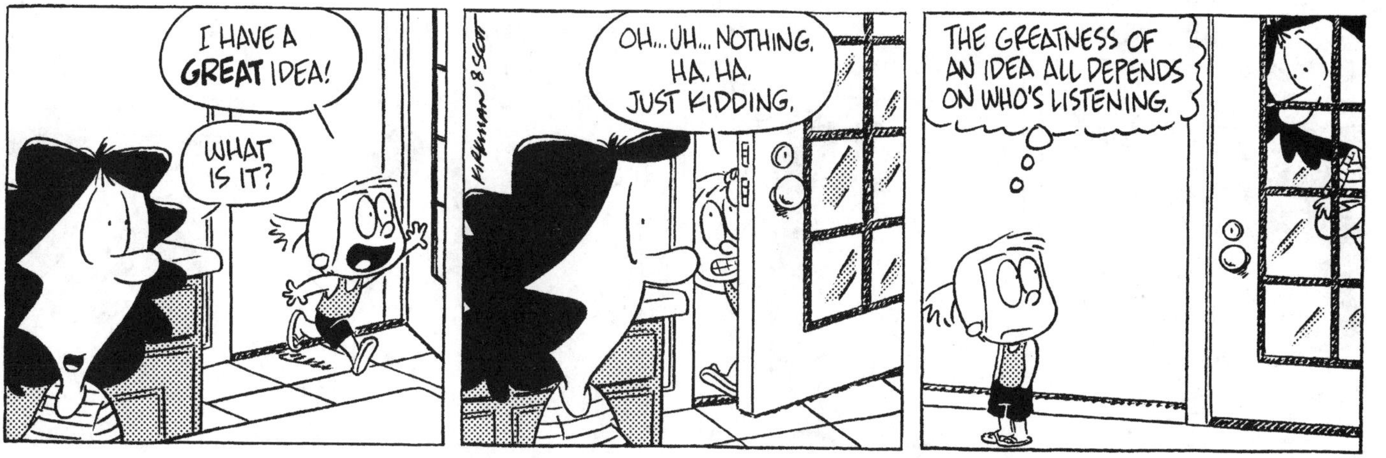
I HAVE A **GREAT** IDEA!
WHAT IS IT?
OH... UH... NOTHING. HA. HA. JUST KIDDING.
THE GREATNESS OF AN IDEA ALL DEPENDS ON WHO'S LISTENING.

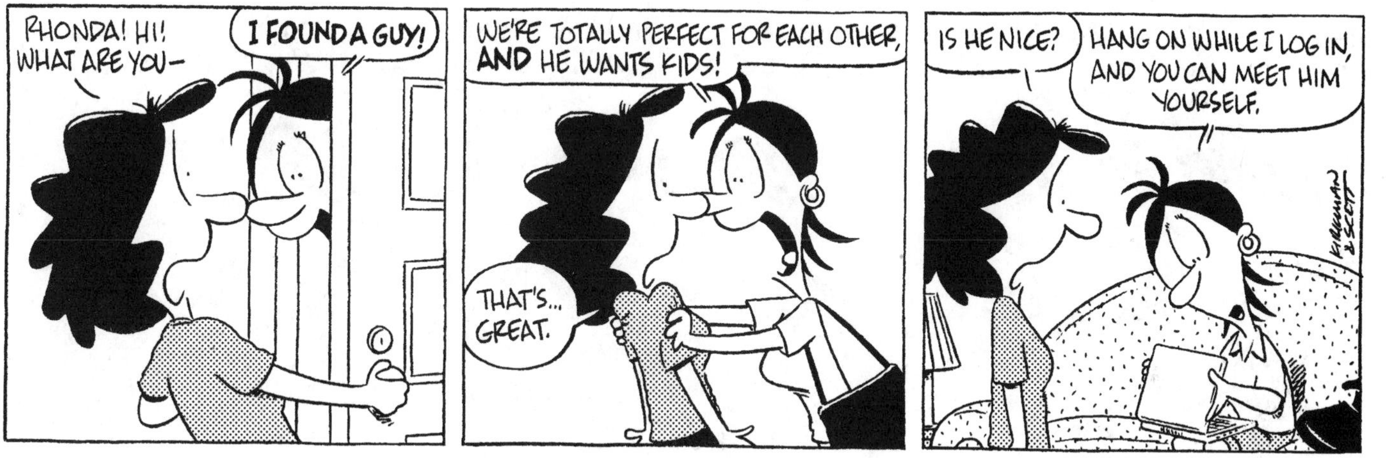
RHONDA! HI! WHAT ARE YOU—
I FOUND A GUY!
WE'RE TOTALLY PERFECT FOR EACH OTHER, **AND** HE WANTS KIDS!
THAT'S... GREAT.
IS HE NICE?
HANG ON WHILE I LOG IN, AND YOU CAN MEET HIM YOURSELF.

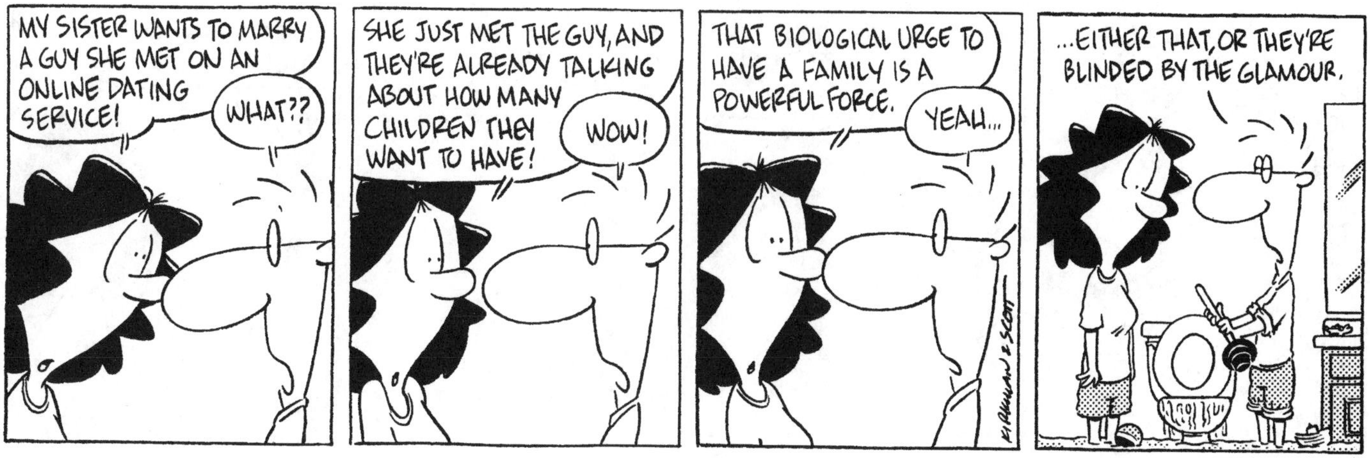
MY SISTER WANTS TO MARRY A GUY SHE MET ON AN ONLINE DATING SERVICE!
WHAT??
SHE JUST MET THE GUY, AND THEY'RE ALREADY TALKING ABOUT HOW MANY CHILDREN THEY WANT TO HAVE!
WOW!
THAT BIOLOGICAL URGE TO HAVE A FAMILY IS A POWERFUL FORCE.
YEAH...
...EITHER THAT, OR THEY'RE BLINDED BY THE GLAMOUR.

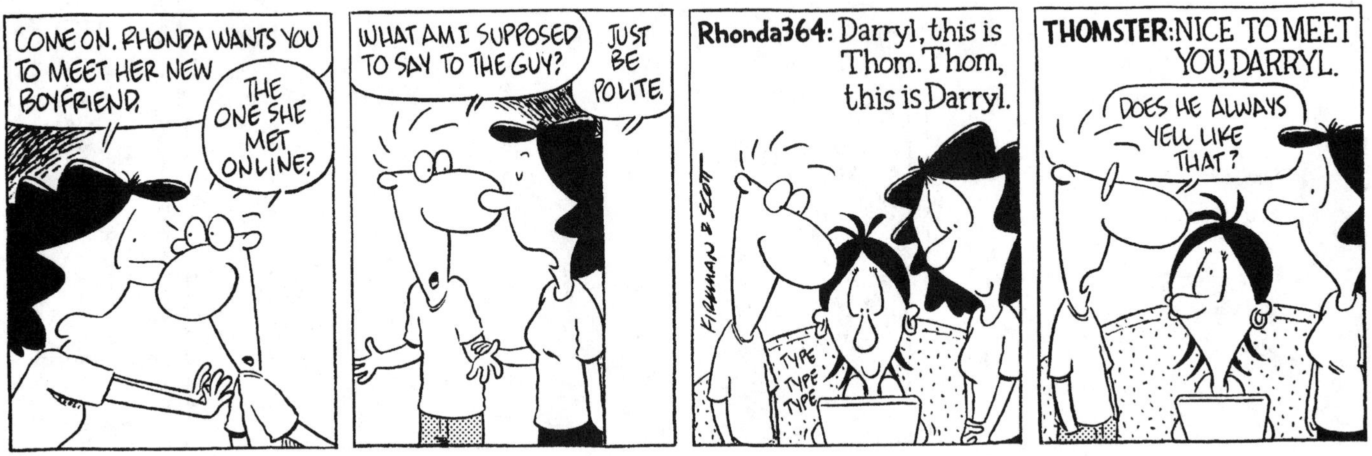

COME ON. RHONDA WANTS YOU TO MEET HER NEW BOYFRIEND.
THE ONE SHE MET ONLINE?
WHAT AM I SUPPOSED TO SAY TO THE GUY?
JUST BE POLITE.
Rhonda364: Darryl, this is Thom. Thom, this is Darryl.
KIRKMAN & SCOTT
TYPE TYPE TYPE
THOMSTER: NICE TO MEET YOU, DARRYL.
DOES HE ALWAYS YELL LIKE THAT?

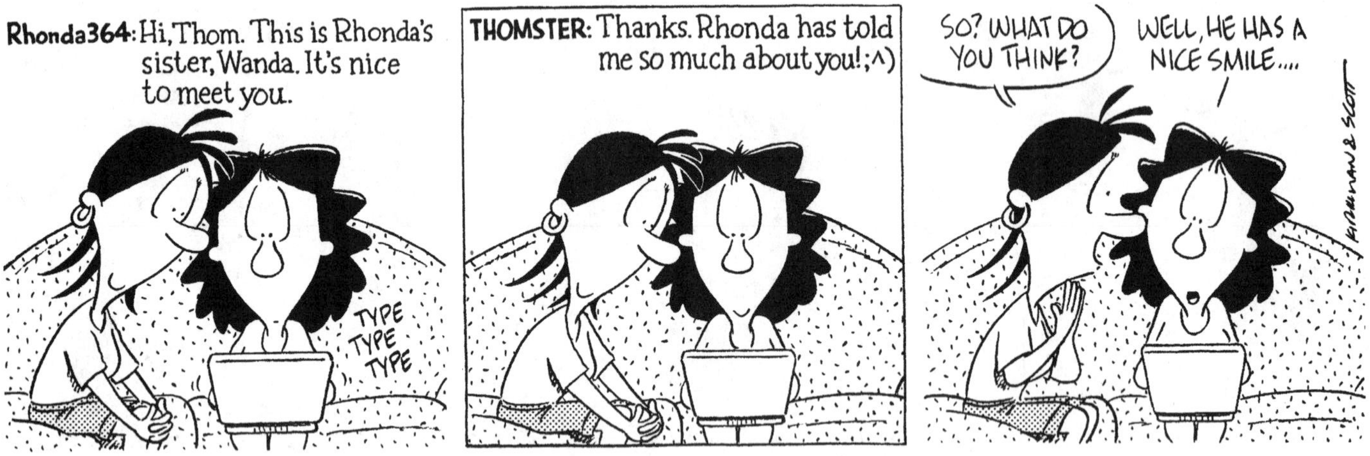

Rhonda364: Hi, Thom. This is Rhonda's sister, Wanda. It's nice to meet you.
TYPE TYPE TYPE
THOMSTER: Thanks. Rhonda has told me so much about you! ;^)
SO? WHAT DO YOU THINK?
WELL, HE HAS A NICE SMILE....
KIRKMAN & SCOTT

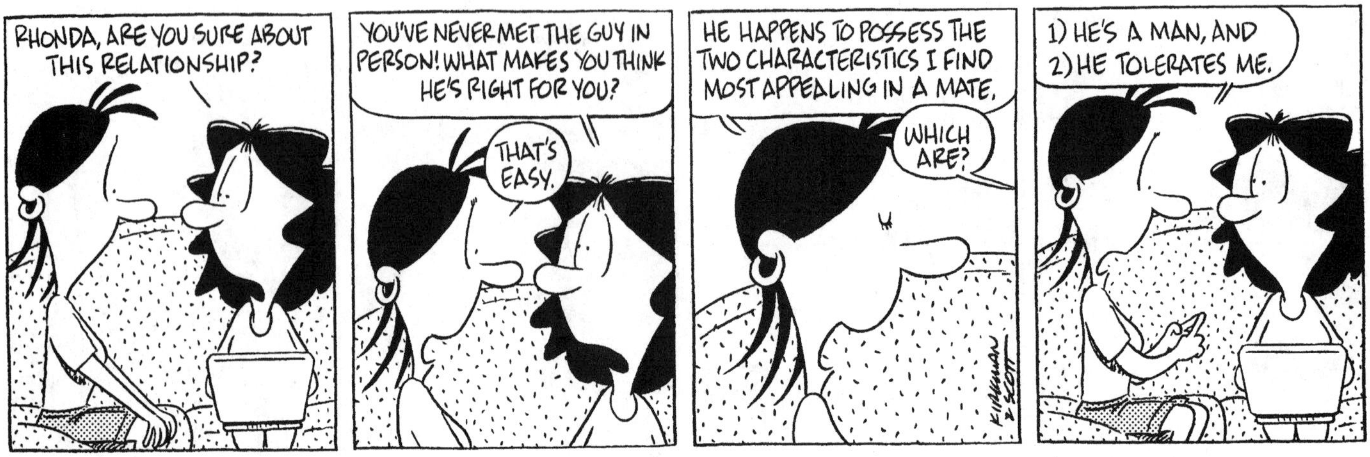

RHONDA, ARE YOU SURE ABOUT THIS RELATIONSHIP?
YOU'VE NEVER MET THE GUY IN PERSON! WHAT MAKES YOU THINK HE'S RIGHT FOR YOU?
THAT'S EASY.
HE HAPPENS TO POSSESS THE TWO CHARACTERISTICS I FIND MOST APPEALING IN A MATE.
WHICH ARE?
KIRKMAN & SCOTT
1) HE'S A MAN, AND
2) HE TOLERATES ME.

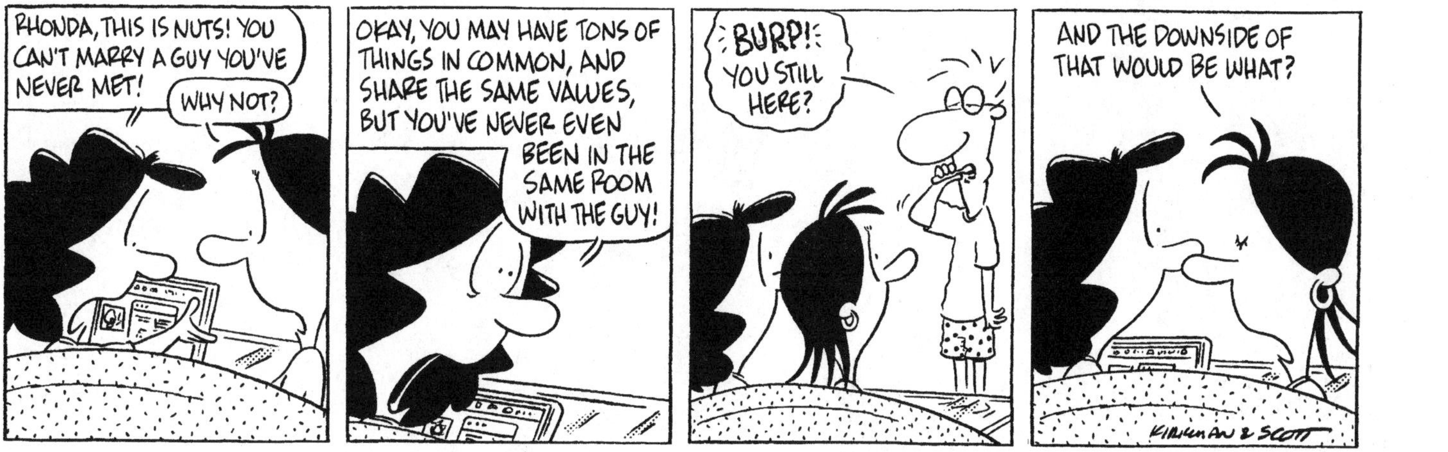
RHONDA, THIS IS NUTS! YOU CAN'T MARRY A GUY YOU'VE NEVER MET!
WHY NOT?
OKAY, YOU MAY HAVE TONS OF THINGS IN COMMON, AND SHARE THE SAME VALUES, BUT YOU'VE NEVER EVEN BEEN IN THE SAME ROOM WITH THE GUY!
BURP!
YOU STILL HERE?
AND THE DOWNSIDE OF THAT WOULD BE WHAT?
KIRKMAN & SCOTT

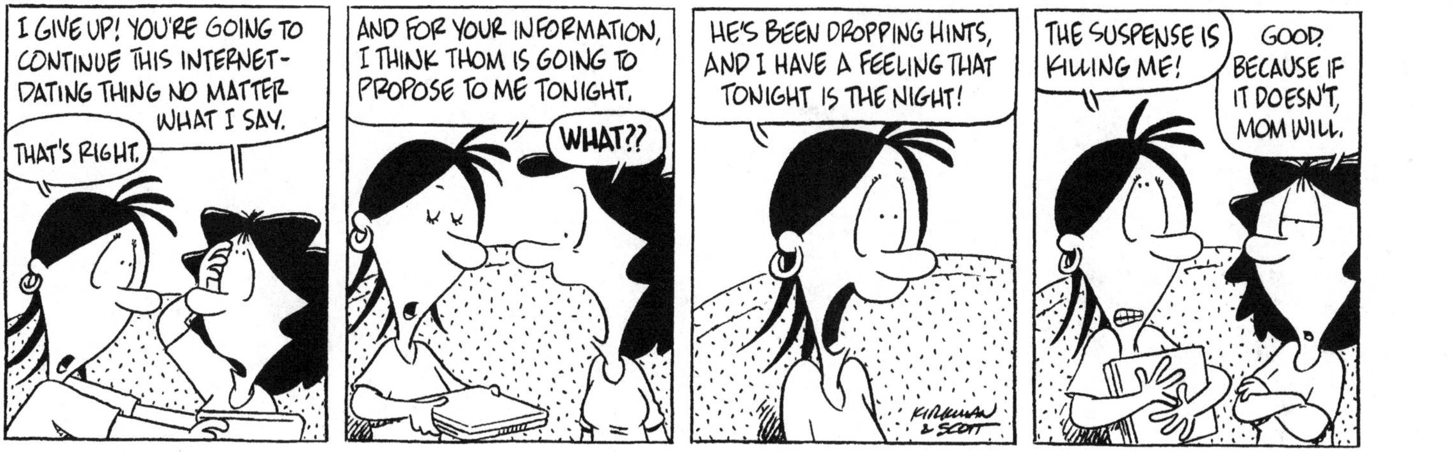
I GIVE UP! YOU'RE GOING TO CONTINUE THIS INTERNET-DATING THING NO MATTER WHAT I SAY.
THAT'S RIGHT.
AND FOR YOUR INFORMATION, I THINK THOM IS GOING TO PROPOSE TO ME TONIGHT.
WHAT??
HE'S BEEN DROPPING HINTS, AND I HAVE A FEELING THAT TONIGHT IS THE NIGHT!
KIRKMAN & SCOTT
THE SUSPENSE IS KILLING ME!
GOOD. BECAUSE IF IT DOESN'T, MOM WILL.

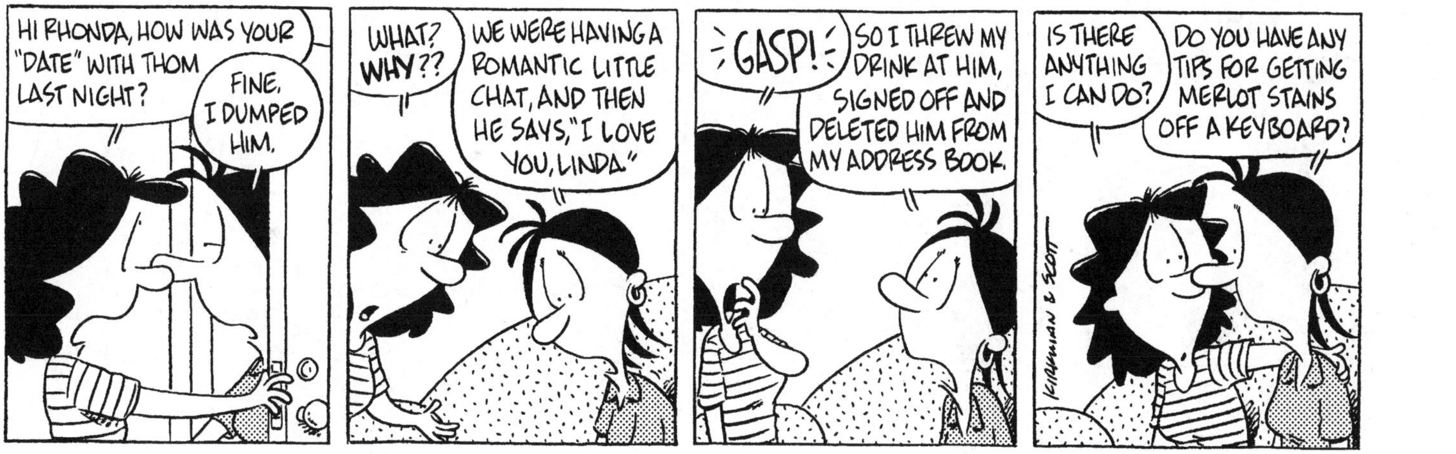
HI RHONDA, HOW WAS YOUR "DATE" WITH THOM LAST NIGHT?
FINE. I DUMPED HIM.
WHAT? WHY??
WE WERE HAVING A ROMANTIC LITTLE CHAT, AND THEN HE SAYS, "I LOVE YOU, LINDA."
GASP!
SO I THREW MY DRINK AT HIM, SIGNED OFF AND DELETED HIM FROM MY ADDRESS BOOK.
KIRKMAN & SCOTT
IS THERE ANYTHING I CAN DO?
DO YOU HAVE ANY TIPS FOR GETTING MERLOT STAINS OFF A KEYBOARD?

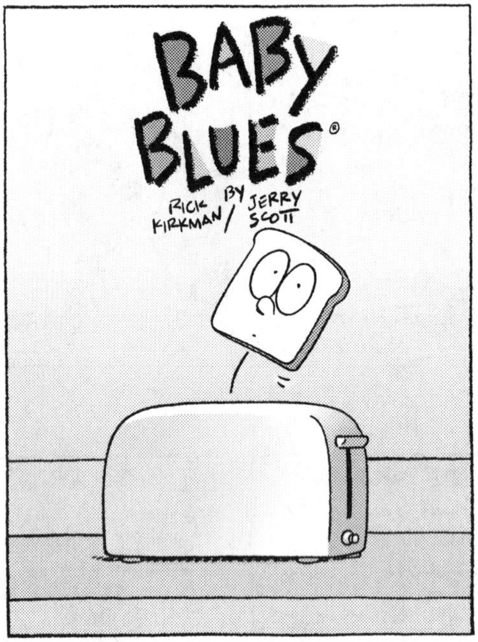
BABY BLUES®
RICK KIRKMAN / BY JERRY SCOTT

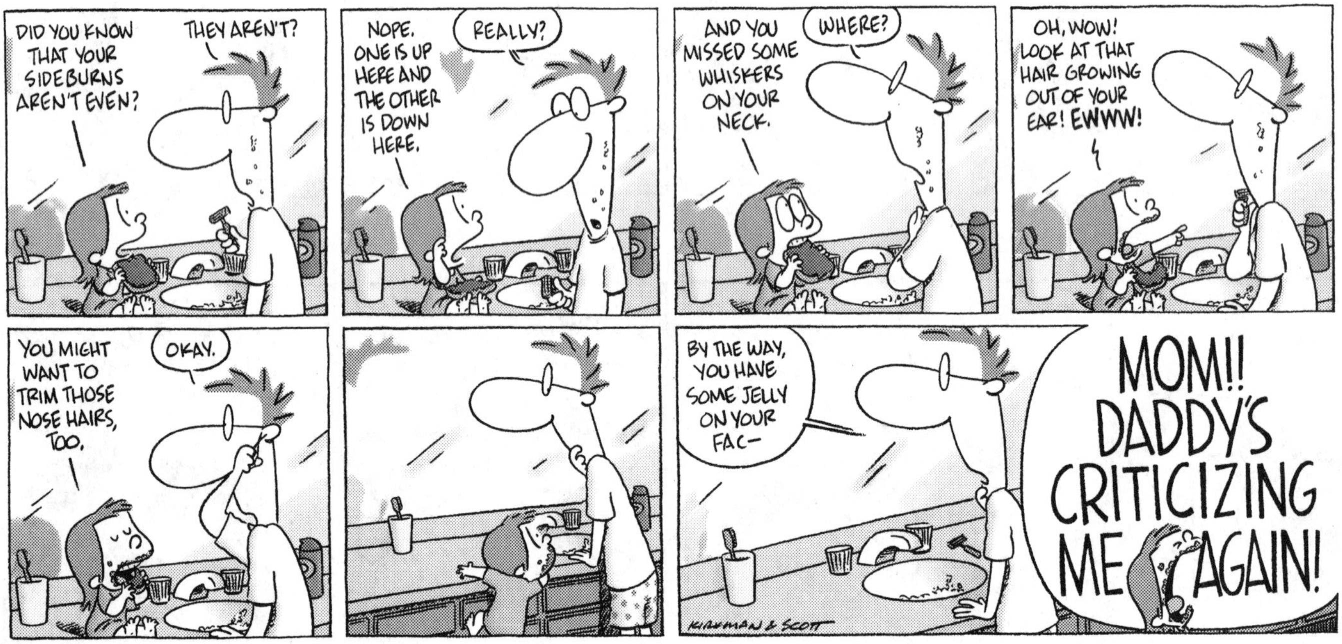
DID YOU KNOW THAT YOUR SIDEBURNS AREN'T EVEN?
THEY AREN'T?
NOPE. ONE IS UP HERE AND THE OTHER IS DOWN HERE.
REALLY?
AND YOU MISSED SOME WHISKERS ON YOUR NECK.
WHERE?
OH, WOW! LOOK AT THAT HAIR GROWING OUT OF YOUR EAR! EWWW!
YOU MIGHT WANT TO TRIM THOSE NOSE HAIRS, TOO.
OKAY.
BY THE WAY, YOU HAVE SOME JELLY ON YOUR FAC—
MOM!! DADDY'S CRITICIZING ME AGAIN!
KIRKMAN & SCOTT

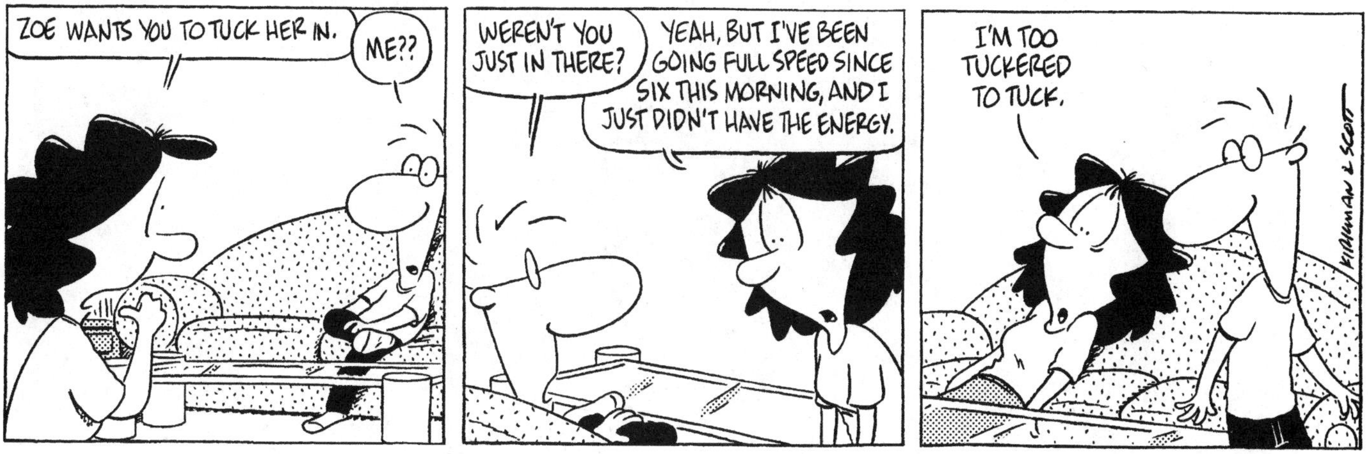
ZOE WANTS YOU TO TUCK HER IN.
ME??
WEREN'T YOU JUST IN THERE?
YEAH, BUT I'VE BEEN GOING FULL SPEED SINCE SIX THIS MORNING, AND I JUST DIDN'T HAVE THE ENERGY.
I'M TOO TUCKERED TO TUCK.
KIRKMAN & SCOTT

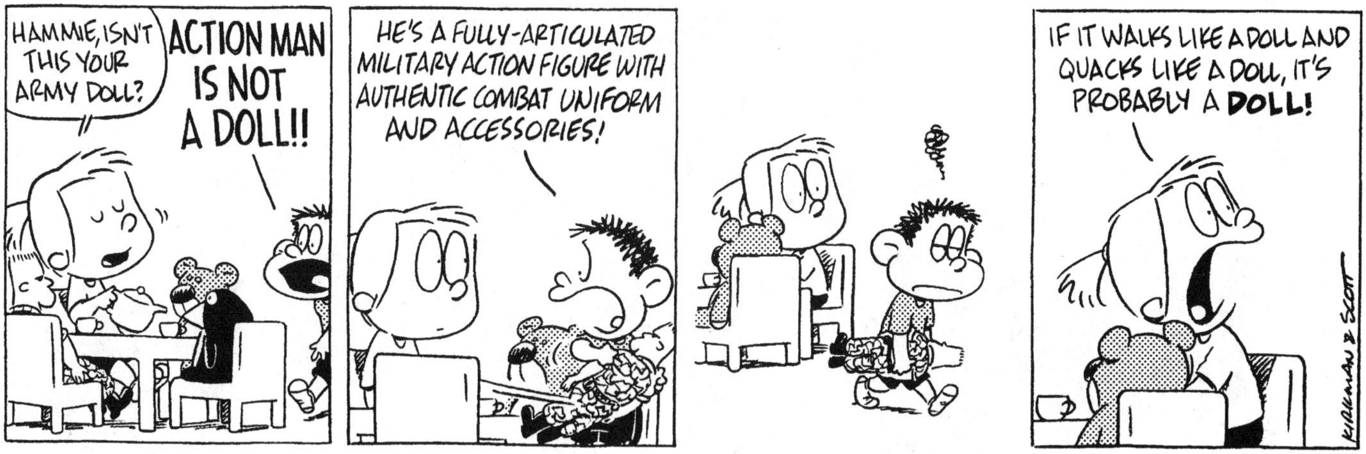
HAMMIE, ISN'T THIS YOUR ARMY DOLL?
ACTION MAN IS NOT A DOLL!!
HE'S A FULLY-ARTICULATED MILITARY ACTION FIGURE WITH AUTHENTIC COMBAT UNIFORM AND ACCESSORIES!
IF IT WALKS LIKE A DOLL AND QUACKS LIKE A DOLL, IT'S PROBABLY A **DOLL!**
KIRKMAN & SCOTT

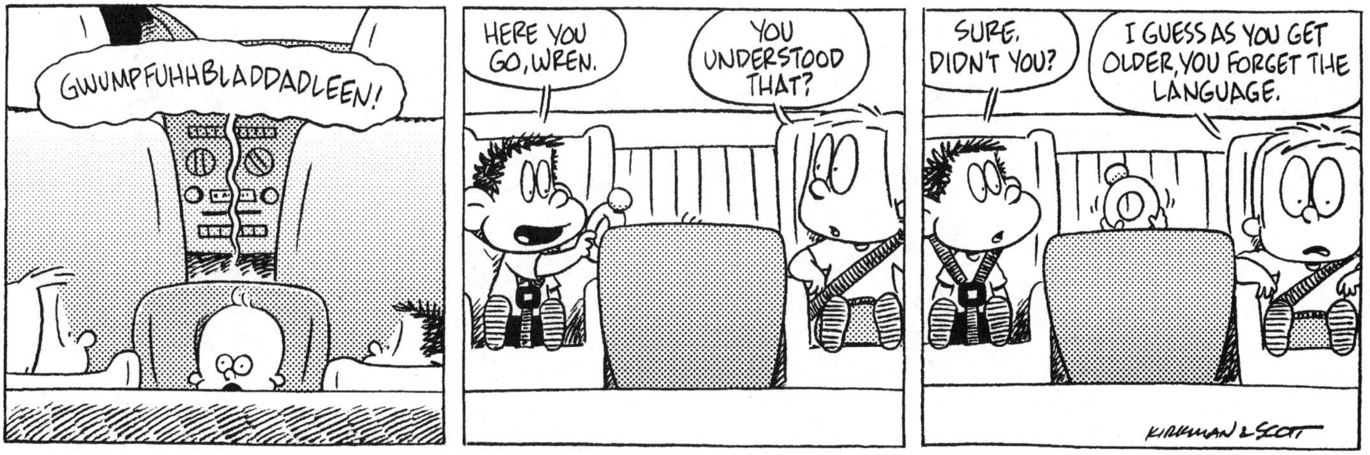
GWUMPFUHHBLADDADLEEN!
HERE YOU GO, WREN.
YOU UNDERSTOOD THAT?
SURE. DIDN'T YOU?
I GUESS AS YOU GET OLDER, YOU FORGET THE LANGUAGE.
KIRKMAN & SCOTT

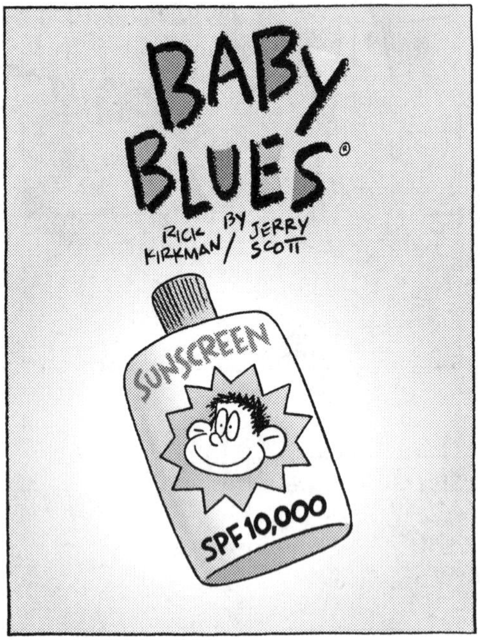
BABY BLUES®
BY RICK KIRKMAN / JERRY SCOTT
SUNSCREEN
SPF 10,000

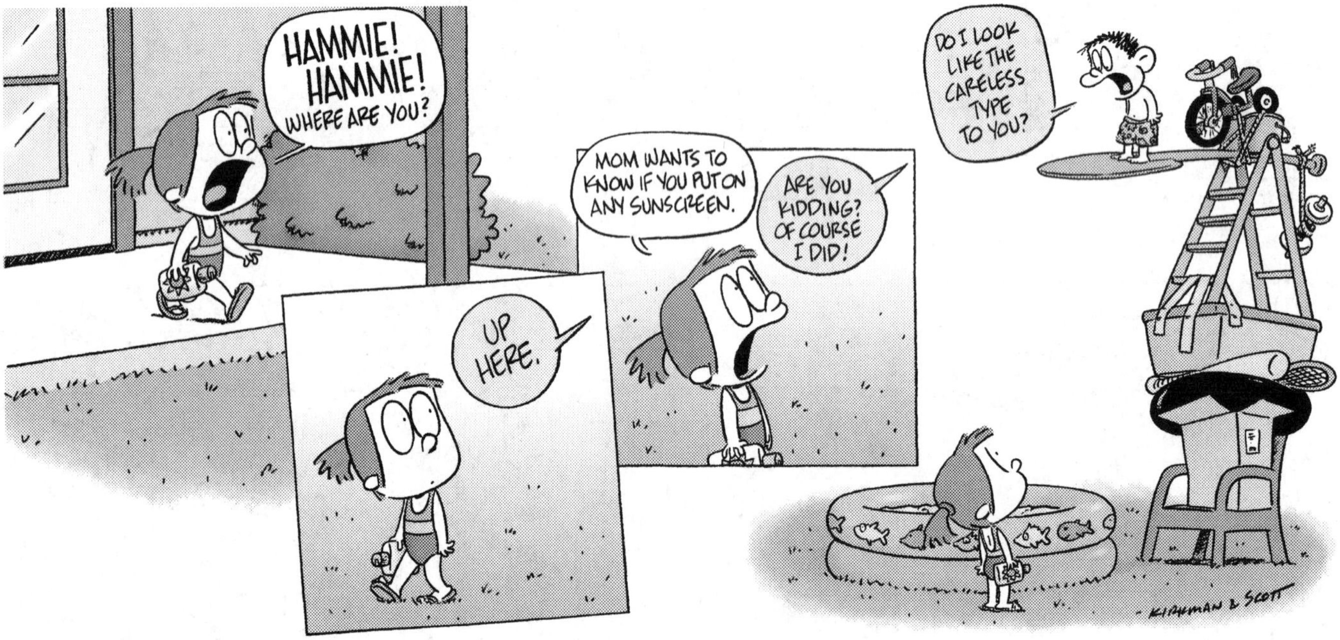
HAMMIE! HAMMIE! WHERE ARE YOU?
UP HERE.
MOM WANTS TO KNOW IF YOU PUT ON ANY SUNSCREEN.
ARE YOU KIDDING? OF COURSE I DID!
DO I LOOK LIKE THE CARELESS TYPE TO YOU?
KIRKMAN & SCOTT

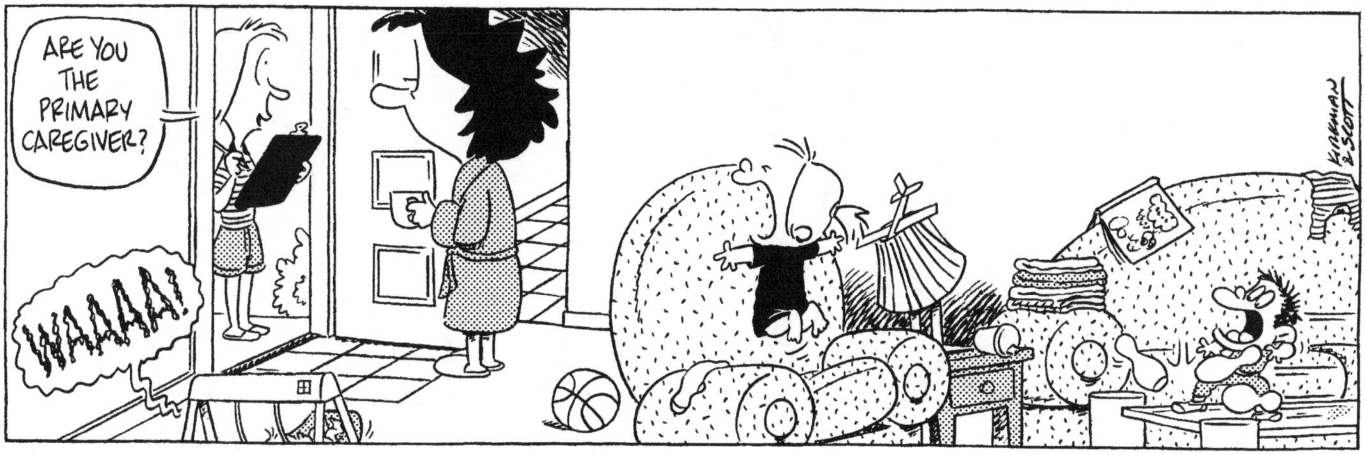
ARE YOU THE PRIMARY CAREGIVER?
WAAAA!
KIRKMAN & SCOTT

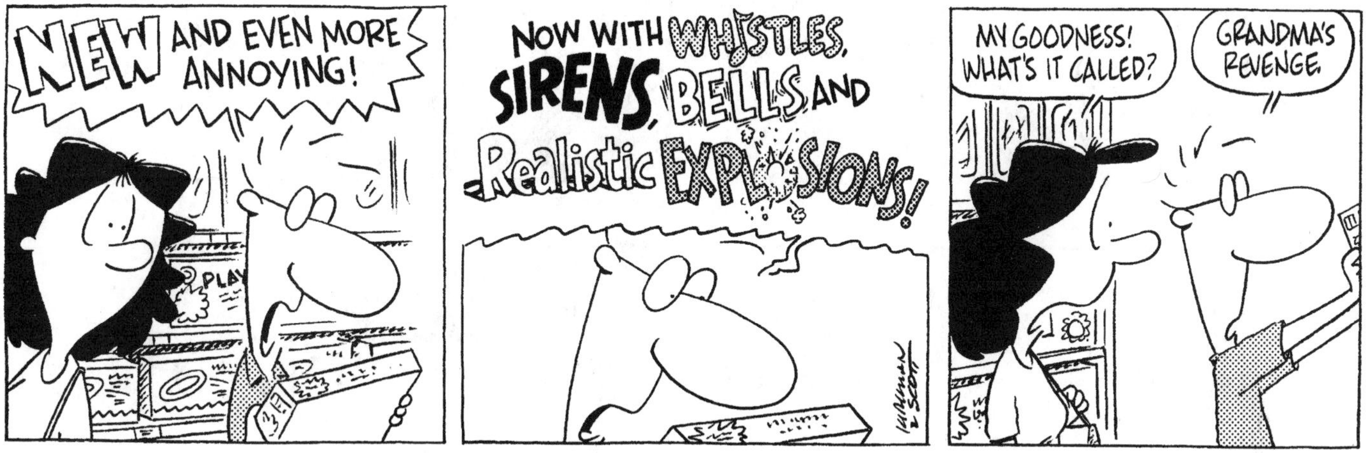
NEW AND EVEN MORE ANNOYING!
NOW WITH WHISTLES, SIRENS, BELLS AND Realistic EXPLOSIONS!
KIRKMAN & SCOTT
MY GOODNESS! WHAT'S IT CALLED?
GRANDMA'S REVENGE.

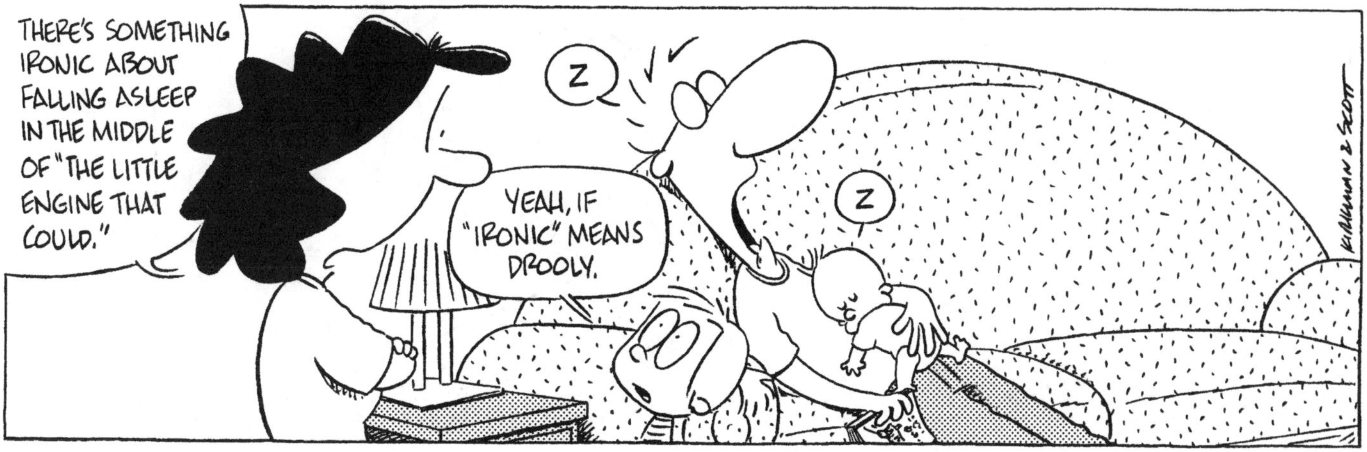
THERE'S SOMETHING IRONIC ABOUT FALLING ASLEEP IN THE MIDDLE OF "THE LITTLE ENGINE THAT COULD."
Z
YEAH, IF "IRONIC" MEANS DROOLY.
Z
KIRKMAN & SCOTT

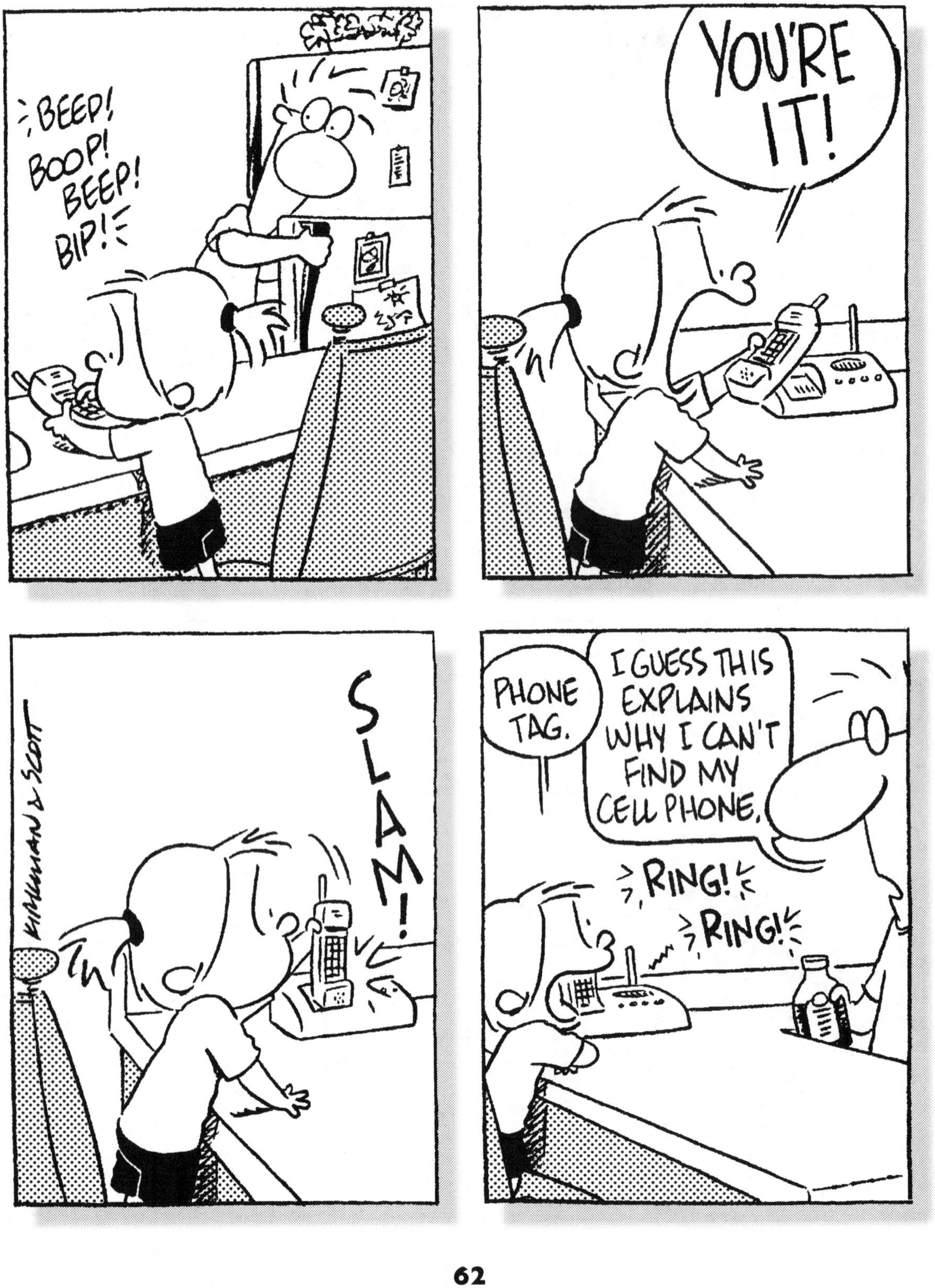
BEEP! BOOP! BEEP! BIP!
YOU'RE IT!
KIRKMAN & SCOTT
SLAM!
PHONE TAG.
I GUESS THIS EXPLAINS WHY I CAN'T FIND MY CELL PHONE.
RING!
RING!

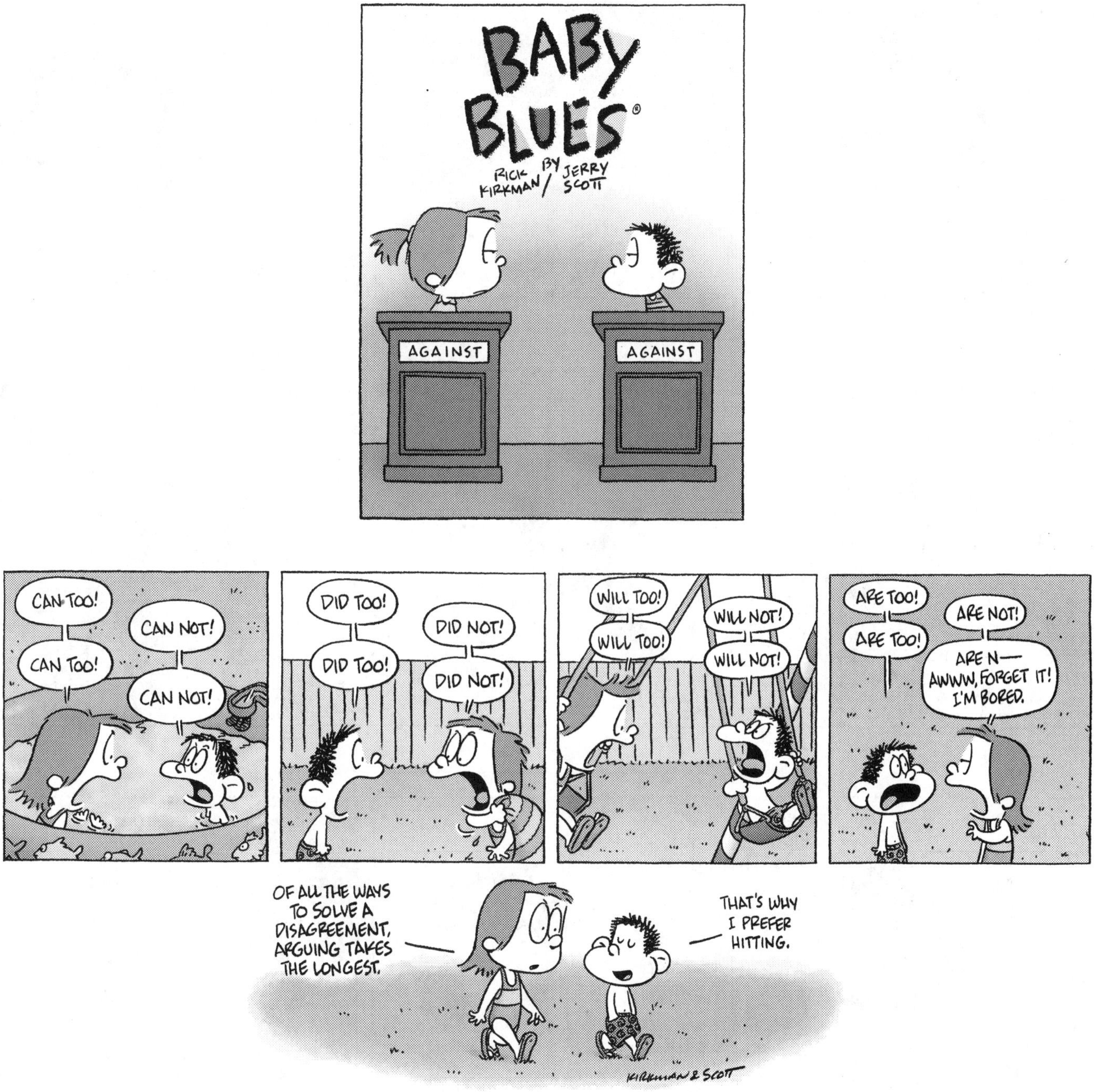
BABY BLUES®
BY RICK KIRKMAN / JERRY SCOTT
AGAINST
AGAINST
CAN TOO!
CAN TOO!
CAN NOT!
CAN NOT!
DID TOO!
DID TOO!
DID NOT!
DID NOT!
WILL TOO!
WILL TOO!
WILL NOT!
WILL NOT!
ARE TOO!
ARE TOO!
ARE NOT!
ARE N— AWWW, FORGET IT! I'M BORED.
OF ALL THE WAYS TO SOLVE A DISAGREEMENT, ARGUING TAKES THE LONGEST.
THAT'S WHY I PREFER HITTING.
KIRKMAN & SCOTT

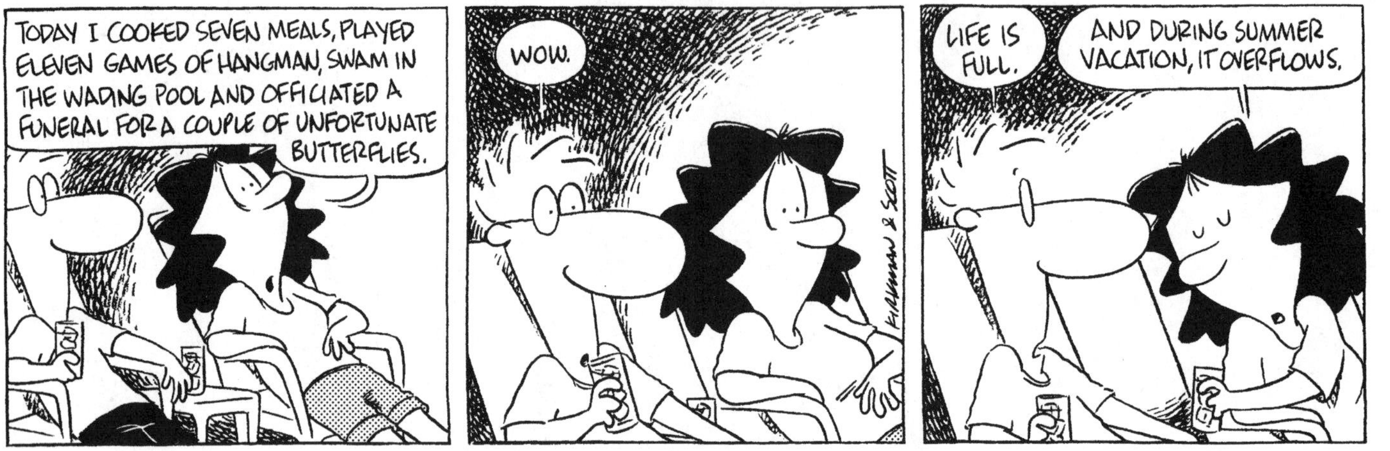
TODAY I COOKED SEVEN MEALS, PLAYED ELEVEN GAMES OF HANGMAN, SWAM IN THE WADING POOL AND OFFICIATED A FUNERAL FOR A COUPLE OF UNFORTUNATE BUTTERFLIES.
WOW.
KIRKMAN & SCOTT
LIFE IS FULL.
AND DURING SUMMER VACATION, IT OVERFLOWS.

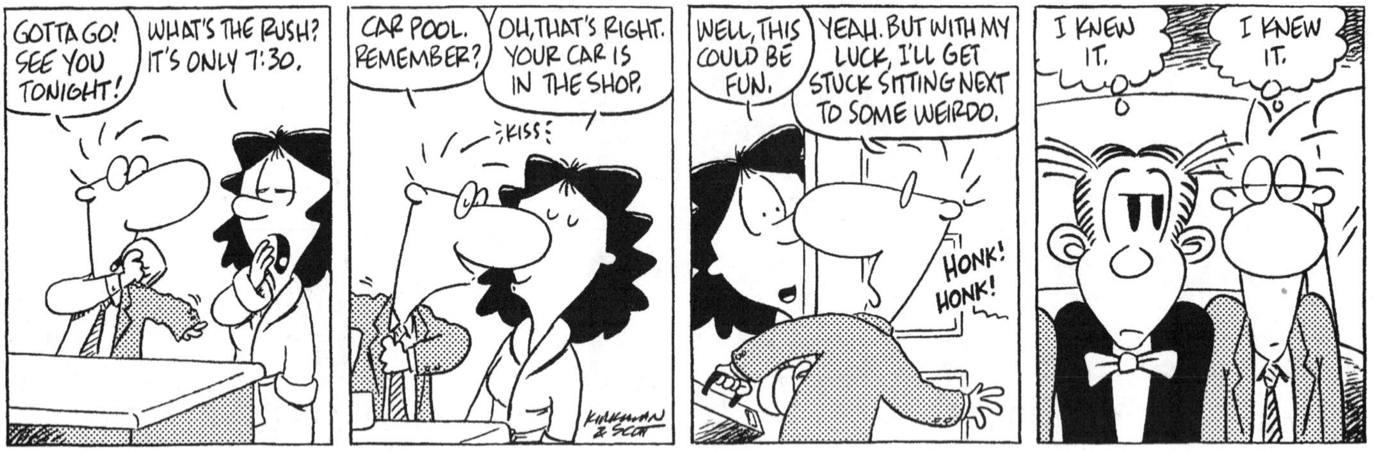
GOTTA GO! SEE YOU TONIGHT!
WHAT'S THE RUSH? IT'S ONLY 7:30.
CAR POOL. REMEMBER?
OH, THAT'S RIGHT. YOUR CAR IS IN THE SHOP.
KISS
KIRKMAN & SCOTT
WELL, THIS COULD BE FUN.
YEAH. BUT WITH MY LUCK, I'LL GET STUCK SITTING NEXT TO SOME WEIRDO.
HONK! HONK!
I KNEW IT.
I KNEW IT.

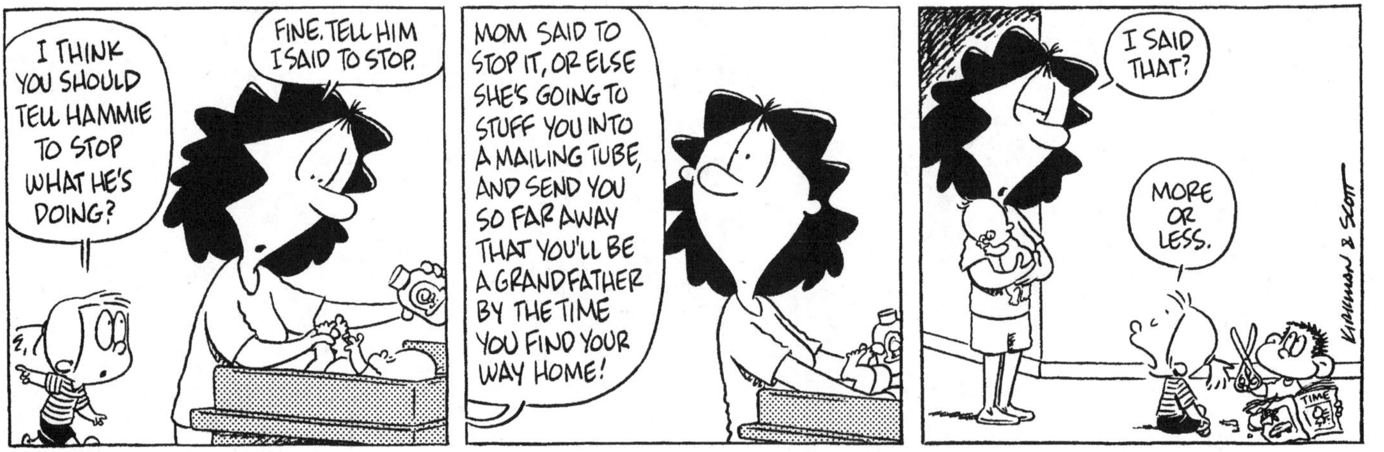
I THINK YOU SHOULD TELL HAMMIE TO STOP WHAT HE'S DOING?
FINE. TELL HIM I SAID TO STOP.
MOM SAID TO STOP IT, OR ELSE SHE'S GOING TO STUFF YOU INTO A MAILING TUBE, AND SEND YOU SO FAR AWAY THAT YOU'LL BE A GRANDFATHER BY THE TIME YOU FIND YOUR WAY HOME!
I SAID THAT?
MORE OR LESS.
KIRKMAN & SCOTT
TIME

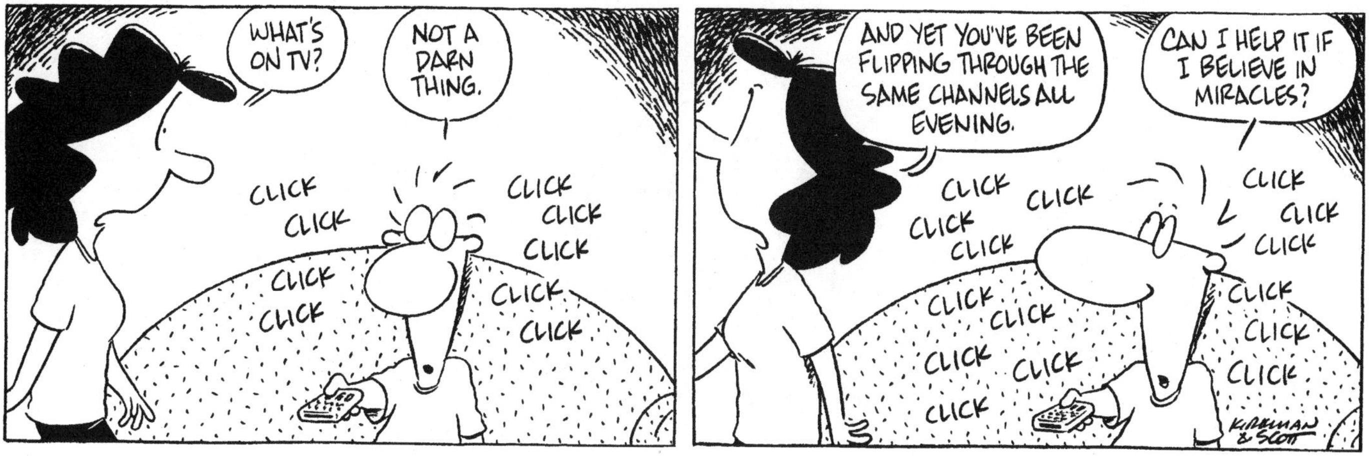
WHAT'S ON TV?
NOT A DARN THING.
CLICK CLICK CLICK CLICK
CLICK CLICK CLICK CLICK CLICK
AND YET YOU'VE BEEN FLIPPING THROUGH THE SAME CHANNELS ALL EVENING.
CAN I HELP IT IF I BELIEVE IN MIRACLES?
CLICK CLICK CLICK CLICK CLICK CLICK CLICK CLICK
CLICK CLICK CLICK CLICK CLICK CLICK
KIRKMAN & SCOTT

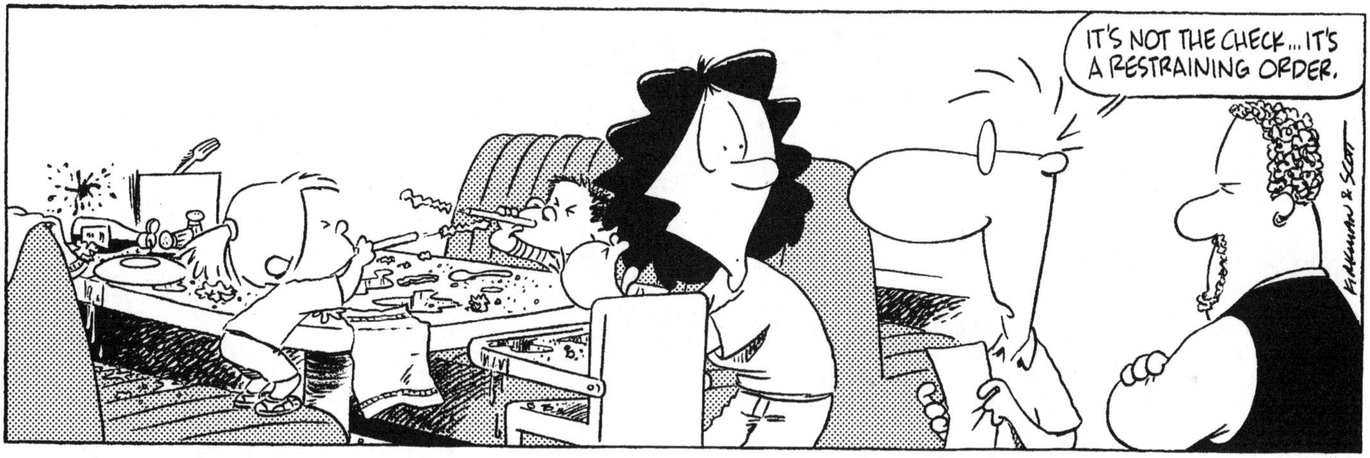
IT'S NOT THE CHECK... IT'S A RESTRAINING ORDER.
KIRKMAN & SCOTT

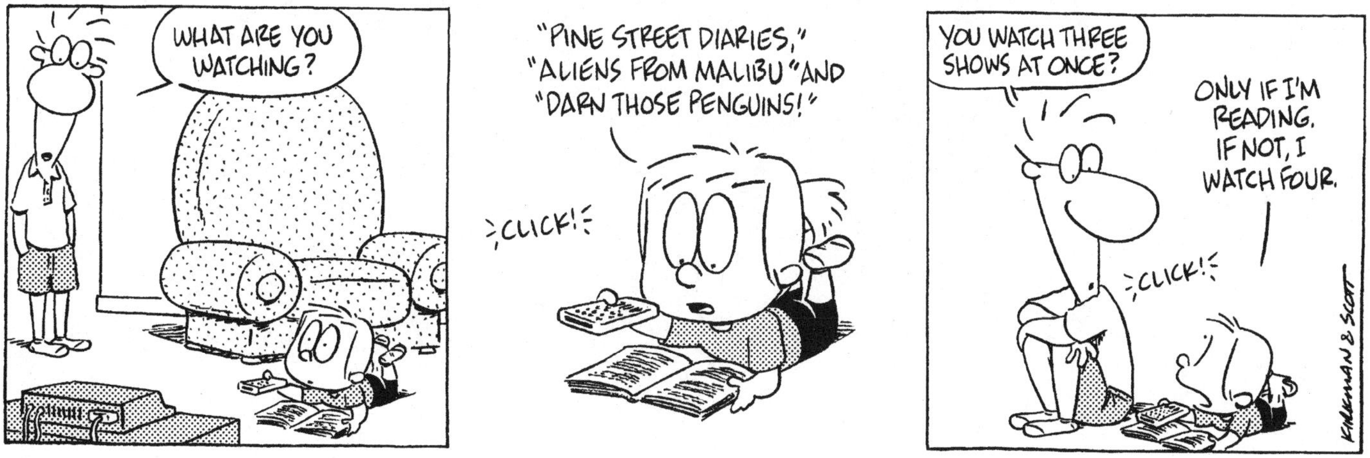
WHAT ARE YOU WATCHING?
"PINE STREET DIARIES," "ALIENS FROM MALIBU" AND "DARN THOSE PENGUINS!"
CLICK!
YOU WATCH THREE SHOWS AT ONCE?
ONLY IF I'M READING. IF NOT, I WATCH FOUR.
CLICK!
KIRKMAN & SCOTT

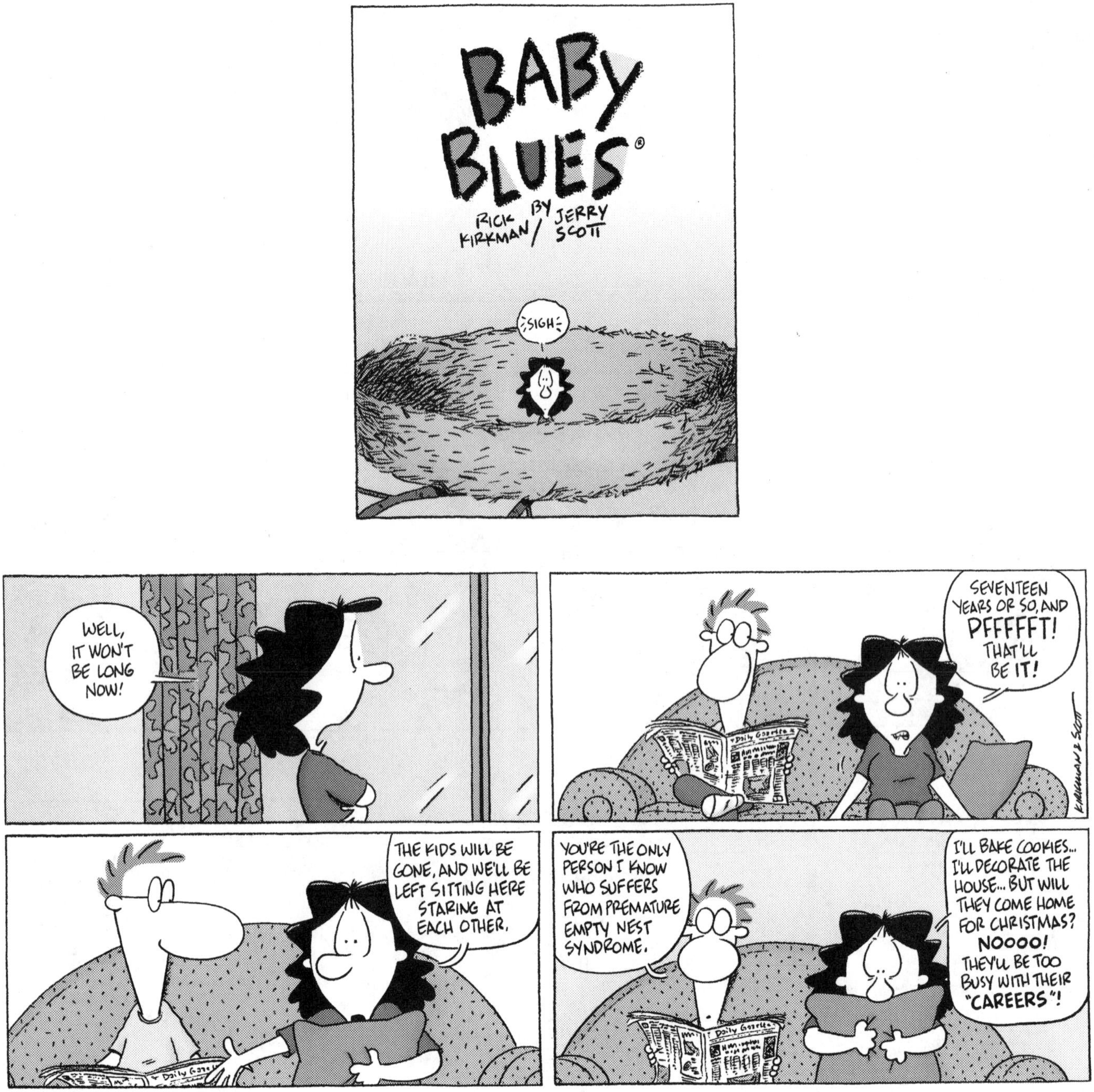
BABY BLUES®
BY RICK KIRKMAN / JERRY SCOTT
SIGH
WELL, IT WON'T BE LONG NOW!
SEVENTEEN YEARS OR SO, AND PFFFFFT! THAT'LL BE IT!
KIRKMAN & SCOTT
THE KIDS WILL BE GONE, AND WE'LL BE LEFT SITTING HERE STARING AT EACH OTHER.
YOU'RE THE ONLY PERSON I KNOW WHO SUFFERS FROM PREMATURE EMPTY NEST SYNDROME.
I'LL BAKE COOKIES... I'LL DECORATE THE HOUSE... BUT WILL THEY COME HOME FOR CHRISTMAS? NOOOO! THEY'LL BE TOO BUSY WITH THEIR "CAREERS"!

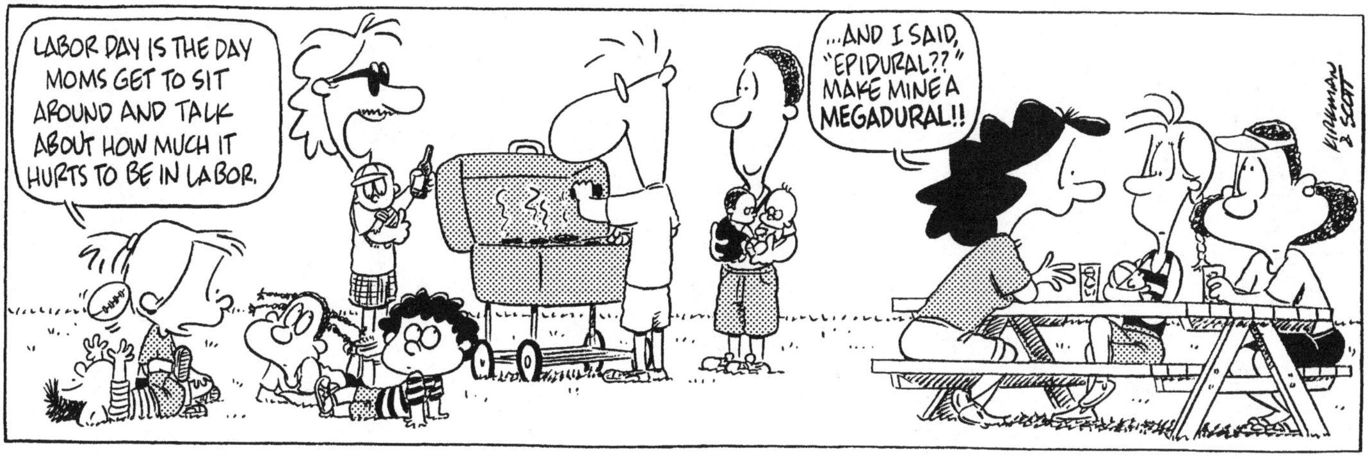
LABOR DAY IS THE DAY MOMS GET TO SIT AROUND AND TALK ABOUT HOW MUCH IT HURTS TO BE IN LABOR.
...AND I SAID, "EPIDURAL??" MAKE MINE A MEGADURAL!!
KIRKMAN & SCOTT

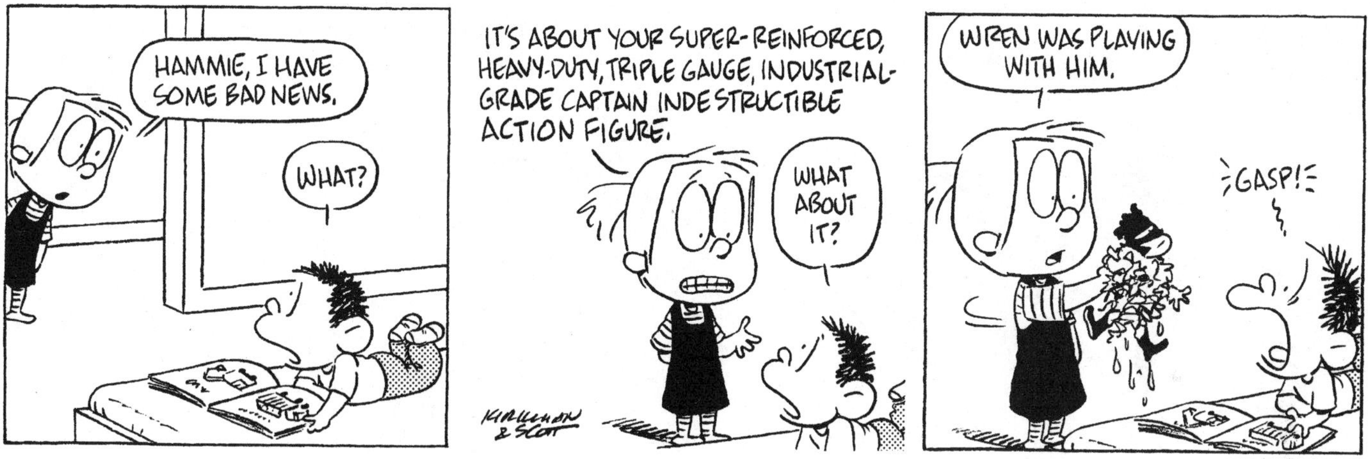
HAMMIE, I HAVE SOME BAD NEWS.
WHAT?
IT'S ABOUT YOUR SUPER-REINFORCED, HEAVY-DUTY, TRIPLE GAUGE, INDUSTRIAL-GRADE CAPTAIN INDESTRUCTIBLE ACTION FIGURE.
WHAT ABOUT IT?
KIRKMAN & SCOTT
WREN WAS PLAYING WITH HIM.
GASP!

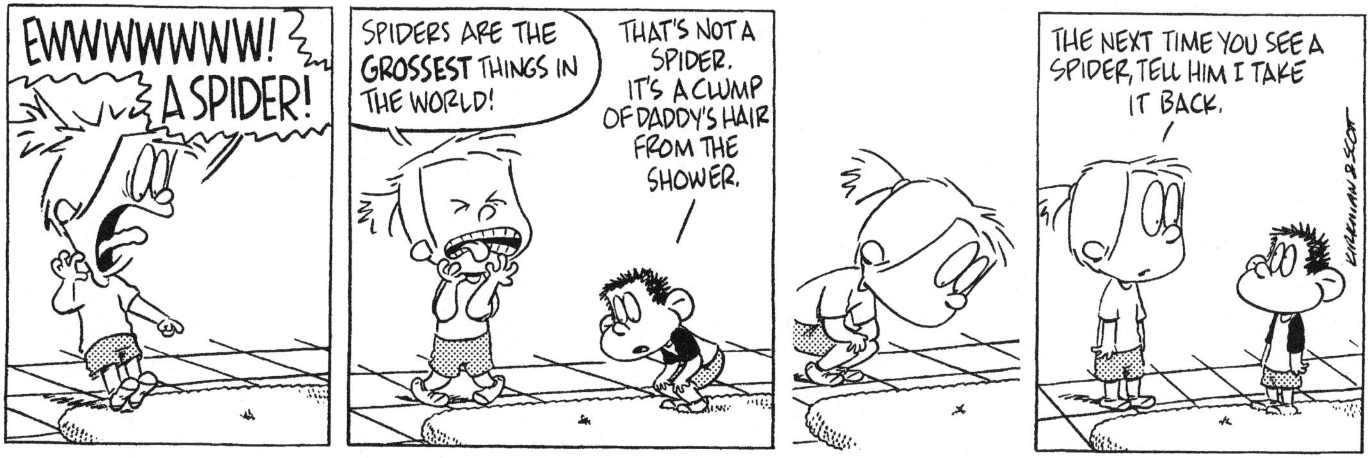
EWWWWWWW! A SPIDER!
SPIDERS ARE THE GROSSEST THINGS IN THE WORLD!
THAT'S NOT A SPIDER. IT'S A CLUMP OF DADDY'S HAIR FROM THE SHOWER.
THE NEXT TIME YOU SEE A SPIDER, TELL HIM I TAKE IT BACK.
KIRKMAN & SCOTT

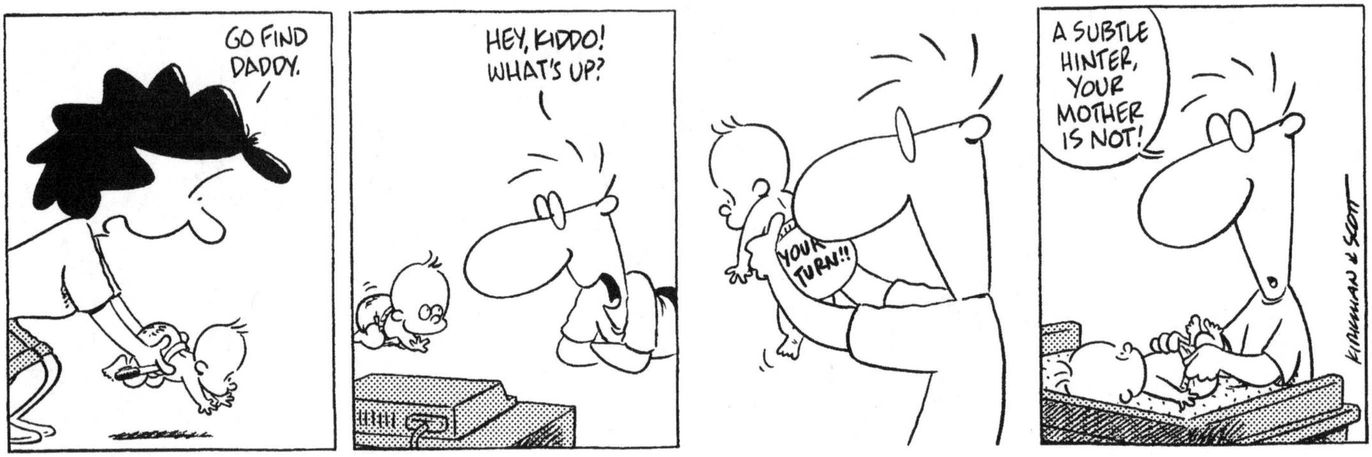
GO FIND DADDY.
HEY, KIDDO! WHAT'S UP?
YOUR TURN!!
A SUBTLE HINTER, YOUR MOTHER IS NOT!
KIRKMAN & SCOTT

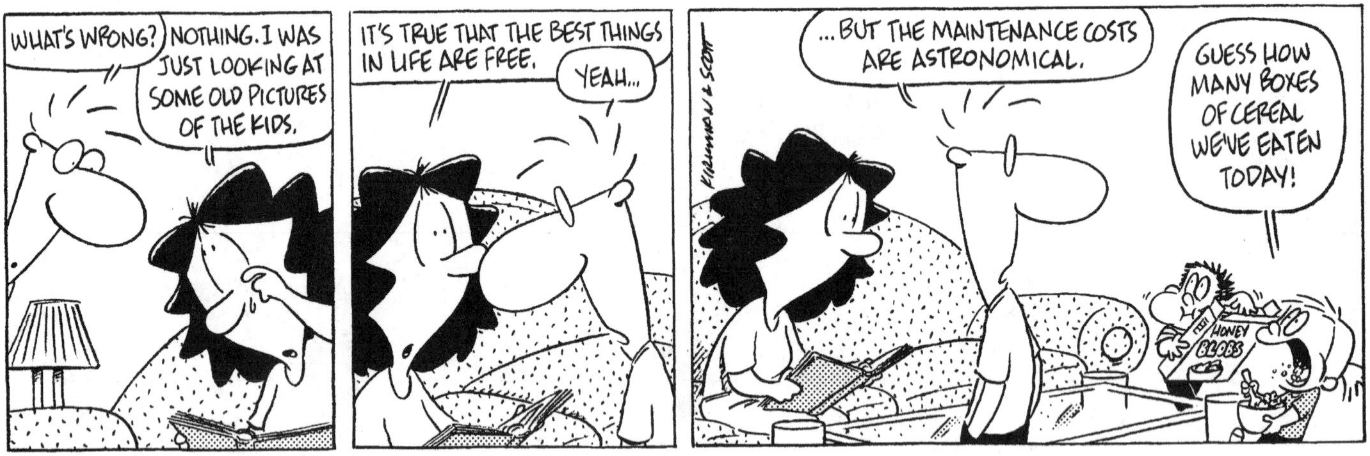
WHAT'S WRONG?
NOTHING. I WAS JUST LOOKING AT SOME OLD PICTURES OF THE KIDS.
IT'S TRUE THAT THE BEST THINGS IN LIFE ARE FREE.
YEAH...
KIRKMAN & SCOTT
...BUT THE MAINTENANCE COSTS ARE ASTRONOMICAL.
GUESS HOW MANY BOXES OF CEREAL WE'VE EATEN TODAY!
HONEY BLOBS

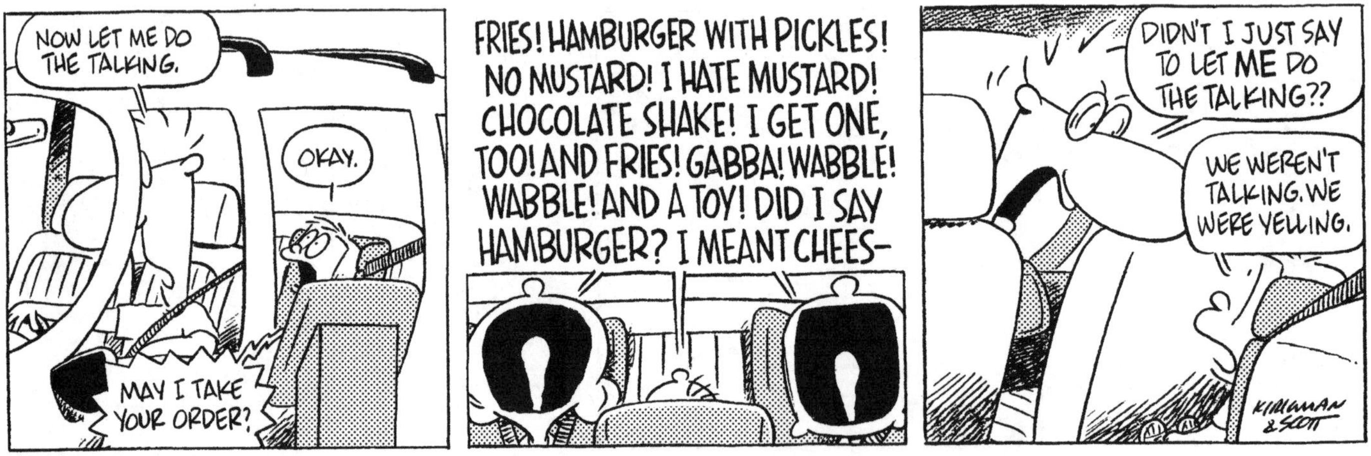
NOW LET ME DO THE TALKING.
OKAY.
MAY I TAKE YOUR ORDER?
FRIES! HAMBURGER WITH PICKLES! NO MUSTARD! I HATE MUSTARD! CHOCOLATE SHAKE! I GET ONE, TOO! AND FRIES! GABBA! WABBLE! WABBLE! AND A TOY! DID I SAY HAMBURGER? I MEANT CHEES-
DIDN'T I JUST SAY TO LET ME DO THE TALKING??
WE WEREN'T TALKING. WE WERE YELLING.
KIRKMAN & SCOTT

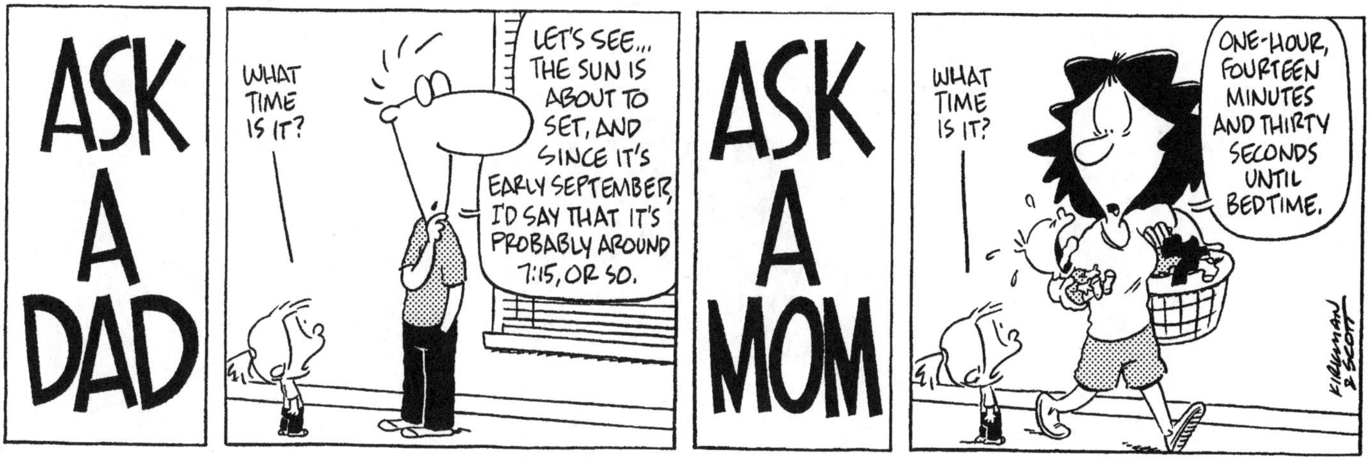
ASK A DAD
WHAT TIME IS IT?
LET'S SEE... THE SUN IS ABOUT TO SET, AND SINCE IT'S EARLY SEPTEMBER, I'D SAY THAT IT'S PROBABLY AROUND 7:15, OR SO.
ASK A MOM
WHAT TIME IS IT?
ONE-HOUR, FOURTEEN MINUTES AND THIRTY SECONDS UNTIL BEDTIME.
KIRKMAN & SCOTT

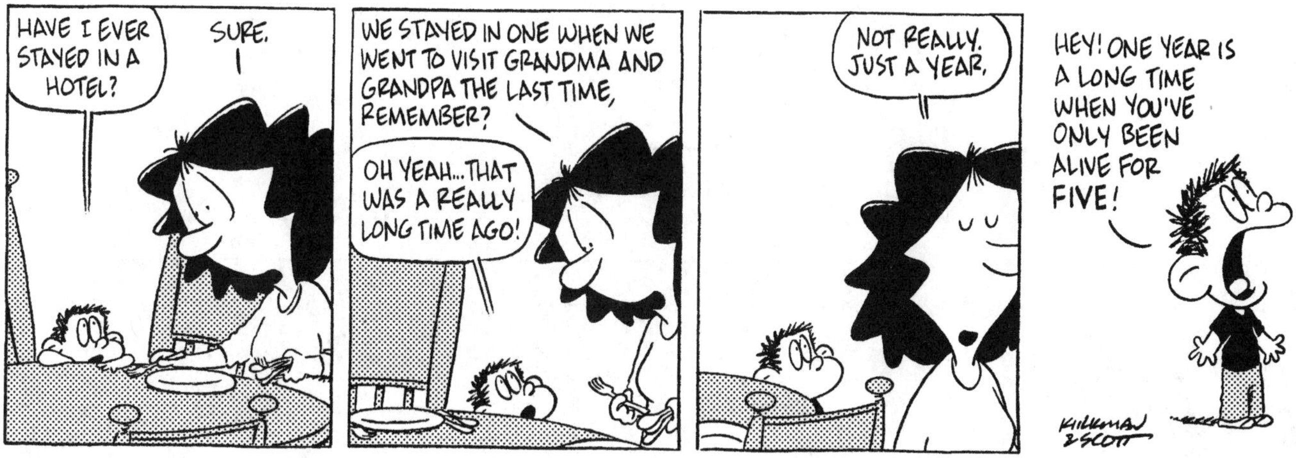
HAVE I EVER STAYED IN A HOTEL?
SURE.
WE STAYED IN ONE WHEN WE WENT TO VISIT GRANDMA AND GRANDPA THE LAST TIME, REMEMBER?
OH YEAH...THAT WAS A REALLY LONG TIME AGO!
NOT REALLY. JUST A YEAR.
HEY! ONE YEAR IS A LONG TIME WHEN YOU'VE ONLY BEEN ALIVE FOR FIVE!
KIRKMAN & SCOTT

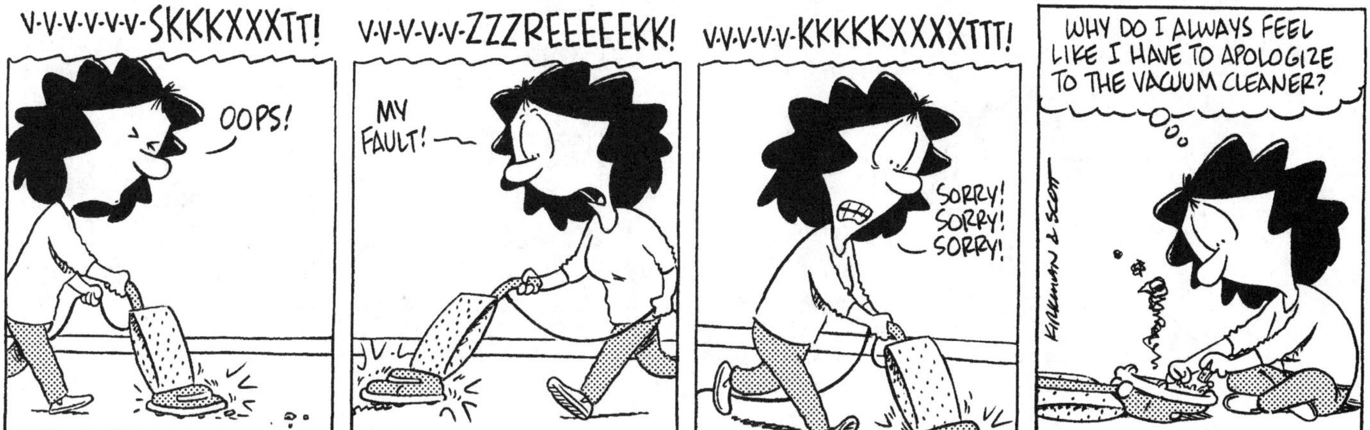
V-V-V-V-V-V-SKKKXXXTT!
OOPS!
V-V-V-V-V-ZZZREEEEEKK!
MY FAULT!
V-V-V-V-V-KKKKKXXXXTTT!
SORRY! SORRY! SORRY!
WHY DO I ALWAYS FEEL LIKE I HAVE TO APOLOGIZE TO THE VACUUM CLEANER?
KIRKMAN & SCOTT

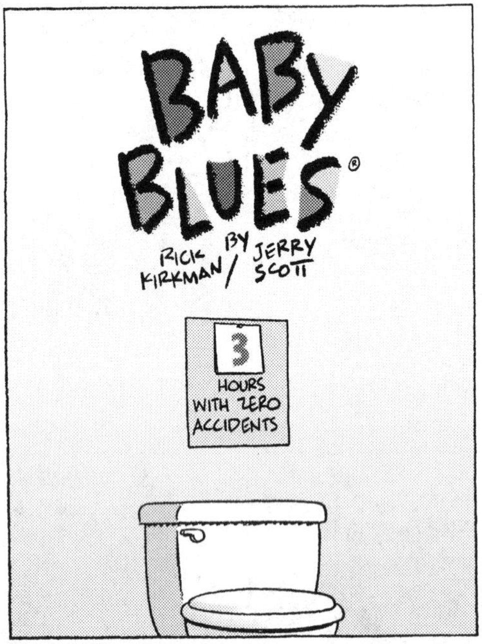
BABY BLUES®
BY RICK KIRKMAN / JERRY SCOTT
3 HOURS WITH ZERO ACCIDENTS

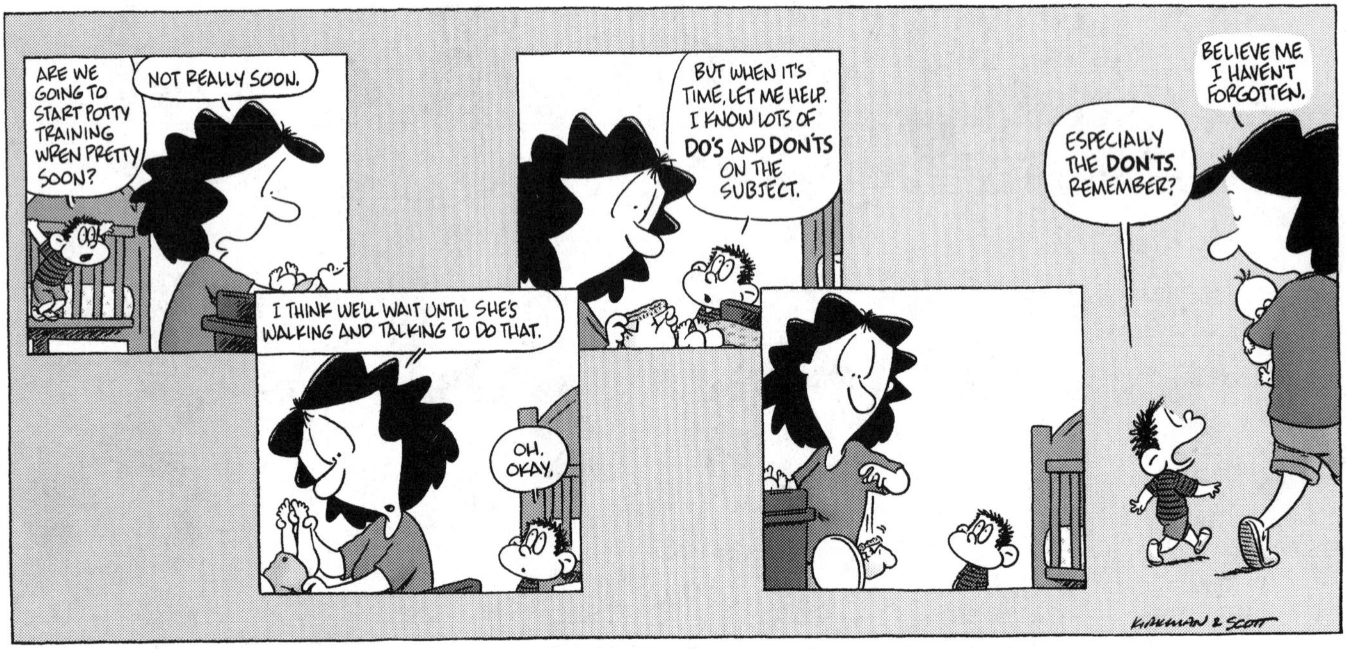
ARE WE GOING TO START POTTY TRAINING WREN PRETTY SOON?
NOT REALLY SOON.
BUT WHEN IT'S TIME, LET ME HELP. I KNOW LOTS OF **DO'S** AND **DON'TS** ON THE SUBJECT.
I THINK WE'LL WAIT UNTIL SHE'S WALKING AND TALKING TO DO THAT.
OH. OKAY.
ESPECIALLY THE **DON'TS**. REMEMBER?
BELIEVE ME. I HAVEN'T FORGOTTEN.
KIRKMAN & SCOTT

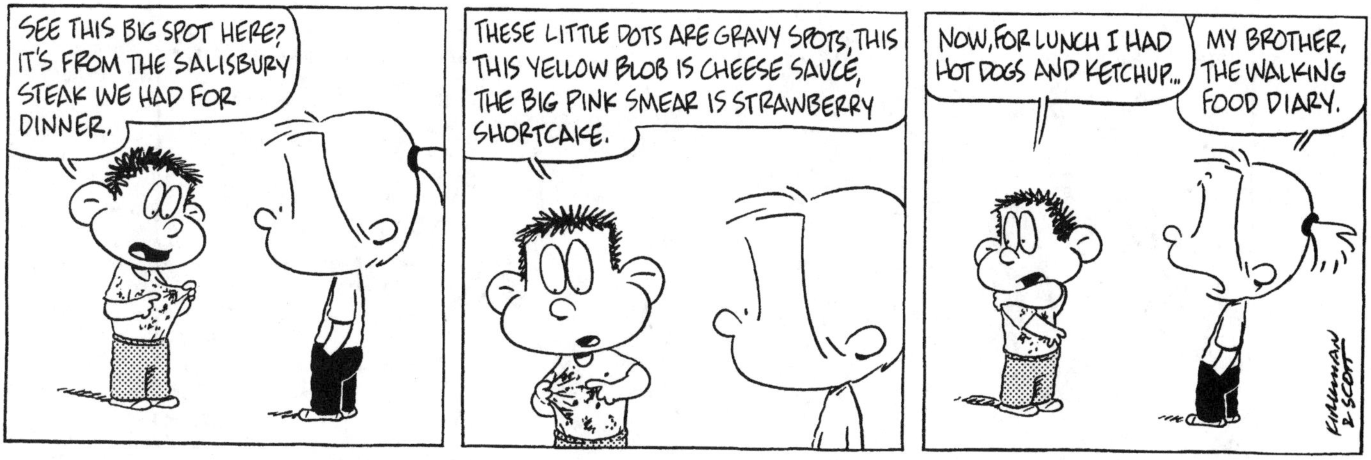
SEE THIS BIG SPOT HERE? IT'S FROM THE SALISBURY STEAK WE HAD FOR DINNER.
THESE LITTLE DOTS ARE GRAVY SPOTS, THIS THIS YELLOW BLOB IS CHEESE SAUCE, THE BIG PINK SMEAR IS STRAWBERRY SHORTCAKE.
NOW, FOR LUNCH I HAD HOT DOGS AND KETCHUP...
MY BROTHER, THE WALKING FOOD DIARY.
KIRKMAN & SCOTT

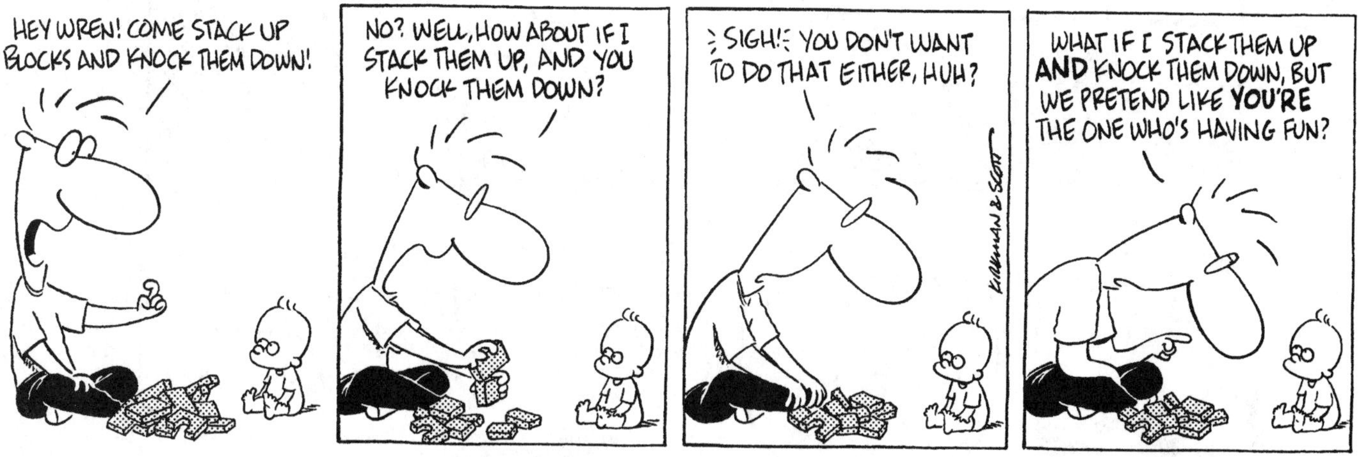
HEY WREN! COME STACK UP BLOCKS AND KNOCK THEM DOWN!
NO? WELL, HOW ABOUT IF I STACK THEM UP, AND YOU KNOCK THEM DOWN?
SIGH! YOU DON'T WANT TO DO THAT EITHER, HUH?
KIRKMAN & SCOTT
WHAT IF I STACK THEM UP **AND** KNOCK THEM DOWN, BUT WE PRETEND LIKE **YOU'RE** THE ONE WHO'S HAVING FUN?

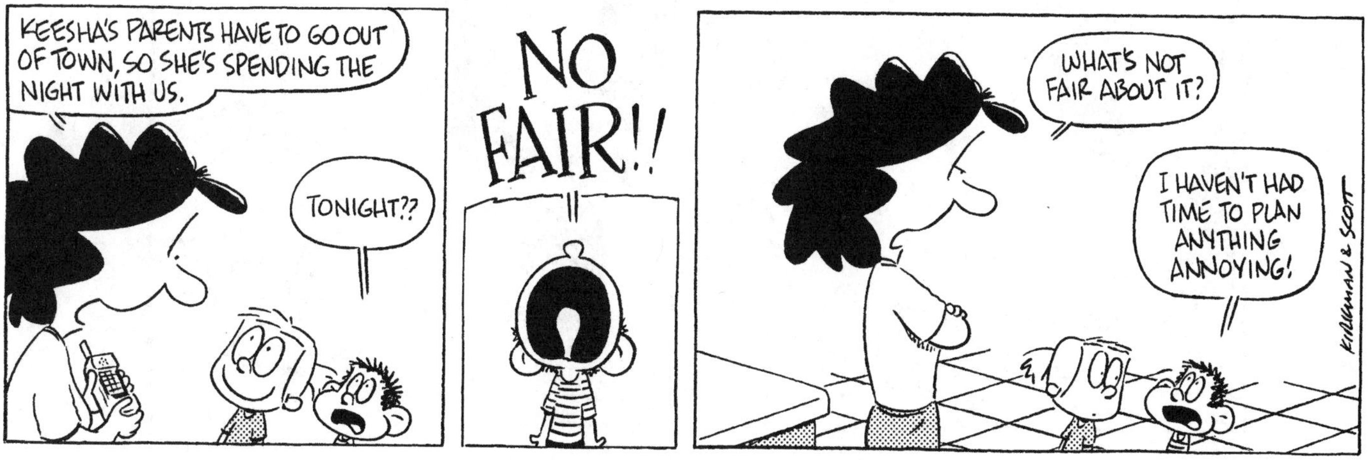
KEESHA'S PARENTS HAVE TO GO OUT OF TOWN, SO SHE'S SPENDING THE NIGHT WITH US.
TONIGHT??
NO FAIR!!
WHAT'S NOT FAIR ABOUT IT?
I HAVEN'T HAD TIME TO PLAN ANYTHING ANNOYING!
KIRKMAN & SCOTT

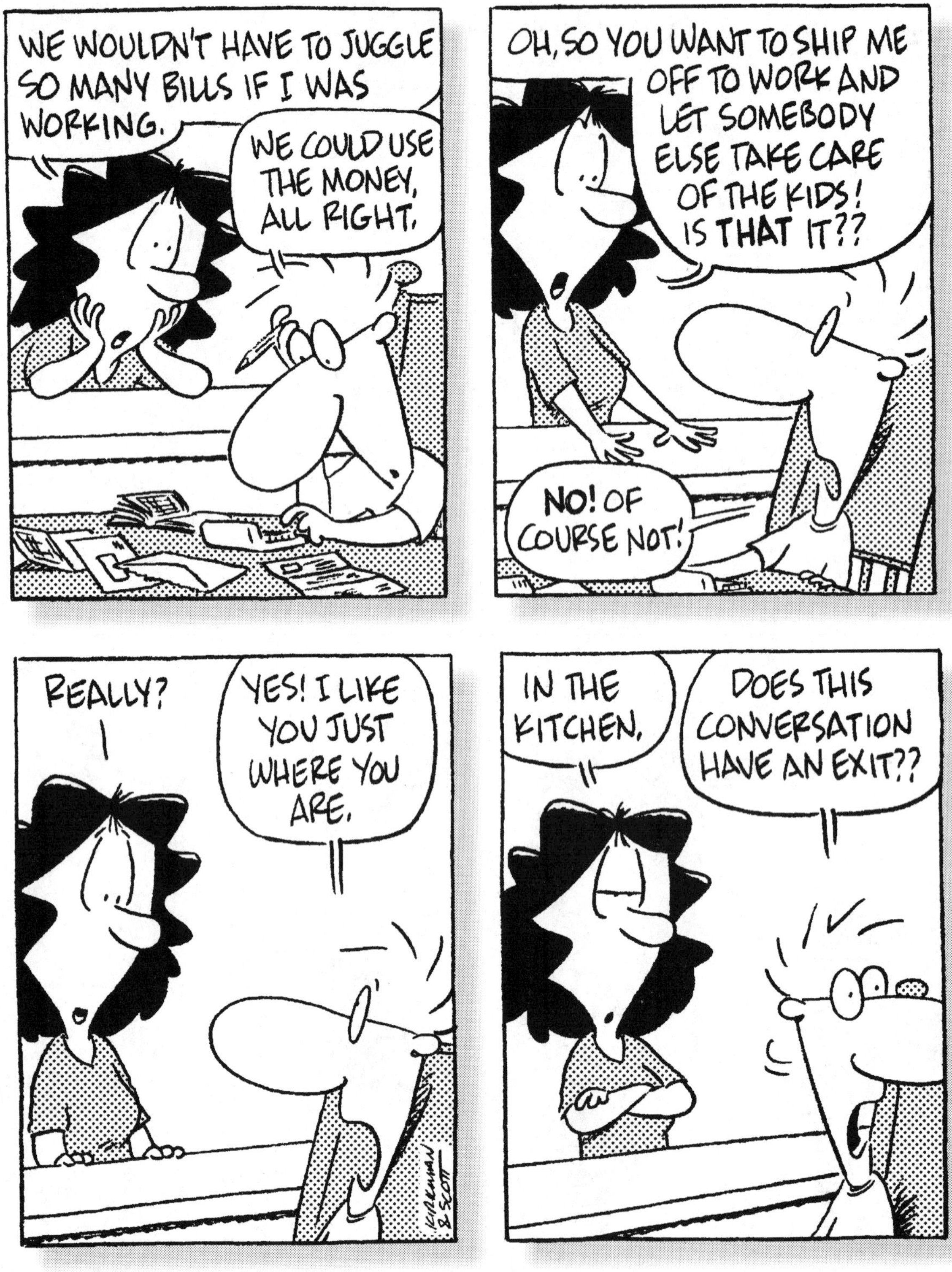
WE WOULDN'T HAVE TO JUGGLE SO MANY BILLS IF I WAS WORKING.
WE COULD USE THE MONEY, ALL RIGHT.
OH, SO YOU WANT TO SHIP ME OFF TO WORK AND LET SOMEBODY ELSE TAKE CARE OF THE KIDS! IS THAT IT??
NO! OF COURSE NOT!
REALLY?
YES! I LIKE YOU JUST WHERE YOU ARE.
KIRKMAN & SCOTT
IN THE KITCHEN.
DOES THIS CONVERSATION HAVE AN EXIT??

BABY BLUES®
BY RICK KIRKMAN / JERRY SCOTT

OKAY. SO THE CHICKEN IS LONELY, RIGHT?
HE DECIDES TO GO AROUND ASKING DIFFERENT ANIMALS IF THEY WANT TO BE HIS FRIEND.
FLIP! FLIP! FLIP!
THE LONELY LITTLE CHICKEN
...AND SO BLAH-DE-BLAH-DE-BLAH... SOME STUFF HAPPENS, THEN SOME MORE STUFF HAPPENS, AND THE CHICKEN LIVES HAPPILY EVER AFTER, OR WHATEVER. THE END.
FLIP! FLIP! FLIP! FLIP! FLIP! FLIP!
FLIP! FLIP! FLIP! FLIP!
FUMP!
I THINK I LIKED THE MOVIE BETTER.
ME, TOO. THE BOOK DIDN'T SEEM TO HAVE AS MUCH DETAIL.
KIRKMAN & SCOTT

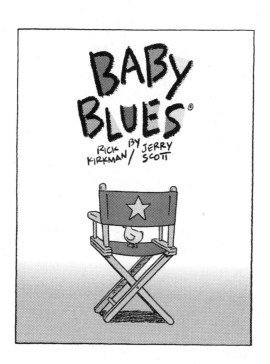

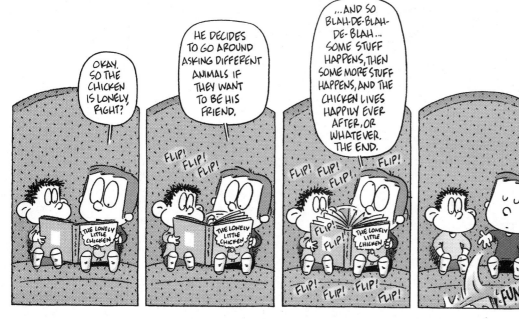

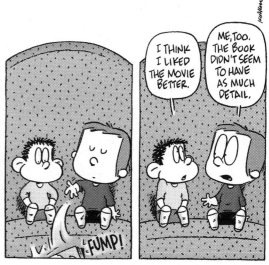

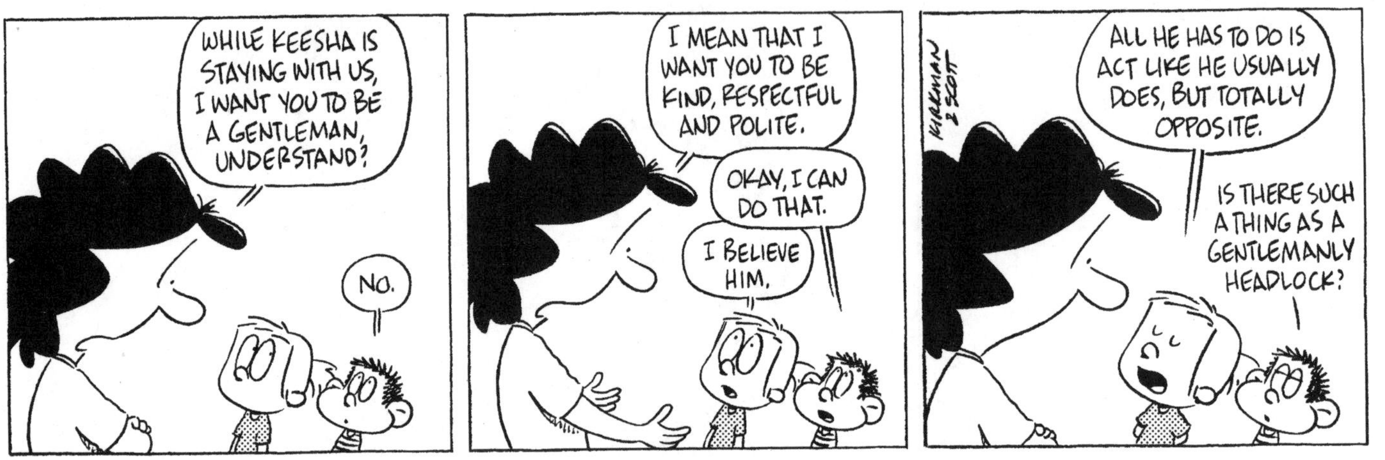
WHILE KEESHA IS STAYING WITH US, I WANT YOU TO BE A GENTLEMAN, UNDERSTAND?
NO.
I MEAN THAT I WANT YOU TO BE KIND, RESPECTFUL AND POLITE.
OKAY, I CAN DO THAT.
I BELIEVE HIM.
KIRKMAN & SCOTT
ALL HE HAS TO DO IS ACT LIKE HE USUALLY DOES, BUT TOTALLY OPPOSITE.
IS THERE SUCH A THING AS A GENTLEMANLY HEADLOCK?

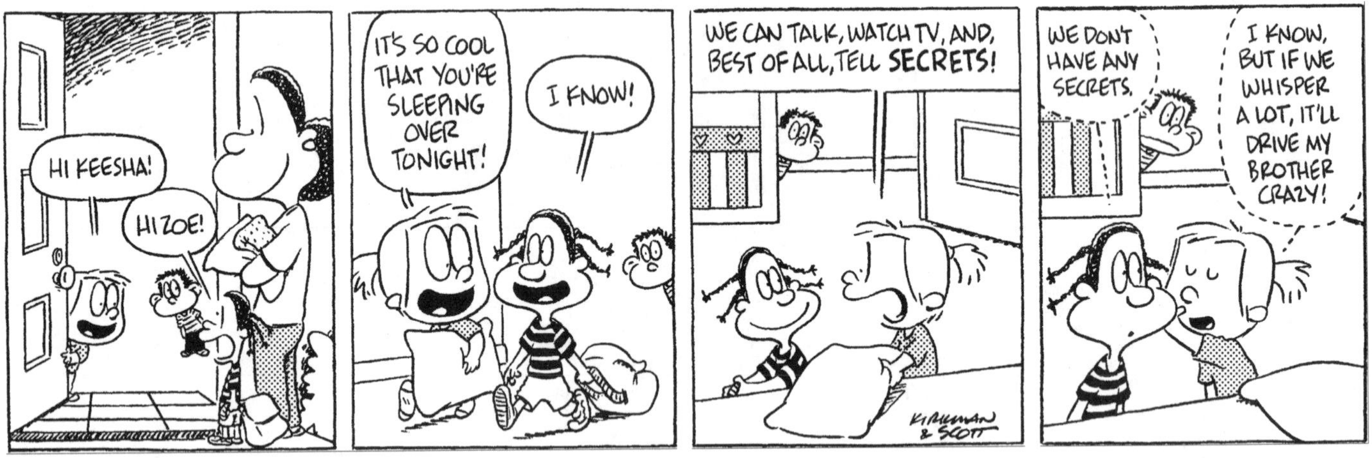
HI KEESHA!
HI ZOE!
IT'S SO COOL THAT YOU'RE SLEEPING OVER TONIGHT!
I KNOW!
WE CAN TALK, WATCH TV, AND, BEST OF ALL, TELL SECRETS!
KIRKMAN & SCOTT
WE DON'T HAVE ANY SECRETS.
I KNOW, BUT IF WE WHISPER A LOT, IT'LL DRIVE MY BROTHER CRAZY!

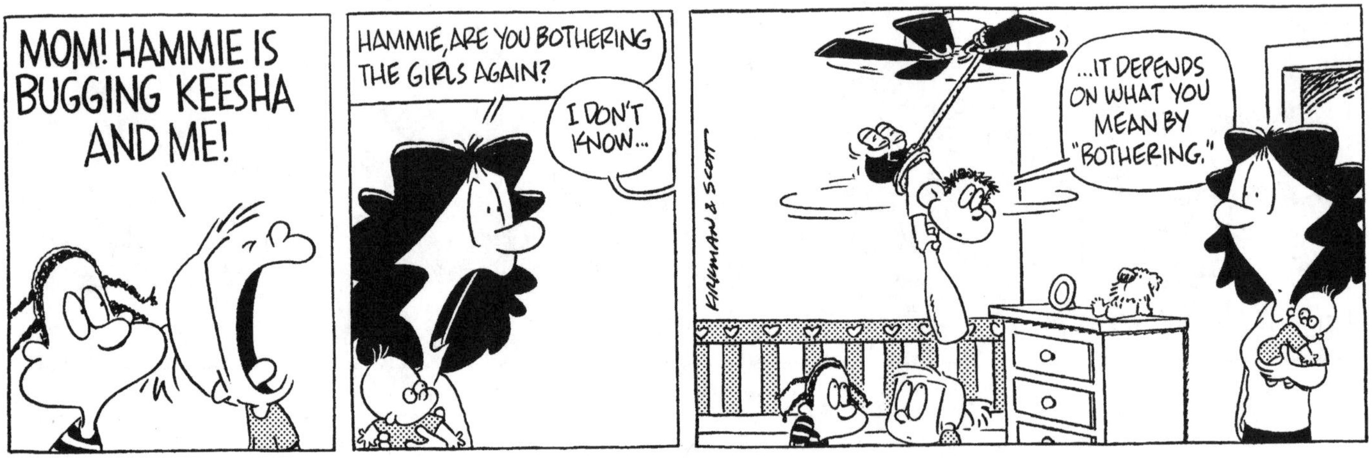
MOM! HAMMIE IS BUGGING KEESHA AND ME!
HAMMIE, ARE YOU BOTHERING THE GIRLS AGAIN?
I DON'T KNOW...
KIRKMAN & SCOTT
...IT DEPENDS ON WHAT YOU MEAN BY "BOTHERING."

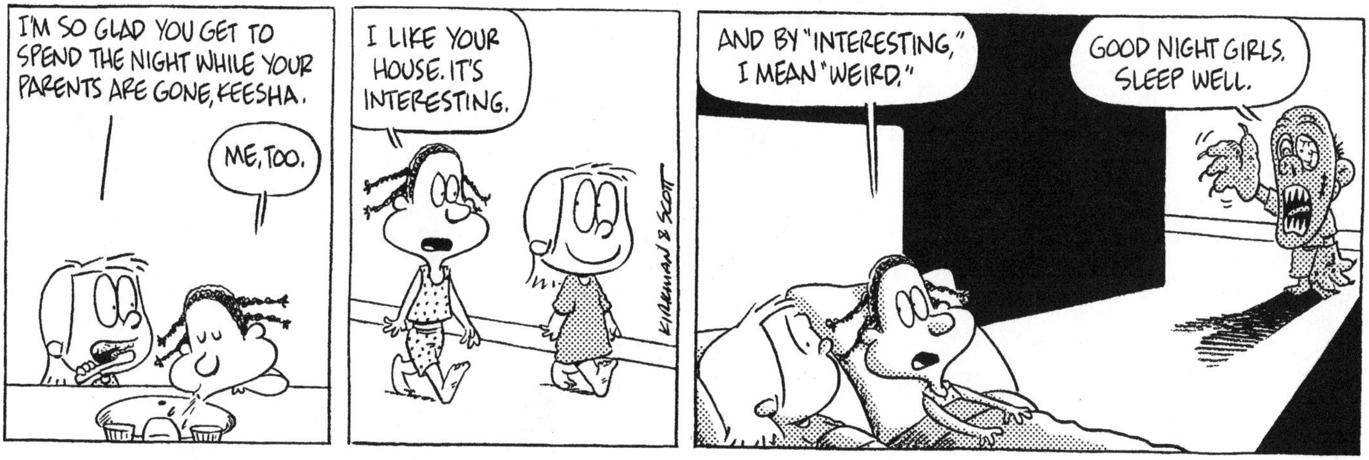
I'M SO GLAD YOU GET TO SPEND THE NIGHT WHILE YOUR PARENTS ARE GONE, KEESHA.
ME, TOO.
I LIKE YOUR HOUSE. IT'S INTERESTING.
KIRKMAN & SCOTT
AND BY "INTERESTING," I MEAN "WEIRD."
GOOD NIGHT GIRLS. SLEEP WELL.

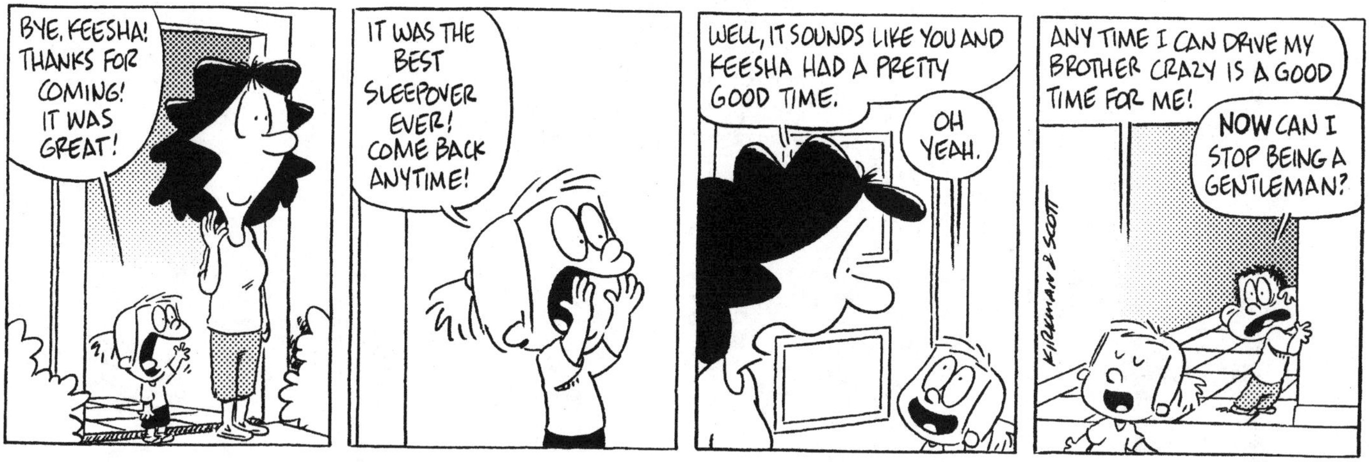
BYE, KEESHA! THANKS FOR COMING! IT WAS GREAT!
IT WAS THE BEST SLEEPOVER EVER! COME BACK ANYTIME!
WELL, IT SOUNDS LIKE YOU AND KEESHA HAD A PRETTY GOOD TIME.
OH YEAH.
KIRKMAN & SCOTT
ANY TIME I CAN DRIVE MY BROTHER CRAZY IS A GOOD TIME FOR ME!
NOW CAN I STOP BEING A GENTLEMAN?

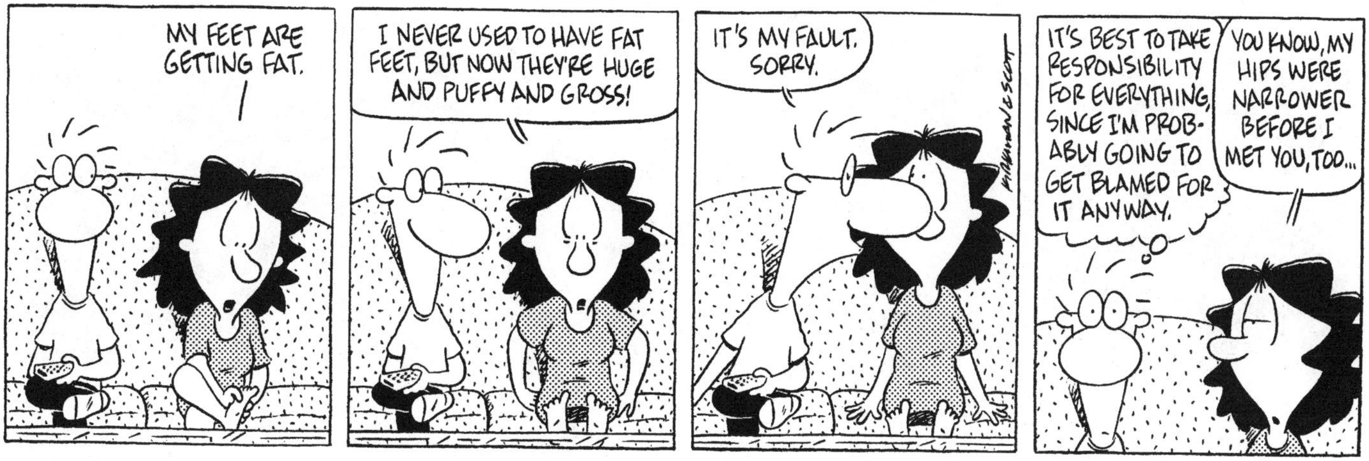
MY FEET ARE GETTING FAT.
I NEVER USED TO HAVE FAT FEET, BUT NOW THEY'RE HUGE AND PUFFY AND GROSS!
IT'S MY FAULT. SORRY.
KIRKMAN & SCOTT
IT'S BEST TO TAKE RESPONSIBILITY FOR EVERYTHING, SINCE I'M PROBABLY GOING TO GET BLAMED FOR IT ANYWAY.
YOU KNOW, MY HIPS WERE NARROWER BEFORE I MET YOU, TOO...

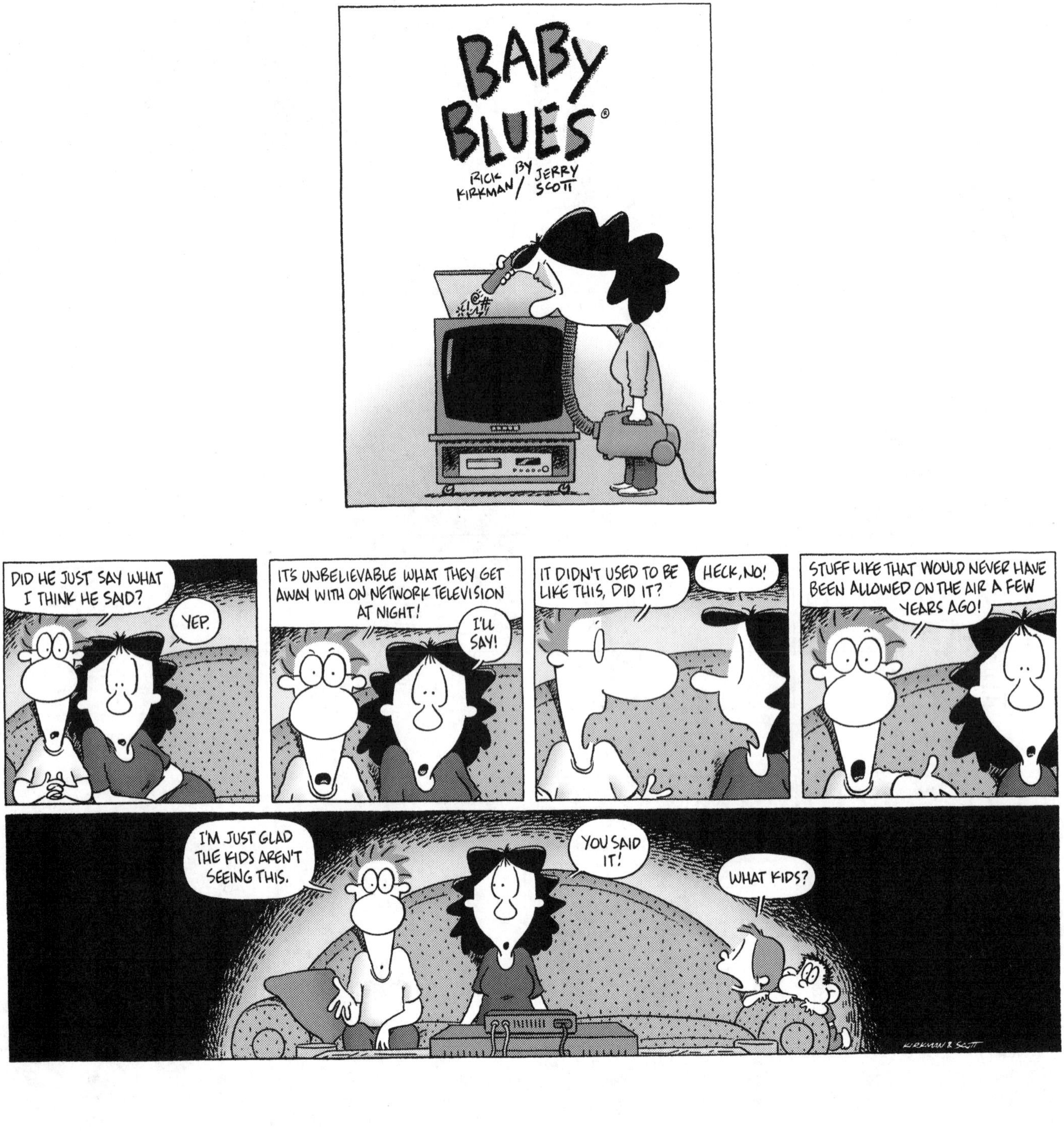
BABY BLUES®
BY RICK KIRKMAN / JERRY SCOTT
DID HE JUST SAY WHAT I THINK HE SAID?
YEP.
IT'S UNBELIEVABLE WHAT THEY GET AWAY WITH ON NETWORK TELEVISION AT NIGHT!
I'LL SAY!
IT DIDN'T USED TO BE LIKE THIS, DID IT?
HECK, NO!
STUFF LIKE THAT WOULD NEVER HAVE BEEN ALLOWED ON THE AIR A FEW YEARS AGO!
I'M JUST GLAD THE KIDS AREN'T SEEING THIS.
YOU SAID IT!
WHAT KIDS?
KIRKMAN & SCOTT

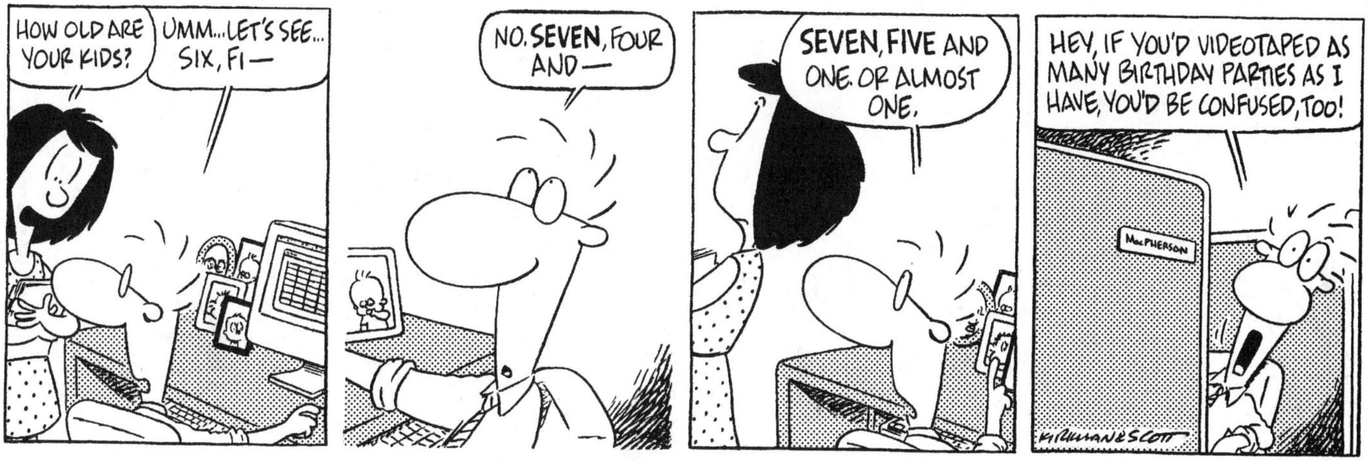
HOW OLD ARE YOUR KIDS?
UMM...LET'S SEE... SIX, FI—
NO. **SEVEN**, FOUR AND—
SEVEN, **FIVE** AND ONE. OR ALMOST ONE.
HEY, IF YOU'D VIDEOTAPED AS MANY BIRTHDAY PARTIES AS I HAVE, YOU'D BE CONFUSED, TOO!
MacPHERSON
KIRKMAN & SCOTT

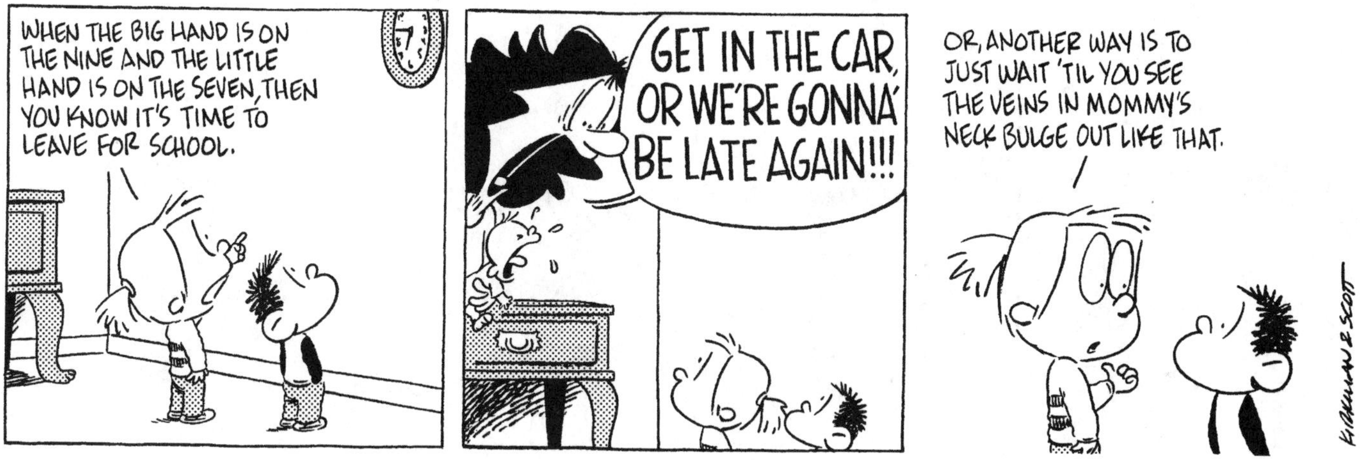
WHEN THE BIG HAND IS ON THE NINE AND THE LITTLE HAND IS ON THE SEVEN, THEN YOU KNOW IT'S TIME TO LEAVE FOR SCHOOL.
GET IN THE CAR, OR WE'RE GONNA' BE LATE AGAIN!!!
OR, ANOTHER WAY IS TO JUST WAIT 'TIL YOU SEE THE VEINS IN MOMMY'S NECK BULGE OUT LIKE THAT.
KIRKMAN & SCOTT

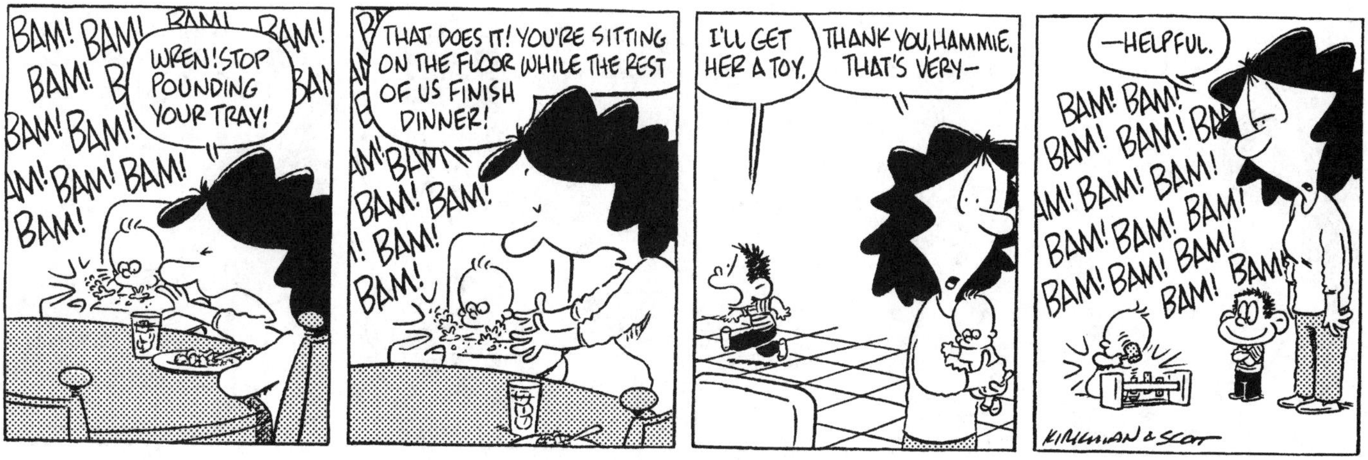
BAM! BAM! BAM! BAM! BAM! BAM! BAM! BAM! BAM! BAM!
WREN! STOP POUNDING YOUR TRAY!
THAT DOES IT! YOU'RE SITTING ON THE FLOOR WHILE THE REST OF US FINISH DINNER!
BAM! BAM! BAM! BAM!
I'LL GET HER A TOY.
THANK YOU, HAMMIE. THAT'S VERY—
—HELPFUL.
BAM! BAM! BAM! BAM! BAM! BAM! BAM! BAM! BAM! BAM! BAM! BAM! BAM!
KIRKMAN & SCOTT

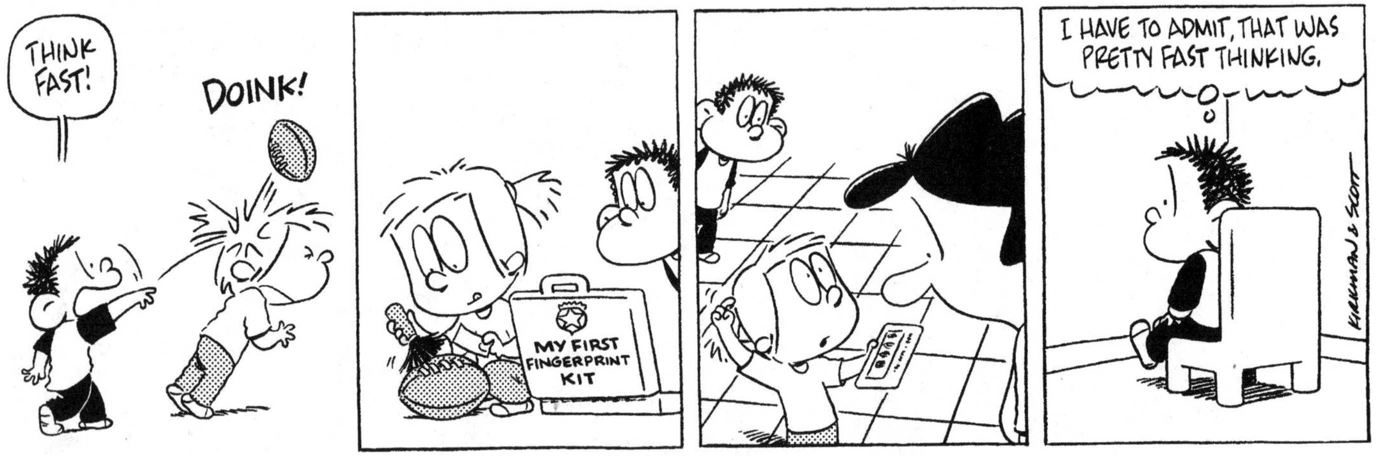
THINK FAST!
DOINK!
MY FIRST FINGERPRINT KIT
I HAVE TO ADMIT, THAT WAS PRETTY FAST THINKING.
KIRKMAN & SCOTT

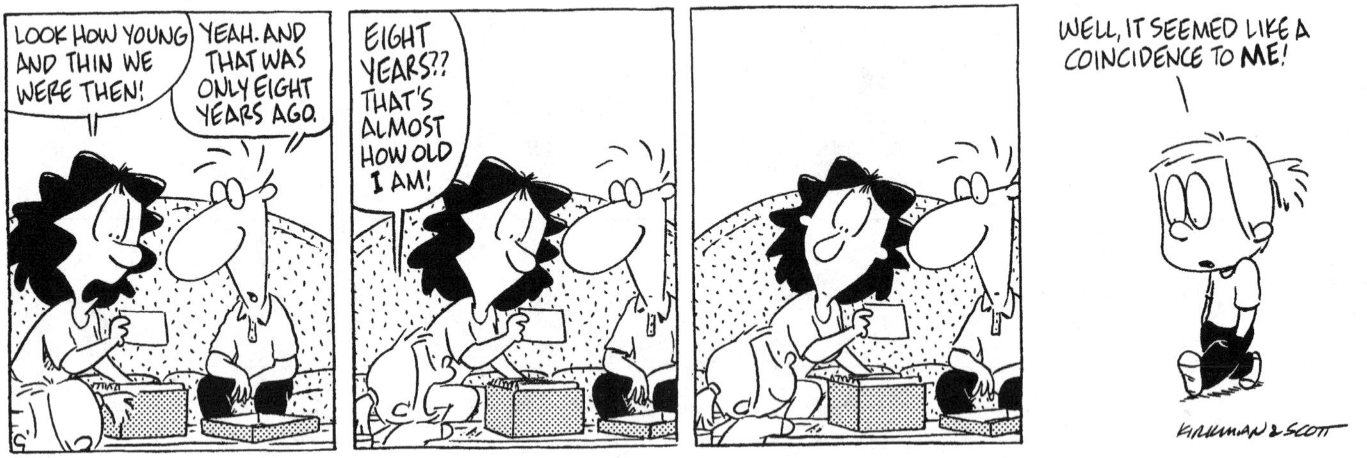
LOOK HOW YOUNG AND THIN WE WERE THEN!
YEAH. AND THAT WAS ONLY EIGHT YEARS AGO.
EIGHT YEARS?? THAT'S ALMOST HOW OLD I AM!
WELL, IT SEEMED LIKE A COINCIDENCE TO ME!
KIRKMAN & SCOTT

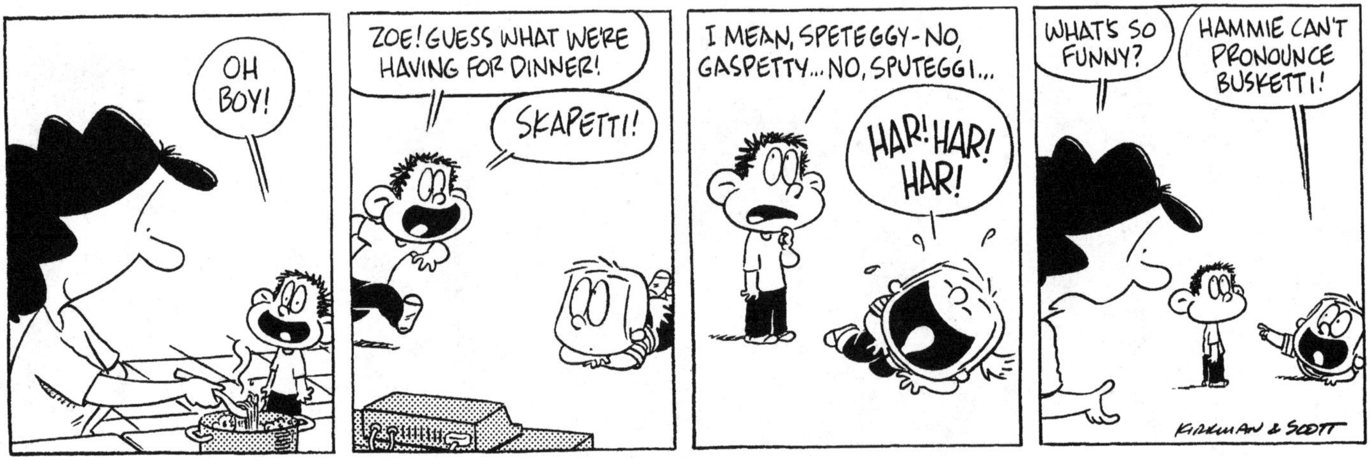
OH BOY!
ZOE! GUESS WHAT WE'RE HAVING FOR DINNER!
SKAPETTI!
I MEAN, SPETEGGY- NO, GASPETTY... NO, SPUTEGGI...
HAR! HAR! HAR!
WHAT'S SO FUNNY?
HAMMIE CAN'T PRONOUNCE BUSKETTI!
KIRKMAN & SCOTT

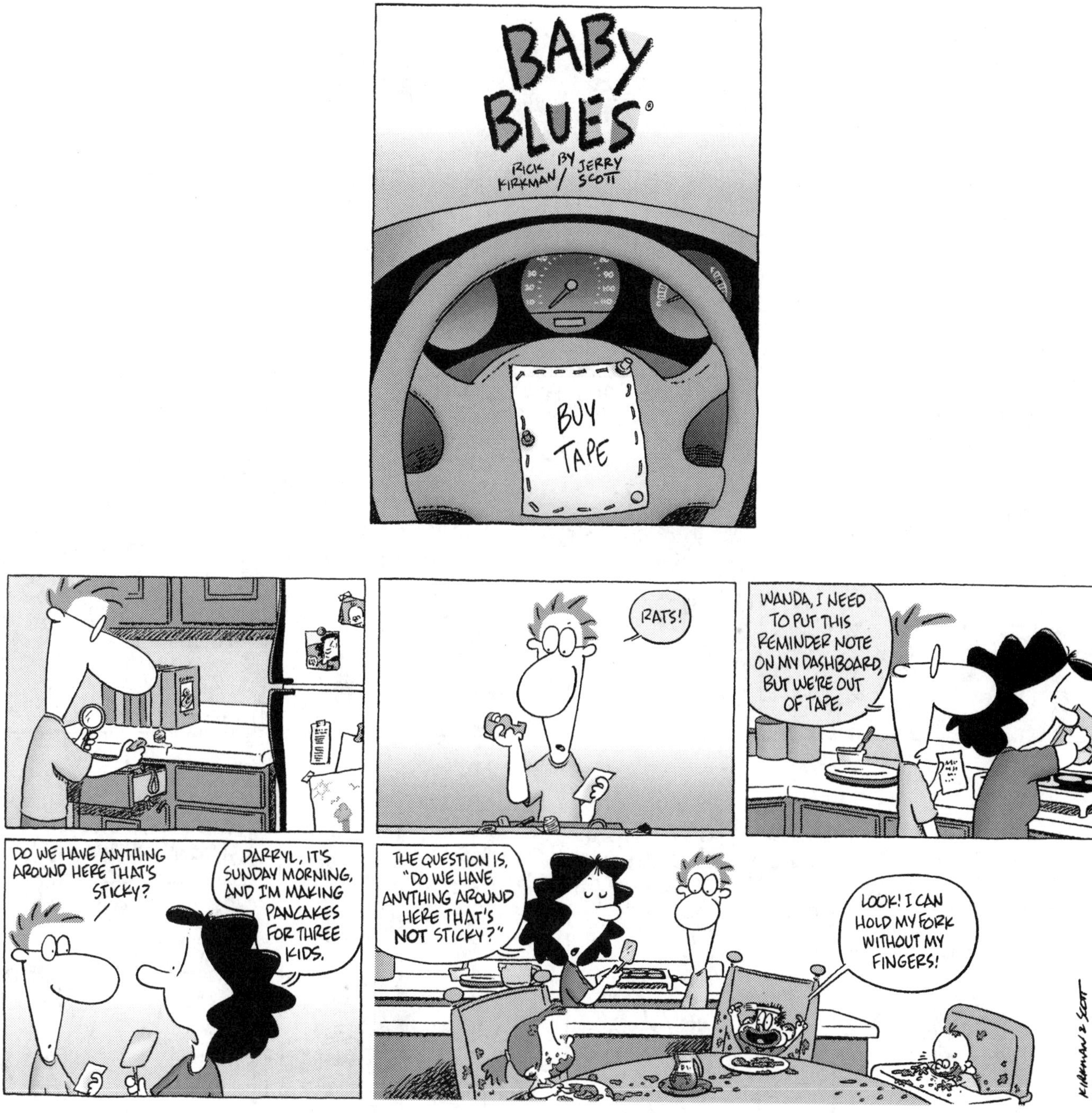
BABY BLUES®
BY RICK KIRKMAN / JERRY SCOTT
BUY TAPE
RATS!
WANDA, I NEED TO PUT THIS REMINDER NOTE ON MY DASHBOARD, BUT WE'RE OUT OF TAPE.
DO WE HAVE ANYTHING AROUND HERE THAT'S STICKY?
DARRYL, IT'S SUNDAY MORNING, AND I'M MAKING PANCAKES FOR THREE KIDS.
THE QUESTION IS, "DO WE HAVE ANYTHING AROUND HERE THAT'S NOT STICKY?"
LOOK! I CAN HOLD MY FORK WITHOUT MY FINGERS!
KIRKMAN & SCOTT

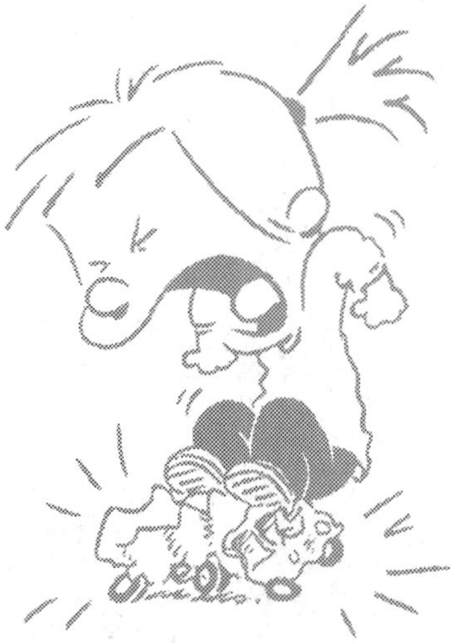

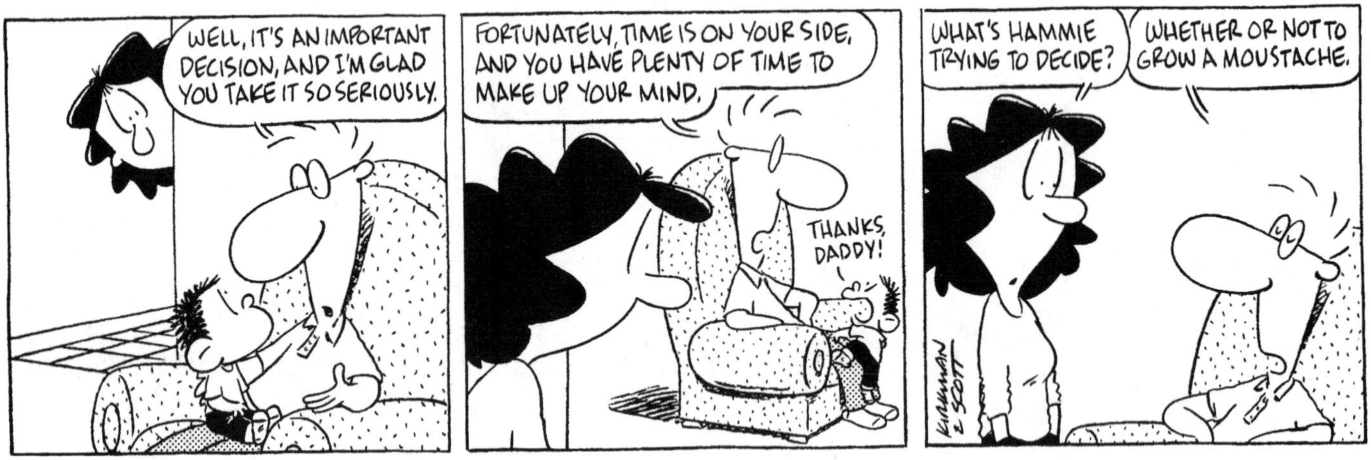
WELL, IT'S AN IMPORTANT DECISION, AND I'M GLAD YOU TAKE IT SO SERIOUSLY.
FORTUNATELY, TIME IS ON YOUR SIDE, AND YOU HAVE PLENTY OF TIME TO MAKE UP YOUR MIND.
THANKS, DADDY!
WHAT'S HAMMIE TRYING TO DECIDE?
WHETHER OR NOT TO GROW A MOUSTACHE.
KIRKMAN & SCOTT

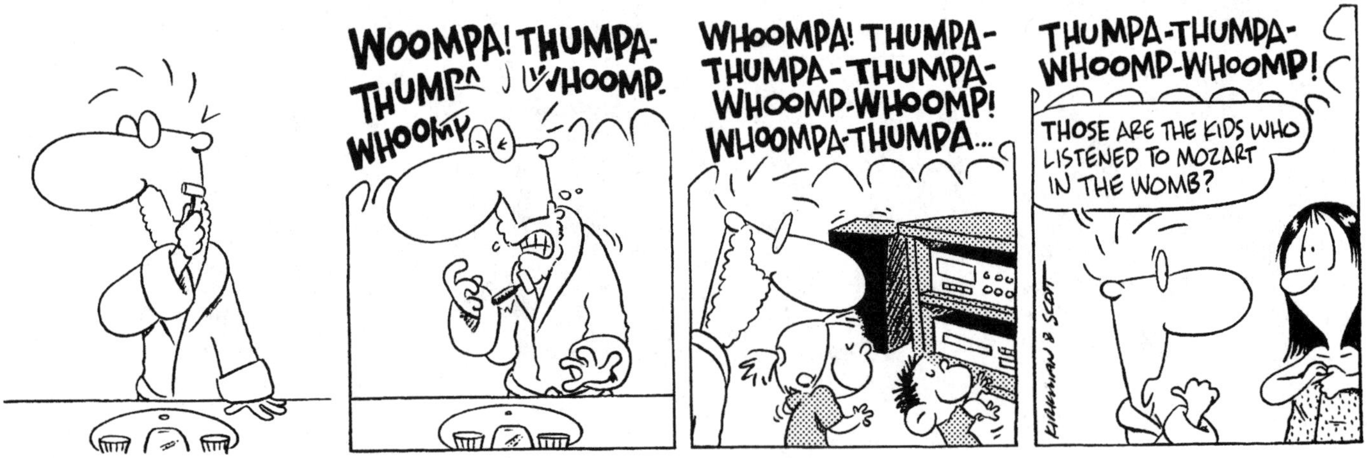
WOOMPA! THUMPA-
WHOOMP.
WHOOMPA! THUMPA-THUMPA-THUMPA-THUMPA-WHOOMP-WHOOMP! WHOOMPA-THUMPA...
THUMPA-THUMPA-WHOOMP-WHOOMP!
THOSE ARE THE KIDS WHO LISTENED TO MOZART IN THE WOMB?
KIRKMAN & SCOTT

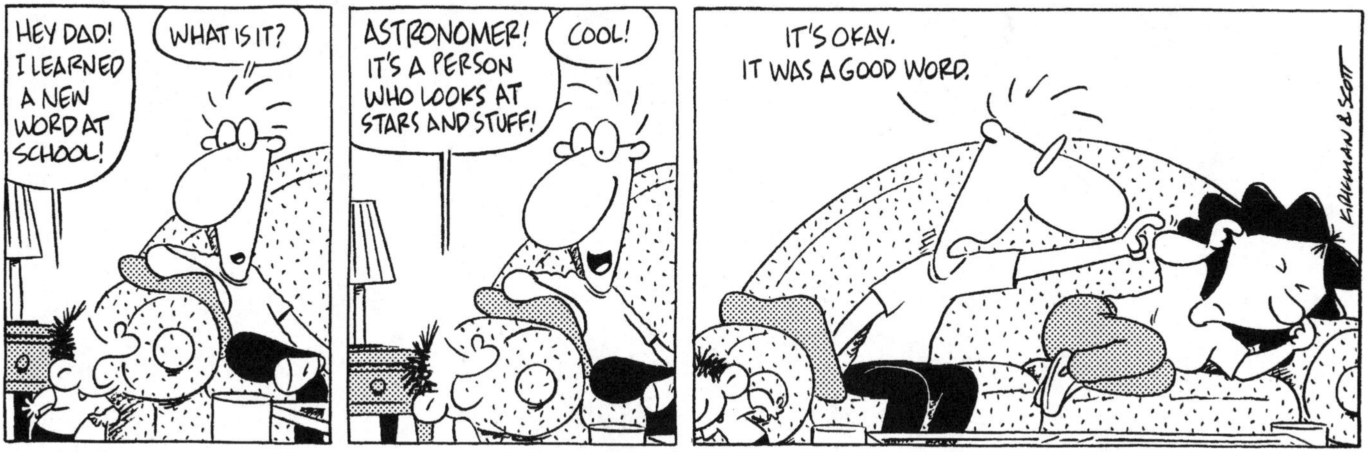
HEY DAD! I LEARNED A NEW WORD AT SCHOOL!
WHAT IS IT?
ASTRONOMER! IT'S A PERSON WHO LOOKS AT STARS AND STUFF!
COOL!
IT'S OKAY. IT WAS A GOOD WORD.
KIRKMAN & SCOTT

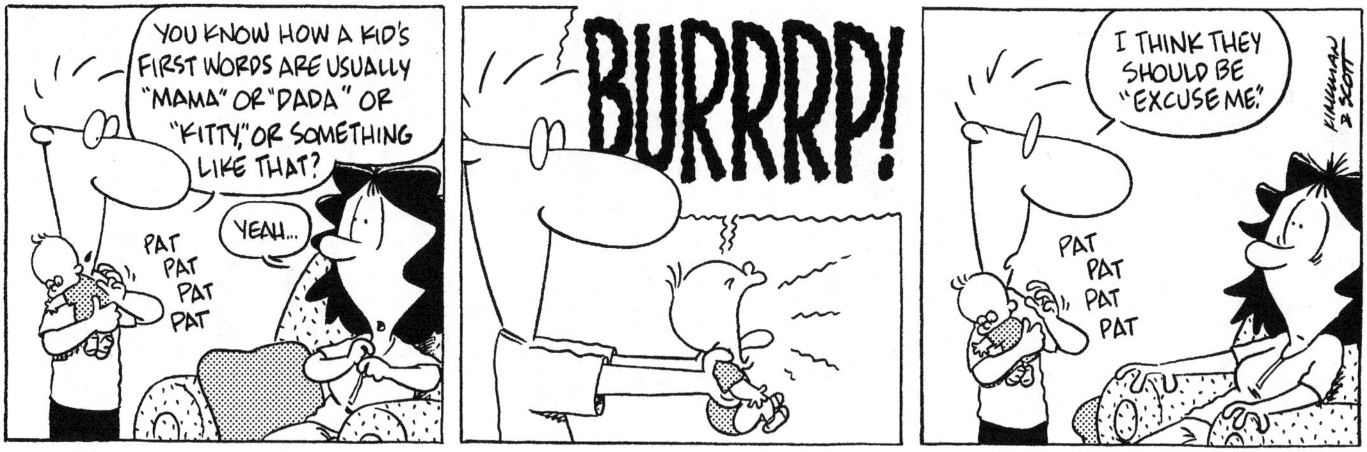
YOU KNOW HOW A KID'S FIRST WORDS ARE USUALLY "MAMA" OR "DADA" OR "KITTY," OR SOMETHING LIKE THAT?
YEAH...
PAT PAT PAT PAT
BURRRP!
I THINK THEY SHOULD BE "EXCUSE ME."
PAT PAT PAT PAT
KIRKMAN & SCOTT

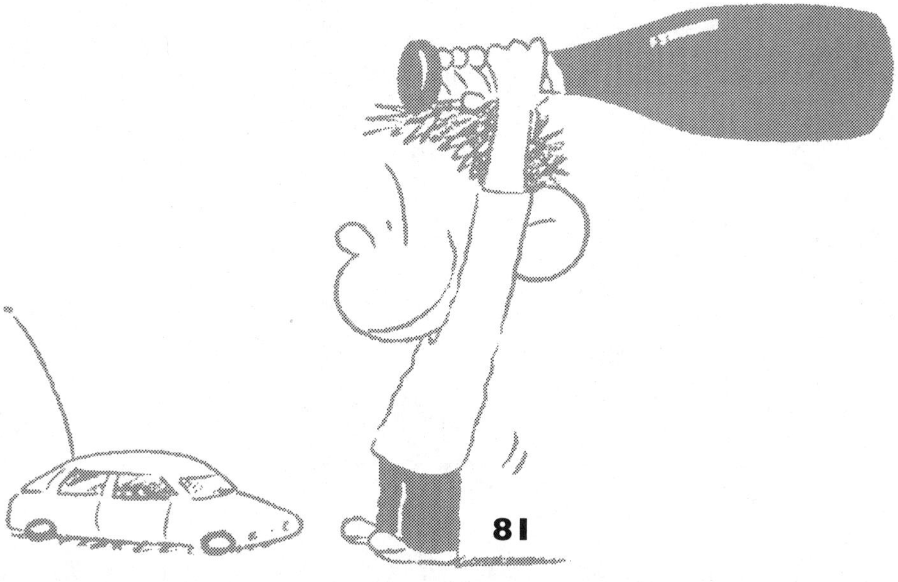

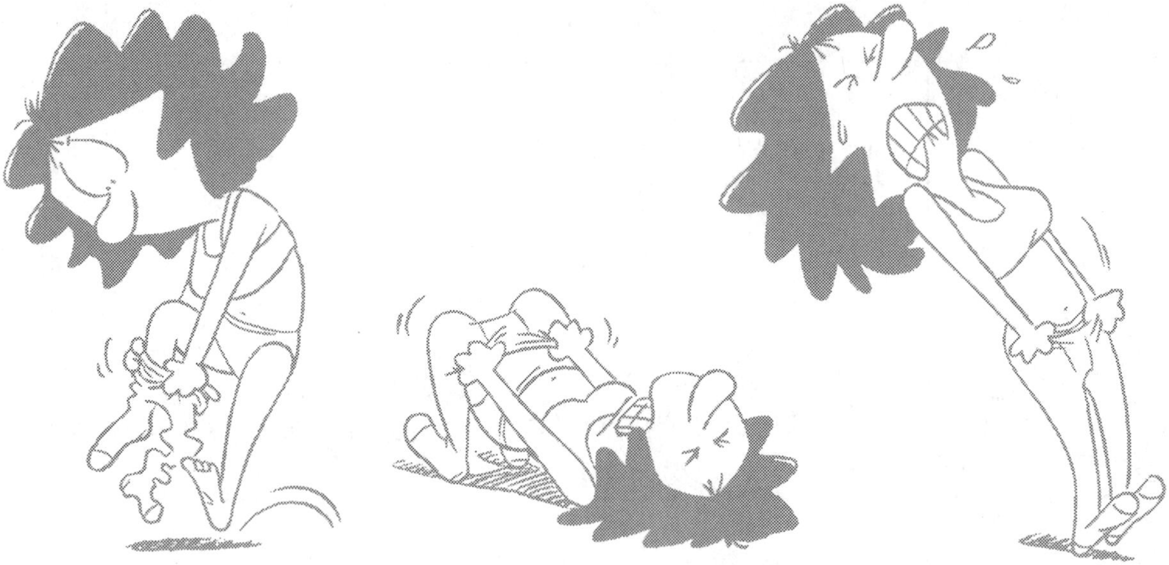

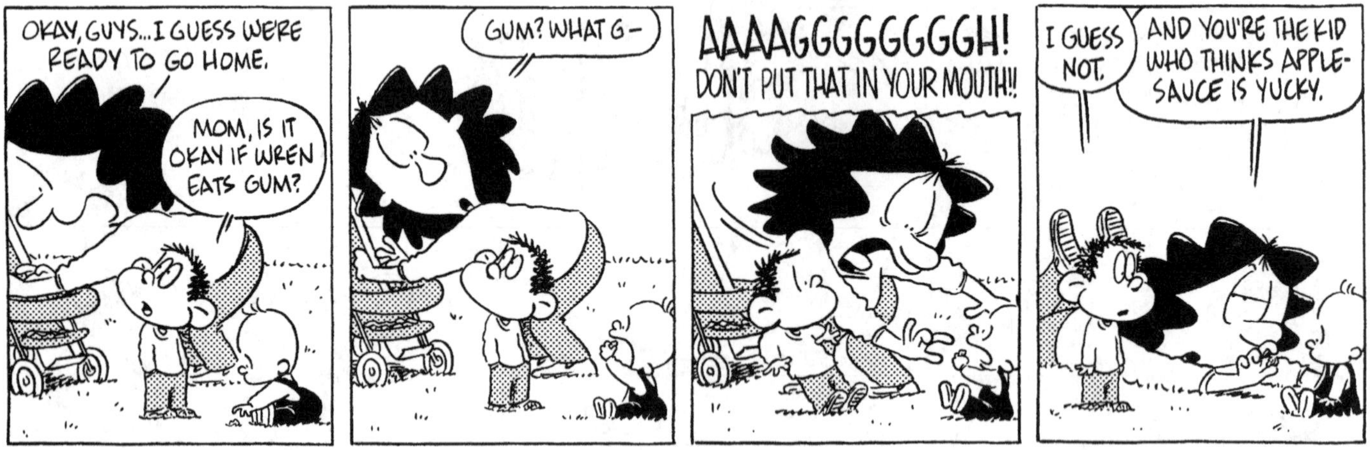

OKAY, GUYS... I GUESS WE'RE READY TO GO HOME.
MOM, IS IT OKAY IF WREN EATS GUM?
GUM? WHAT G–
AAAAGGGGGGGH! DON'T PUT THAT IN YOUR MOUTH!!
I GUESS NOT.
AND YOU'RE THE KID WHO THINKS APPLE-SAUCE IS YUCKY.

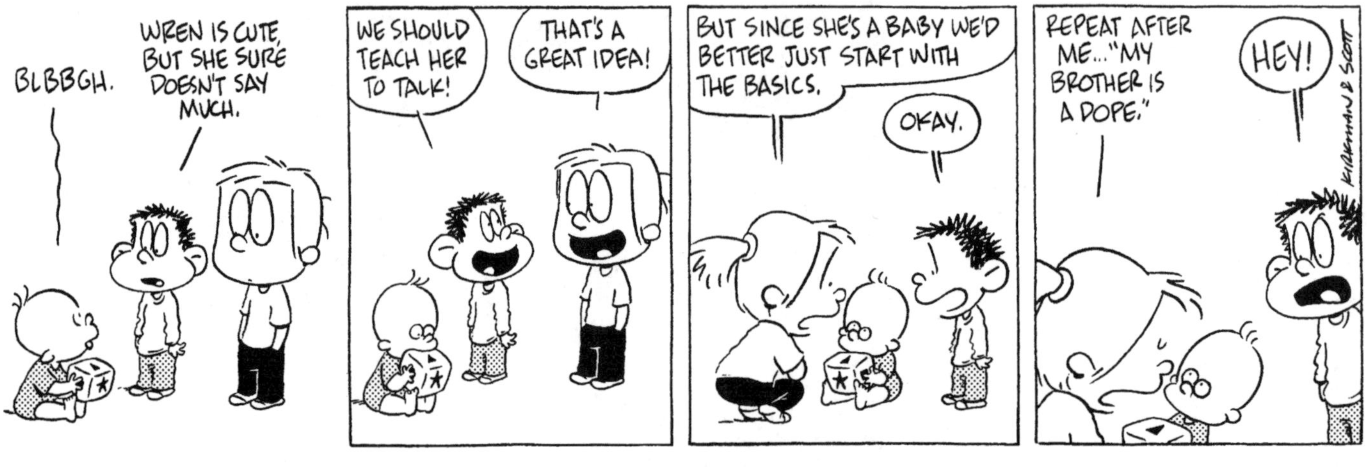

BLBBGH.
WREN IS CUTE, BUT SHE SURE DOESN'T SAY MUCH.
WE SHOULD TEACH HER TO TALK!
THAT'S A GREAT IDEA!
BUT SINCE SHE'S A BABY WE'D BETTER JUST START WITH THE BASICS.
OKAY.
REPEAT AFTER ME... "MY BROTHER IS A DOPE."
HEY!
KIRKMAN & SCOTT

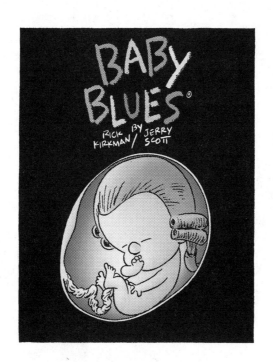

BABY BLUES
by Rick Kirkman / Jerry Scott

MOZART?

MM-HMM.

WHEN MY FIRST BABY WAS BORN, MY PLAN WAS FOR HER TO PLAY THE PIANO AND BE FLUENT IN AT LEAST TWO LANGUAGES BY THE AGE OF FIVE.

WOW!

THEN WHEN I HAD MY SECOND BABY, I WAS A LITTLE MORE REALISTIC.

OH?

YEAH. I SCALED BACK MY EXPECTATIONS TO JUST READING AND WRITING BY AGE FIVE.

INTERESTING. AND WITH YOUR THIRD?

POTTY-TRAINED AND WEANED BY THE TIME SHE GRADUATES FROM COLLEGE.

¡BBTHHHHHH!

KIRKMAN & SCOTT

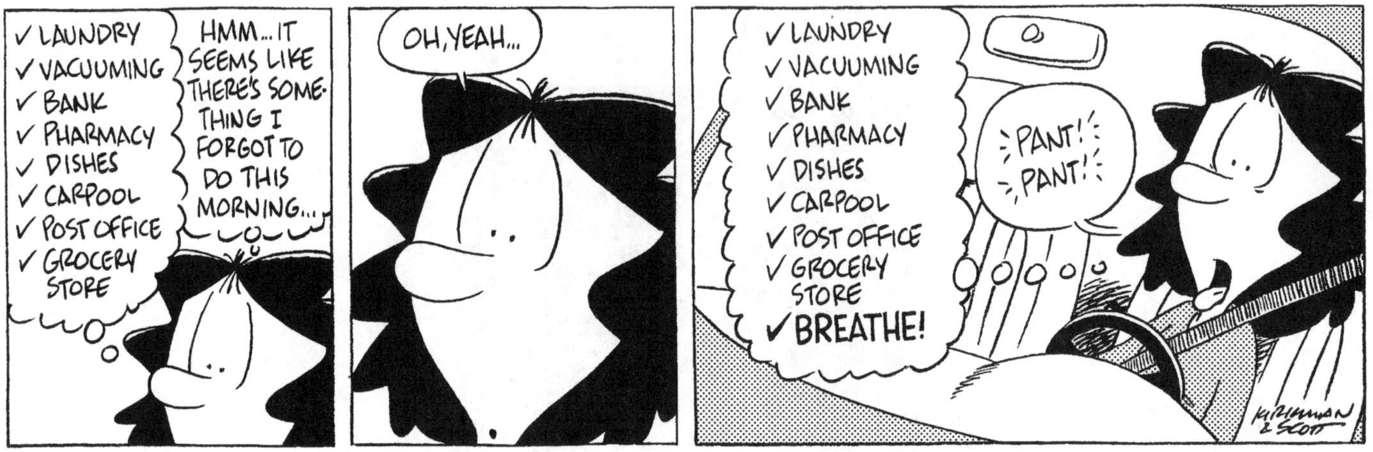
✓ LAUNDRY
✓ VACUUMING
✓ BANK
✓ PHARMACY
✓ DISHES
✓ CARPOOL
✓ POST OFFICE
✓ GROCERY STORE
HMM... IT SEEMS LIKE THERE'S SOMETHING I FORGOT TO DO THIS MORNING...
OH, YEAH...
✓ LAUNDRY
✓ VACUUMING
✓ BANK
✓ PHARMACY
✓ DISHES
✓ CARPOOL
✓ POST OFFICE
✓ GROCERY STORE
✓ BREATHE!
PANT! PANT!
KIRKMAN & SCOTT

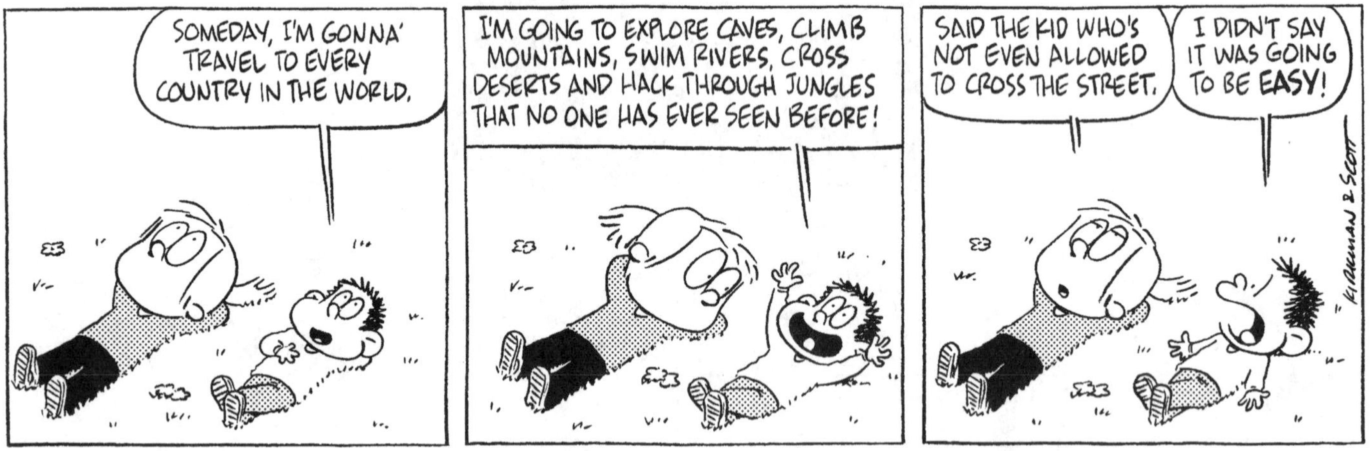
SOMEDAY, I'M GONNA' TRAVEL TO EVERY COUNTRY IN THE WORLD.
I'M GOING TO EXPLORE CAVES, CLIMB MOUNTAINS, SWIM RIVERS, CROSS DESERTS AND HACK THROUGH JUNGLES THAT NO ONE HAS EVER SEEN BEFORE!
SAID THE KID WHO'S NOT EVEN ALLOWED TO CROSS THE STREET.
I DIDN'T SAY IT WAS GOING TO BE EASY!
KIRKMAN & SCOTT

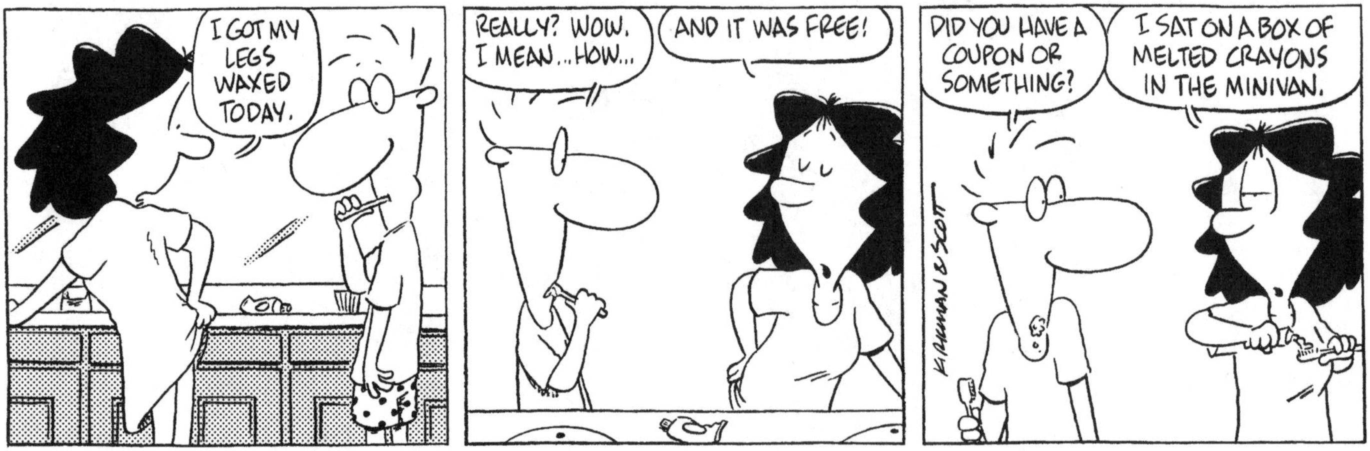
I GOT MY LEGS WAXED TODAY.
REALLY? WOW. I MEAN... HOW...
AND IT WAS FREE!
DID YOU HAVE A COUPON OR SOMETHING?
I SAT ON A BOX OF MELTED CRAYONS IN THE MINIVAN.
KIRKMAN & SCOTT

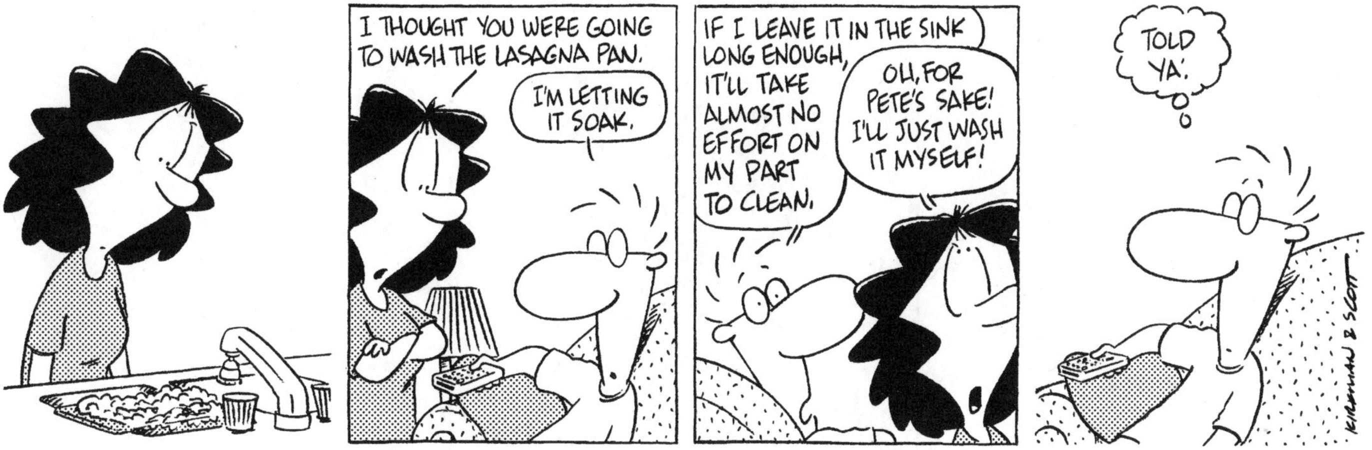
I THOUGHT YOU WERE GOING TO WASH THE LASAGNA PAN.
I'M LETTING IT SOAK.
IF I LEAVE IT IN THE SINK LONG ENOUGH, IT'LL TAKE ALMOST NO EFFORT ON MY PART TO CLEAN.
OH, FOR PETE'S SAKE! I'LL JUST WASH IT MYSELF!
TOLD YA.
KIRKMAN & SCOTT

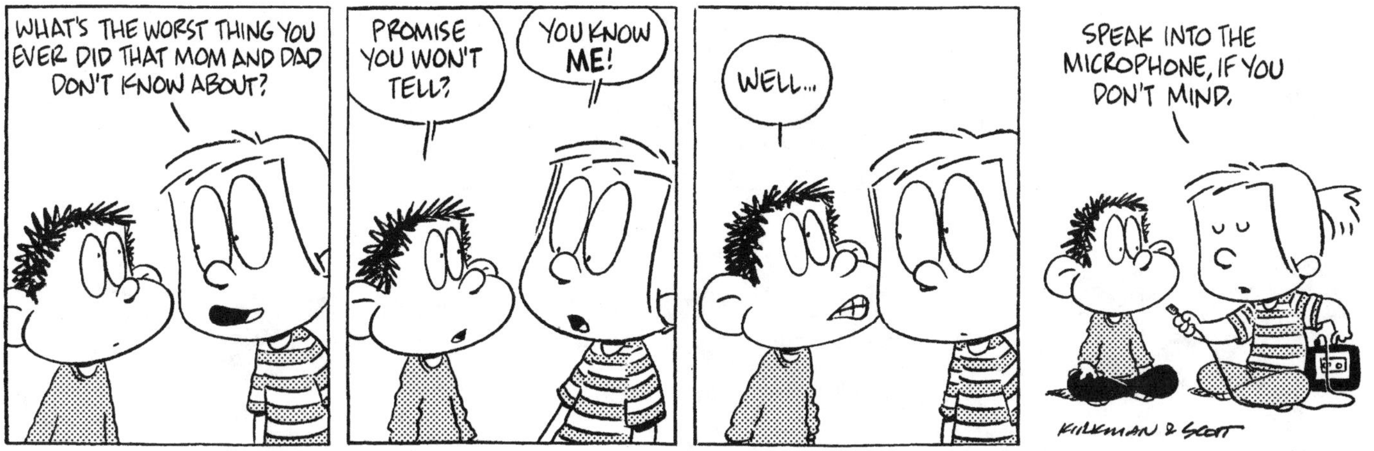
WHAT'S THE WORST THING YOU EVER DID THAT MOM AND DAD DON'T KNOW ABOUT?
PROMISE YOU WON'T TELL?
YOU KNOW ME!
WELL...
SPEAK INTO THE MICROPHONE, IF YOU DON'T MIND.
KIRKMAN & SCOTT

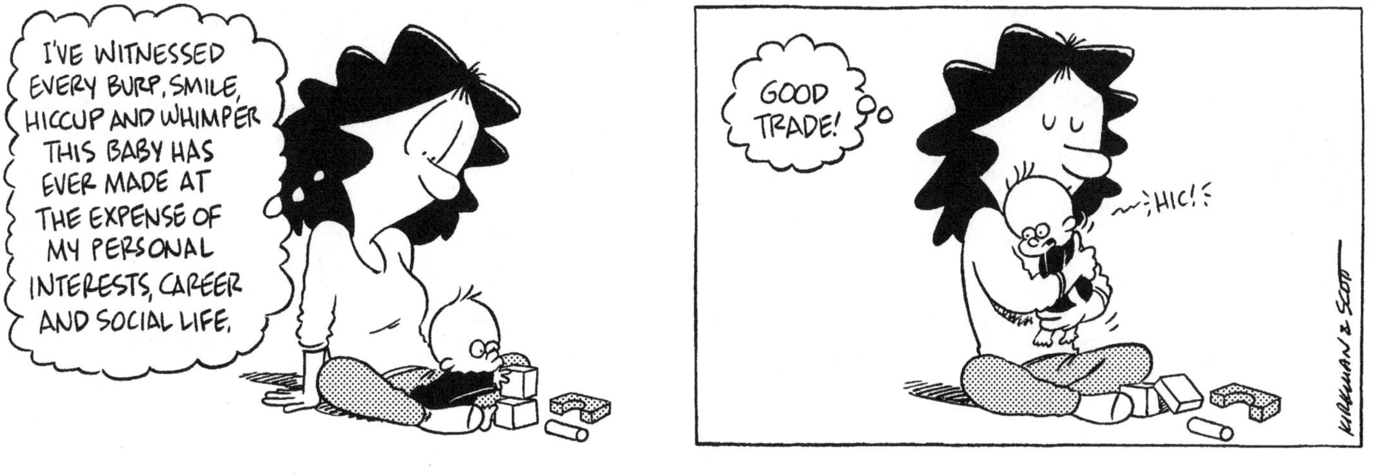
I'VE WITNESSED EVERY BURP, SMILE, HICCUP AND WHIMPER THIS BABY HAS EVER MADE AT THE EXPENSE OF MY PERSONAL INTERESTS, CAREER AND SOCIAL LIFE.
GOOD TRADE!
HIC!
KIRKMAN & SCOTT

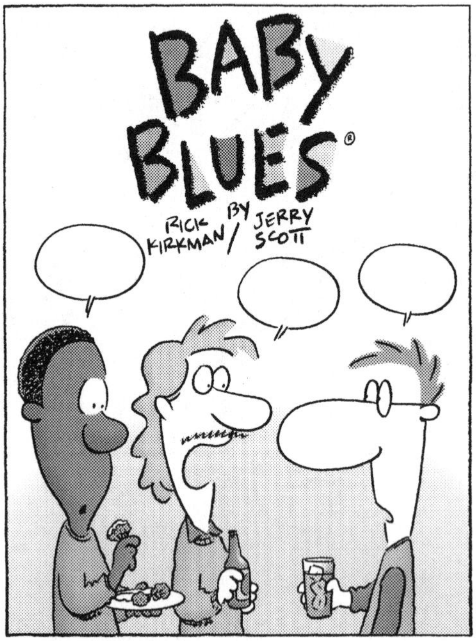
BABY BLUES®
BY RICK KIRKMAN / JERRY SCOTT

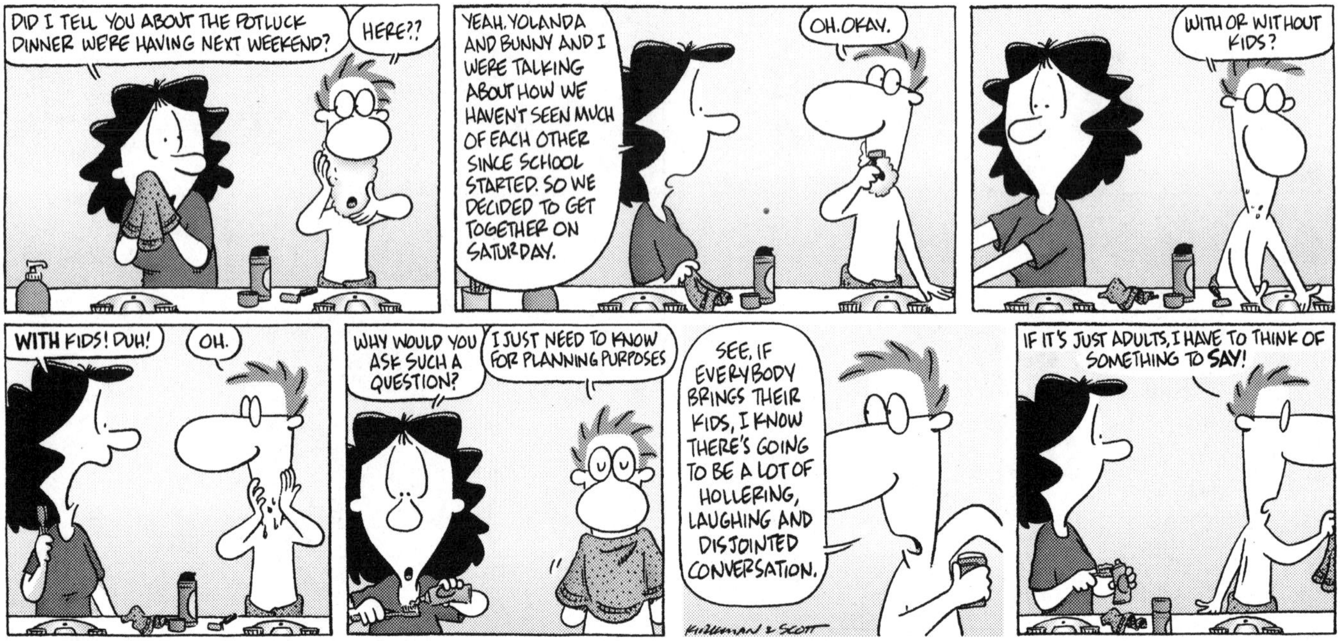
DID I TELL YOU ABOUT THE POTLUCK DINNER WE'RE HAVING NEXT WEEKEND?
HERE??
YEAH. YOLANDA AND BUNNY AND I WERE TALKING ABOUT HOW WE HAVEN'T SEEN MUCH OF EACH OTHER SINCE SCHOOL STARTED. SO WE DECIDED TO GET TOGETHER ON SATURDAY.
OH. OKAY.
WITH OR WITHOUT KIDS?
WITH KIDS! DUH!
OH.
WHY WOULD YOU ASK SUCH A QUESTION?
I JUST NEED TO KNOW FOR PLANNING PURPOSES
SEE, IF EVERYBODY BRINGS THEIR KIDS, I KNOW THERE'S GOING TO BE A LOT OF HOLLERING, LAUGHING AND DISJOINTED CONVERSATION.
KIRKMAN & SCOTT
IF IT'S JUST ADULTS, I HAVE TO THINK OF SOMETHING TO SAY!

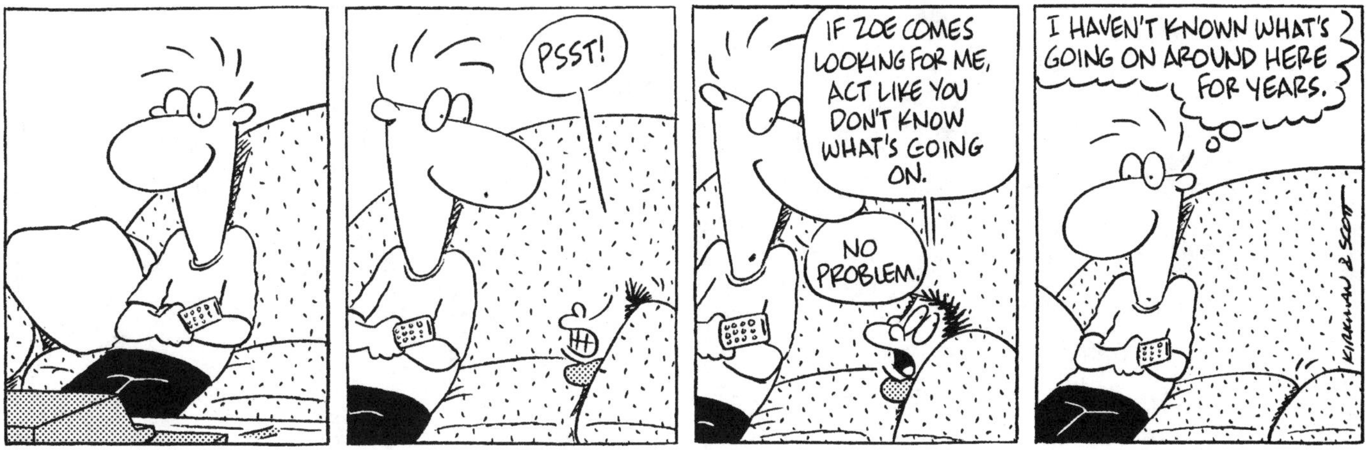

PSST!
IF ZOE COMES LOOKING FOR ME, ACT LIKE YOU DON'T KNOW WHAT'S GOING ON.
NO PROBLEM.
I HAVEN'T KNOWN WHAT'S GOING ON AROUND HERE FOR YEARS.
KIRKMAN & SCOTT

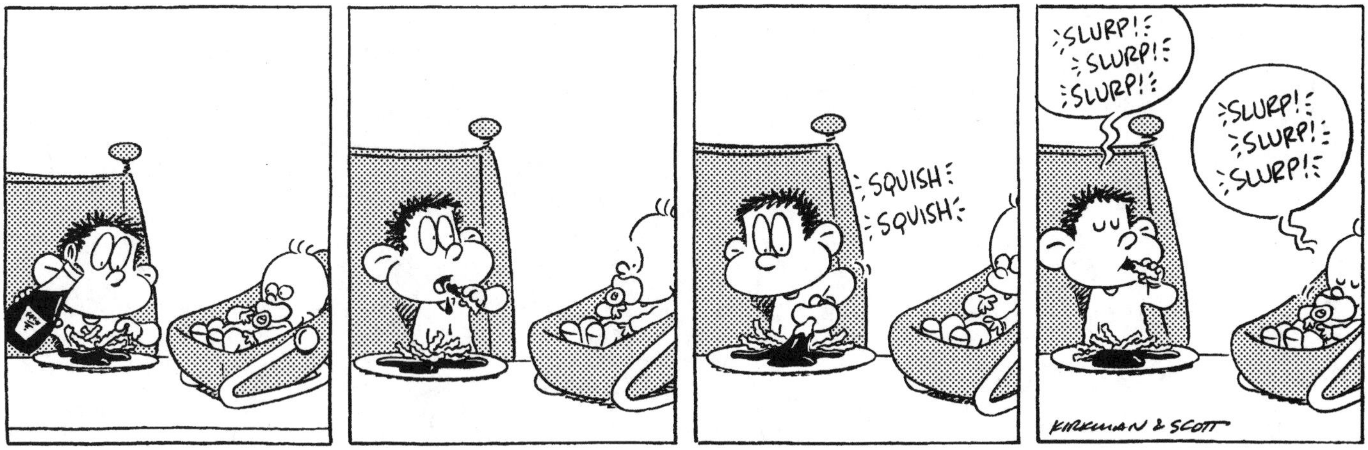

SQUISH SQUISH
SLURP! SLURP! SLURP!
SLURP! SLURP! SLURP!
KIRKMAN & SCOTT

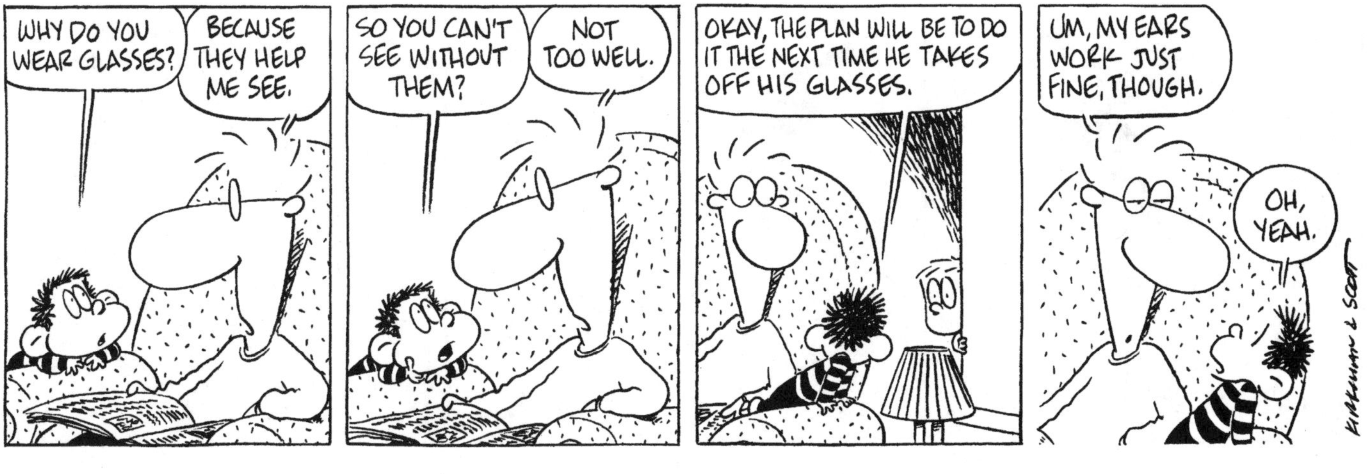

WHY DO YOU WEAR GLASSES?
BECAUSE THEY HELP ME SEE.
SO YOU CAN'T SEE WITHOUT THEM?
NOT TOO WELL.
OKAY, THE PLAN WILL BE TO DO IT THE NEXT TIME HE TAKES OFF HIS GLASSES.
UM, MY EARS WORK JUST FINE, THOUGH.
OH, YEAH.
KIRKMAN & SCOTT

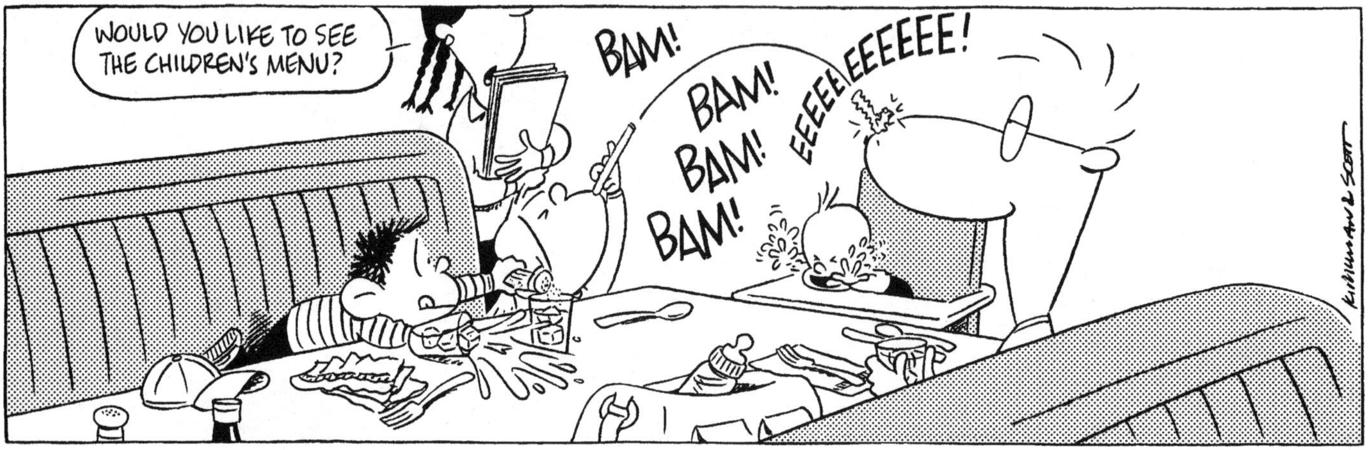
WOULD YOU LIKE TO SEE THE CHILDREN'S MENU?
BAM!
BAM!
BAM!
BAM!
EEEEEEEEEEE!
KIRKMAN & SCOTT

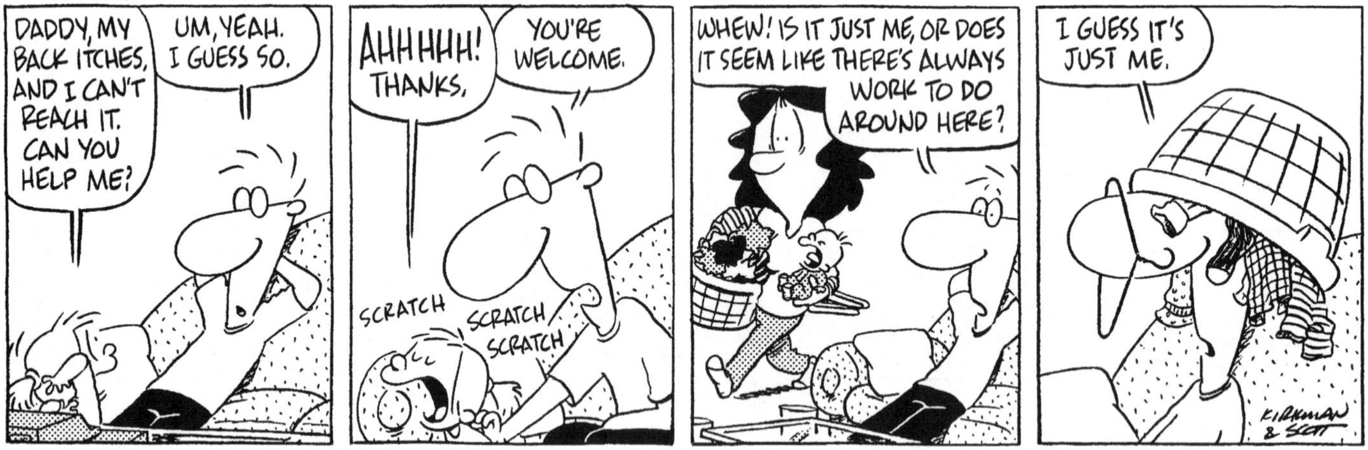
DADDY, MY BACK ITCHES, AND I CAN'T REACH IT. CAN YOU HELP ME?
UM, YEAH. I GUESS SO.
AHHHHH! THANKS.
YOU'RE WELCOME.
SCRATCH
SCRATCH
SCRATCH
WHEW! IS IT JUST ME, OR DOES IT SEEM LIKE THERE'S ALWAYS WORK TO DO AROUND HERE?
I GUESS IT'S JUST ME.
KIRKMAN & SCOTT

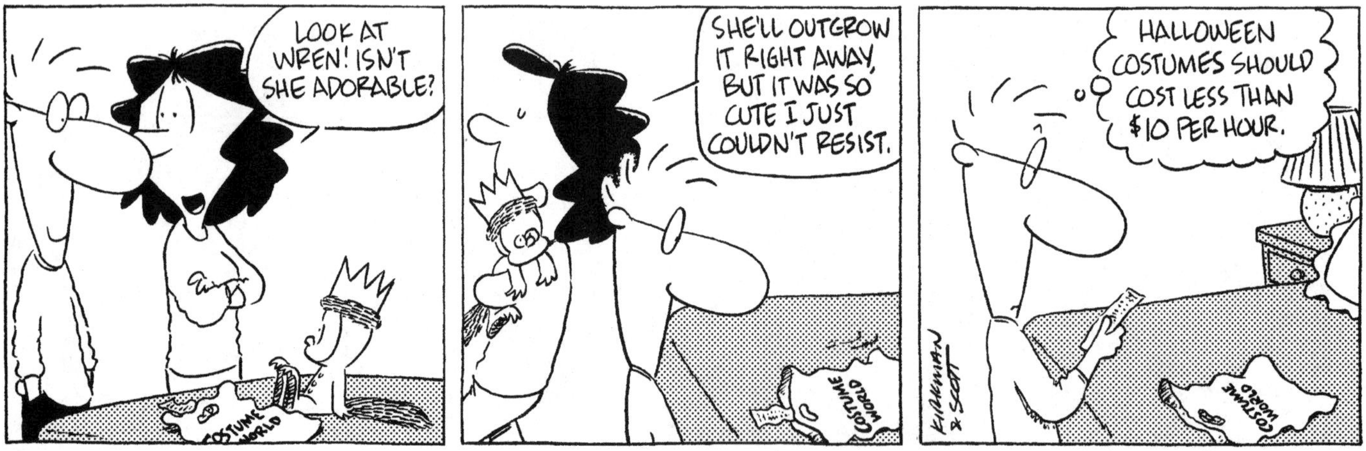
LOOK AT WREN! ISN'T SHE ADORABLE?
COSTUME WORLD
SHE'LL OUTGROW IT RIGHT AWAY, BUT IT WAS SO CUTE I JUST COULDN'T RESIST.
COSTUME WORLD
KIRKMAN & SCOTT
HALLOWEEN COSTUMES SHOULD COST LESS THAN $10 PER HOUR.
COSTUME WORLD

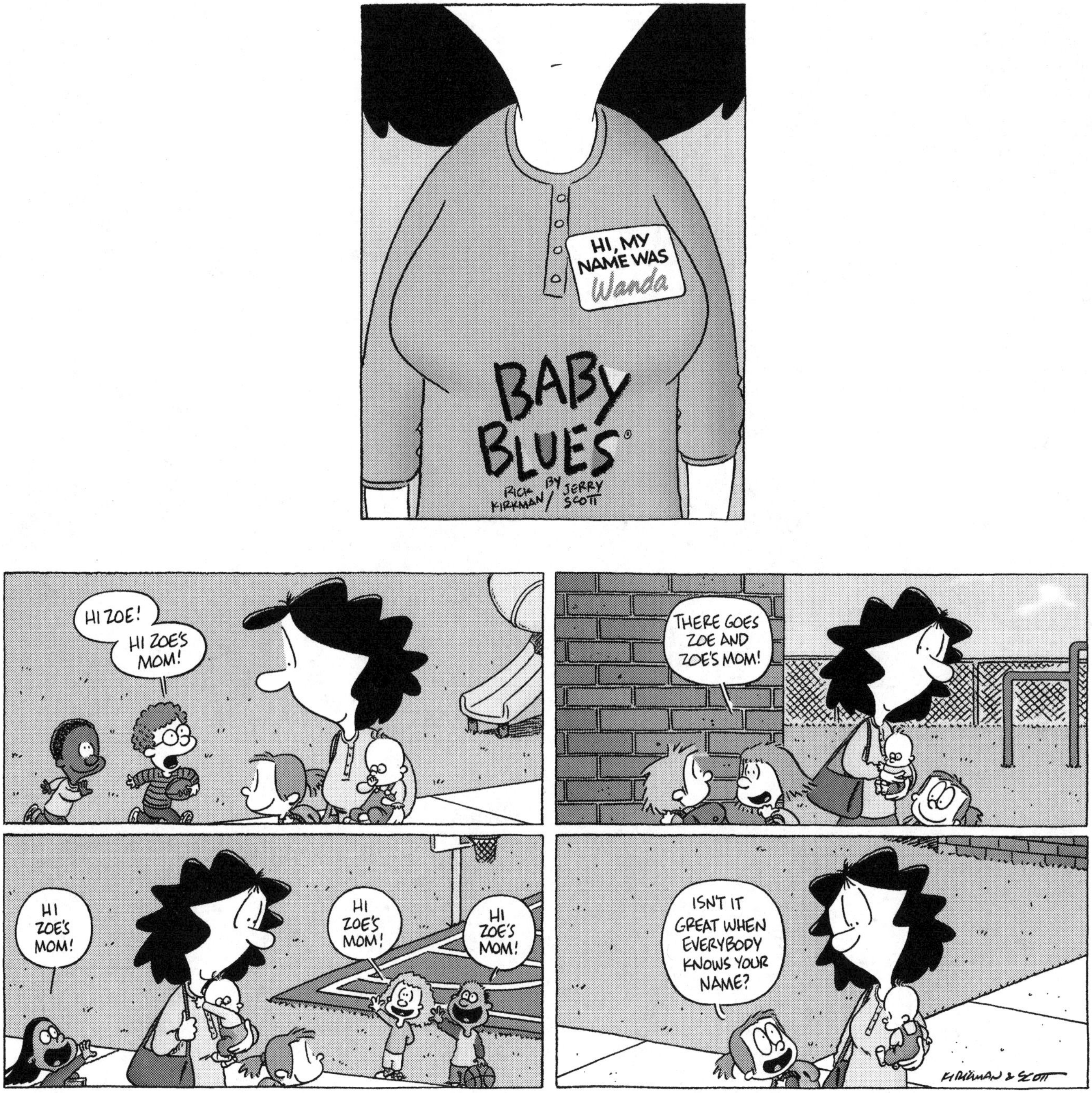
HI, MY NAME WAS Wanda
BABY BLUES®
BY RICK KIRKMAN / JERRY SCOTT
HI ZOE!
HI ZOE'S MOM!
THERE GOES ZOE AND ZOE'S MOM!
HI ZOE'S MOM!
HI ZOE'S MOM!
HI ZOE'S MOM!
ISN'T IT GREAT WHEN EVERYBODY KNOWS YOUR NAME?
KIRKMAN & SCOTT

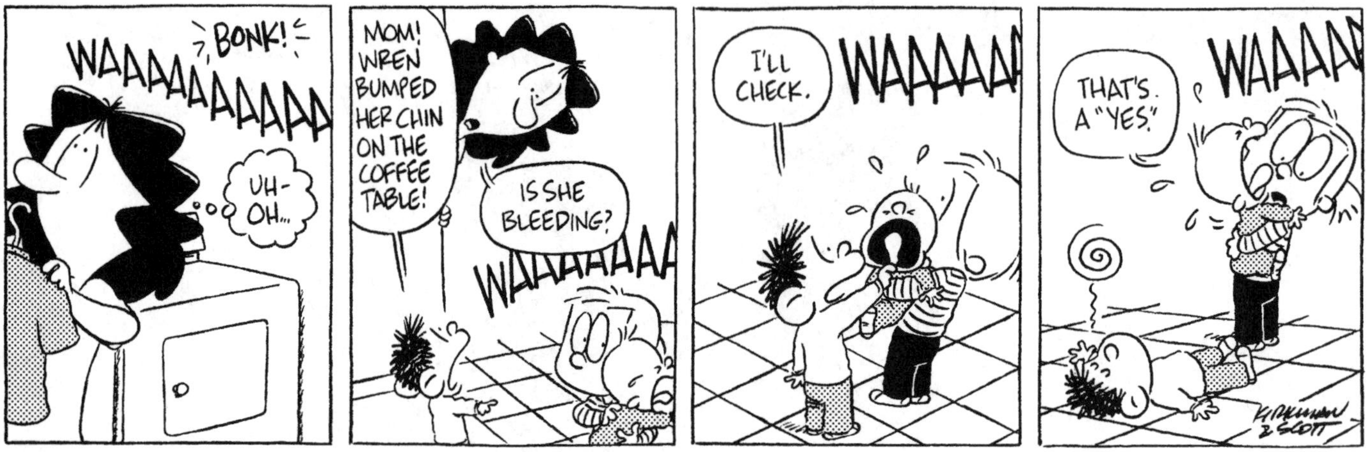
BONK!
WAAAAAAAAAAA
UH-OH...
MOM! WREN BUMPED HER CHIN ON THE COFFEE TABLE!
IS SHE BLEEDING?
WAAAAAAA
I'LL CHECK.
WAAAAAA
THAT'S A "YES."
WAAAA
KIRKMAN & SCOTT

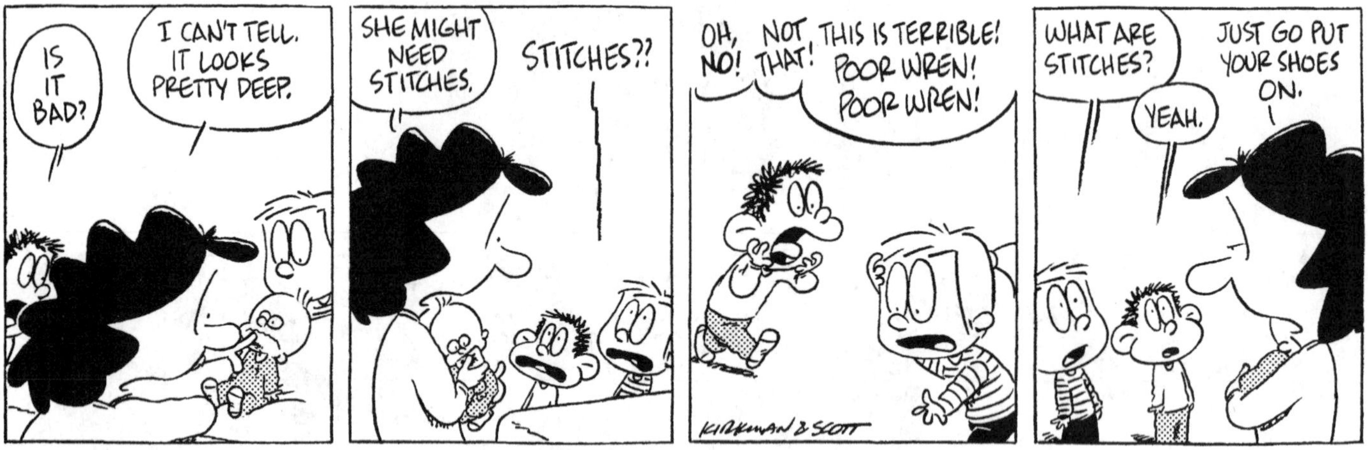
IS IT BAD?
I CAN'T TELL. IT LOOKS PRETTY DEEP.
SHE MIGHT NEED STITCHES.
STITCHES??
OH, NO!
NOT THAT!
THIS IS TERRIBLE! POOR WREN! POOR WREN!
KIRKMAN & SCOTT
WHAT ARE STITCHES?
YEAH.
JUST GO PUT YOUR SHOES ON.

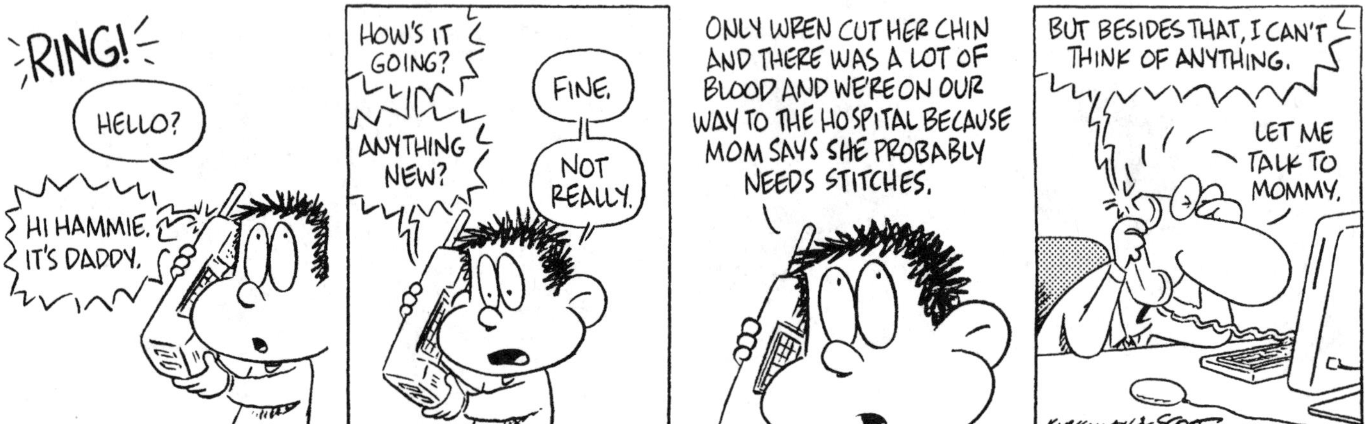
RING!
HELLO?
HI HAMMIE. IT'S DADDY.
HOW'S IT GOING?
FINE.
ANYTHING NEW?
NOT REALLY.
ONLY WREN CUT HER CHIN AND THERE WAS A LOT OF BLOOD AND WE'RE ON OUR WAY TO THE HOSPITAL BECAUSE MOM SAYS SHE PROBABLY NEEDS STITCHES.
BUT BESIDES THAT, I CAN'T THINK OF ANYTHING.
LET ME TALK TO MOMMY.
KIRKMAN & SCOTT

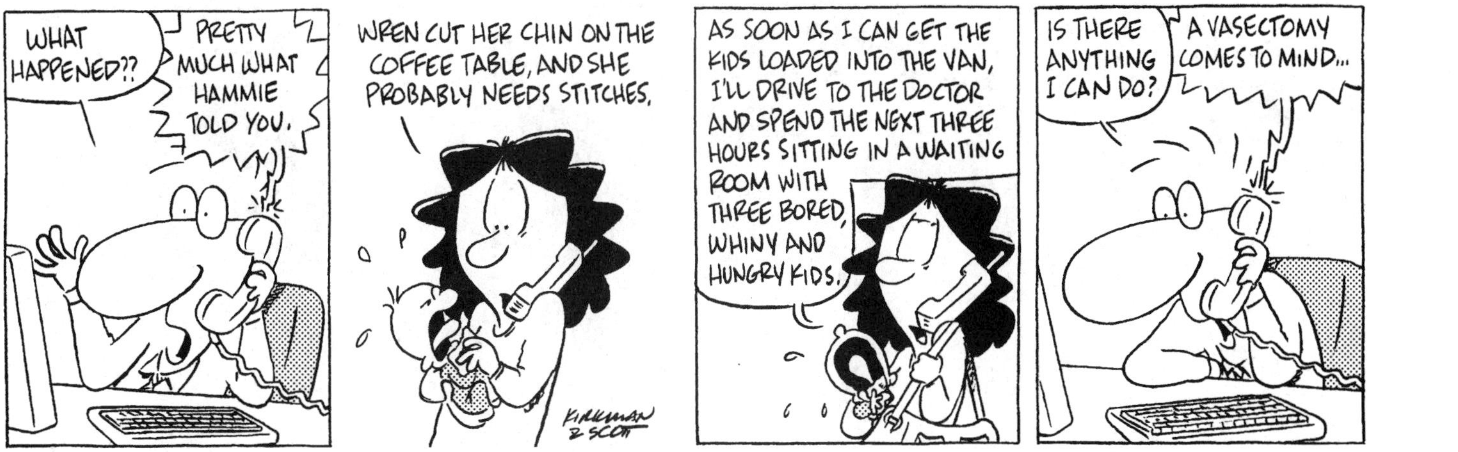
WHAT HAPPENED??
PRETTY MUCH WHAT HAMMIE TOLD YOU.
WREN CUT HER CHIN ON THE COFFEE TABLE, AND SHE PROBABLY NEEDS STITCHES.
KIRKMAN & SCOTT
AS SOON AS I CAN GET THE KIDS LOADED INTO THE VAN, I'LL DRIVE TO THE DOCTOR AND SPEND THE NEXT THREE HOURS SITTING IN A WAITING ROOM WITH THREE BORED, WHINY AND HUNGRY KIDS.
IS THERE ANYTHING I CAN DO?
A VASECTOMY COMES TO MIND...

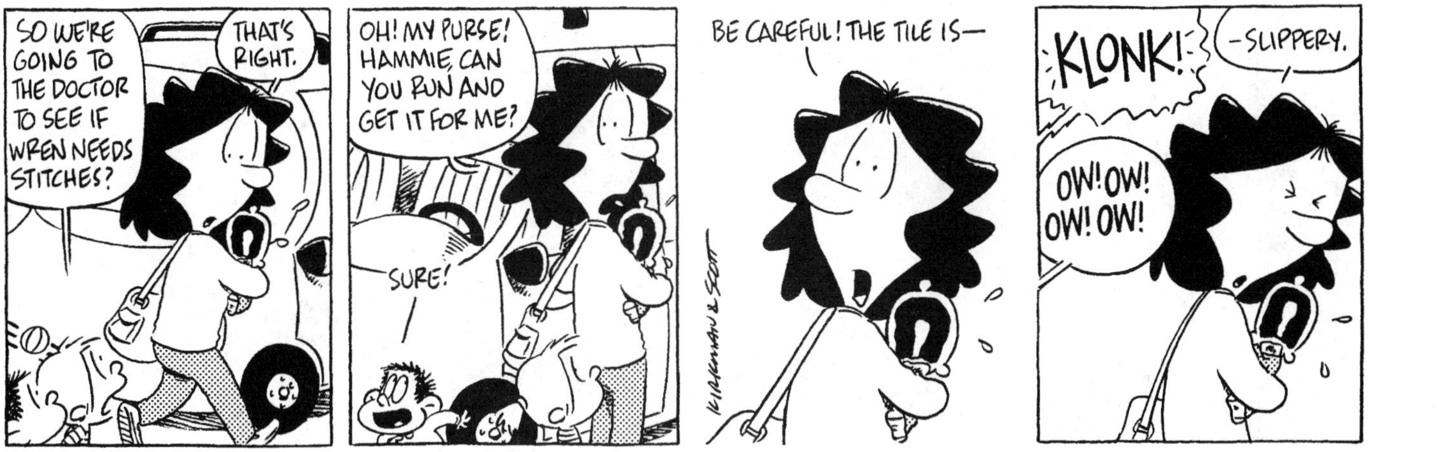
SO WE'RE GOING TO THE DOCTOR TO SEE IF WREN NEEDS STITCHES?
THAT'S RIGHT.
OH! MY PURSE! HAMMIE, CAN YOU RUN AND GET IT FOR ME?
SURE!
BE CAREFUL! THE TILE IS—
KIRKMAN & SCOTT
KLONK!
-SLIPPERY.
OW! OW! OW! OW!

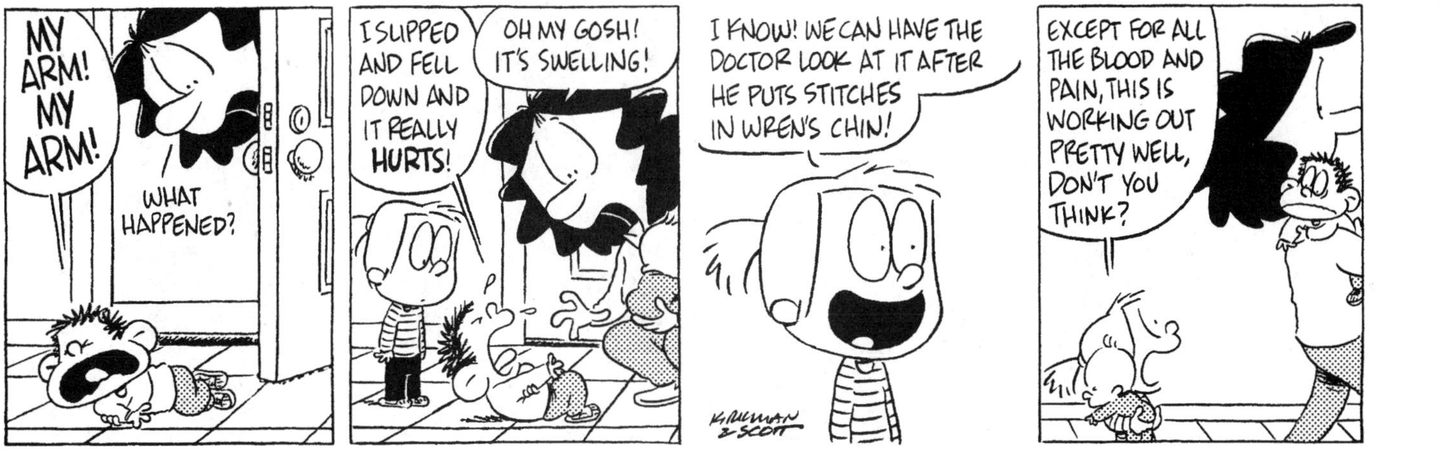
MY ARM! MY ARM!
WHAT HAPPENED?
I SLIPPED AND FELL DOWN AND IT REALLY HURTS!
OH MY GOSH! IT'S SWELLING!
I KNOW! WE CAN HAVE THE DOCTOR LOOK AT IT AFTER HE PUTS STITCHES IN WREN'S CHIN!
KIRKMAN & SCOTT
EXCEPT FOR ALL THE BLOOD AND PAIN, THIS IS WORKING OUT PRETTY WELL, DON'T YOU THINK?

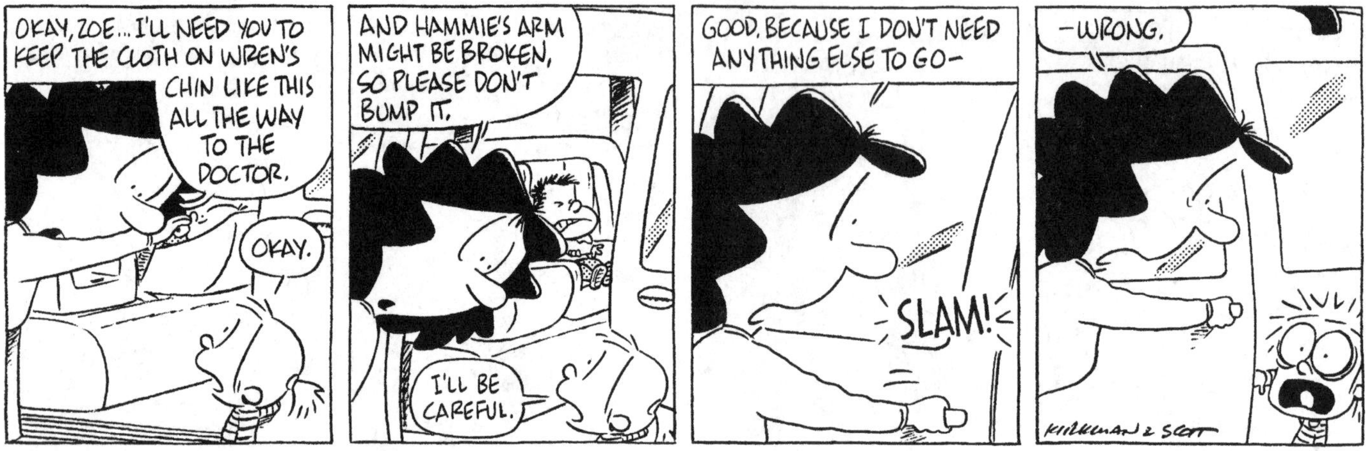
OKAY, ZOE... I'LL NEED YOU TO KEEP THE CLOTH ON WREN'S CHIN LIKE THIS ALL THE WAY TO THE DOCTOR.
OKAY.
AND HAMMIE'S ARM MIGHT BE BROKEN, SO PLEASE DON'T BUMP IT.
I'LL BE CAREFUL.
GOOD. BECAUSE I DON'T NEED ANYTHING ELSE TO GO-
SLAM!
-WRONG.
KIRKMAN & SCOTT

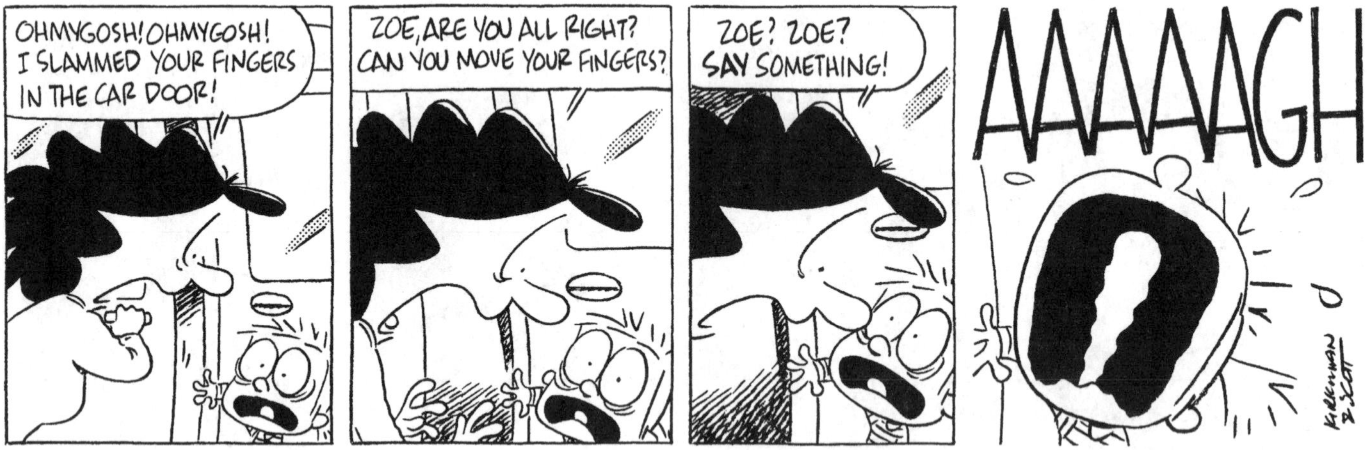
OHMYGOSH! OHMYGOSH! I SLAMMED YOUR FINGERS IN THE CAR DOOR!
ZOE, ARE YOU ALL RIGHT? CAN YOU MOVE YOUR FINGERS?
ZOE? ZOE? SAY SOMETHING!
AAAAAAGH
KIRKMAN & SCOTT

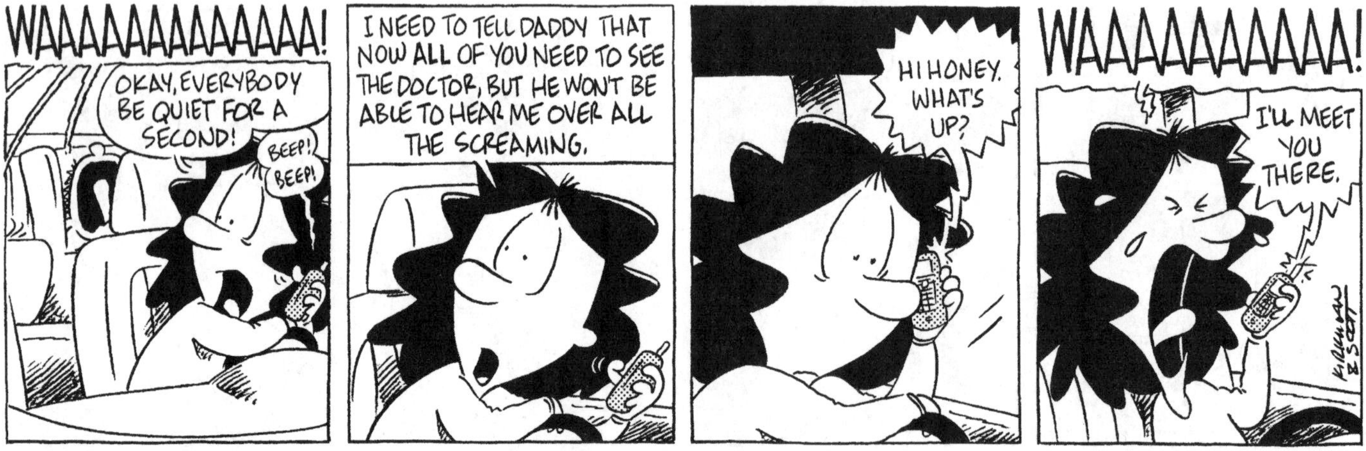
WAAAAAAAAAAAAA!
OKAY, EVERYBODY BE QUIET FOR A SECOND!
BEEP! BEEP!
I NEED TO TELL DADDY THAT NOW ALL OF YOU NEED TO SEE THE DOCTOR, BUT HE WON'T BE ABLE TO HEAR ME OVER ALL THE SCREAMING.
HI HONEY. WHAT'S UP?
WAAAAAAAAAA!
I'LL MEET YOU THERE.
KIRKMAN & SCOTT

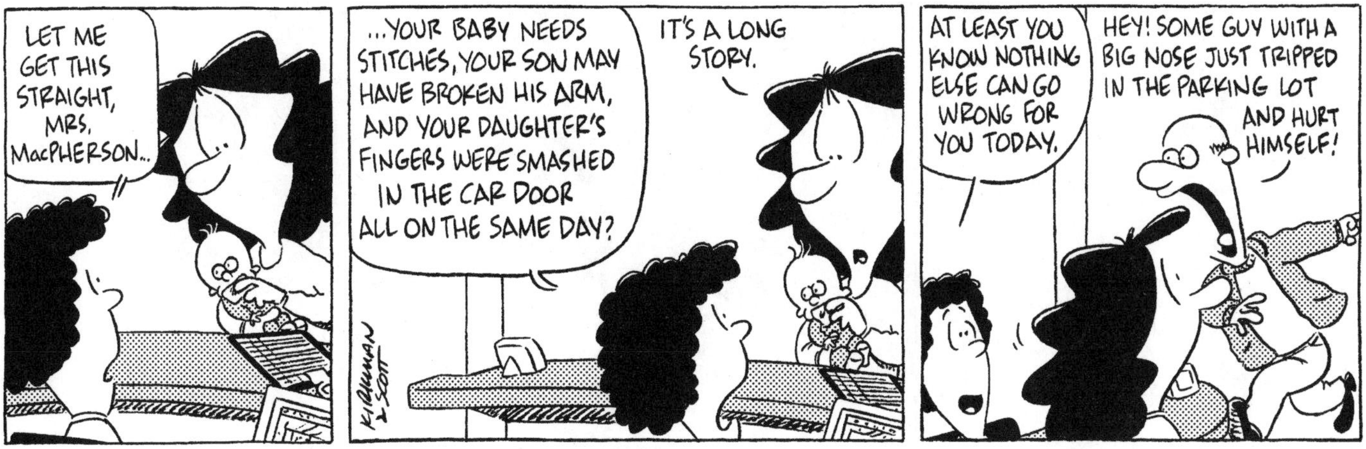
LET ME GET THIS STRAIGHT, MRS. MacPHERSON...
...YOUR BABY NEEDS STITCHES, YOUR SON MAY HAVE BROKEN HIS ARM, AND YOUR DAUGHTER'S FINGERS WERE SMASHED IN THE CAR DOOR ALL ON THE SAME DAY?
IT'S A LONG STORY.
AT LEAST YOU KNOW NOTHING ELSE CAN GO WRONG FOR YOU TODAY.
HEY! SOME GUY WITH A BIG NOSE JUST TRIPPED IN THE PARKING LOT AND HURT HIMSELF!
KIRKMAN & SCOTT

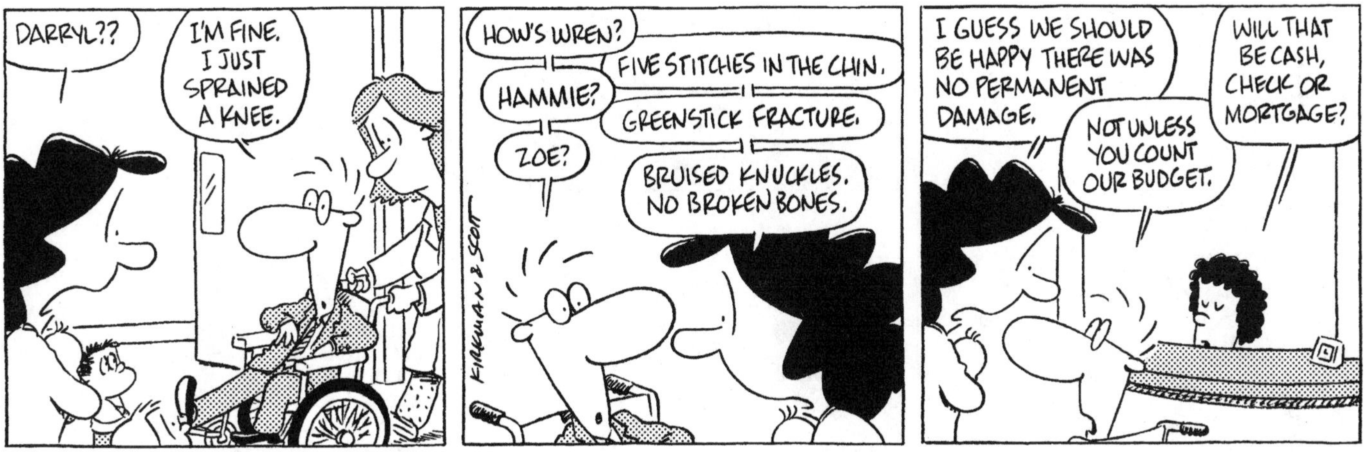
DARRYL??
I'M FINE. I JUST SPRAINED A KNEE.
HOW'S WREN?
FIVE STITCHES IN THE CHIN.
HAMMIE?
GREENSTICK FRACTURE.
ZOE?
BRUISED KNUCKLES. NO BROKEN BONES.
KIRKMAN & SCOTT
I GUESS WE SHOULD BE HAPPY THERE WAS NO PERMANENT DAMAGE.
NOT UNLESS YOU COUNT OUR BUDGET.
WILL THAT BE CASH, CHECK OR MORTGAGE?

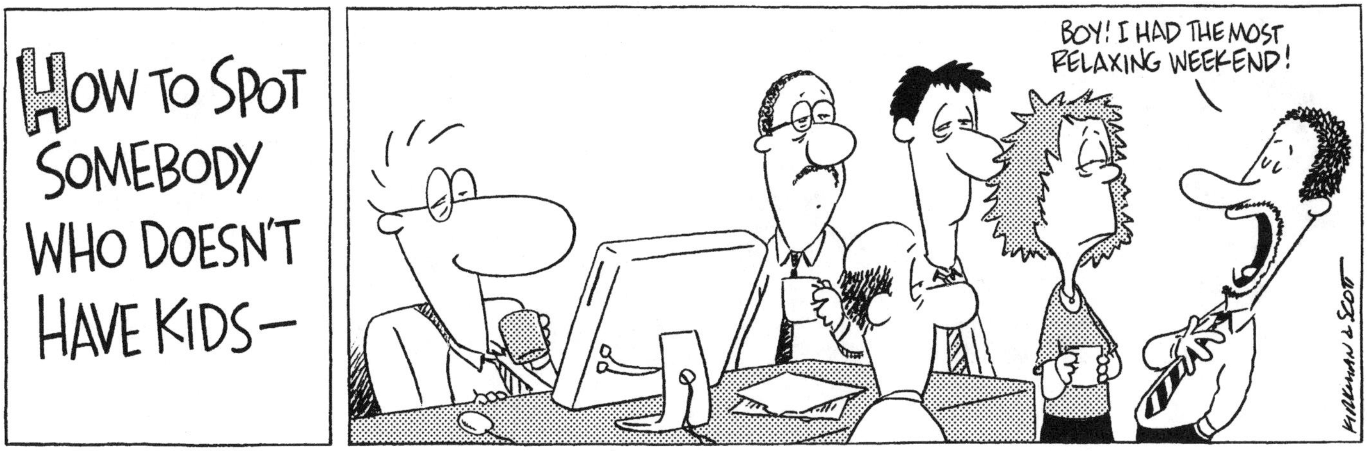
HOW TO SPOT SOMEBODY WHO DOESN'T HAVE KIDS—
BOY! I HAD THE MOST RELAXING WEEKEND!
KIRKMAN & SCOTT

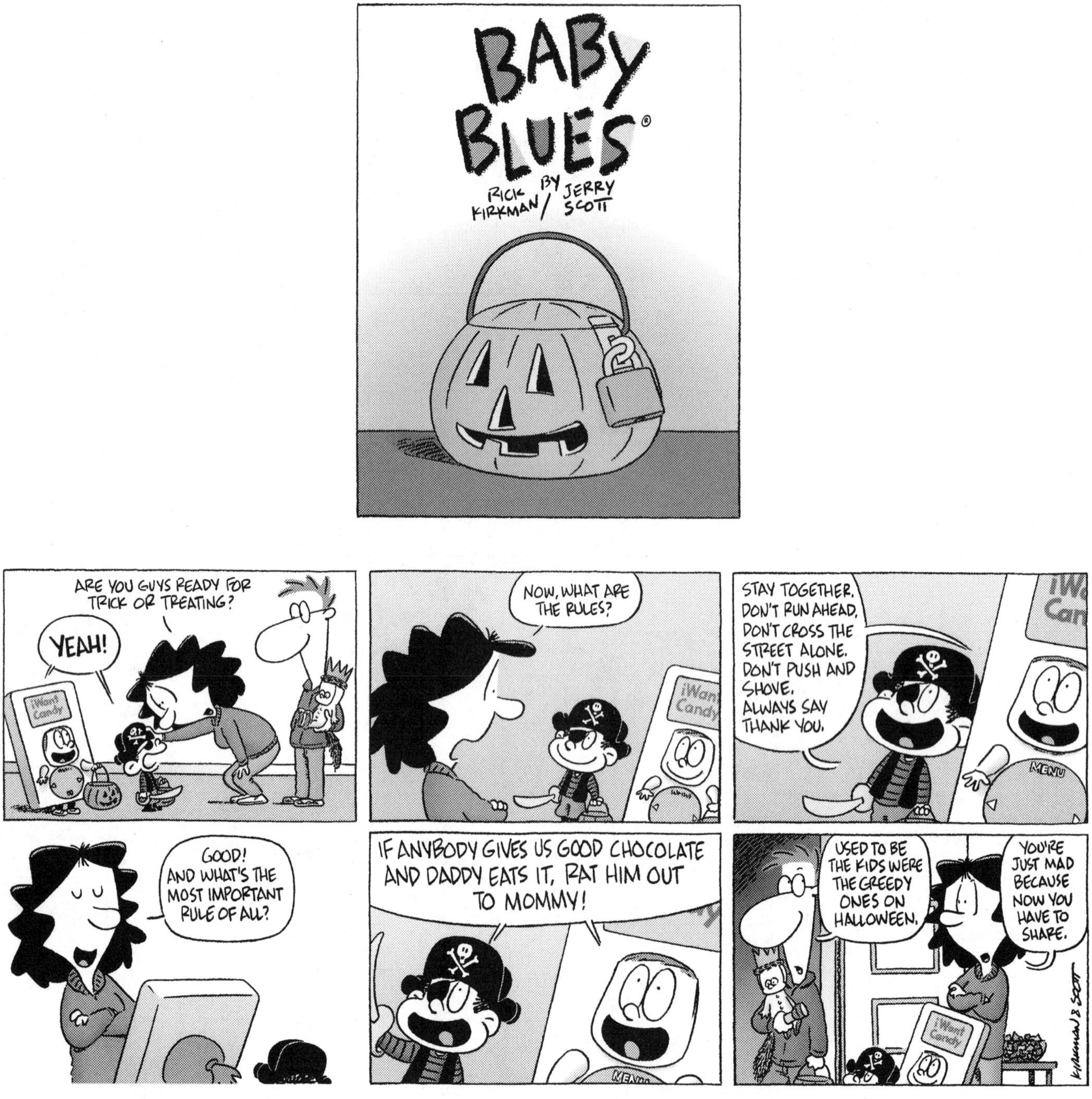
BABY BLUES®
BY RICK KIRKMAN / JERRY SCOTT
ARE YOU GUYS READY FOR TRICK OR TREATING?
YEAH!
iWant Candy
NOW, WHAT ARE THE RULES?
STAY TOGETHER. DON'T RUN AHEAD, DON'T CROSS THE STREET ALONE. DON'T PUSH AND SHOVE. ALWAYS SAY THANK YOU.
MENU
GOOD! AND WHAT'S THE MOST IMPORTANT RULE OF ALL?
IF ANYBODY GIVES US GOOD CHOCOLATE AND DADDY EATS IT, RAT HIM OUT TO MOMMY!
USED TO BE THE KIDS WERE THE GREEDY ONES ON HALLOWEEN.
YOU'RE JUST MAD BECAUSE NOW YOU HAVE TO SHARE.
KIRKMAN & SCOTT

BABY BLUES®
BY RICK KIRKMAN / JERRY SCOTT
37

MATH MATH MATH!
MATH MATH MATH!
MATH MATH MATH MATH MATH!
WHAT ARE YOU DOING?
SINGING.
ABOUT MATH??
YEAH. I MADE UP A SONG ABOUT MATH BECAUSE IT'S MY NEW FAVORITE SUBJECT.
REALLY?
OH YEAH. I LOVE IT.
NUMBERS, NUMBERS, NUMBERS! I JUST LOVE NUMBERS!
WOW!
KIRKMAN & SCOTT
CAN I HAVE SOME MONEY TO PRACTICE ON?

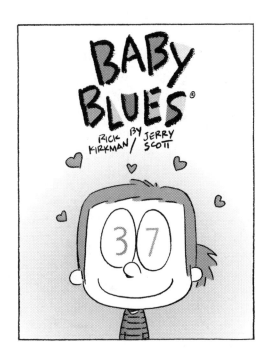

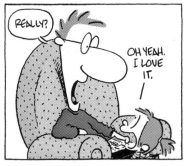

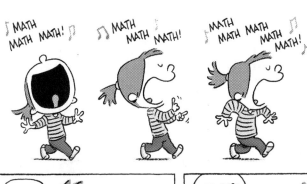

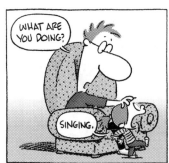

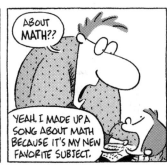

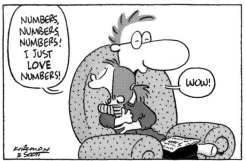

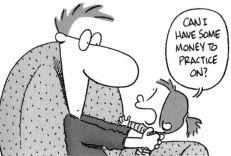

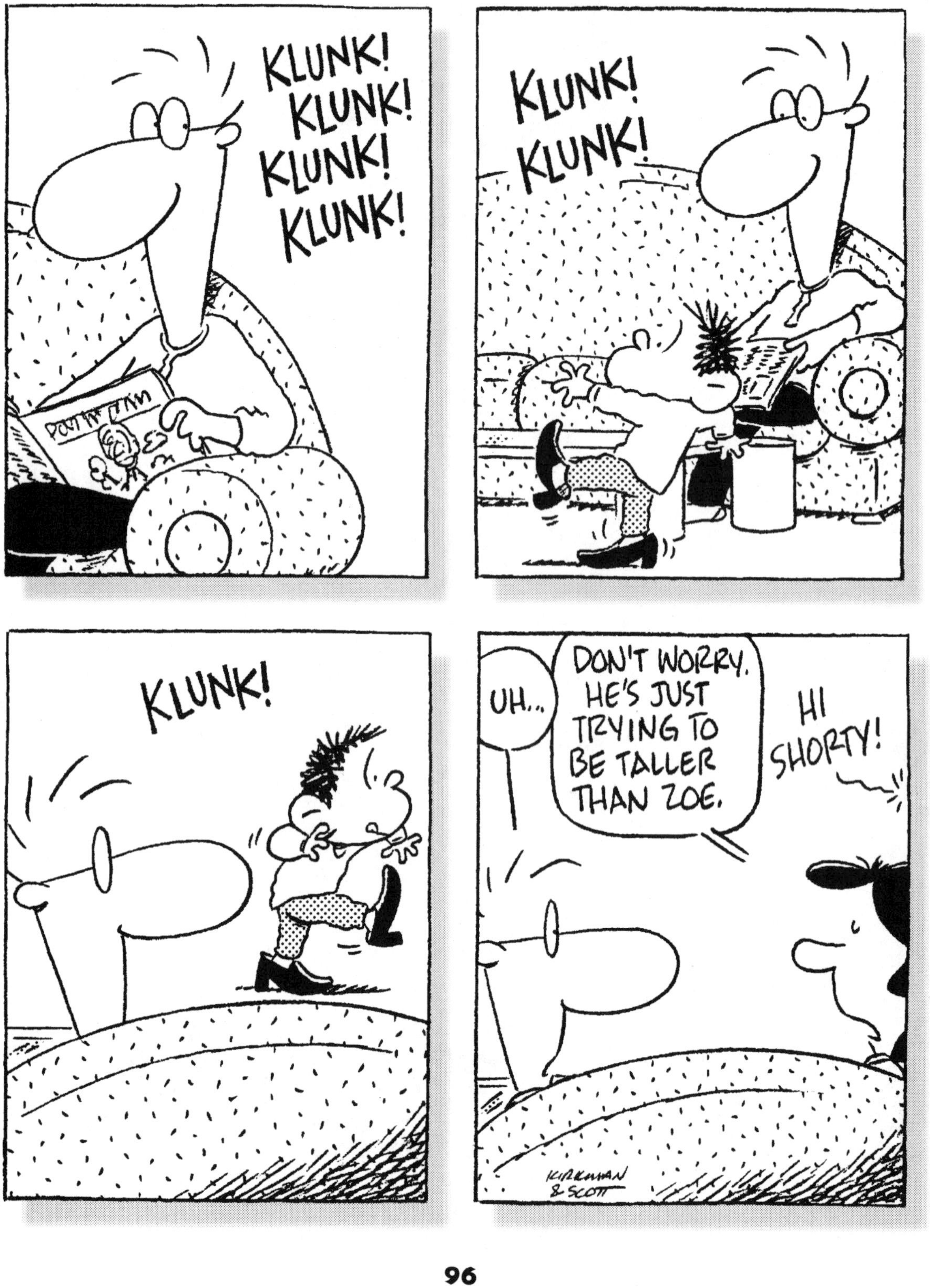
KLUNK! KLUNK! KLUNK! KLUNK!
KLUNK! KLUNK!
KLUNK!
UH...
DON'T WORRY. HE'S JUST TRYING TO BE TALLER THAN ZOE.
HI SHORTY!
KIRKMAN & SCOTT

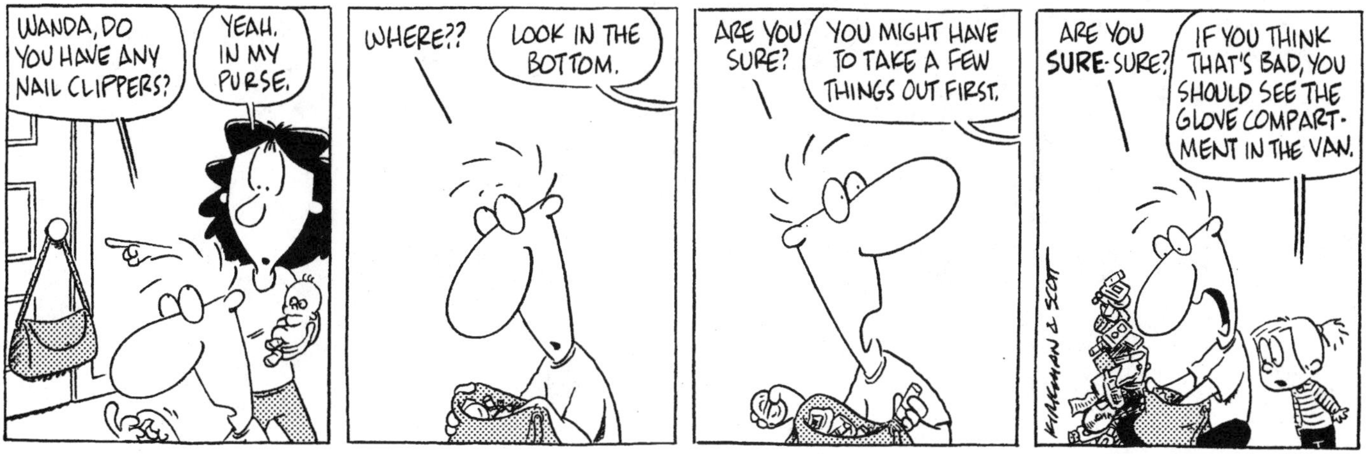
WANDA, DO YOU HAVE ANY NAIL CLIPPERS?
YEAH. IN MY PURSE.
WHERE??
LOOK IN THE BOTTOM.
ARE YOU SURE?
YOU MIGHT HAVE TO TAKE A FEW THINGS OUT FIRST.
ARE YOU **SURE**-SURE?
IF YOU THINK THAT'S BAD, YOU SHOULD SEE THE GLOVE COMPARTMENT IN THE VAN.
KIRKMAN & SCOTT

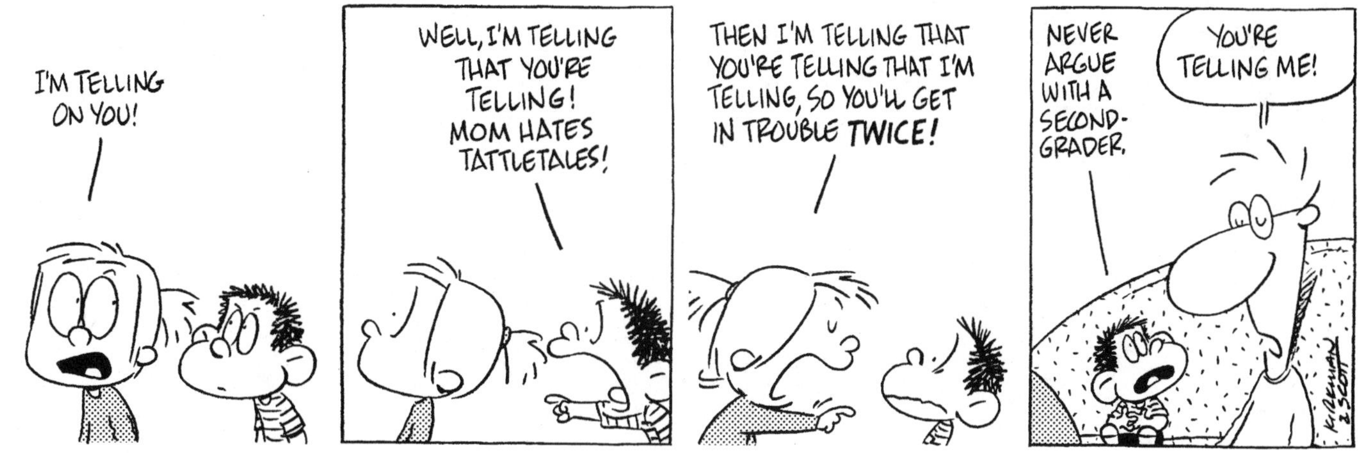
I'M TELLING ON YOU!
WELL, I'M TELLING THAT YOU'RE TELLING! MOM HATES TATTLETALES!
THEN I'M TELLING THAT YOU'RE TELLING THAT I'M TELLING, SO YOU'LL GET IN TROUBLE **TWICE**!
NEVER ARGUE WITH A SECOND-GRADER.
YOU'RE TELLING ME!
KIRKMAN & SCOTT

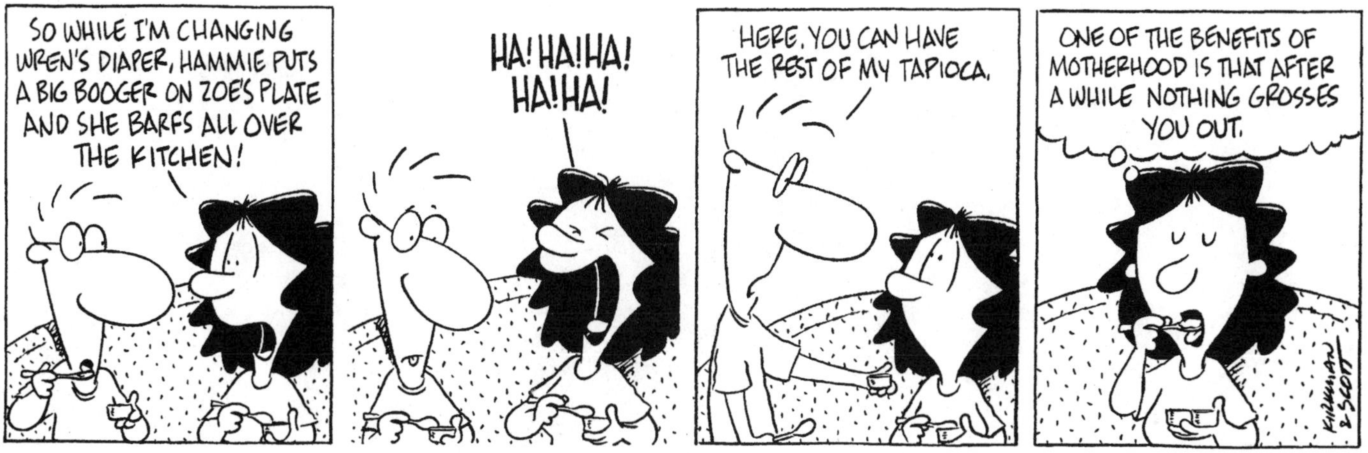
SO WHILE I'M CHANGING WREN'S DIAPER, HAMMIE PUTS A BIG BOOGER ON ZOE'S PLATE AND SHE BARFS ALL OVER THE KITCHEN!
HA! HA! HA! HA! HA!
HERE. YOU CAN HAVE THE REST OF MY TAPIOCA.
ONE OF THE BENEFITS OF MOTHERHOOD IS THAT AFTER A WHILE NOTHING GROSSES YOU OUT.
KIRKMAN & SCOTT

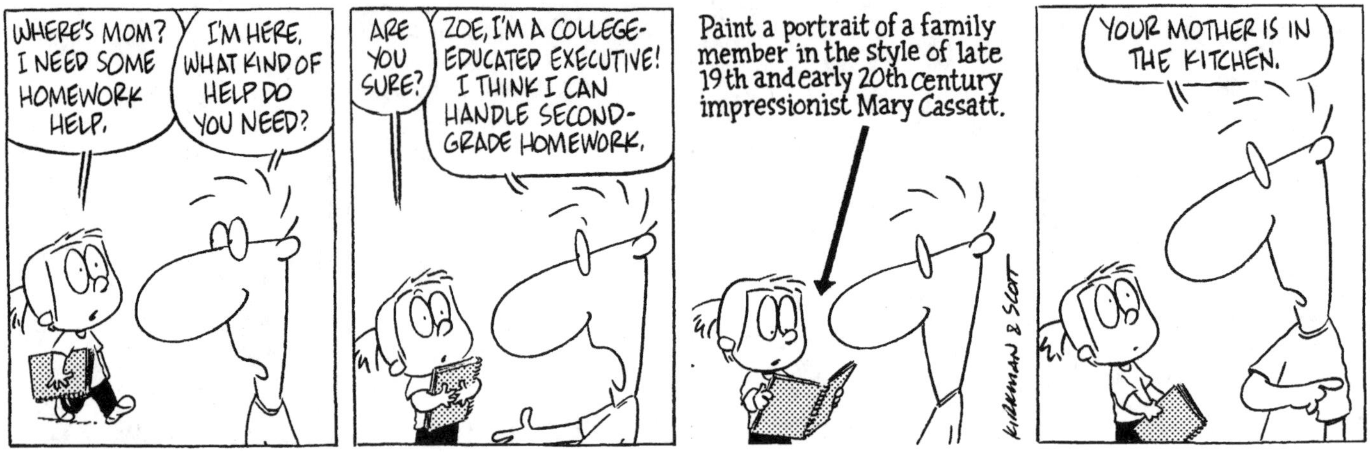
WHERE'S MOM? I NEED SOME HOMEWORK HELP.
I'M HERE. WHAT KIND OF HELP DO YOU NEED?
ARE YOU SURE?
ZOE, I'M A COLLEGE-EDUCATED EXECUTIVE! I THINK I CAN HANDLE SECOND-GRADE HOMEWORK.
Paint a portrait of a family member in the style of late 19th and early 20th century impressionist Mary Cassatt.
KIRKMAN & SCOTT
YOUR MOTHER IS IN THE KITCHEN.

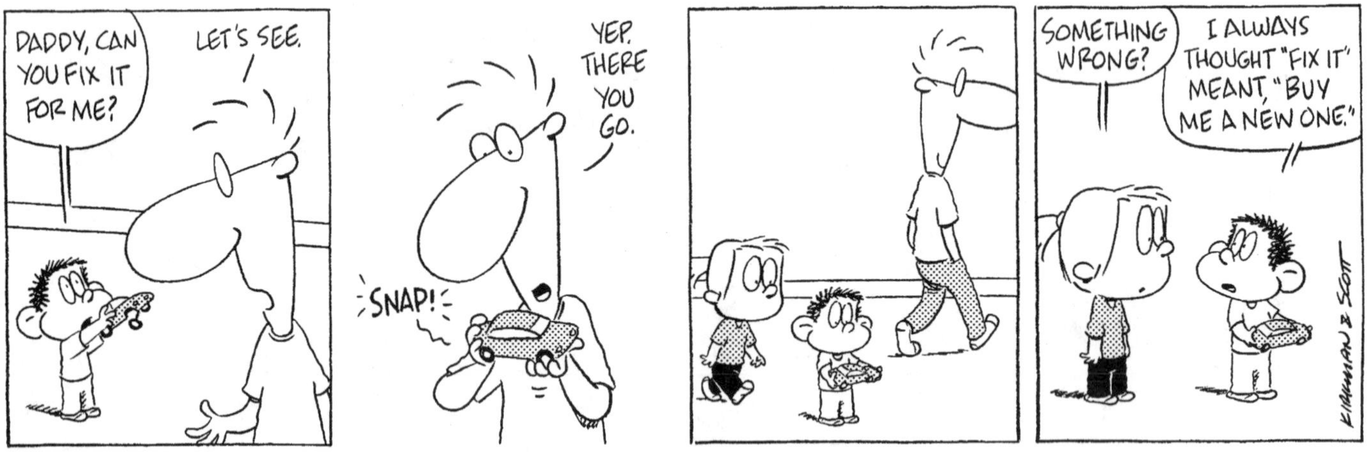
DADDY, CAN YOU FIX IT FOR ME?
LET'S SEE.
YEP. THERE YOU GO.
SNAP!
SOMETHING WRONG?
I ALWAYS THOUGHT "FIX IT" MEANT, "BUY ME A NEW ONE."
KIRKMAN & SCOTT

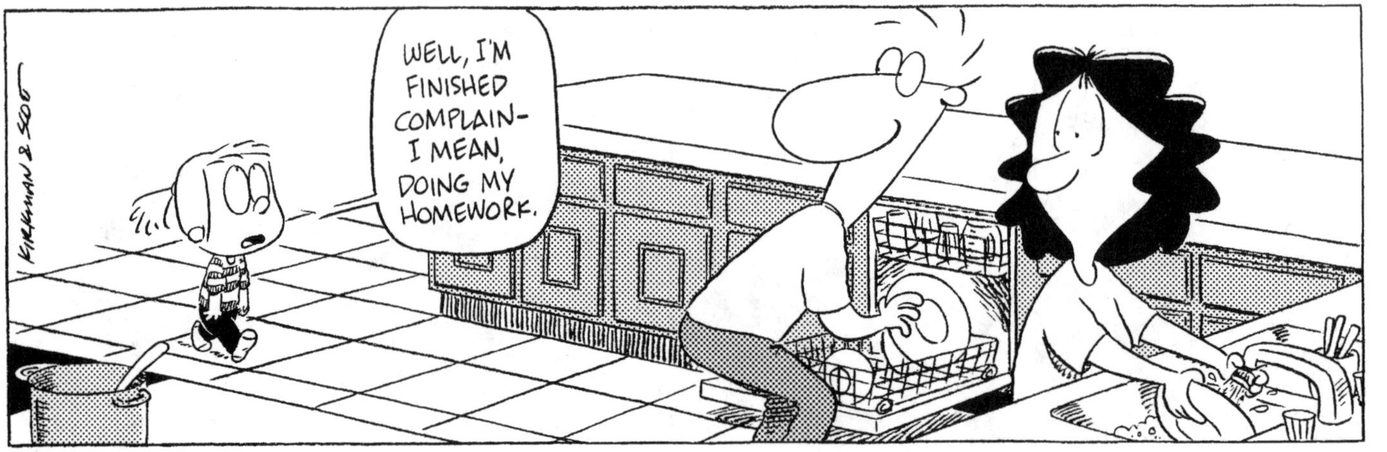
KIRKMAN & SCOTT
WELL, I'M FINISHED COMPLAIN- I MEAN, DOING MY HOMEWORK.

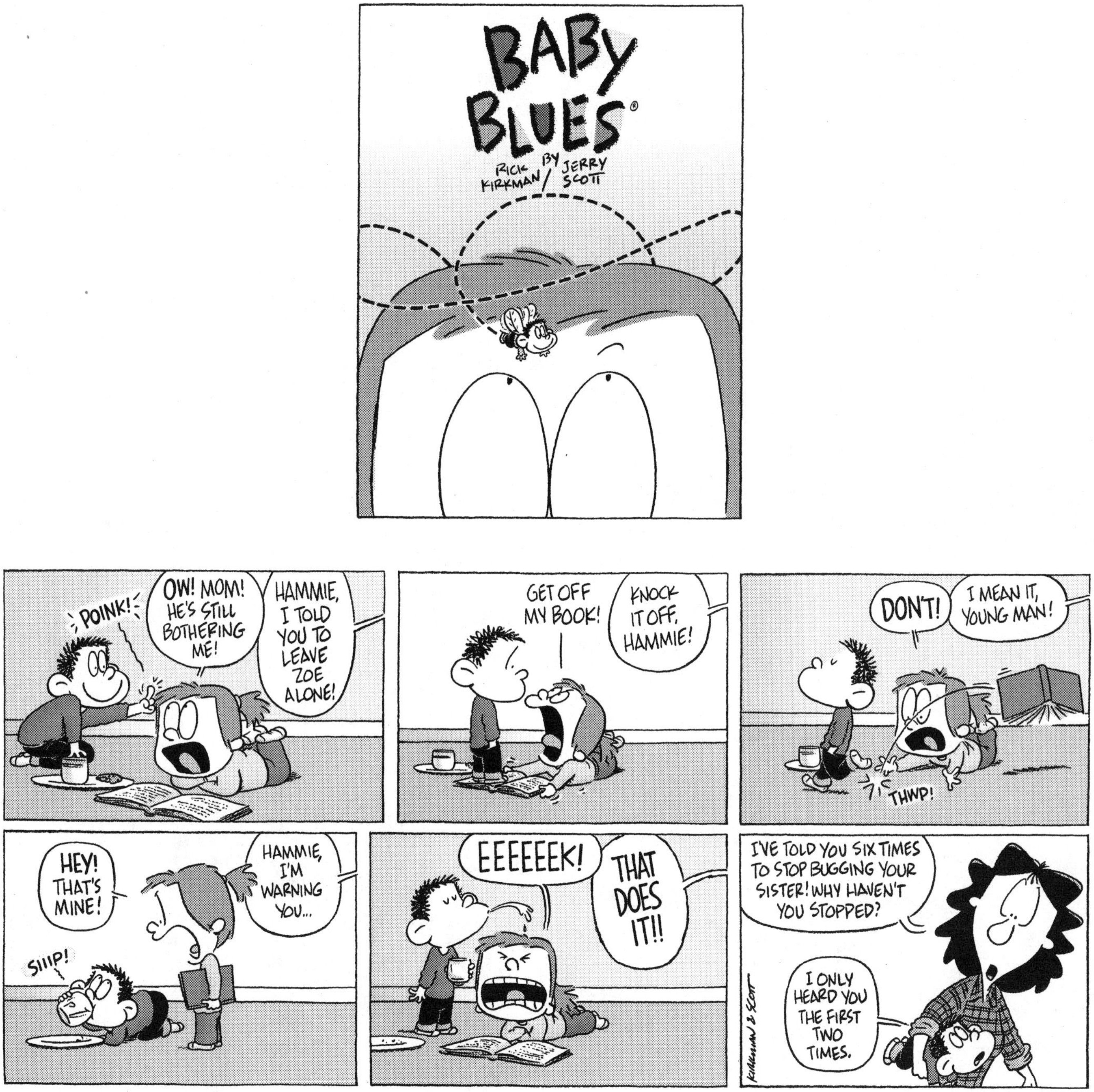
BABY BLUES®
BY RICK KIRKMAN / JERRY SCOTT
POINK!
OW! MOM! HE'S STILL BOTHERING ME!
HAMMIE, I TOLD YOU TO LEAVE ZOE ALONE!
GET OFF MY BOOK!
KNOCK IT OFF, HAMMIE!
DON'T!
I MEAN IT, YOUNG MAN!
THWP!
HEY! THAT'S MINE!
SIIIP!
HAMMIE, I'M WARNING YOU...
EEEEEEK!
THAT DOES IT!!
I'VE TOLD YOU SIX TIMES TO STOP BUGGING YOUR SISTER! WHY HAVEN'T YOU STOPPED?
I ONLY HEARD YOU THE FIRST TWO TIMES.
KIRKMAN & SCOTT

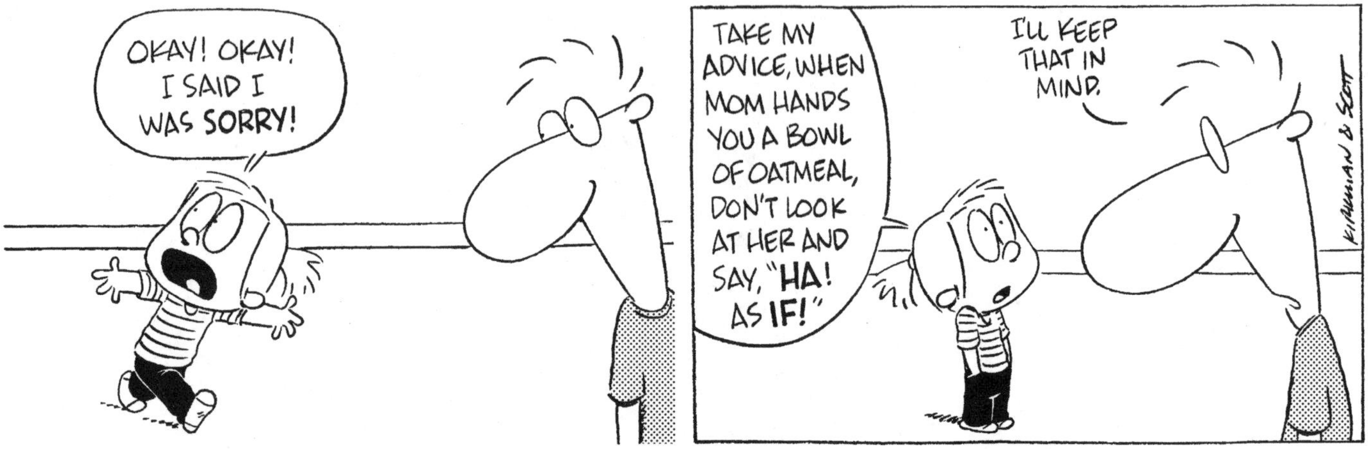
OKAY! OKAY! I SAID I WAS SORRY!
TAKE MY ADVICE, WHEN MOM HANDS YOU A BOWL OF OATMEAL, DON'T LOOK AT HER AND SAY, "HA! AS IF!"
I'LL KEEP THAT IN MIND.
KIRKMAN & SCOTT

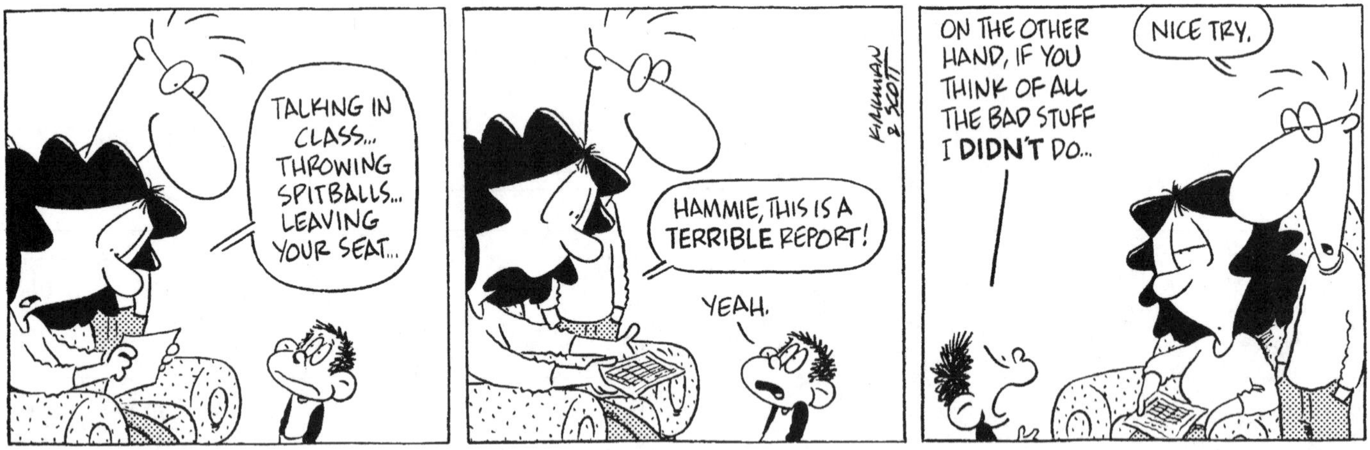
TALKING IN CLASS... THROWING SPITBALLS... LEAVING YOUR SEAT...
HAMMIE, THIS IS A TERRIBLE REPORT!
YEAH.
KIRKMAN & SCOTT
ON THE OTHER HAND, IF YOU THINK OF ALL THE BAD STUFF I DIDN'T DO...
NICE TRY.

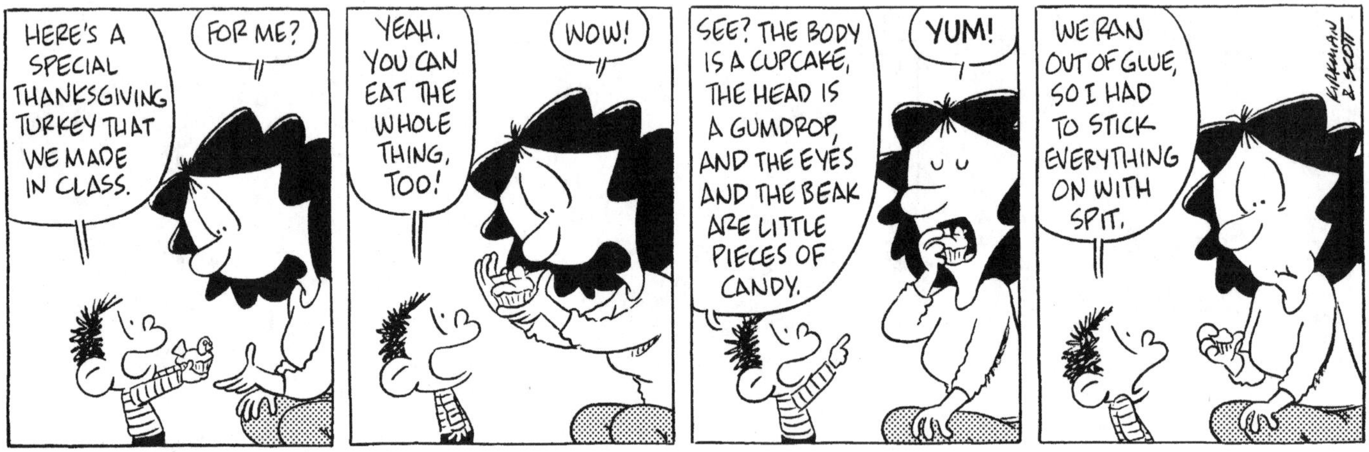
HERE'S A SPECIAL THANKSGIVING TURKEY THAT WE MADE IN CLASS.
FOR ME?
YEAH. YOU CAN EAT THE WHOLE THING, TOO!
WOW!
SEE? THE BODY IS A CUPCAKE, THE HEAD IS A GUMDROP, AND THE EYES AND THE BEAK ARE LITTLE PIECES OF CANDY.
YUM!
WE RAN OUT OF GLUE, SO I HAD TO STICK EVERYTHING ON WITH SPIT.
KIRKMAN & SCOTT

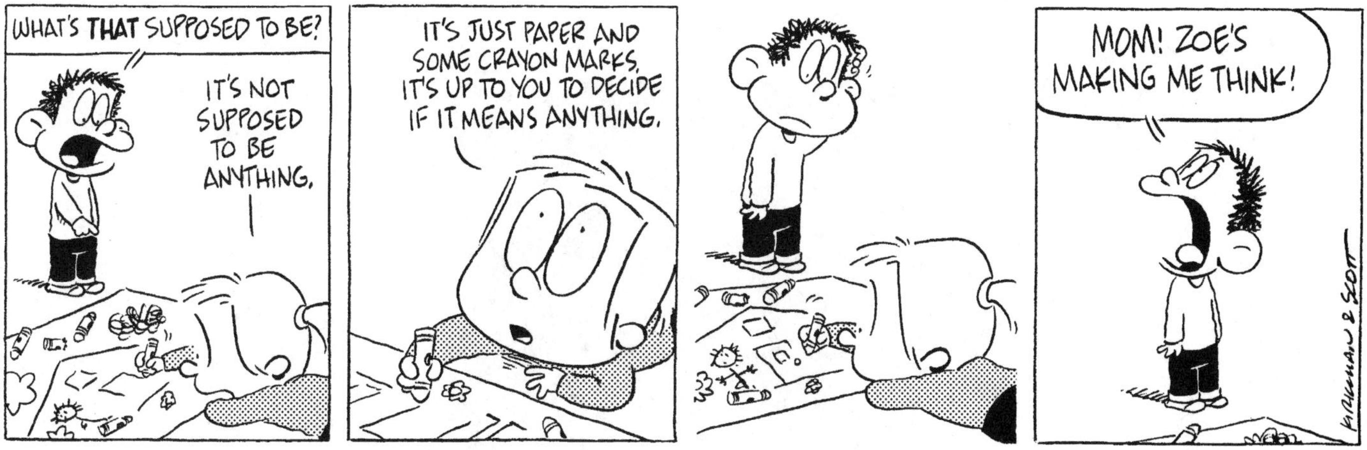
WHAT'S THAT SUPPOSED TO BE?
IT'S NOT SUPPOSED TO BE ANYTHING.
IT'S JUST PAPER AND SOME CRAYON MARKS. IT'S UP TO YOU TO DECIDE IF IT MEANS ANYTHING.
MOM! ZOE'S MAKING ME THINK!

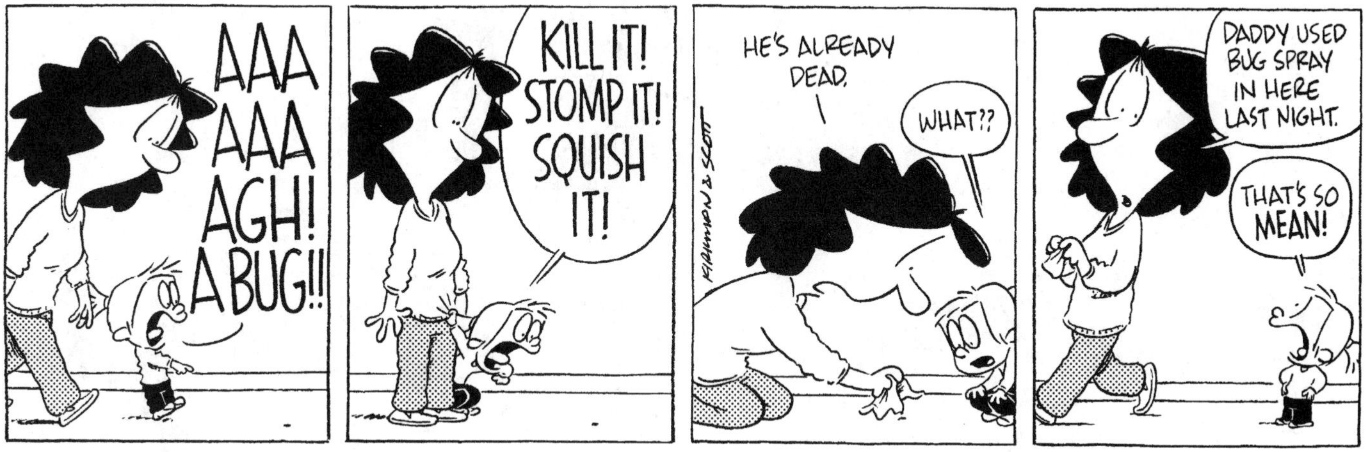
AAAAAAAGH! A BUG!!
KILL IT! STOMP IT! SQUISH IT!
HE'S ALREADY DEAD.
WHAT??
DADDY USED BUG SPRAY IN HERE LAST NIGHT.
THAT'S SO MEAN!

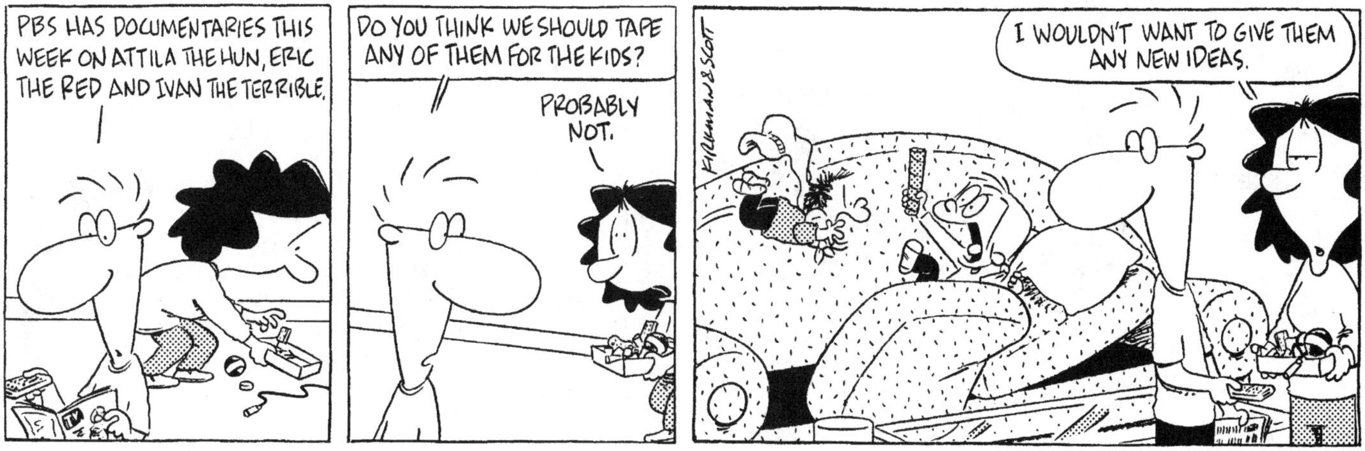
PBS HAS DOCUMENTARIES THIS WEEK ON ATTILA THE HUN, ERIC THE RED AND IVAN THE TERRIBLE.
DO YOU THINK WE SHOULD TAPE ANY OF THEM FOR THE KIDS?
PROBABLY NOT.
I WOULDN'T WANT TO GIVE THEM ANY NEW IDEAS.

BABY BLUES
By
Rick Kirkman
& Jerry Scott

IT'S QUIET. WHERE ARE THE KIDS?
WATCHING CARTOONS.
WHAT??
WANDA, I THOUGHT WE DIDN'T WANT THEM WATCHING TV ON THE WEEKEND!
WE DON'T...
...BUT I HAVE TO GET SOME THINGS DONE AROUND HERE, AND IT'S THE ONLY THING THAT WILL KEEP THEM QUIET AND IN ONE PLACE.
KIRKMAN & SCOTT
BESIDES, WHAT HARM CAN A FEW MINUTES OF CARTOONS DO?
KNOCK! KNOCK! KNOCK!
HERE'S A LIST OF OUR CEREAL AND TOY DEMANDS.

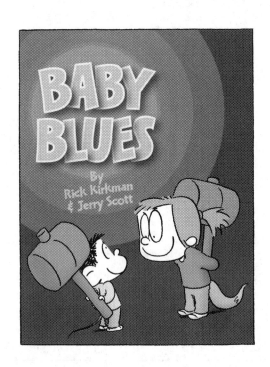

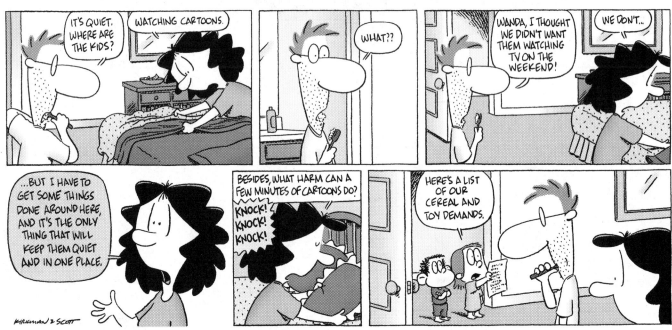

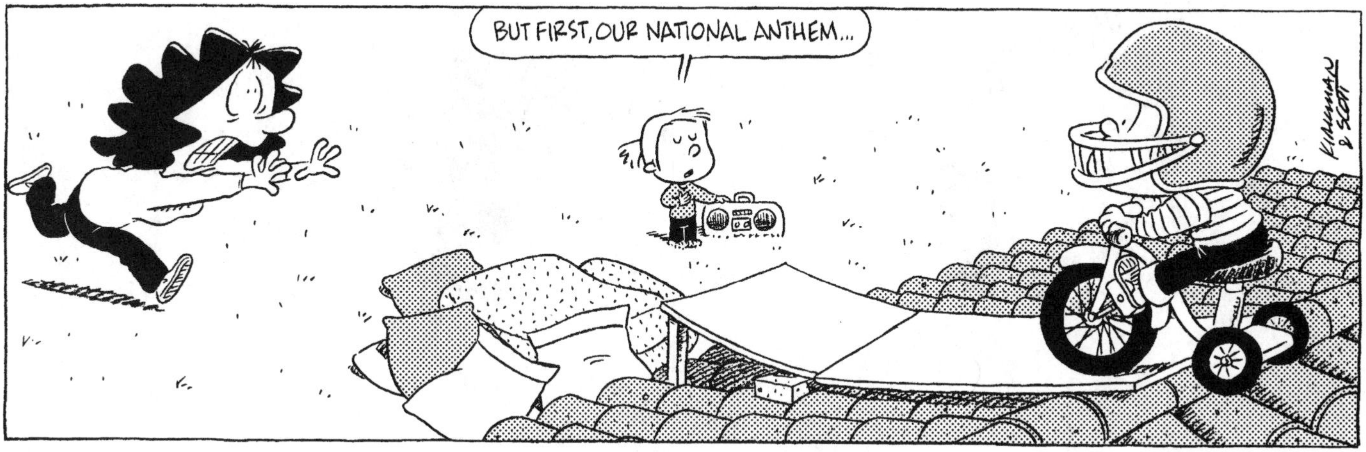
BUT FIRST, OUR NATIONAL ANTHEM...
KIRKMAN & SCOTT

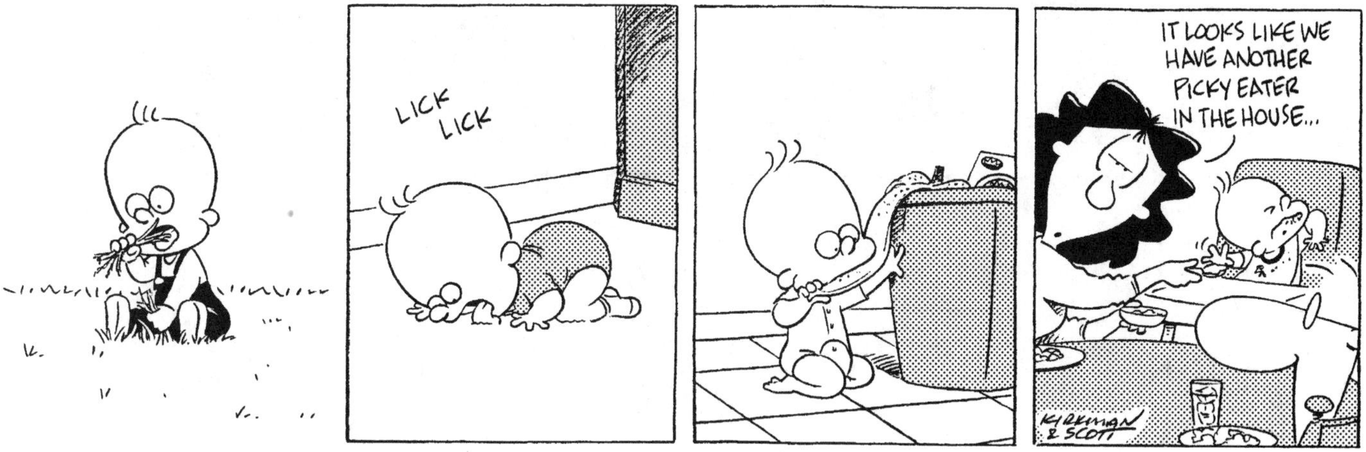
LICK
LICK
IT LOOKS LIKE WE HAVE ANOTHER PICKY EATER IN THE HOUSE...
KIRKMAN & SCOTT

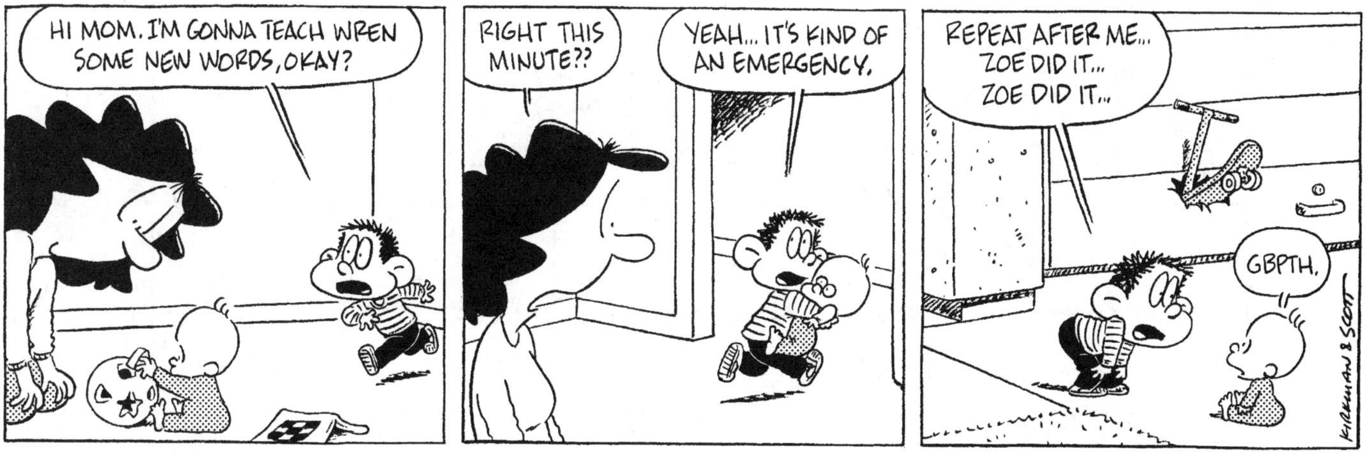
HI MOM. I'M GONNA TEACH WREN SOME NEW WORDS, OKAY?
RIGHT THIS MINUTE??
YEAH... IT'S KIND OF AN EMERGENCY.
REPEAT AFTER ME... ZOE DID IT... ZOE DID IT...
GBPTH.
KIRKMAN & SCOTT

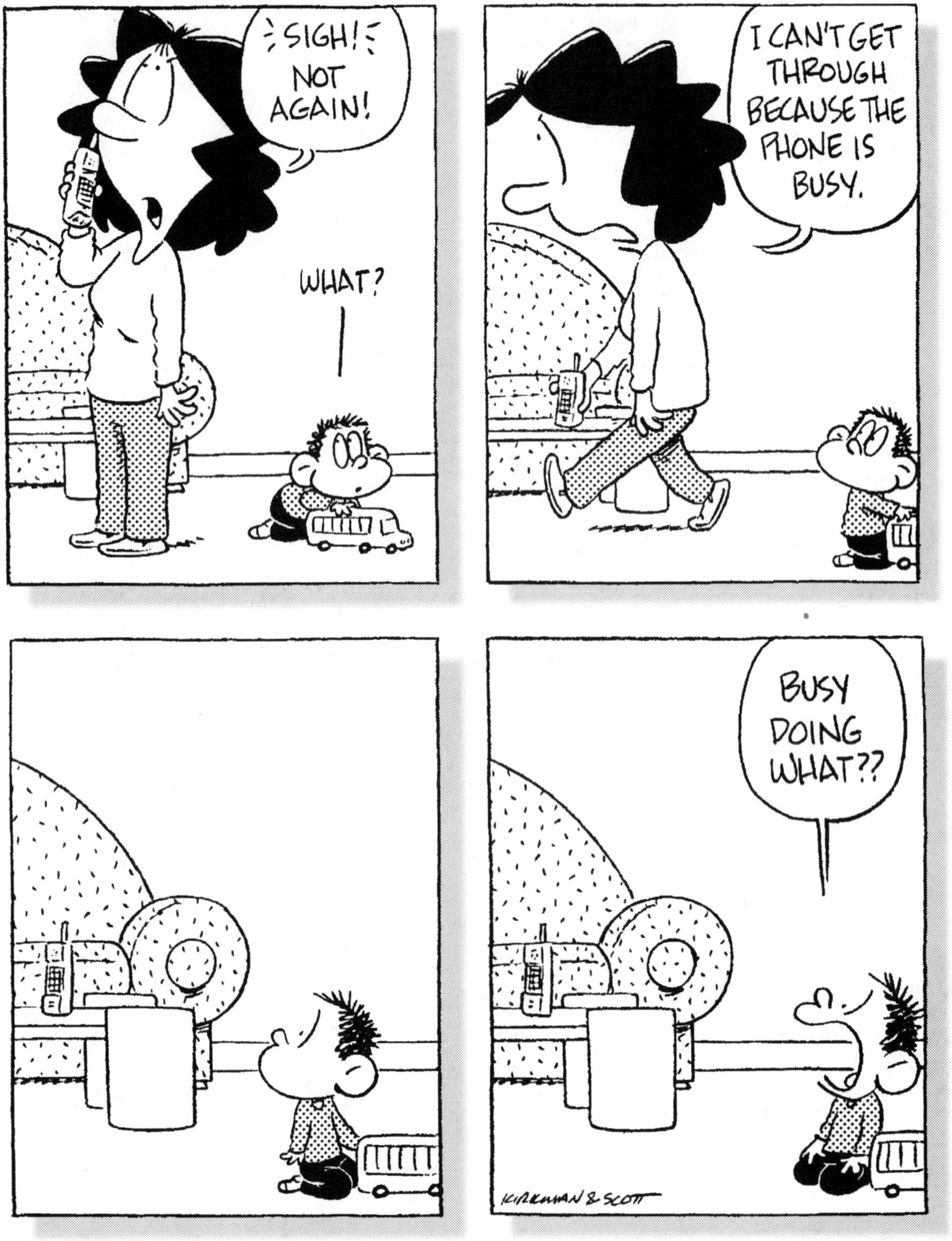
SIGH! NOT AGAIN!
WHAT?
I CAN'T GET THROUGH BECAUSE THE PHONE IS BUSY.
BUSY DOING WHAT??
KIRKMAN & SCOTT

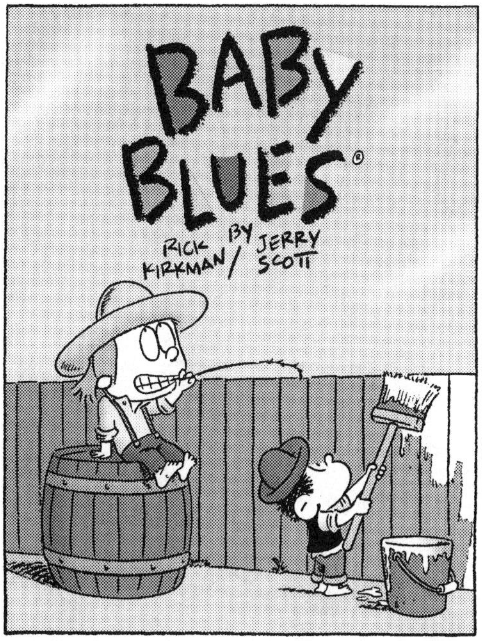
BABY BLUES®
BY RICK KIRKMAN / JERRY SCOTT

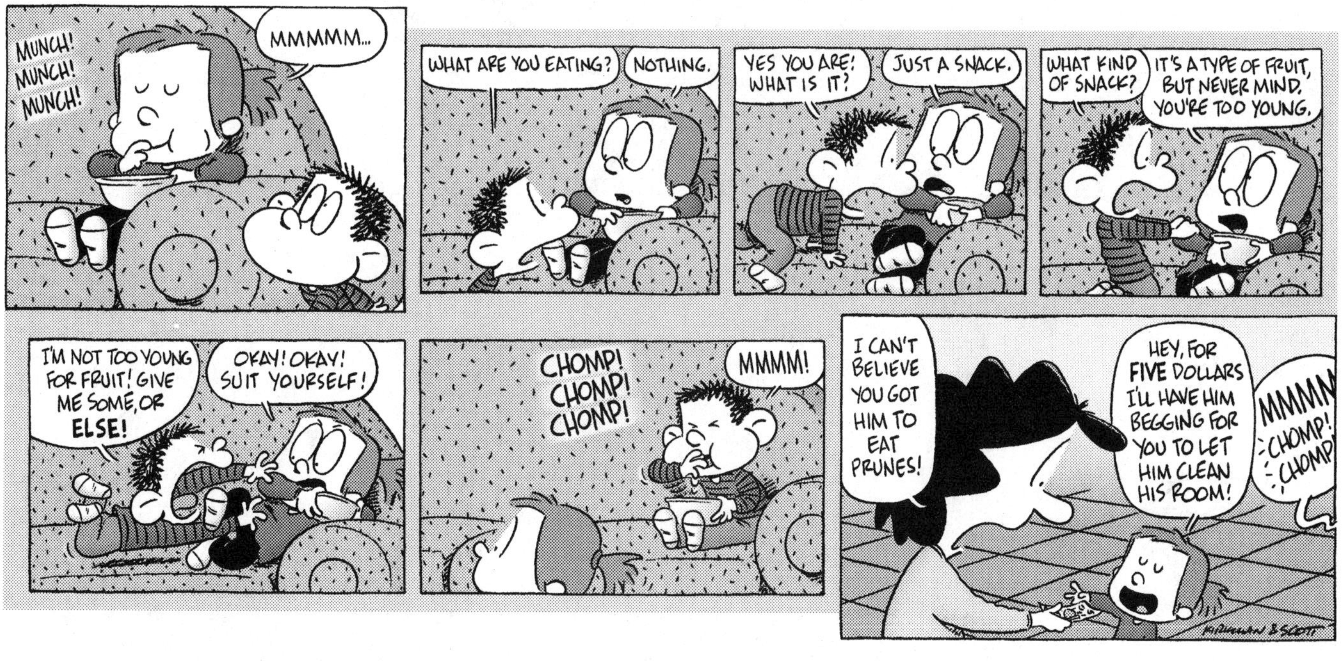
MUNCH! MUNCH! MUNCH!
MMMMM...
WHAT ARE YOU EATING?
NOTHING.
YES YOU ARE! WHAT IS IT?
JUST A SNACK.
WHAT KIND OF SNACK?
IT'S A TYPE OF FRUIT, BUT NEVER MIND. YOU'RE TOO YOUNG.
I'M NOT TOO YOUNG FOR FRUIT! GIVE ME SOME, OR ELSE!
OKAY! OKAY! SUIT YOURSELF!
CHOMP! CHOMP! CHOMP!
MMMM!
I CAN'T BELIEVE YOU GOT HIM TO EAT PRUNES!
HEY, FOR FIVE DOLLARS I'LL HAVE HIM BEGGING FOR YOU TO LET HIM CLEAN HIS ROOM!
MMMM
CHOMP! CHOMP!
KIRKMAN & SCOTT

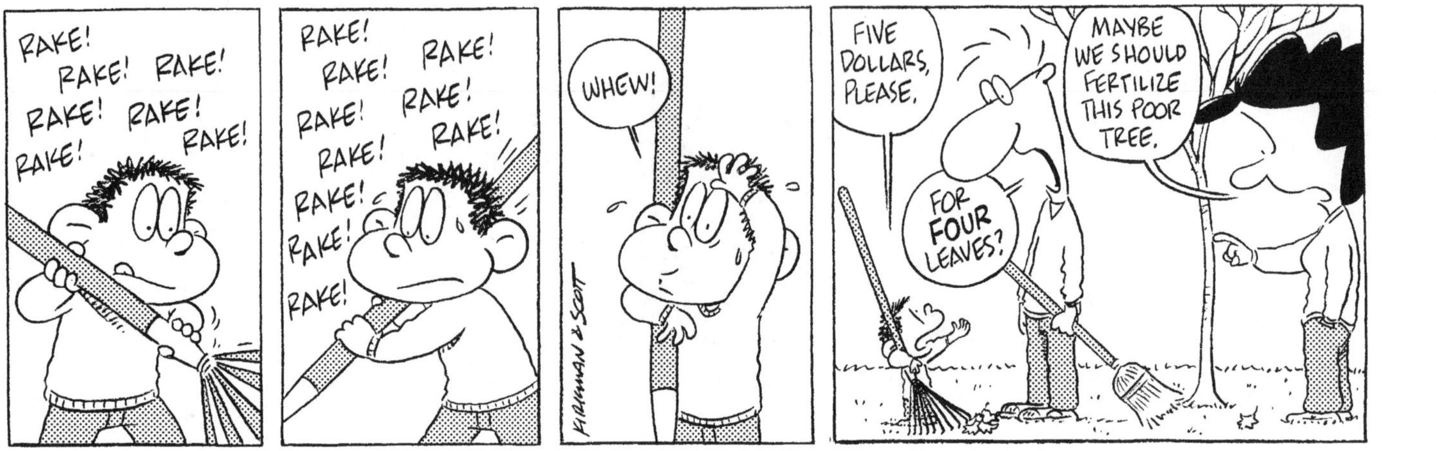
RAKE! RAKE! RAKE! RAKE! RAKE! RAKE! RAKE!
RAKE! RAKE! RAKE! RAKE! RAKE! RAKE! RAKE! RAKE! RAKE! RAKE!
WHEW!
KIRKMAN & SCOTT
FIVE DOLLARS, PLEASE.
FOR **FOUR** LEAVES?
MAYBE WE SHOULD FERTILIZE THIS POOR TREE.

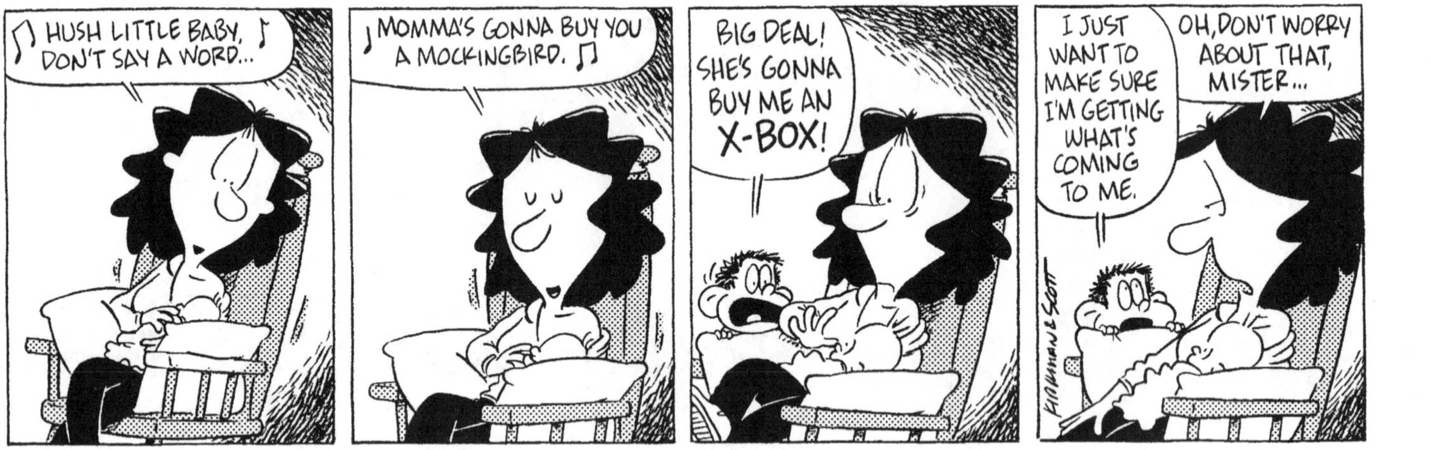
♫ HUSH LITTLE BABY, DON'T SAY A WORD... ♪
♪ MOMMA'S GONNA BUY YOU A MOCKINGBIRD. ♫
BIG DEAL! SHE'S GONNA BUY ME AN **X-BOX**!
I JUST WANT TO MAKE SURE I'M GETTING WHAT'S COMING TO ME.
OH, DON'T WORRY ABOUT THAT, MISTER...
KIRKMAN & SCOTT

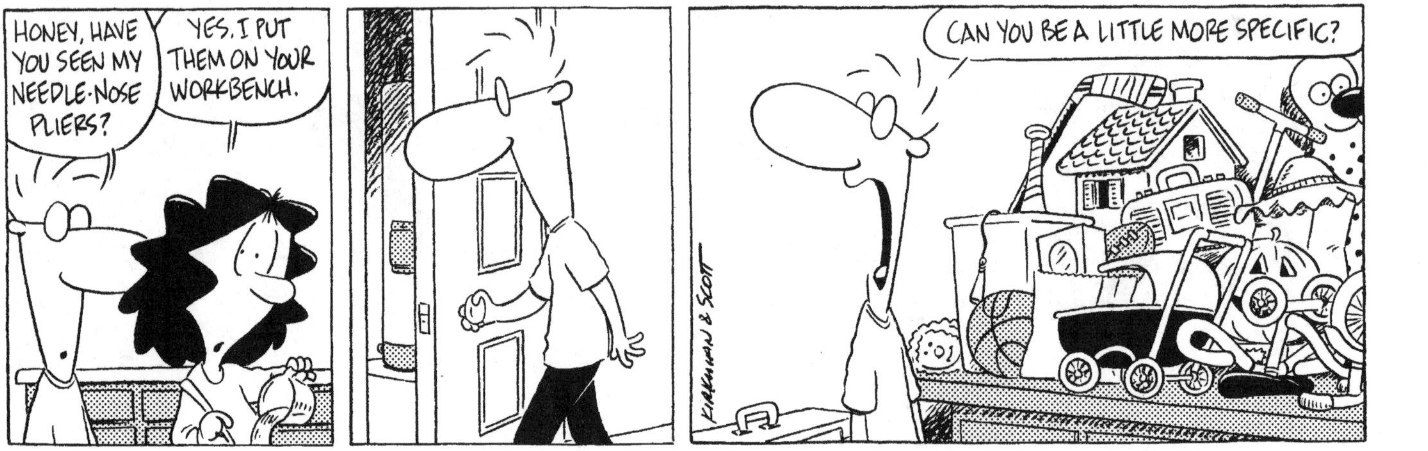
HONEY, HAVE YOU SEEN MY NEEDLE-NOSE PLIERS?
YES. I PUT THEM ON YOUR WORKBENCH.
KIRKMAN & SCOTT
CAN YOU BE A LITTLE MORE SPECIFIC?

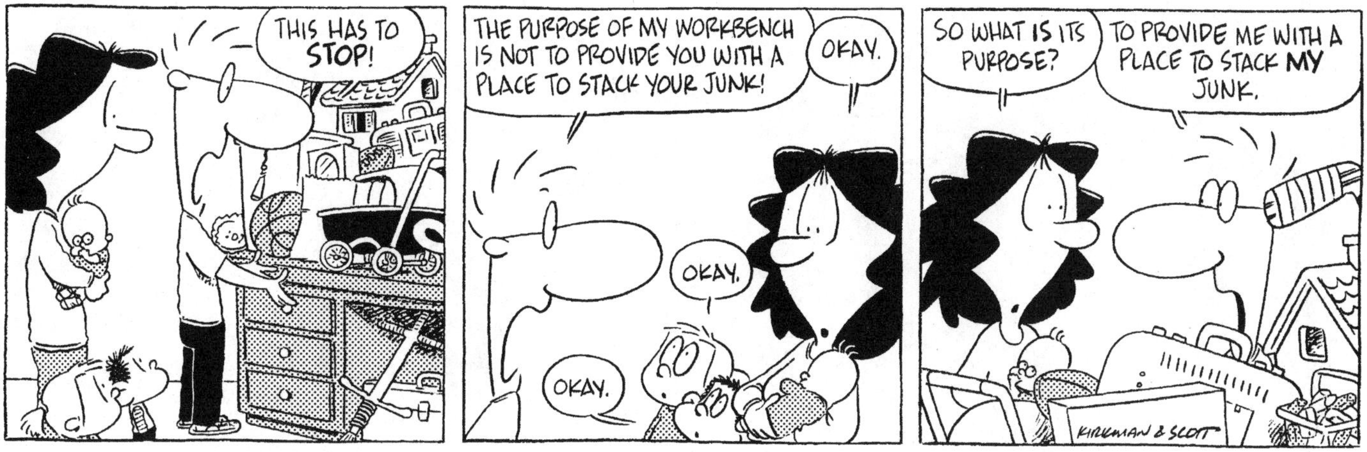
THIS HAS TO STOP!
THE PURPOSE OF MY WORKBENCH IS NOT TO PROVIDE YOU WITH A PLACE TO STACK YOUR JUNK!
OKAY.
OKAY.
OKAY.
SO WHAT IS ITS PURPOSE?
TO PROVIDE ME WITH A PLACE TO STACK MY JUNK.
KIRKMAN & SCOTT

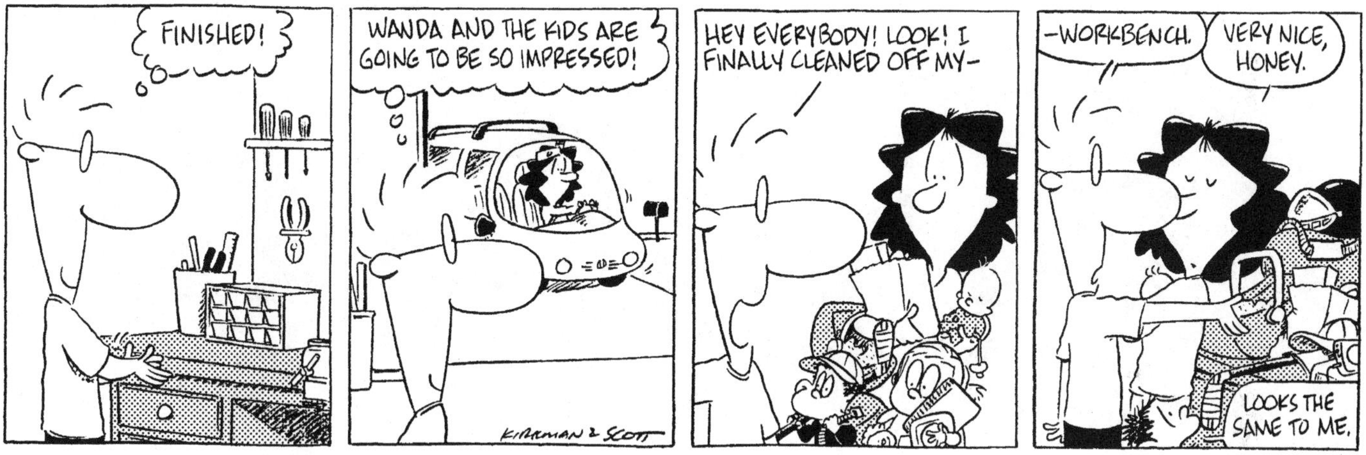
FINISHED!
WANDA AND THE KIDS ARE GOING TO BE SO IMPRESSED!
KIRKMAN & SCOTT
HEY EVERYBODY! LOOK! I FINALLY CLEANED OFF MY-
-WORKBENCH.
VERY NICE, HONEY.
LOOKS THE SAME TO ME.

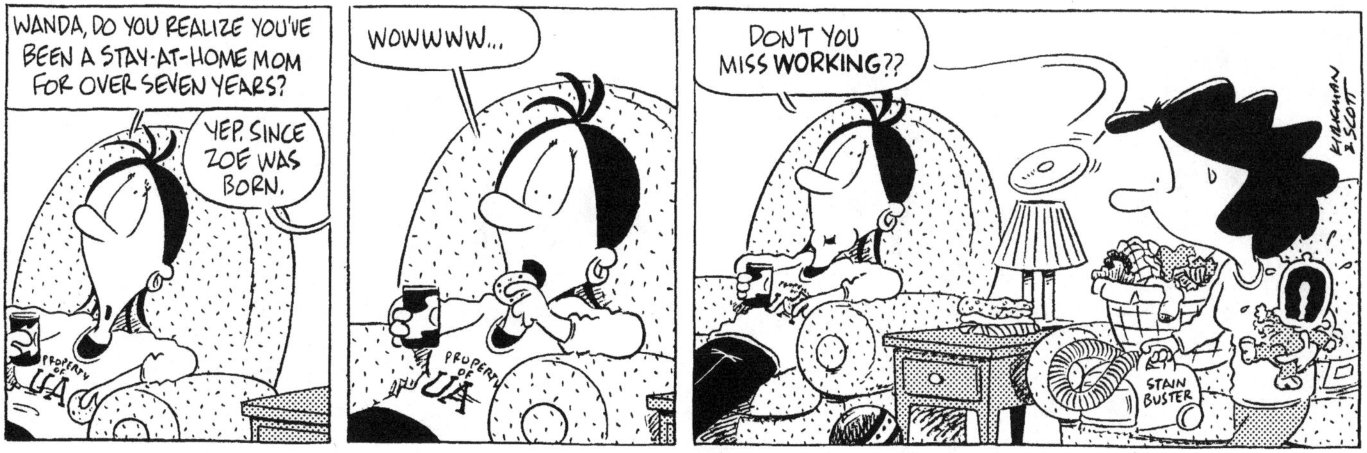
WANDA, DO YOU REALIZE YOU'VE BEEN A STAY-AT-HOME MOM FOR OVER SEVEN YEARS?
YEP. SINCE ZOE WAS BORN.
PROPERTY OF UA
WOWWWW...
PROPERTY OF UA
DON'T YOU MISS WORKING??
KIRKMAN & SCOTT
STAIN BUSTER

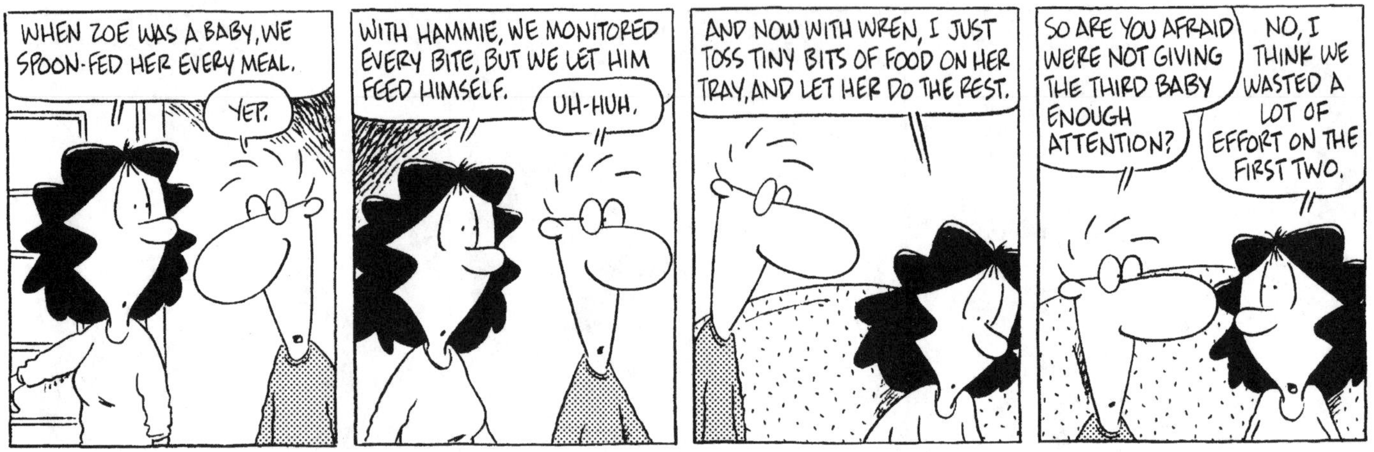
WHEN ZOE WAS A BABY, WE SPOON-FED HER EVERY MEAL.
YEP.
WITH HAMMIE, WE MONITORED EVERY BITE, BUT WE LET HIM FEED HIMSELF.
UH-HUH.
AND NOW WITH WREN, I JUST TOSS TINY BITS OF FOOD ON HER TRAY, AND LET HER DO THE REST.
SO ARE YOU AFRAID WE'RE NOT GIVING THE THIRD BABY ENOUGH ATTENTION?
NO, I THINK WE WASTED A LOT OF EFFORT ON THE FIRST TWO.

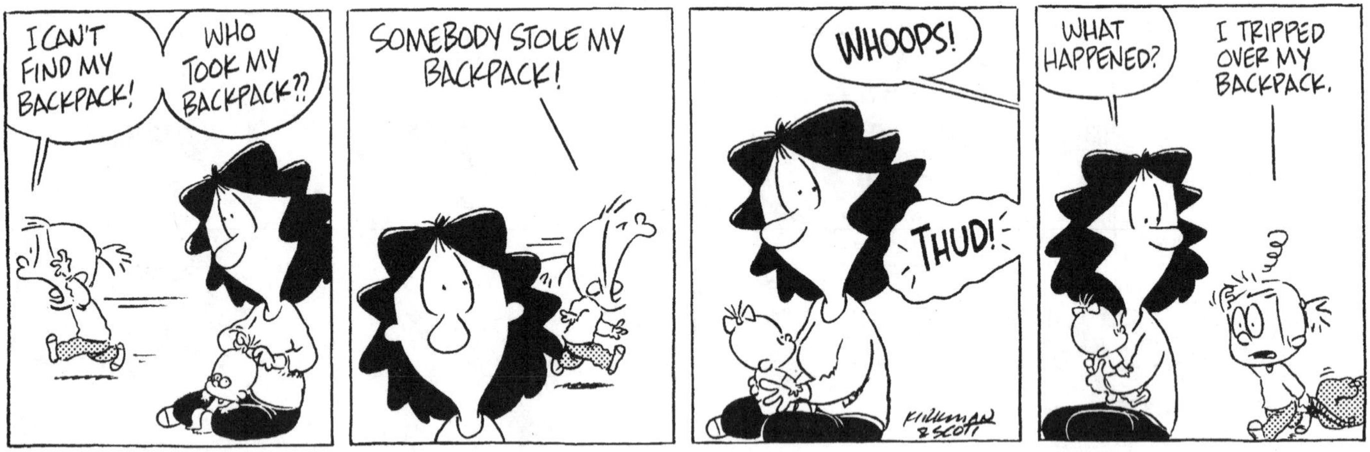
I CAN'T FIND MY BACKPACK!
WHO TOOK MY BACKPACK??
SOMEBODY STOLE MY BACKPACK!
WHOOPS!
THUD!
WHAT HAPPENED?
I TRIPPED OVER MY BACKPACK.

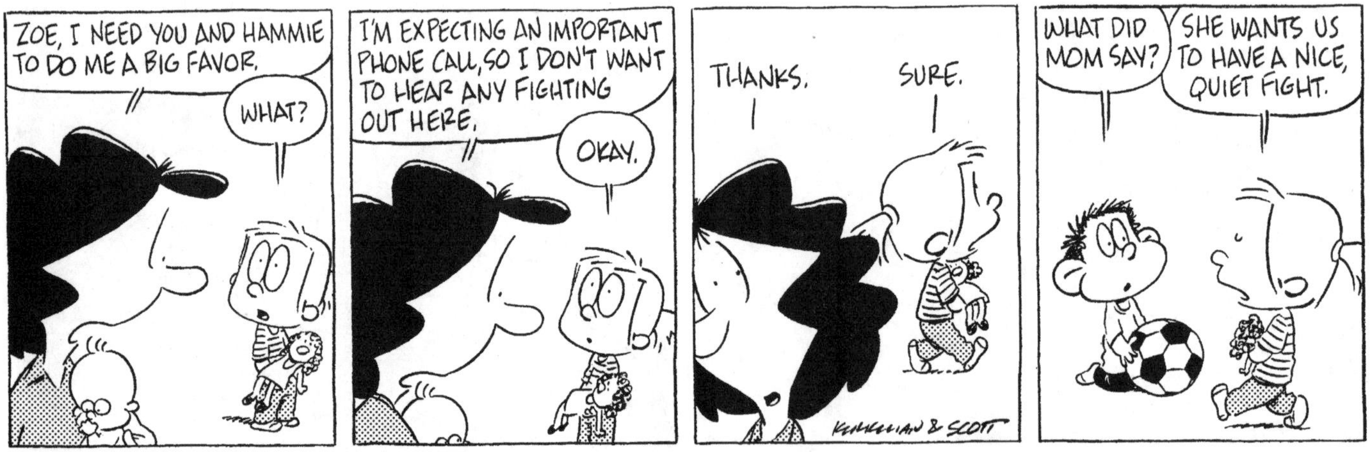
ZOE, I NEED YOU AND HAMMIE TO DO ME A BIG FAVOR.
WHAT?
I'M EXPECTING AN IMPORTANT PHONE CALL, SO I DON'T WANT TO HEAR ANY FIGHTING OUT HERE.
OKAY.
THANKS.
SURE.
WHAT DID MOM SAY?
SHE WANTS US TO HAVE A NICE, QUIET FIGHT.

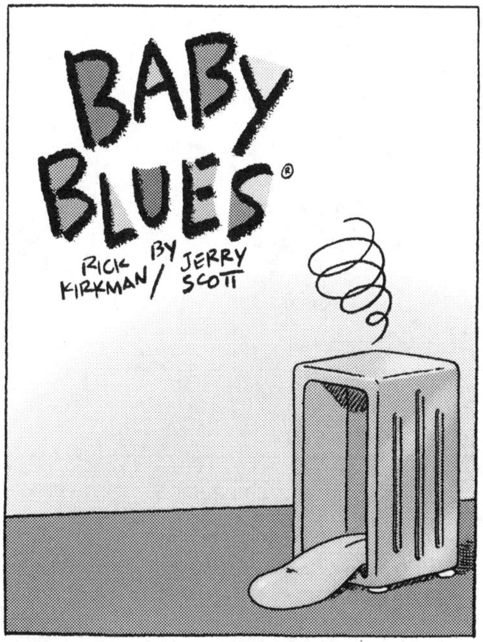
BABY BLUES®
BY
RICK KIRKMAN / JERRY SCOTT

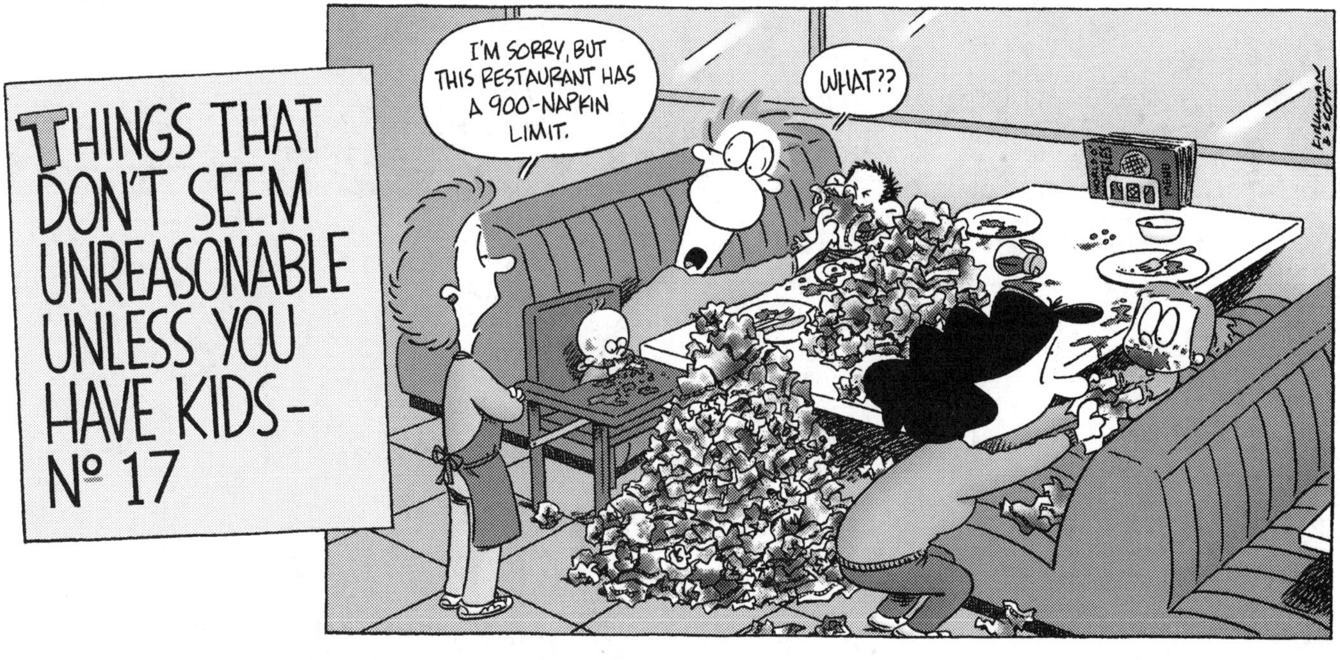
THINGS THAT DON'T SEEM UNREASONABLE UNLESS YOU HAVE KIDS— № 17
I'M SORRY, BUT THIS RESTAURANT HAS A 900-NAPKIN LIMIT.
WHAT??

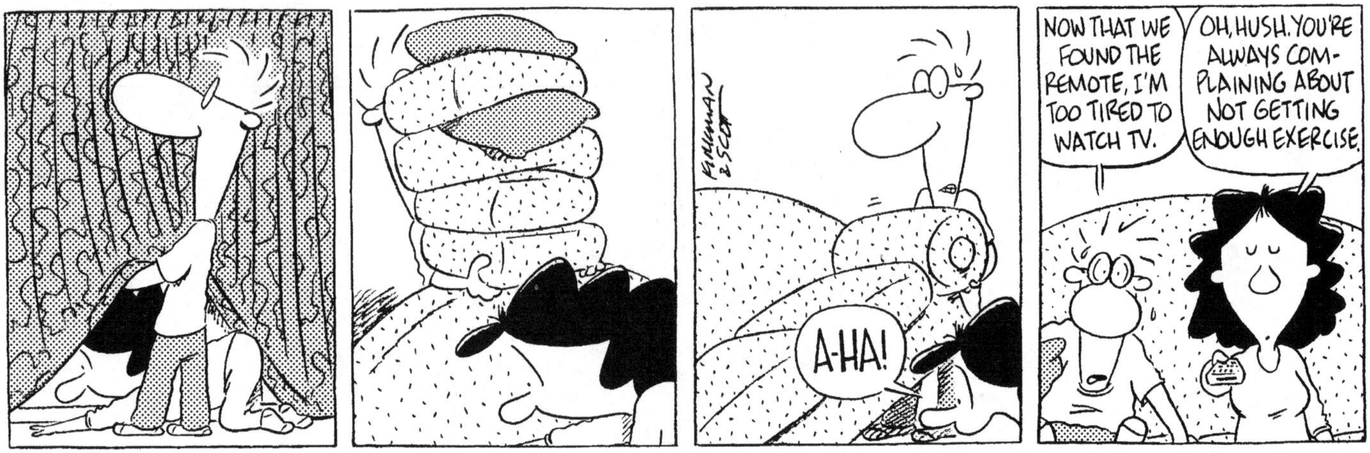
A-HA!
NOW THAT WE FOUND THE REMOTE, I'M TOO TIRED TO WATCH TV.
OH, HUSH. YOU'RE ALWAYS COMPLAINING ABOUT NOT GETTING ENOUGH EXERCISE.

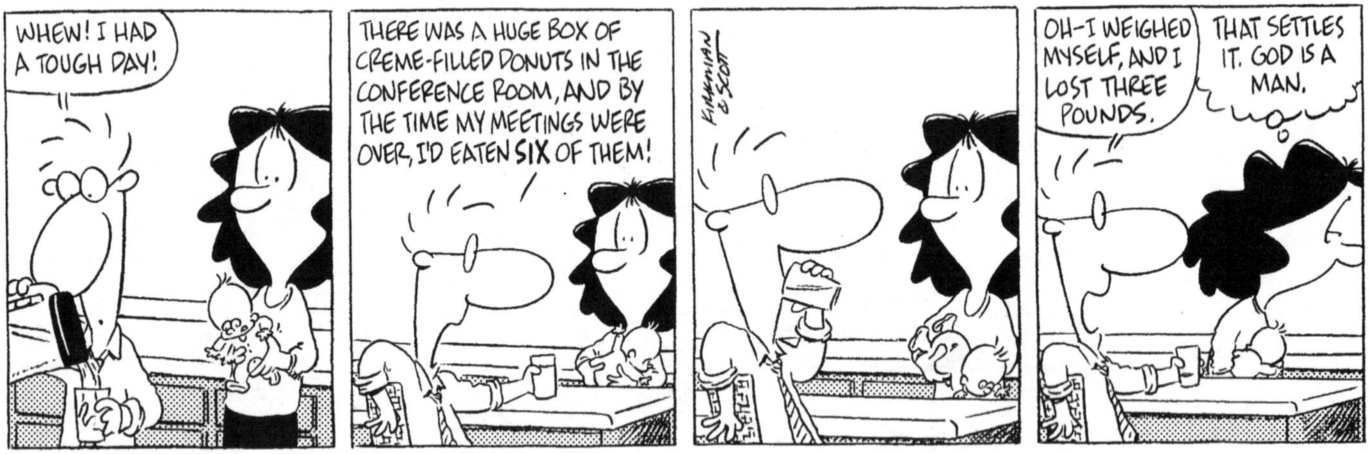
WHEW! I HAD A TOUGH DAY!
THERE WAS A HUGE BOX OF CREME-FILLED DONUTS IN THE CONFERENCE ROOM, AND BY THE TIME MY MEETINGS WERE OVER, I'D EATEN **SIX** OF THEM!
OH-I WEIGHED MYSELF, AND I LOST THREE POUNDS.
THAT SETTLES IT. GOD IS A MAN.

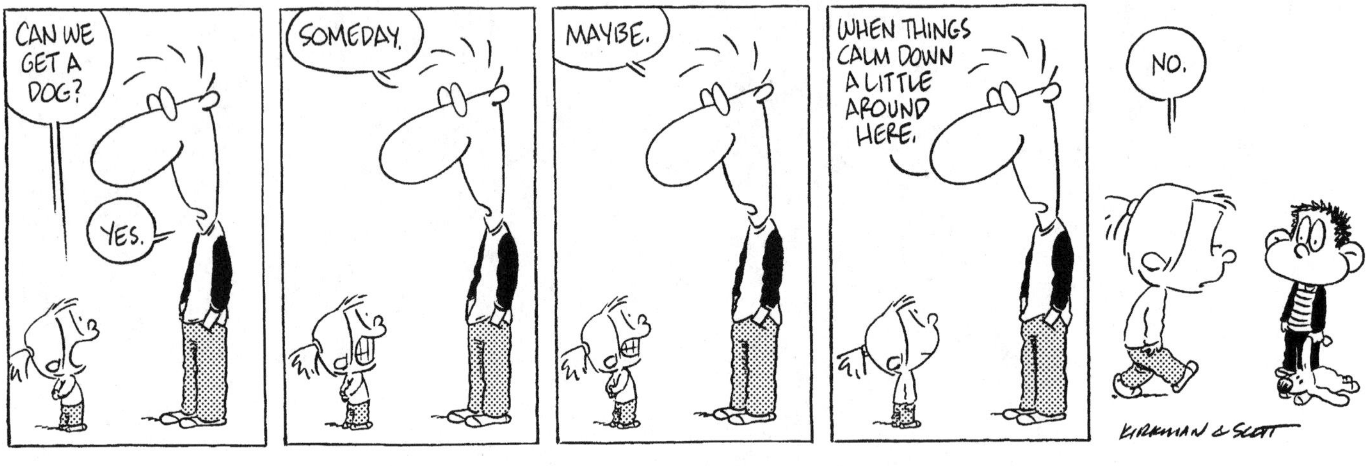
CAN WE GET A DOG?
YES.
SOMEDAY.
MAYBE.
WHEN THINGS CALM DOWN A LITTLE AROUND HERE.
NO.
KIRKMAN & SCOTT

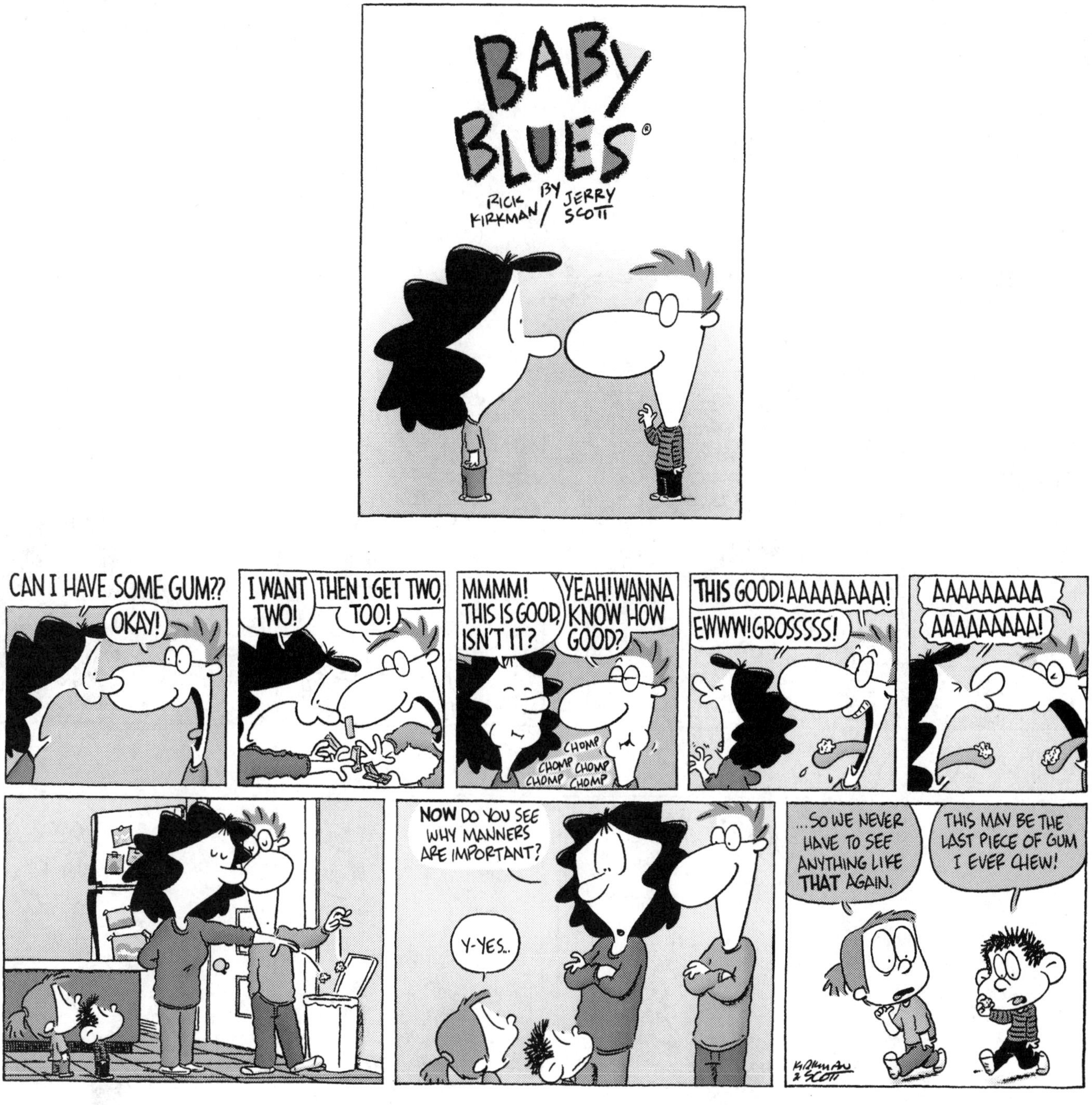
BABY BLUES®
BY RICK KIRKMAN / JERRY SCOTT
CAN I HAVE SOME GUM??
OKAY!
I WANT TWO!
THEN I GET TWO, TOO!
MMMM! THIS IS GOOD, ISN'T IT?
YEAH! WANNA KNOW HOW GOOD?
CHOMP
CHOMP
CHOMP
CHOMP
CHOMP
THIS GOOD! AAAAAAAA!
EWWW! GROSSSSS!
AAAAAAAAA
AAAAAAAAA!
NOW DO YOU SEE WHY MANNERS ARE IMPORTANT?
Y-YES..
...SO WE NEVER HAVE TO SEE ANYTHING LIKE THAT AGAIN.
THIS MAY BE THE LAST PIECE OF GUM I EVER CHEW!
KIRKMAN & SCOTT

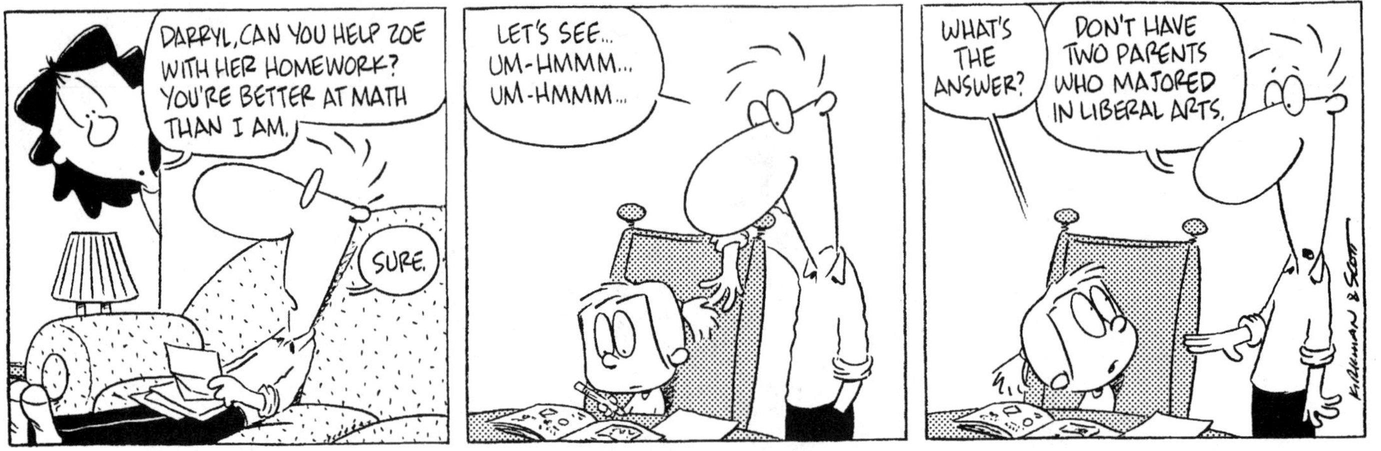
DARRYL, CAN YOU HELP ZOE WITH HER HOMEWORK? YOU'RE BETTER AT MATH THAN I AM.
SURE.
LET'S SEE... UM-HMMM... UM-HMMM...
WHAT'S THE ANSWER?
DON'T HAVE TWO PARENTS WHO MAJORED IN LIBERAL ARTS.
KIRKMAN & SCOTT

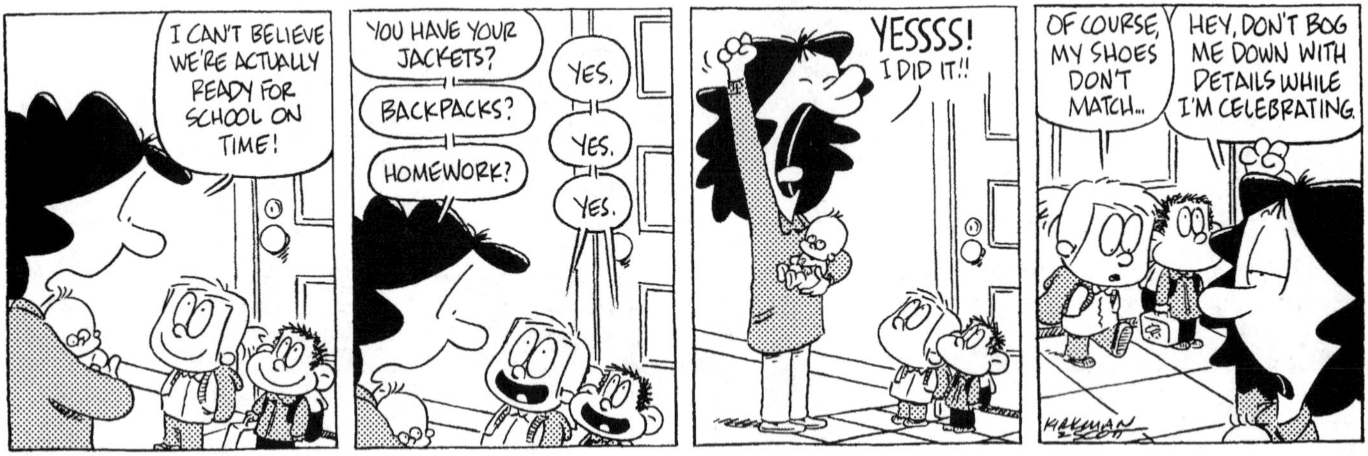
I CAN'T BELIEVE WE'RE ACTUALLY READY FOR SCHOOL ON TIME!
YOU HAVE YOUR JACKETS?
YES.
BACKPACKS?
YES.
HOMEWORK?
YES.
YESSSS! I DID IT!!
OF COURSE, MY SHOES DON'T MATCH...
HEY, DON'T BOG ME DOWN WITH DETAILS WHILE I'M CELEBRATING.
KIRKMAN & SCOTT

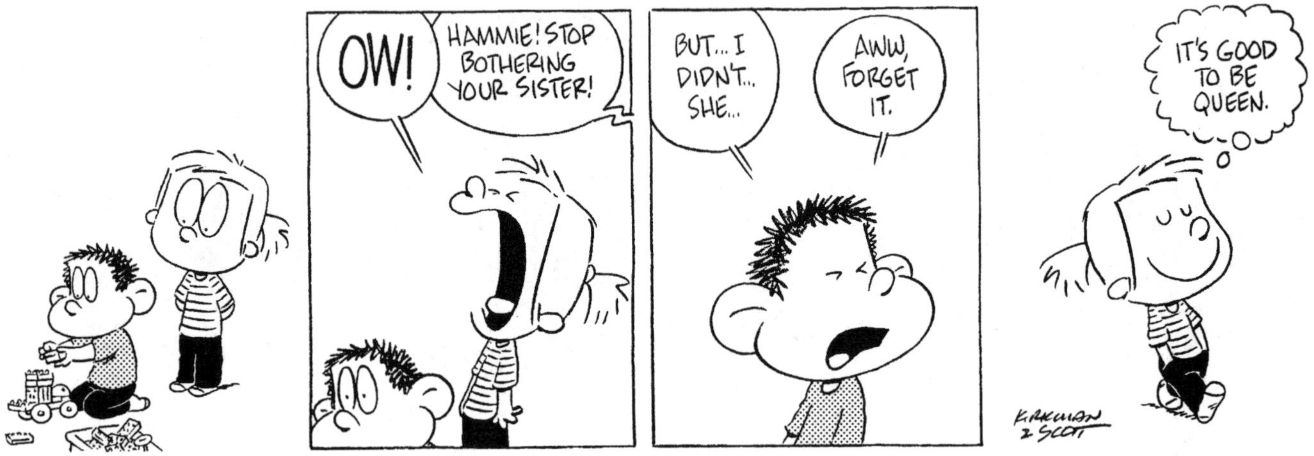
OW!
HAMMIE! STOP BOTHERING YOUR SISTER!
BUT... I DIDN'T... SHE...
AWW, FORGET IT.
IT'S GOOD TO BE QUEEN.
KIRKMAN & SCOTT

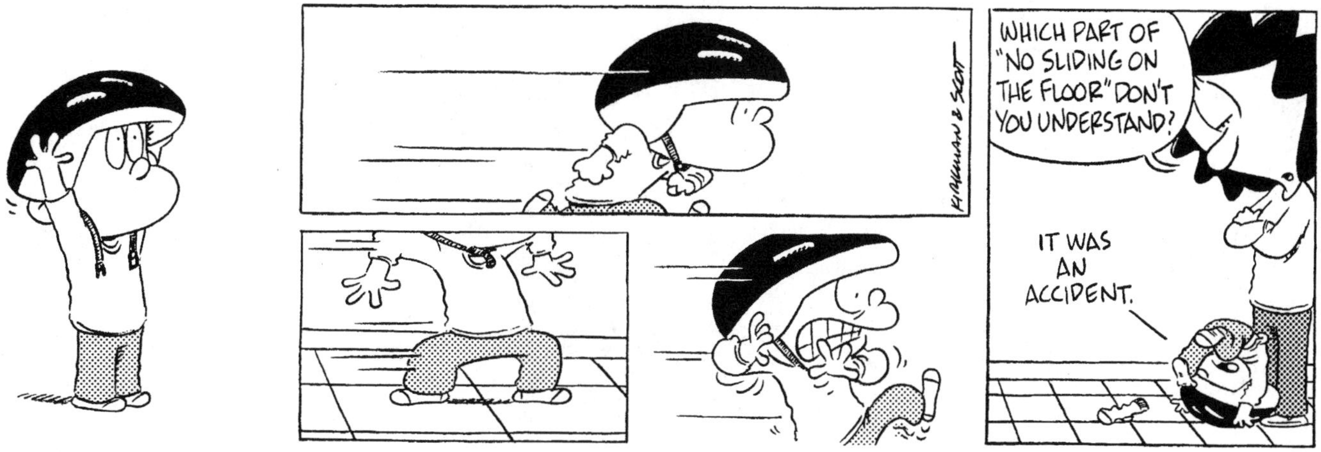
WHICH PART OF "NO SLIDING ON THE FLOOR" DON'T YOU UNDERSTAND?
IT WAS AN ACCIDENT.

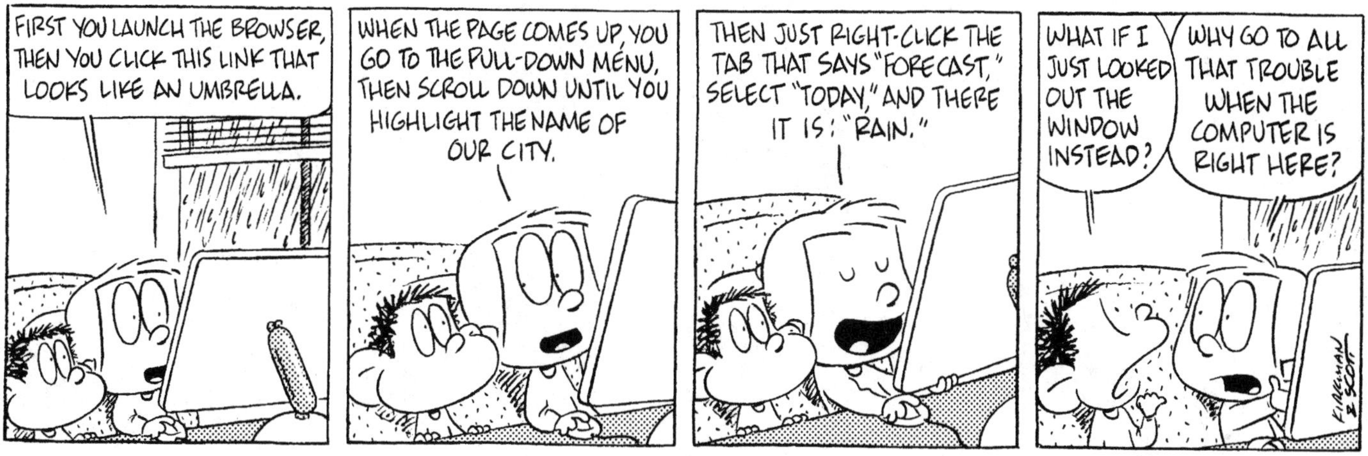
FIRST YOU LAUNCH THE BROWSER, THEN YOU CLICK THIS LINK THAT LOOKS LIKE AN UMBRELLA.
WHEN THE PAGE COMES UP, YOU GO TO THE PULL-DOWN MENU, THEN SCROLL DOWN UNTIL YOU HIGHLIGHT THE NAME OF OUR CITY.
THEN JUST RIGHT-CLICK THE TAB THAT SAYS "FORECAST," SELECT "TODAY," AND THERE IT IS: "RAIN."
WHAT IF I JUST LOOKED OUT THE WINDOW INSTEAD?
WHY GO TO ALL THAT TROUBLE WHEN THE COMPUTER IS RIGHT HERE?

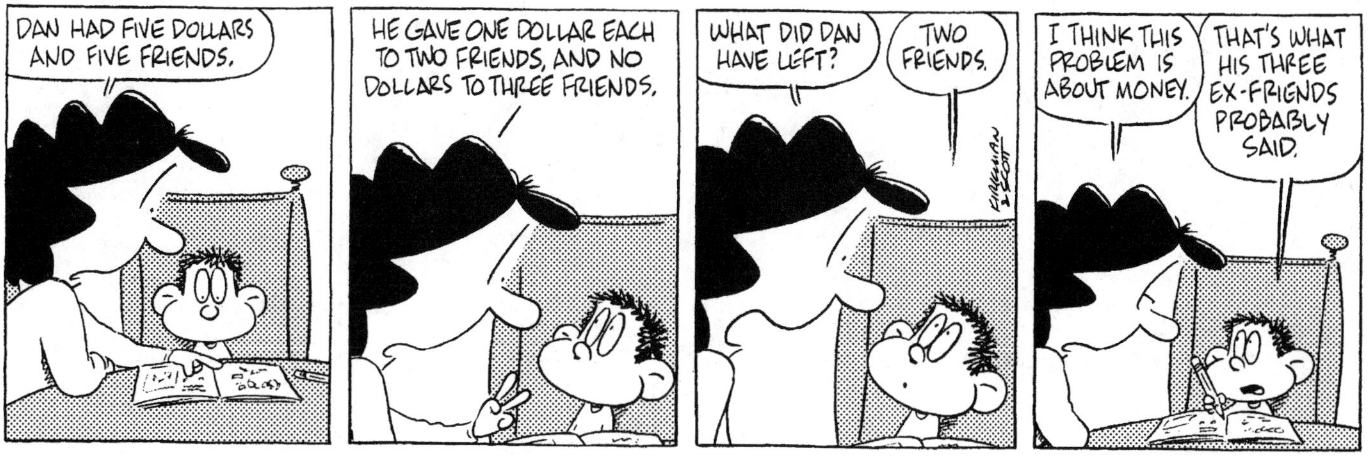
DAN HAD FIVE DOLLARS AND FIVE FRIENDS.
HE GAVE ONE DOLLAR EACH TO TWO FRIENDS, AND NO DOLLARS TO THREE FRIENDS.
WHAT DID DAN HAVE LEFT?
TWO FRIENDS.
I THINK THIS PROBLEM IS ABOUT MONEY.
THAT'S WHAT HIS THREE EX-FRIENDS PROBABLY SAID.

BABY BLUES®
BY
RICK KIRKMAN / JERRY SCOTT

HELLO?
RING RING
HI HONEY. HOW'S IT GOING?
I HAVE A HEADACHE.
I'M SORRY. DID THE PLUMBER SHOW UP?
NOT YET.
YOU POOR THING! I HOPE HE GETS THERE PRETTY SOON.
ME, TOO.
NOTHING CAN DRIVE A PERSON CRAZIER THAN A DRIPPING FAUCET.
WANNA' BET?
DRIP!
KIRKMAN & SCOTT

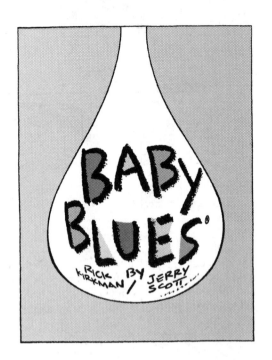

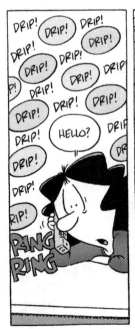

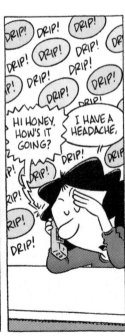

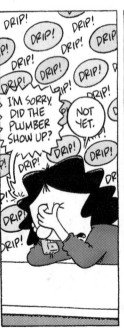

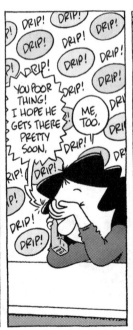

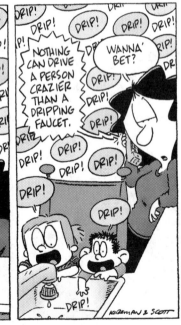

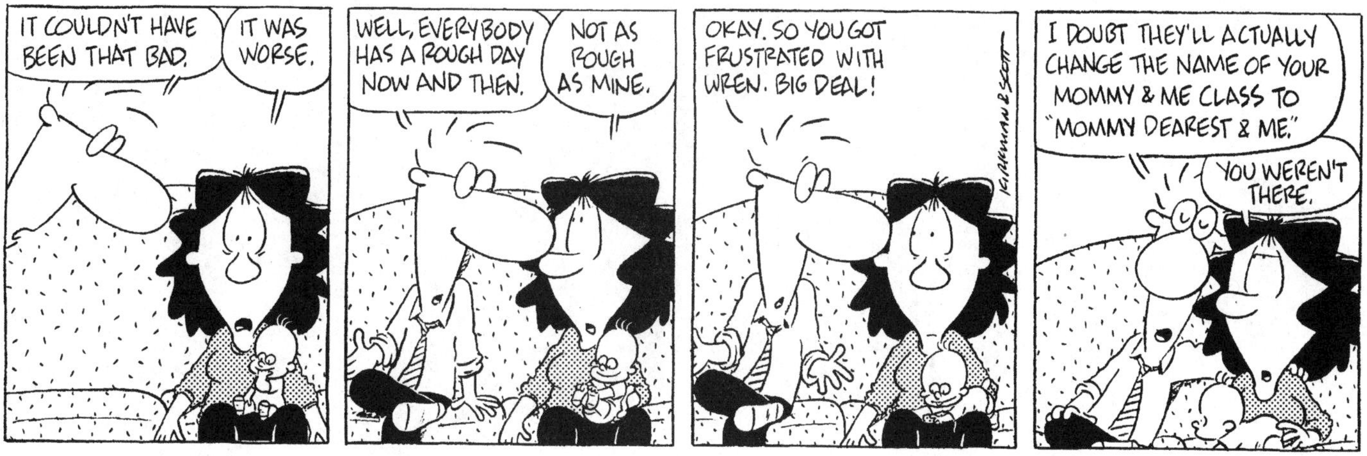
IT COULDN'T HAVE BEEN THAT BAD.
IT WAS WORSE.
WELL, EVERYBODY HAS A ROUGH DAY NOW AND THEN.
NOT AS ROUGH AS MINE.
OKAY. SO YOU GOT FRUSTRATED WITH WREN. BIG DEAL!
KIRKMAN & SCOTT
I DOUBT THEY'LL ACTUALLY CHANGE THE NAME OF YOUR MOMMY & ME CLASS TO "MOMMY DEAREST & ME."
YOU WEREN'T THERE.

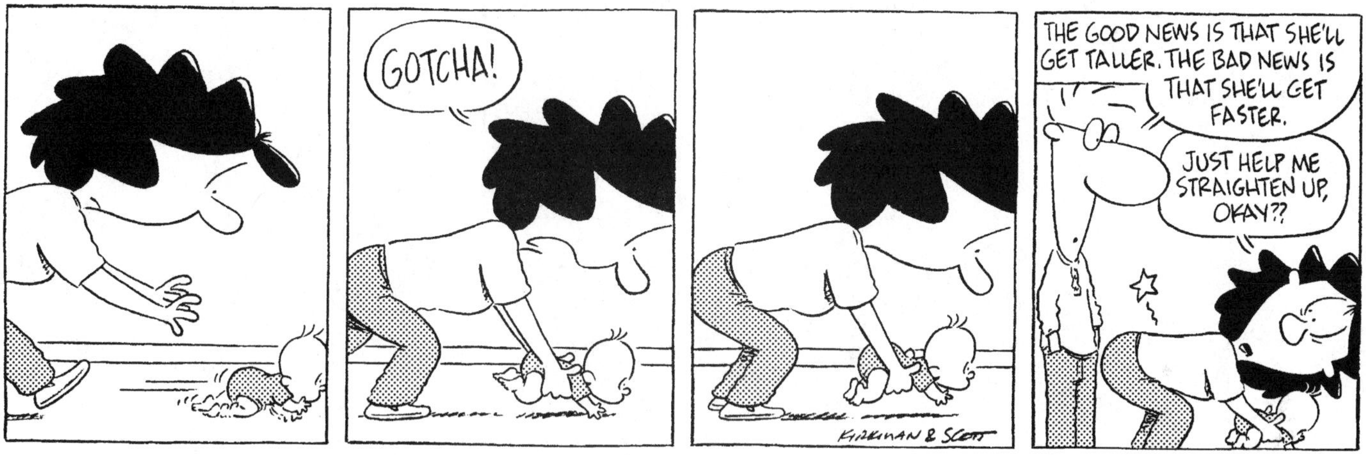
GOTCHA!
KIRKMAN & SCOTT
THE GOOD NEWS IS THAT SHE'LL GET TALLER. THE BAD NEWS IS THAT SHE'LL GET FASTER.
JUST HELP ME STRAIGHTEN UP, OKAY??

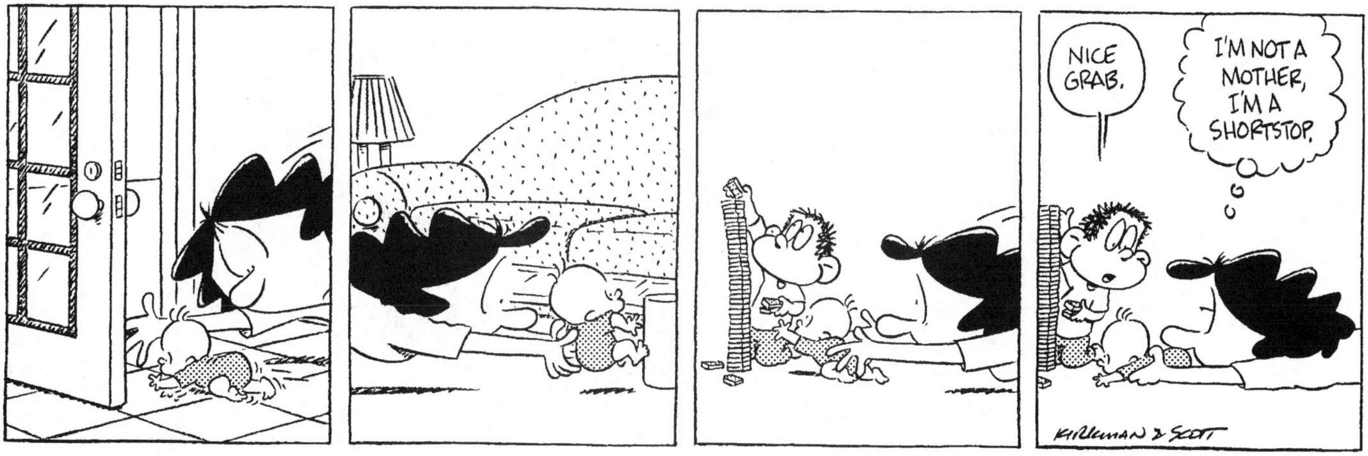
NICE GRAB.
I'M NOT A MOTHER, I'M A SHORTSTOP.
KIRKMAN & SCOTT

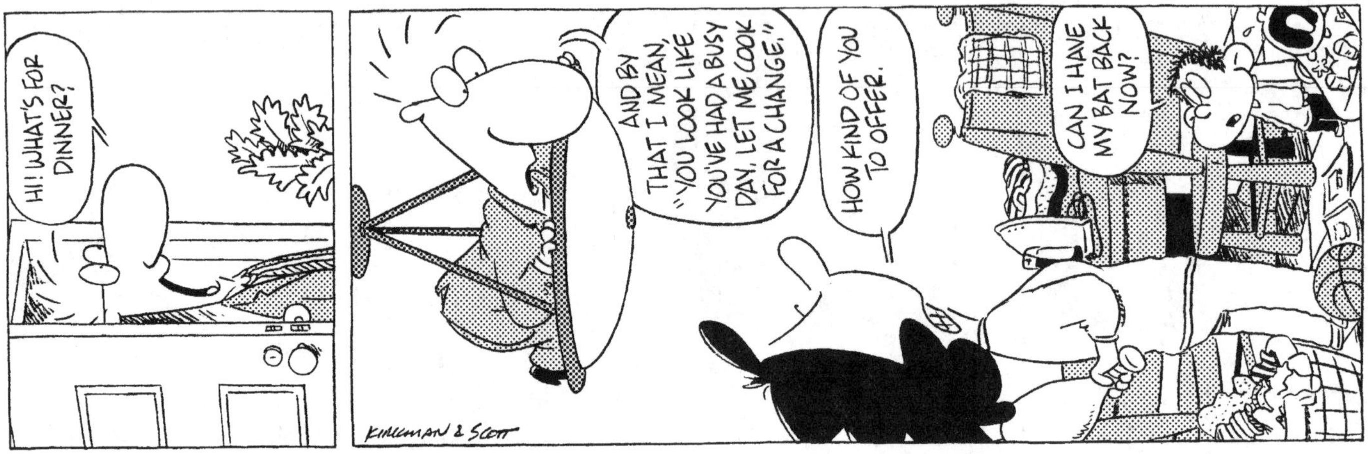
HI! WHAT'S FOR DINNER?
AND BY THAT I MEAN, "YOU LOOK LIKE YOU'VE HAD A BUSY DAY. LET ME COOK FOR A CHANGE."
HOW KIND OF YOU TO OFFER.
CAN I HAVE MY BAT BACK NOW?
KIRKMAN & SCOTT

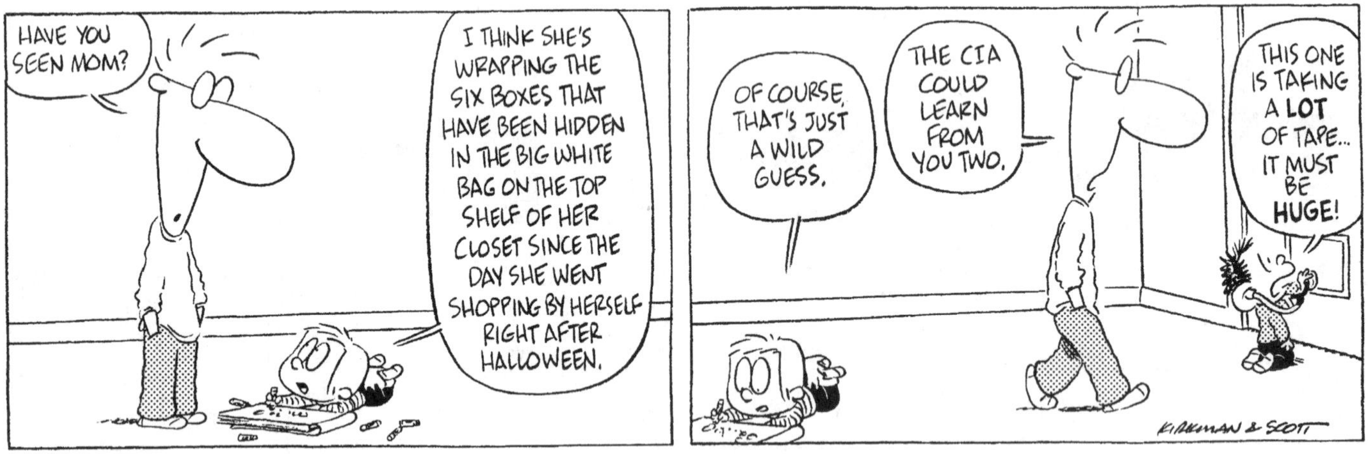
HAVE YOU SEEN MOM?
I THINK SHE'S WRAPPING THE SIX BOXES THAT HAVE BEEN HIDDEN IN THE BIG WHITE BAG ON THE TOP SHELF OF HER CLOSET SINCE THE DAY SHE WENT SHOPPING BY HERSELF RIGHT AFTER HALLOWEEN.
OF COURSE, THAT'S JUST A WILD GUESS.
THE CIA COULD LEARN FROM YOU TWO.
THIS ONE IS TAKING A **LOT** OF TAPE... IT MUST BE **HUGE**!
KIRKMAN & SCOTT

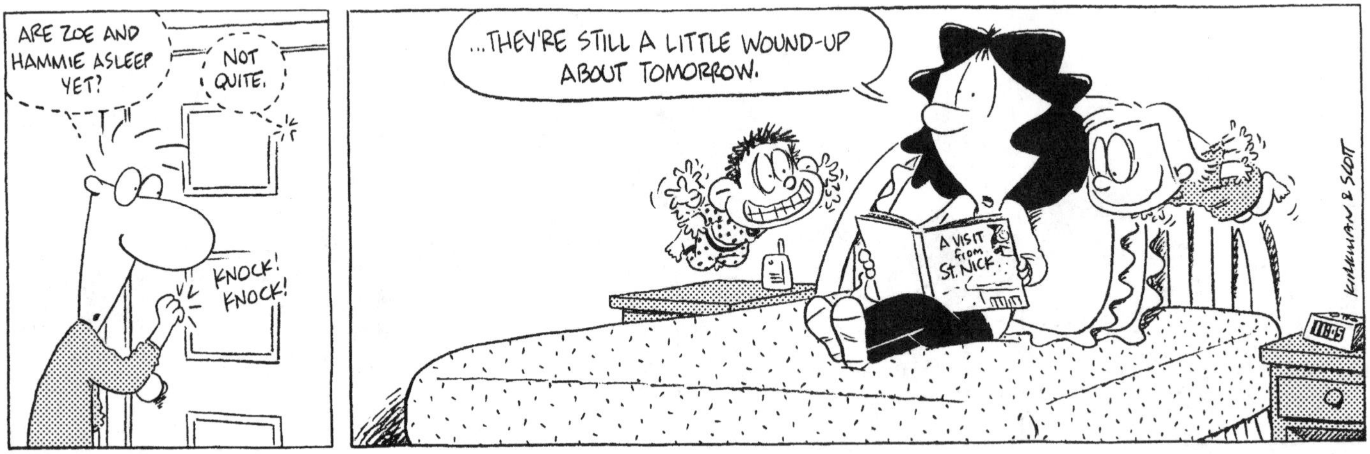
ARE ZOE AND HAMMIE ASLEEP YET?
NOT QUITE.
KNOCK! KNOCK!
...THEY'RE STILL A LITTLE WOUND-UP ABOUT TOMORROW.
A VISIT from ST. NICK
KIRKMAN & SCOTT

BABY BLUES®
BY RICK KIRKMAN / JERRY SCOTT

Assembly Instructions
STEP 1
Obtain a master's degree in mechanical engineering from M.I.T.
UH-OH...
SHOULD I PUT ON SOME MORE COFFEE?
INSTRUCTION MANUAL VOLUME ONE
KIRKMAN & SCOTT

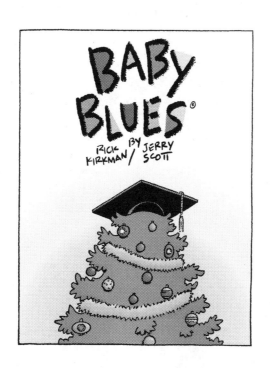

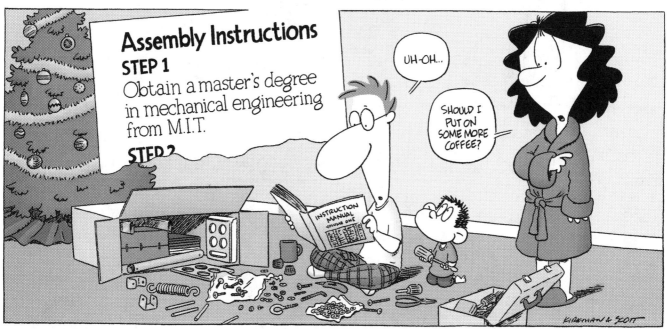

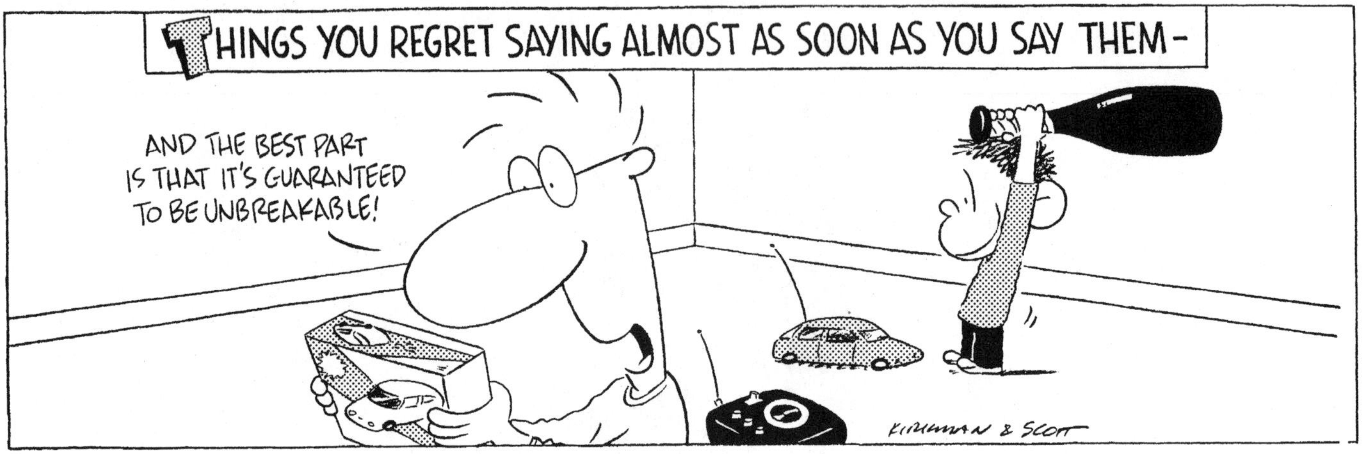
THINGS YOU REGRET SAYING ALMOST AS SOON AS YOU SAY THEM-
AND THE BEST PART IS THAT IT'S GUARANTEED TO BE UNBREAKABLE!
KIRKMAN & SCOTT

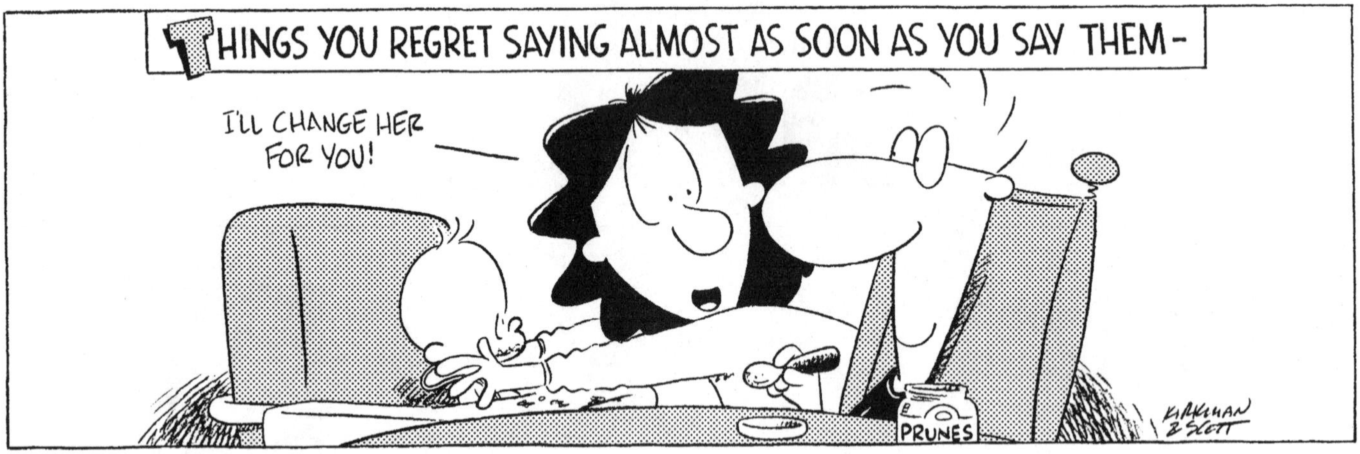
THINGS YOU REGRET SAYING ALMOST AS SOON AS YOU SAY THEM-
I'LL CHANGE HER FOR YOU!
PRUNES
KIRKMAN & SCOTT

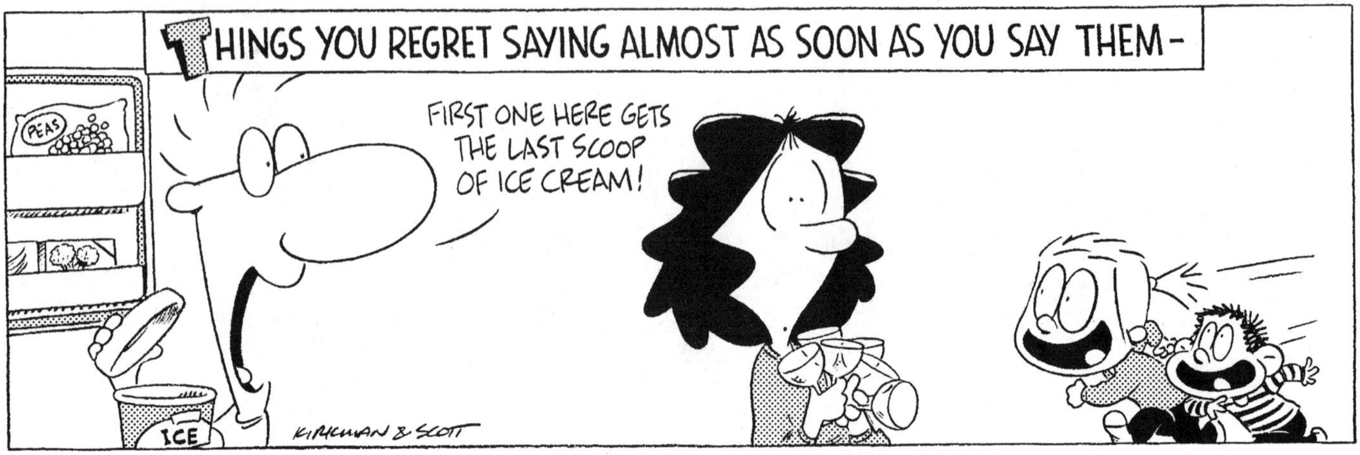
THINGS YOU REGRET SAYING ALMOST AS SOON AS YOU SAY THEM-
PEAS
FIRST ONE HERE GETS THE LAST SCOOP OF ICE CREAM!
ICE
KIRKMAN & SCOTT

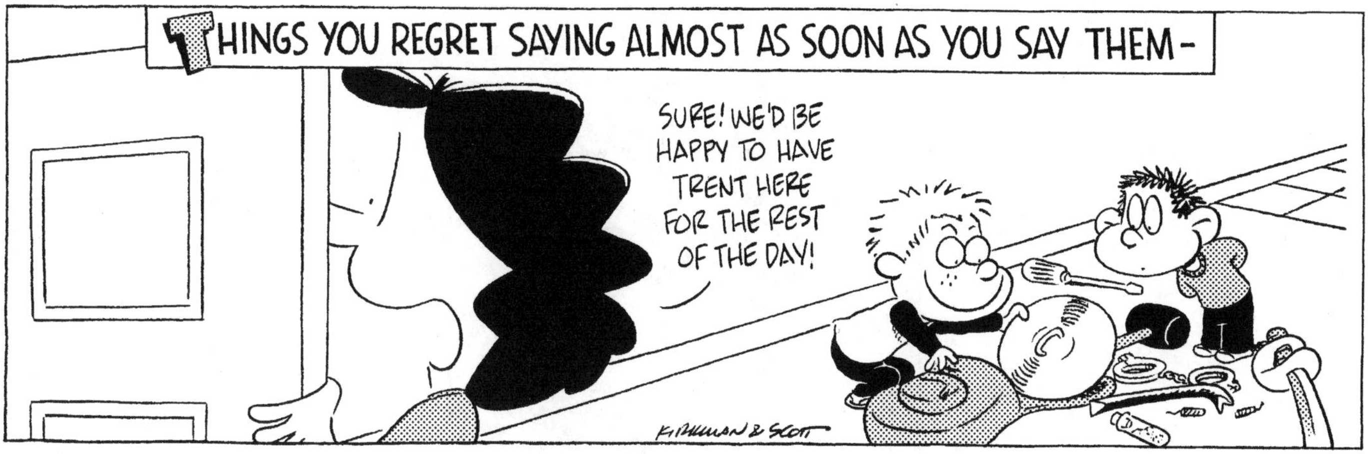
THINGS YOU REGRET SAYING ALMOST AS SOON AS YOU SAY THEM-
SURE! WE'D BE HAPPY TO HAVE TRENT HERE FOR THE REST OF THE DAY!
KIRKMAN & SCOTT

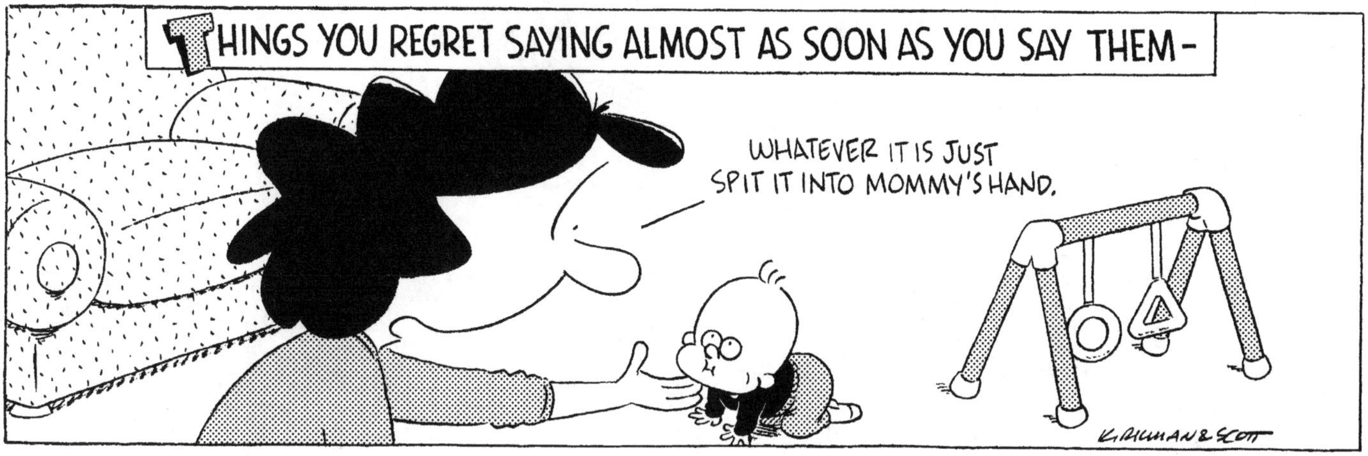
THINGS YOU REGRET SAYING ALMOST AS SOON AS YOU SAY THEM-
WHATEVER IT IS JUST SPIT IT INTO MOMMY'S HAND.
KIRKMAN & SCOTT

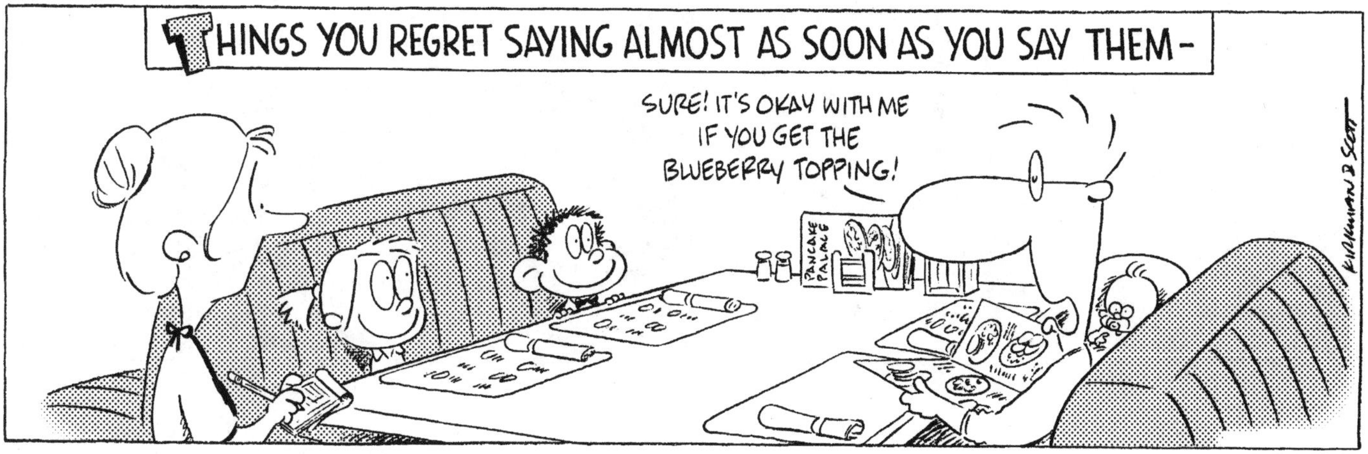
THINGS YOU REGRET SAYING ALMOST AS SOON AS YOU SAY THEM-
SURE! IT'S OKAY WITH ME IF YOU GET THE BLUEBERRY TOPPING!
PANCAKE PALACE
KIRKMAN & SCOTT

BABY BLUES®
BY RICK KIRKMAN / JERRY SCOTT

A LITTLE HAM... A LITTLE TURKEY... A LITTLE SWISS... A LITTLE MORE HAM...
...SOME GREEN OLIVES... A BOWL OF CHIPS... A COLD BEER...
A-A-A-A-AND THE COUCH!
NEW YEAR'S DAY IS THE ONE DAY OF THE YEAR WHEN I CAN SIT BACK, RELAX, AND ENJOY A LONG AFTERNOON OF—
—GUILT.
OH, LOOK! MIKE IS TAKING HIS CHRISTMAS DECORATIONS DOWN, AND PLAYING WITH HIS CHILDREN!
GOOD NEWS, EVERYBODY! CHANNEL 2 IS SHOWING RERUNS OF THE ROSE PARADE ALL AFTERNOON!
CAN WE WATCH IT AGAIN? CAN WE? CAN WE?
KIRKMAN & SCOTT

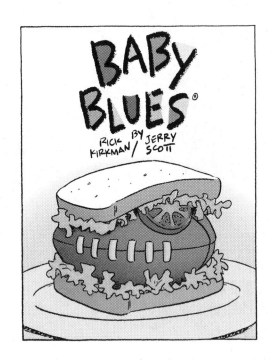

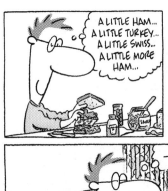

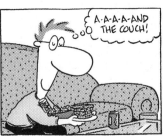

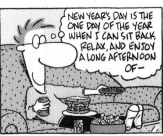

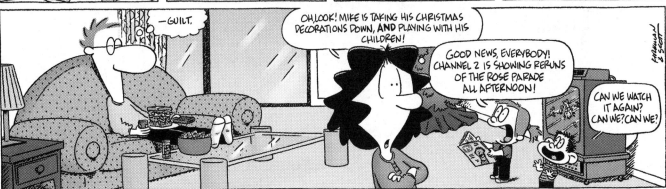

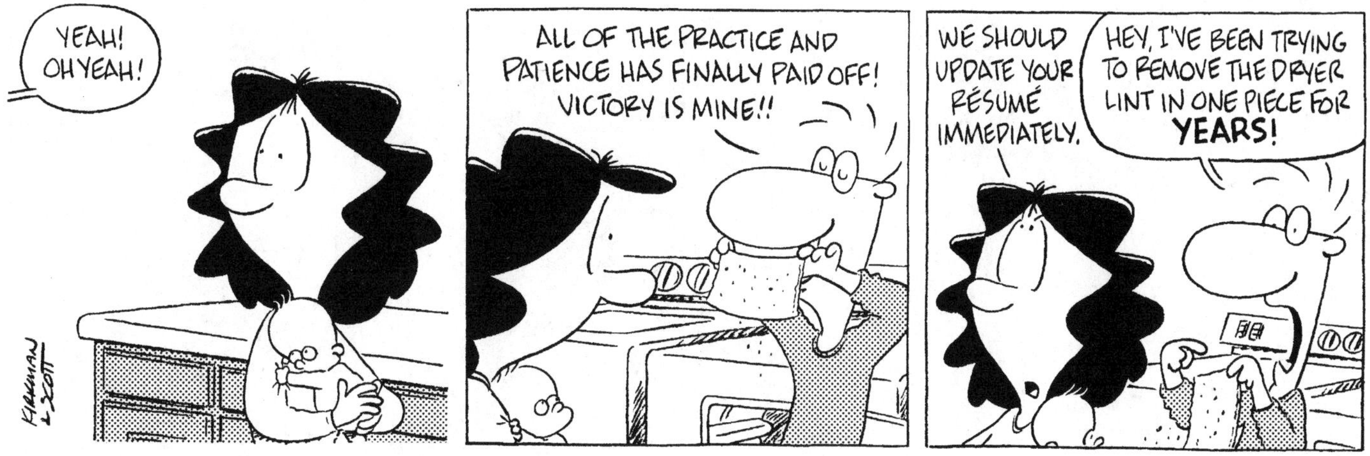
YEAH! OH YEAH!
ALL OF THE PRACTICE AND PATIENCE HAS FINALLY PAID OFF! VICTORY IS MINE!!
WE SHOULD UPDATE YOUR RÉSUMÉ IMMEDIATELY.
HEY, I'VE BEEN TRYING TO REMOVE THE DRYER LINT IN ONE PIECE FOR **YEARS!**
KIRKMAN & SCOTT

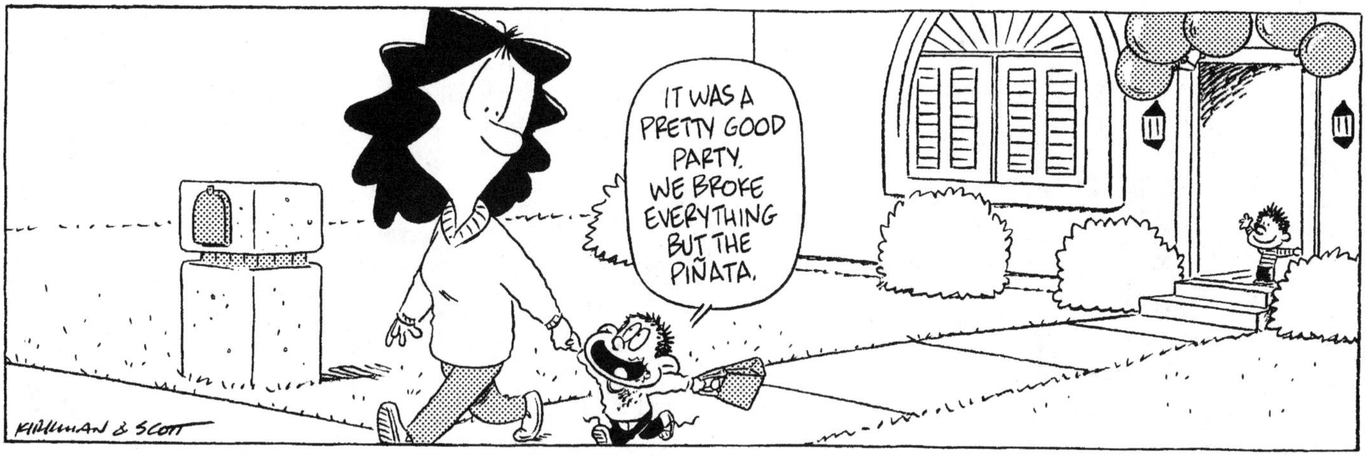
IT WAS A PRETTY GOOD PARTY. WE BROKE EVERYTHING BUT THE PIÑATA.
KIRKMAN & SCOTT

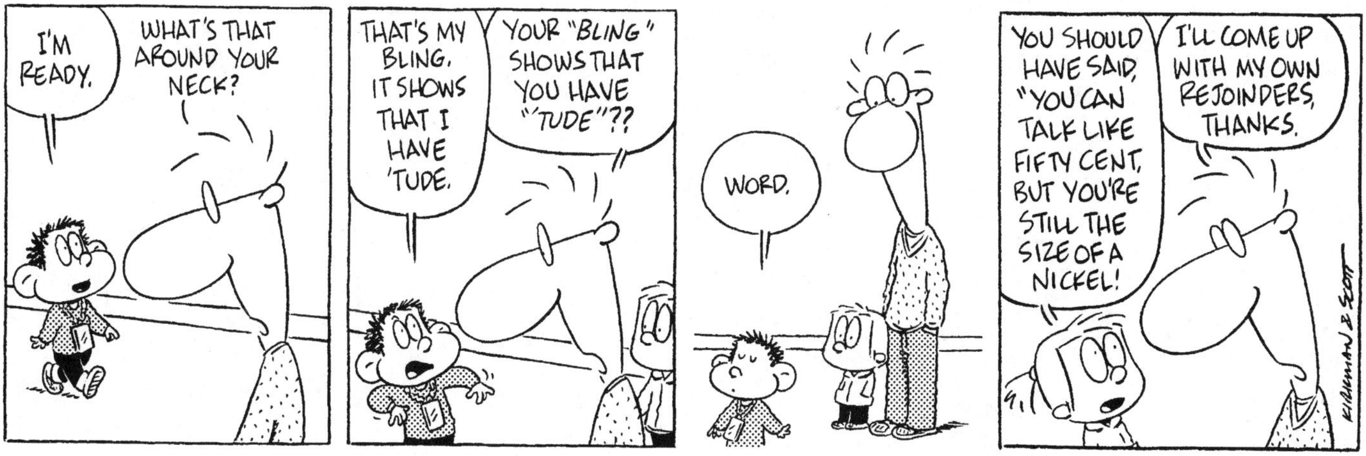
I'M READY.
WHAT'S THAT AROUND YOUR NECK?
THAT'S MY BLING. IT SHOWS THAT I HAVE 'TUDE.
YOUR "BLING" SHOWS THAT YOU HAVE "'TUDE"??
WORD.
YOU SHOULD HAVE SAID, "YOU CAN TALK LIKE FIFTY CENT, BUT YOU'RE STILL THE SIZE OF A NICKEL!
I'LL COME UP WITH MY OWN REJOINDERS, THANKS.
KIRKMAN & SCOTT

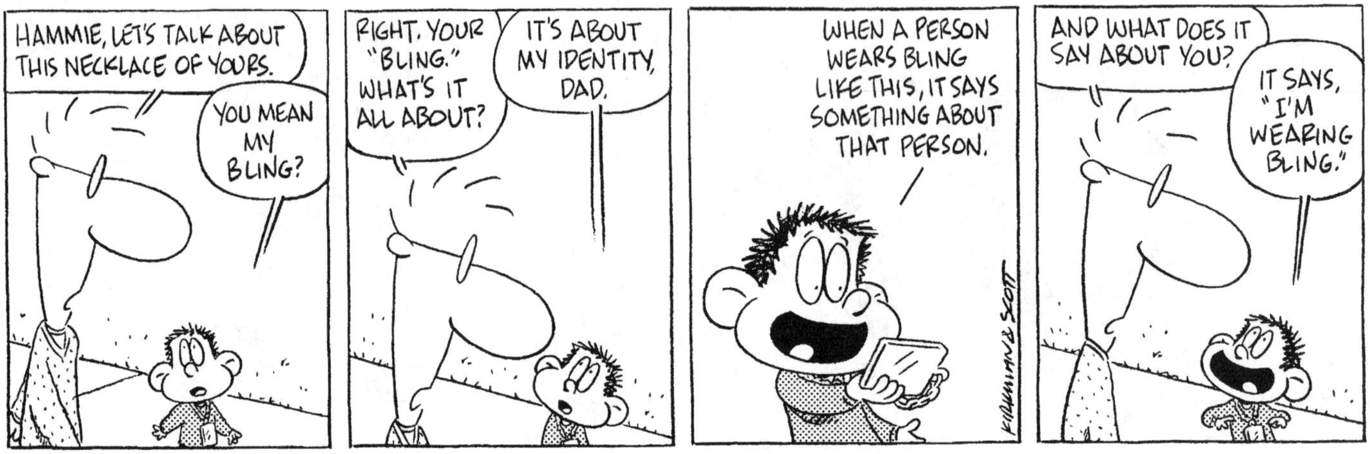
HAMMIE, LET'S TALK ABOUT THIS NECKLACE OF YOURS.
YOU MEAN MY BLING?
RIGHT. YOUR "BLING." WHAT'S IT ALL ABOUT?
IT'S ABOUT MY IDENTITY, DAD.
WHEN A PERSON WEARS BLING LIKE THIS, IT SAYS SOMETHING ABOUT THAT PERSON.
AND WHAT DOES IT SAY ABOUT YOU?
IT SAYS, "I'M WEARING BLING."
KIRKMAN & SCOTT

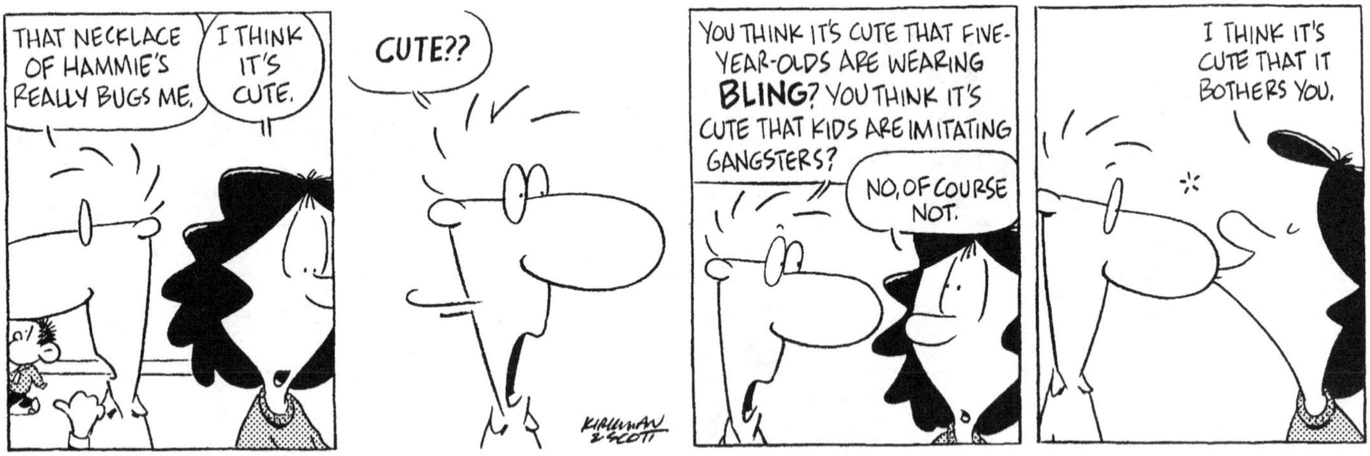
THAT NECKLACE OF HAMMIE'S REALLY BUGS ME.
I THINK IT'S CUTE.
CUTE??
KIRKMAN & SCOTT
YOU THINK IT'S CUTE THAT FIVE-YEAR-OLDS ARE WEARING **BLING**? YOU THINK IT'S CUTE THAT KIDS ARE IMITATING GANGSTERS?
NO, OF COURSE NOT.
I THINK IT'S CUTE THAT IT BOTHERS YOU.

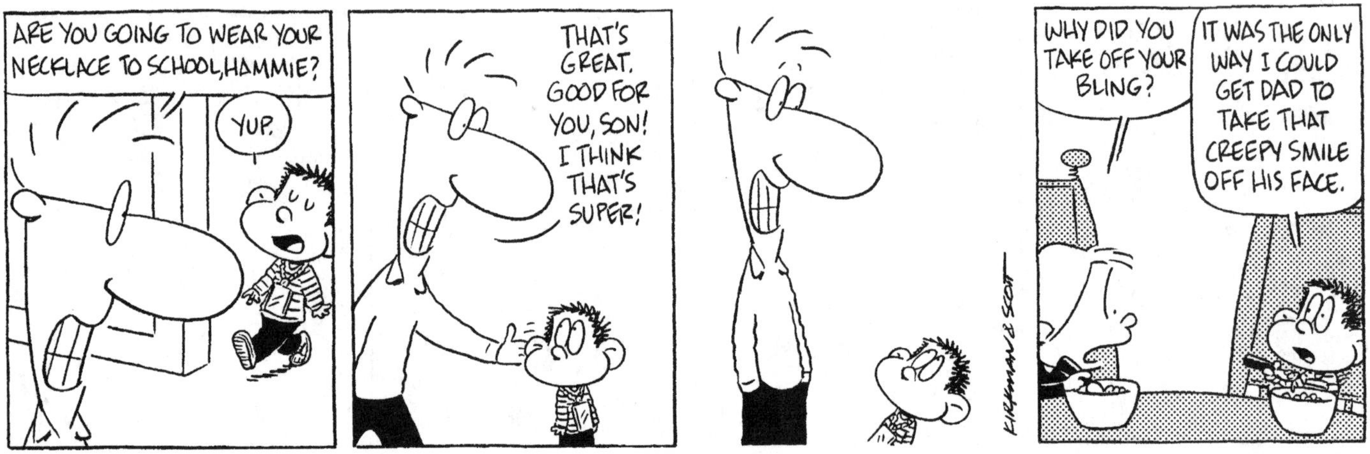
ARE YOU GOING TO WEAR YOUR NECKLACE TO SCHOOL, HAMMIE?
YUP.
THAT'S GREAT. GOOD FOR YOU, SON! I THINK THAT'S SUPER!
KIRKMAN & SCOTT
WHY DID YOU TAKE OFF YOUR BLING?
IT WAS THE ONLY WAY I COULD GET DAD TO TAKE THAT CREEPY SMILE OFF HIS FACE.

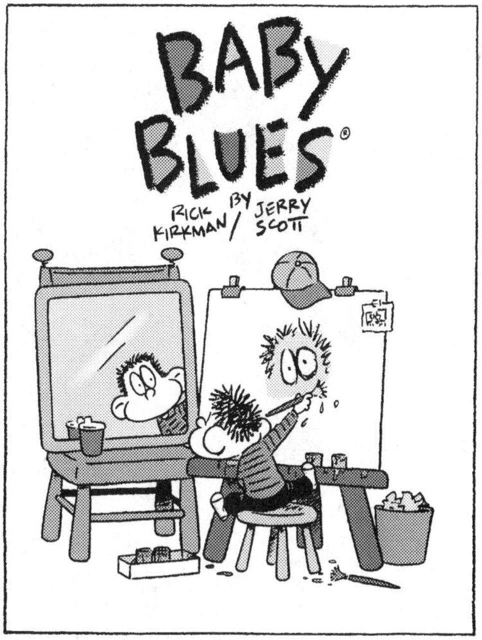
BABY BLUES®
BY RICK KIRKMAN / JERRY SCOTT

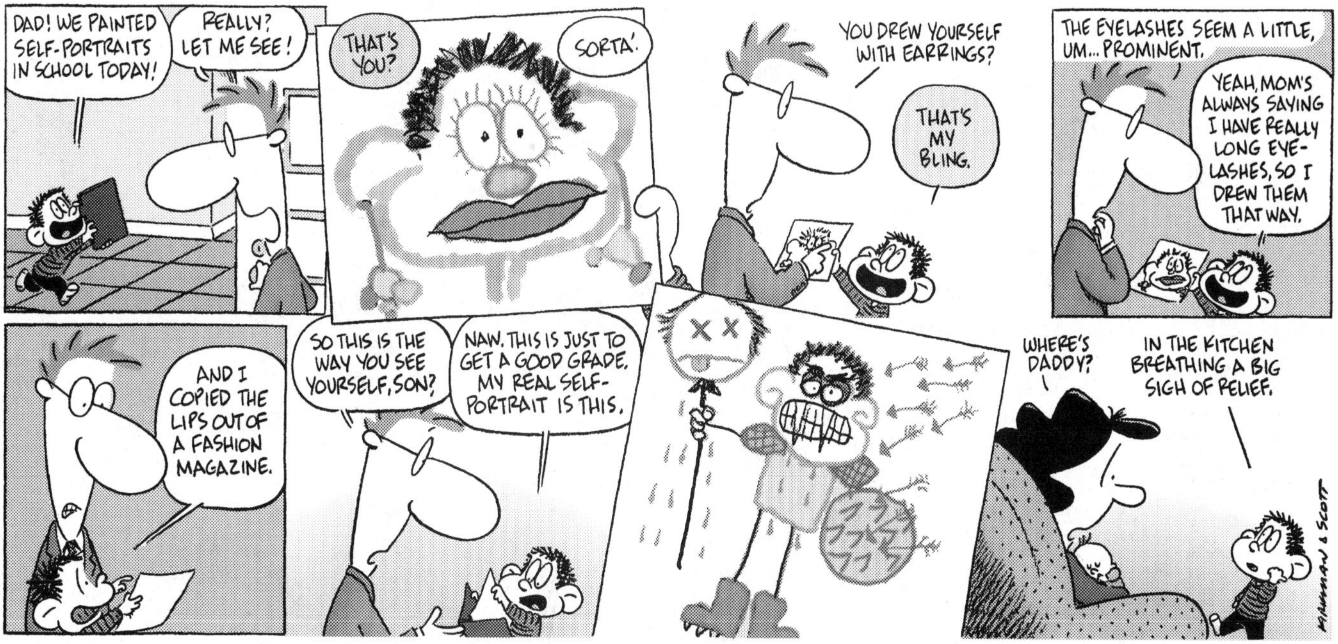
DAD! WE PAINTED SELF-PORTRAITS IN SCHOOL TODAY!
REALLY? LET ME SEE!
THAT'S YOU?
SORTA'.
YOU DREW YOURSELF WITH EARRINGS?
THAT'S MY BLING.
THE EYELASHES SEEM A LITTLE, UM... PROMINENT.
YEAH, MOM'S ALWAYS SAYING I HAVE REALLY LONG EYE-LASHES, SO I DREW THEM THAT WAY.
AND I COPIED THE LIPS OUT OF A FASHION MAGAZINE.
SO THIS IS THE WAY YOU SEE YOURSELF, SON?
NAW. THIS IS JUST TO GET A GOOD GRADE. MY REAL SELF-PORTRAIT IS THIS.
WHERE'S DADDY?
IN THE KITCHEN BREATHING A BIG SIGH OF RELIEF.
KIRKMAN & SCOTT

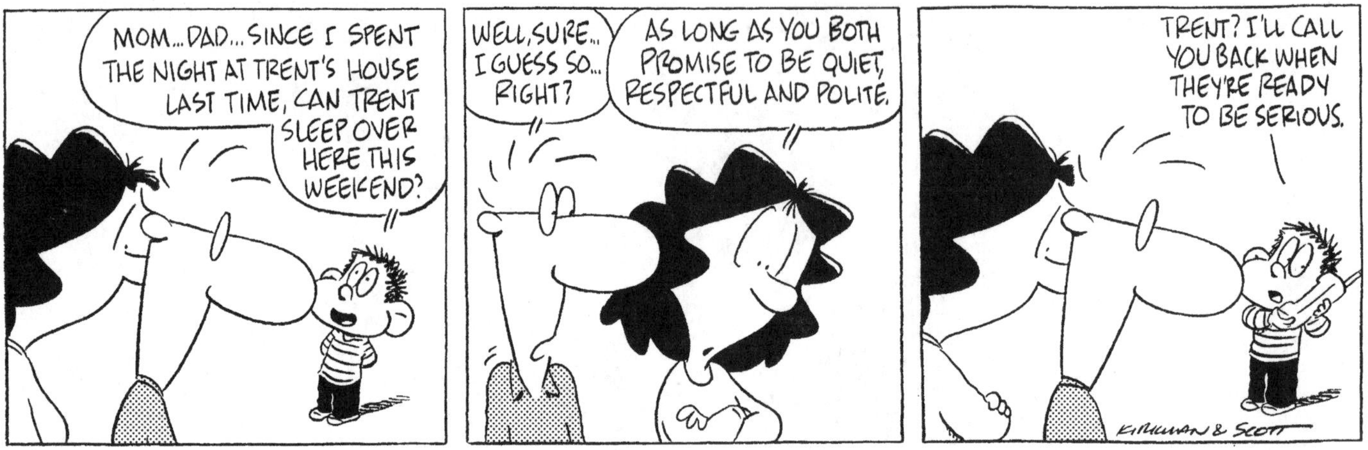
MOM...DAD...SINCE I SPENT THE NIGHT AT TRENT'S HOUSE LAST TIME, CAN TRENT SLEEP OVER HERE THIS WEEKEND?
WELL, SURE... I GUESS SO... RIGHT?
AS LONG AS YOU BOTH PROMISE TO BE QUIET, RESPECTFUL AND POLITE.
TRENT? I'LL CALL YOU BACK WHEN THEY'RE READY TO BE SERIOUS.
KIRKMAN & SCOTT

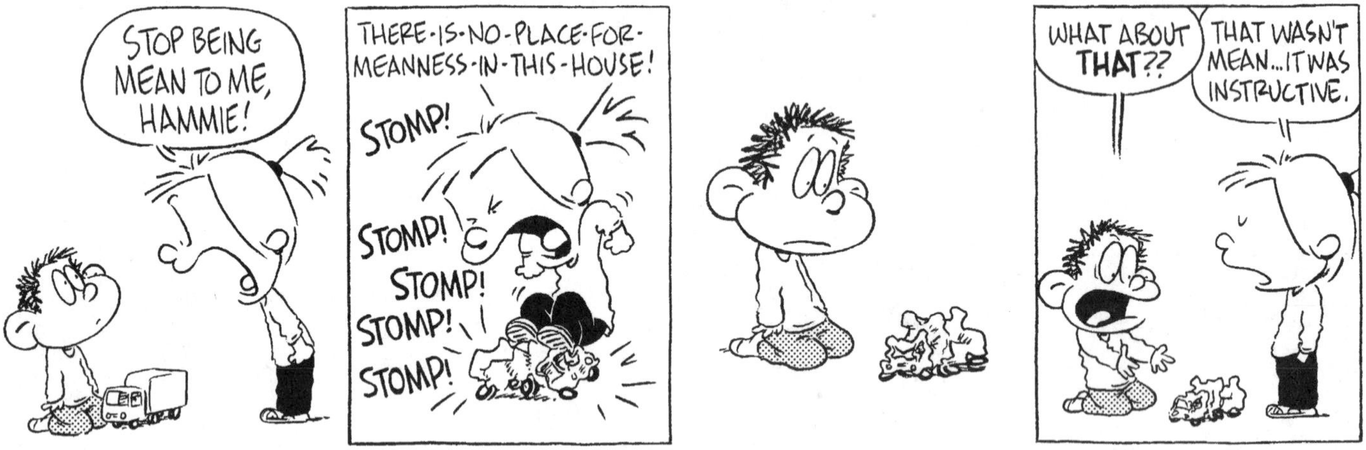
STOP BEING MEAN TO ME, HAMMIE!
THERE-IS-NO-PLACE-FOR-MEANNESS-IN-THIS-HOUSE!
STOMP!
STOMP!
STOMP!
STOMP!
STOMP!
WHAT ABOUT THAT??
THAT WASN'T MEAN...IT WAS INSTRUCTIVE.

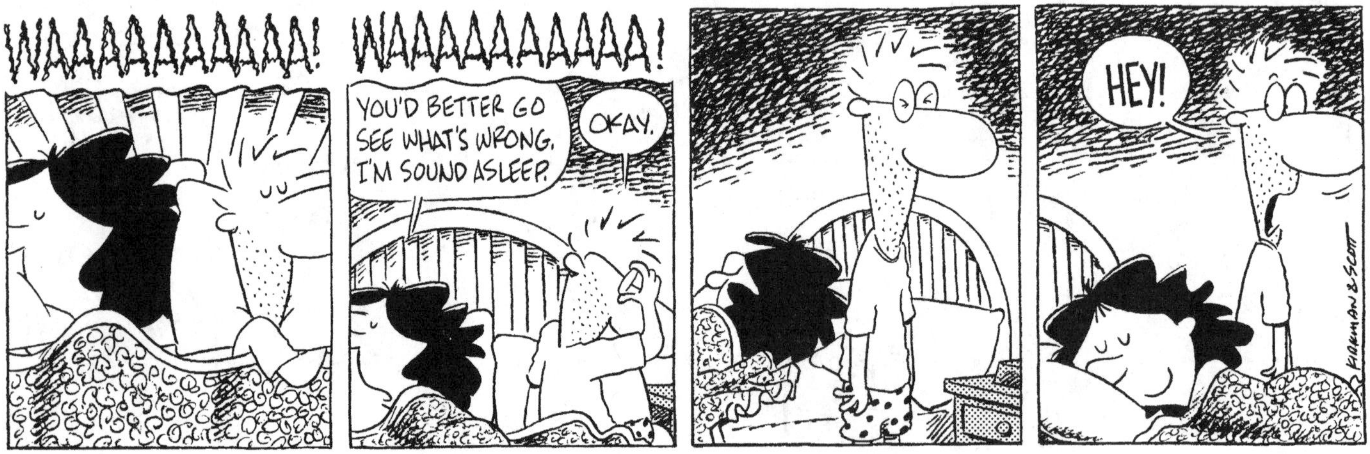
WAAAAAAAAAA!
WAAAAAAAAAA!
YOU'D BETTER GO SEE WHAT'S WRONG. I'M SOUND ASLEEP.
OKAY.
HEY!
KIRKMAN & SCOTT

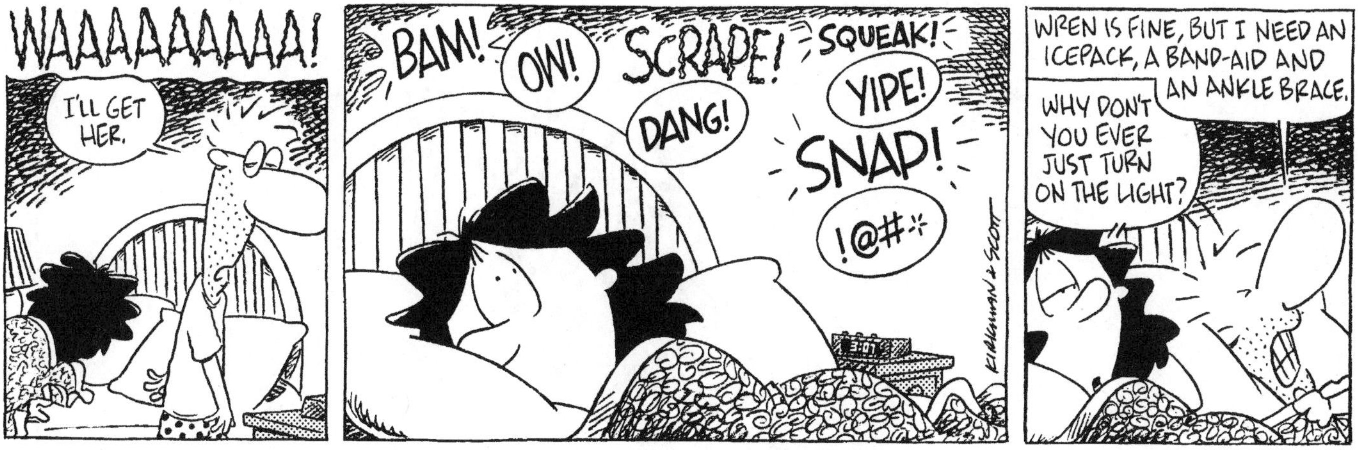
WAAAAAAAAA!
I'LL GET HER.
BAM!
OW!
SCRAPE!
SQUEAK!
DANG!
YIPE!
SNAP!
!@#*
WREN IS FINE, BUT I NEED AN ICEPACK, A BAND-AID AND AN ANKLE BRACE.
WHY DON'T YOU EVER JUST TURN ON THE LIGHT?

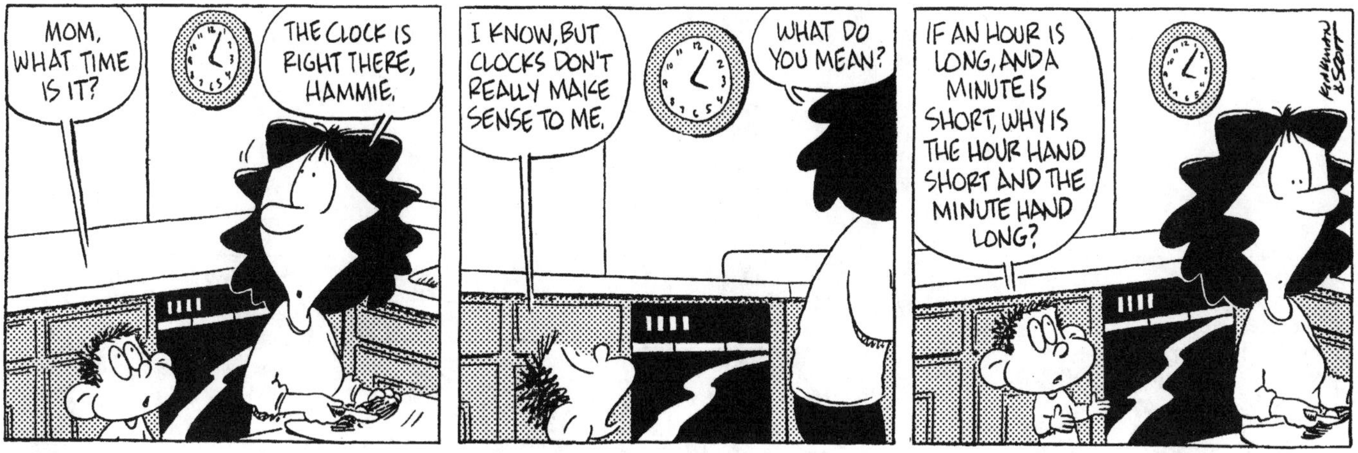
MOM, WHAT TIME IS IT?
THE CLOCK IS RIGHT THERE, HAMMIE.
I KNOW, BUT CLOCKS DON'T REALLY MAKE SENSE TO ME.
WHAT DO YOU MEAN?
IF AN HOUR IS LONG, AND A MINUTE IS SHORT, WHY IS THE HOUR HAND SHORT AND THE MINUTE HAND LONG?

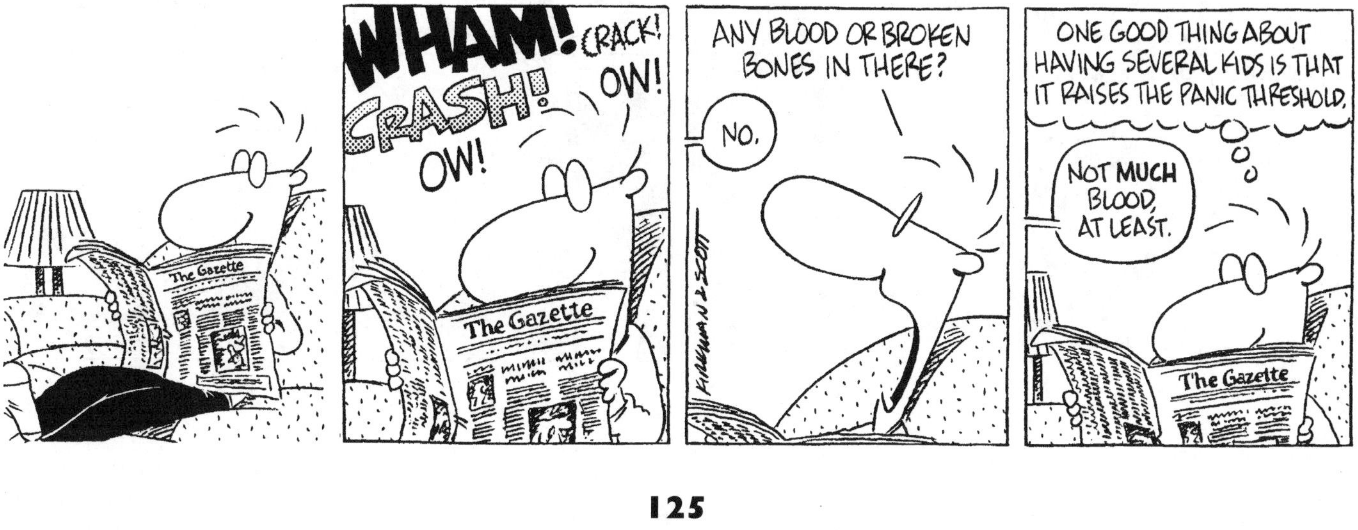
WHAM!
CRACK!
CRASH!
OW!
OW!
ANY BLOOD OR BROKEN BONES IN THERE?
NO.
ONE GOOD THING ABOUT HAVING SEVERAL KIDS IS THAT IT RAISES THE PANIC THRESHOLD.
NOT MUCH BLOOD, AT LEAST.

BABY BLUES®
BY RICK KIRKMAN / JERRY SCOTT

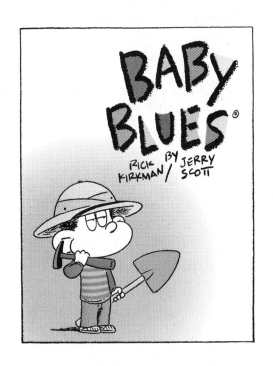

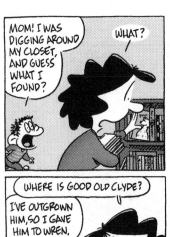

MOM! I WAS DIGGING AROUND MY CLOSET, AND GUESS WHAT I FOUND?
WHAT?
CLYDE!
YOU FOUND CLYDE??
YEAH! HE WAS BURIED UNDER A BUNCH OF OLD STUFFED ANIMALS!
YOU AND CLYDE WERE INSEPARABLE WHEN YOU WERE LITTLE, REMEMBER?
THERE YOU TWO ARE TOGETHER AT THE ZOO... THAT'S WHEN YOU TOOK CLYDE TO THE LAKE... THERE YOU ARE, TUCKING HIM INTO BED...
AWWW!
PHOTOS
WHERE IS GOOD OLD CLYDE?
I'VE OUTGROWN HIM, SO I GAVE HIM TO WREN.
WREN?
OH.
THAT'S REALLY, UM, SWEET OF YOU, HAMMIE, BUT ARE YOU SURE CLYDE IS WREN'S TYPE?
YEAH! OF COURSE!
WHO WOULDN'T LOVE AN EARTHMOVER?
KIRKMAN & SCOTT

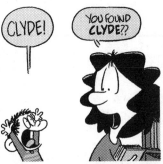

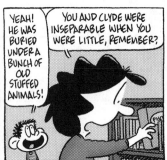

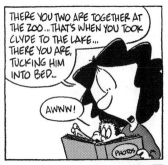

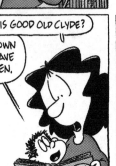

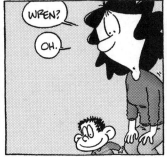

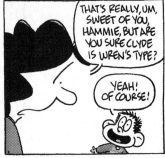

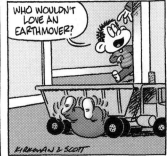

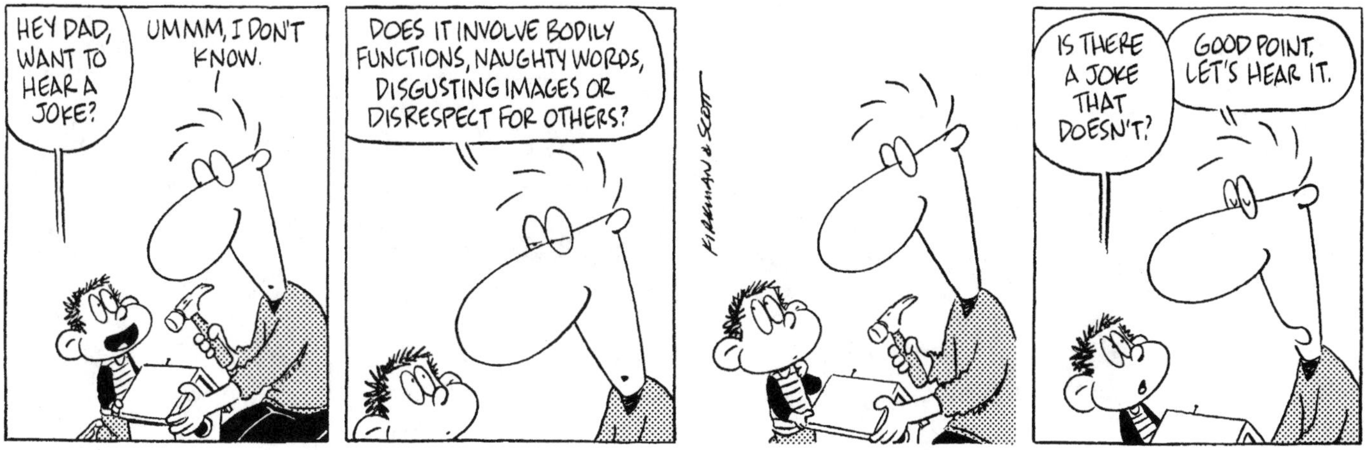
HEY DAD, WANT TO HEAR A JOKE?
UMMM, I DON'T KNOW.
DOES IT INVOLVE BODILY FUNCTIONS, NAUGHTY WORDS, DISGUSTING IMAGES OR DISRESPECT FOR OTHERS?
KIRKMAN & SCOTT
IS THERE A JOKE THAT DOESN'T?
GOOD POINT. LET'S HEAR IT.

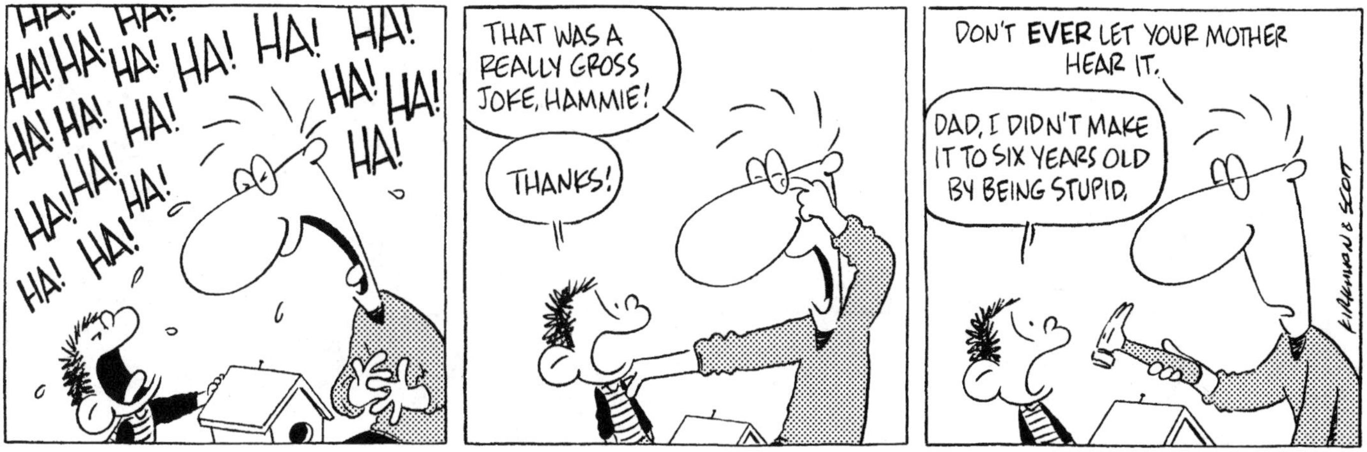
HA! HA! HA! HA! HA! HA! HA! HA! HA! HA! HA! HA! HA! HA! HA! HA! HA! HA! HA! HA! HA!
THAT WAS A REALLY GROSS JOKE, HAMMIE!
THANKS!
DON'T **EVER** LET YOUR MOTHER HEAR IT.
DAD, I DIDN'T MAKE IT TO SIX YEARS OLD BY BEING STUPID.
KIRKMAN & SCOTT

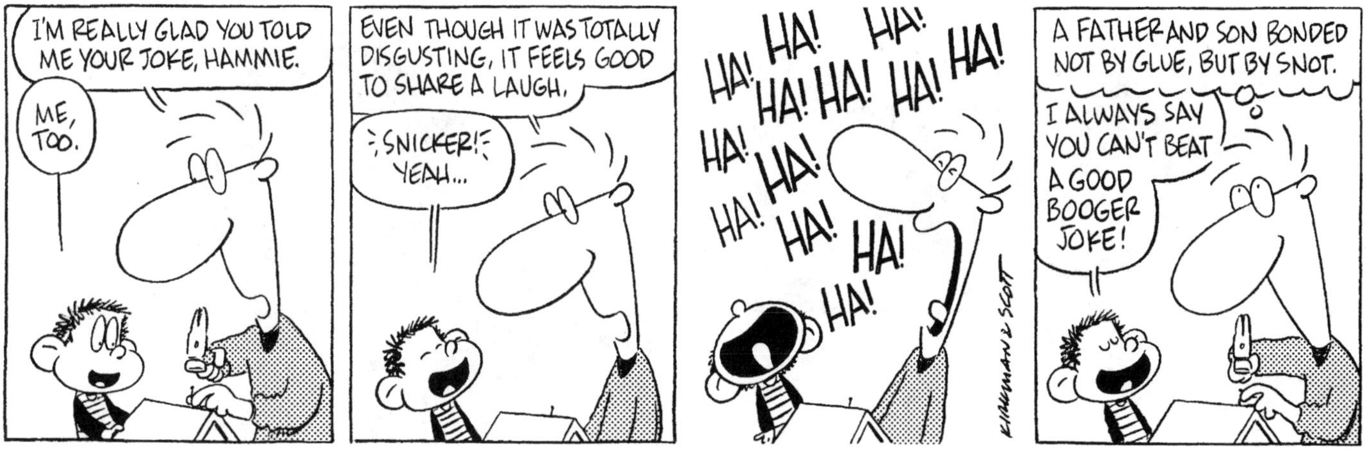
I'M REALLY GLAD YOU TOLD ME YOUR JOKE, HAMMIE.
ME, TOO.
EVEN THOUGH IT WAS TOTALLY DISGUSTING, IT FEELS GOOD TO SHARE A LAUGH.
SNICKER! YEAH...
HA! HA! HA! HA! HA! HA! HA! HA! HA! HA! HA! HA! HA! HA!
KIRKMAN & SCOTT
A FATHER AND SON BONDED NOT BY GLUE, BUT BY SNOT.
I ALWAYS SAY YOU CAN'T BEAT A GOOD BOOGER JOKE!

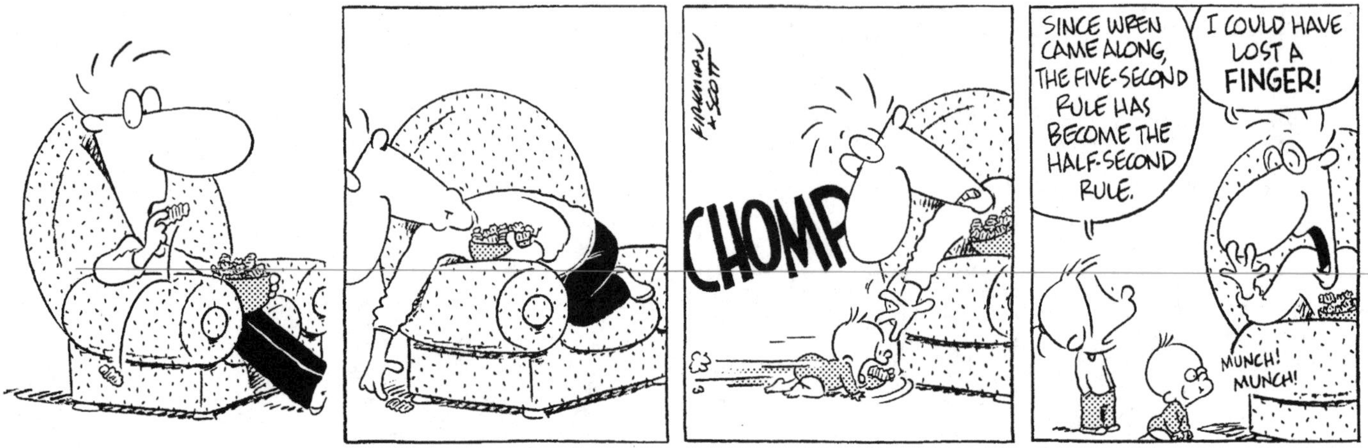
KIRKMAN & SCOTT
CHOMP
SINCE WREN CAME ALONG, THE FIVE-SECOND RULE HAS BECOME THE HALF-SECOND RULE.
I COULD HAVE LOST A **FINGER!**
MUNCH! MUNCH!

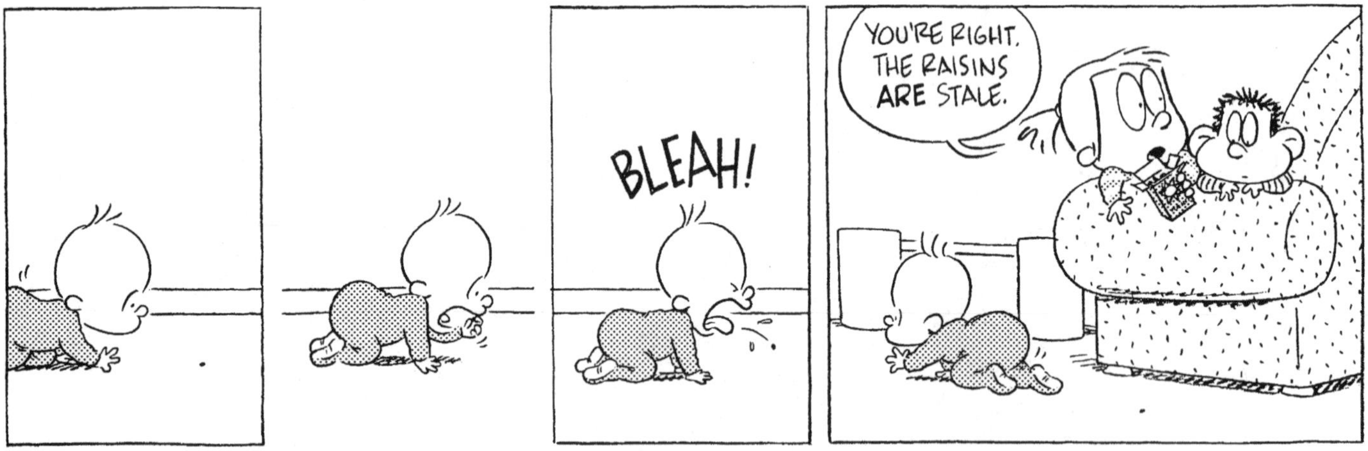
BLEAH!
YOU'RE RIGHT. THE RAISINS **ARE** STALE.

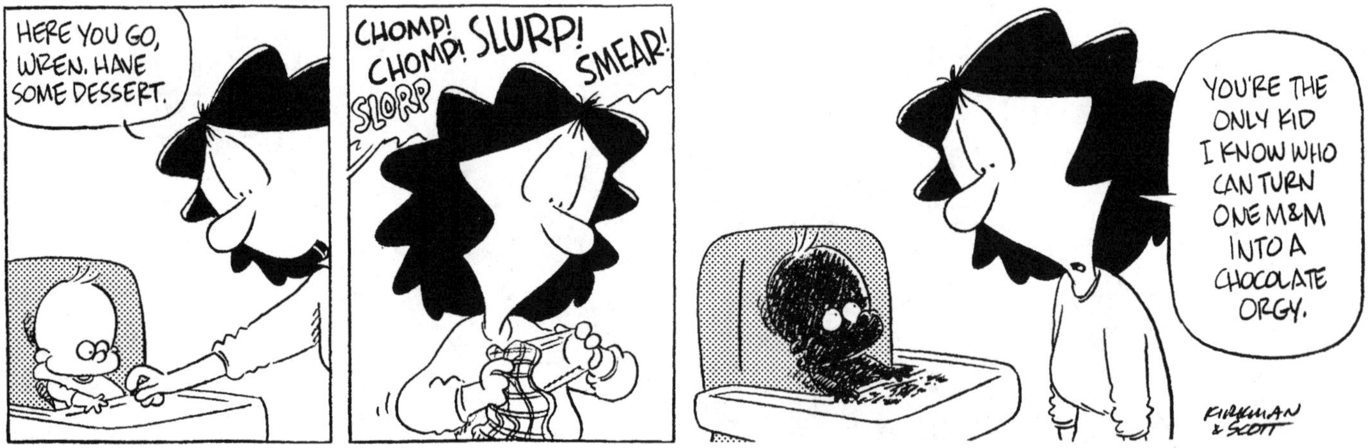
HERE YOU GO, WREN. HAVE SOME DESSERT.
CHOMP! CHOMP! SLURP!
SLORP
SMEAR!
YOU'RE THE ONLY KID I KNOW WHO CAN TURN ONE M&M INTO A CHOCOLATE ORGY.
KIRKMAN & SCOTT